# Health and the
# National Health Service

## Second Edition

## John Carrier and Ian Kendall

Routledge
Taylor & Francis Group

LONDON AND NEW YORK

First published 1998 by The Athlone Press

2 Park Square, Milton Park, Abingdon, Oxon OX14 4RN
711 Third Avenue, New York, NY 10017, USA

*Routledge is an imprint of the Taylor & Francis Group, an informa business*

First issued in paperback 2017

*British Library Cataloguing in Publication Data*
A catalog record for this book is available from the British Library

*Library of Congress Cataloging-in-Publication Data*
Health and the National Health Service / John Carrier, Ian Kendall.
pages cm. -- 1. National health services--Great Britain. 2. Medical care--Great Britain. 3. Health policy--Great Britain. I. Kendall, Ian. II. Title.
RA395.G6C382 2015
362.10941--dc23
2015008196

ISBN: 978-1-904385-14-1 (hbk)
ISBN: 978-1-138-08436-0 (pbk)

Typeset in Baskerville by
Servis Filmsetting Ltd, Stockport, Cheshire

# Contents

# Acknowledgements

The first edition of this book owed much to our long time mentor Professor Brian Abel-Smith, who died before it was completed. We relied heavily on his scholarship, and this second edition still benefits from his wisdom.

We are also indebted to the writings of other scholars, academics and journalists, as well as the King's Fund and the Nuffield Trust, all of whom we refer to in the text and in the updated bibliography. We are particularly grateful to Professor David Downes for his advice, comments and patience during the time it took to complete the book. The lengthy procedures and debates associated with the passage of the Health and Social Care Act 2012 meant that completion of the book took longer than expected.

We have also drawn on Government and parliamentary sources and much of the astute journalism that commented upon the passage of the Act, and the developments that followed. In the first edition, we referred to the continuous changes in the NHS whilst the book was in progress and we faced the same problem whilst writing this new edition.

The Taylor & Francis staff gave us continuous help for which we are grateful.

The support of members of our families was invaluable, especially our wives, Sarah and Eileen, and Kathryn Kendall who typed the updated bibliography.

Any errors of fact or interpretation are ours alone.

*John Carrier*
*Ian Kendall*
*21 April 2015*

## Biographical details

John Carrier is a retired academic who has spent most of his teaching career at the London School of Economics, mainly in the Department of Social Policy and also, since retirement, in the Department of Law. He was also Dean of Graduate Studies. He has long experience as a lay member of NHS Trust Boards, is an

Honorary Fellow of the Royal College of Physicians and an Honorary Bencher of Lincoln's Inn.

Ian Kendall is a retired academic who spent his teaching career at the University of Portsmouth, in the School of Social and Historical Studies, where he was also Dean of the Faculty of Humanities and Social Sciences for several years.

# Preface

This second, much revised and expanded, edition of Carrier's and Kendall's masterly guide to the history and development of the National Health Service (NHS) comes at a time when its very survival seems in jeopardy. For the NHS to continue and, indeed, flourish in a recognisable form, it must retain its core principles of universal health care provision, free at the point of access, to the best attainable levels of service and treatment, and funded overwhelmingly by tax and National Insurance revenue. Yet since its inception, as the authors' document shows all too vividly, these principles have been under siege. It is claimed, by its critics and opponents, to be unduly expensive and therefore economically unsustainable; to be lax and inefficient due to guaranteed State funding; and to have generated unrealistic expectations of health care that no system could meet. The alternative usually proposed is that health care should be left to the market and charitable sources, despite the history of health care on this basis being one of gross market failure.

Carrier's and Kendall's book in effect puts each of these points of criticism to the test, showing how, throughout its 60-year history, they have been found wanting or ill-judged. The cost of the NHS, for example, more than bears comparison with other 'socialised' health care systems in Western Europe, some of which charge at the point of use even if, at some administrative expense, some or all is repaid from the public purse. The NHS is especially both cost and health effective by comparison with the United States, which spends twice as much of its gross domestic product (GDP) on health care as Britain, whilst leaving a large minority bereft of health services, even after the reforms of President Obama diminished that gap in provision. A recent report by the Washington-based Commonwealth Fund declared the NHS 'the best healthcare system ... its care superior to countries which spend far more on health'.[1] In some respects, the NHS has been a victim of its own success, UK governments consistently allocating that sector 1 per cent of GDP or more *below* that of comparable societies. Many of the problems still

---

1 Denis Campbell and Nicholas Watt, 'NHS comes top in healthcare survey', *The Guardian*, 17 June 2014.

afflicting the NHS can be attributed to such relative under-resourcing which, over time, amounts to an immense cumulative comparative shortfall.

Much of the latter part of this edition gives a detailed and judicious account of the Health and Social Care Act 2012, which preoccupied the Coalition Government for an inordinate amount of parliamentary time, all the more remarkable as the Prime Minister, David Cameron, had given a personal pre-election pledge that 'there would be no top-down reorganisation of the NHS'. Nor had the Conservative or the Liberal Democrat manifestoes intimated the possibility. The Health and Social Care Act 2012 gave the lie to this pledge, leading to fears that the NHS was being set up for further privatisation through the back door by, for example, many General Practitioners – who were now to be the prime movers in health care resourcing – resorting to private consultants for advice on competitive tendering for services. After all, the previous New Labour Government had resorted to the Private Finance Initiative to raise levels of spending following a decade in which expenditure on health actually fell under the Thatcher Governments.

This book could not be more timely in enabling students to gauge how well or ill-founded such anxieties may be, as well as providing them with a succinct yet comprehensive history of what Chris Mullin has called 'the one part of the post-war consensus that has survived more or less intact the ravages of Thatcherism and the global market'.[2]

*David Downes and Paul Rock*
*20 January 2015*

---

2 Review by Chris Mullin of 'Nye: The Political Life of Aneurin Bevan' by Nicklaus Thomas-Symonds, *Guardian*, 28 December 2014.

# Tables and figures

## Tables

## Figures

# Introduction

The majority of the population in England consider it ... the most natural thing in the world, when they fall ill, to ... receive free treatment without question or delay ... Americans hold ... that no person is entitled to occupy a free bed unless or until he can prove beyond dispute that he is unable to pay something for the treatment he received in the hospital ward.

(Burdett 1893b: 56)

The new buildings were opened by Queen Victoria who planted a tree with a diamond-studded trowel. But almost immediately the hospital ... [St. Thomas's]... was beset with chronic financial shortage. For several years, 13 of the wards were kept closed for lack funds.

(Harris 1979: 288)

There is no new thing under the sun.

(Ecclesiastes 1: v.8)

This is essentially an historical account of the role of the State in health care. It is not an account of a particular segment of this history, of which there are many excellent examples varying in the range and detail of their focus. We have attempted to provide an overview of how this role has changed, taking in some of the earliest examples (see Chapter 1) concluding with quite recent developments (Chapters 14 and 15). It is also a history of health care within the UK with only a few references to other societies. The connections made are essentially those between different times and different developments in England and Wales. Our history of health care developments within the UK is based on a range of existing accounts. In so doing, the aim has been to search out consensus between scholars. An historical perspective on the State provision of health care in Britain illustrates both very significant changes in the role of the State; and some of the arguments generated by this change. Once political commitment became attached to the provision of health care for the population in the late nineteenth and early twentieth centuries, long and acrimonious debates took place upon exactly what it was the population required to meet their current health needs, how could this best be organised, its cost, and likely outcomes in terms of improvement in health status.

Our history is one of health care rather than health, but concerns regarding the latter are, as one might expect, a feature of the former. We should note in particular the Liberal reforms, the case for health care reform in the 1930s, and the Beveridge Report. But alongside understandable concerns with health care reform, those concerned with the 'health of the nation' have also argued that non-health care interventions have an impact upon life expectancy and lower morbidity with income, housing, education and nutrition all being identified as important factors in this regard. Issues of cost have figured in both sets of arguments. If non-health care interventions can improve health status, then surely they can reduce the need for health care and so reduce the demands on and the cost of our health care. But if health care interventions can also improve health status, then might the right sort of health care service, easily accessible and of a reasonable standard, also reduce the need for health care with a similar impact on the cost of our health care. Both arguments were perhaps most famously combined in the Beveridge Report. Beveridge's 'Five Giants' were clearly 'joined up' in his Report providing the rationale for concerted and wide-ranging social policy reform. The latter included health care reform which was expected to have its own particular impact on health and health care costs. This argument has re-appeared subsequently (Chapter 11) but it is clear that it must be regarded with a degree of scepticism. Whilst changes beyond health care can improve health status, there is a simpler relationship between changes within health care and health status (Chapter 9). The citizenship right to adequate health care is not identical with a citizenship right to adequate health, and the former cannot be taken as a guarantee of the latter.

We have made a conscious effort to re-visit classic texts on the history of health care in the UK, especially Abel-Smith 1964, Brand 1965, Eckstein 1958, Gilbert 1966, Klein 1983, Stevens 1966, Titmuss 1950, 1963, 1968, Webster 1988 and Willcocks 1967. This is partly in recognition of their intrinsic quality but also to ensure we identify some of the continuities in the analysis and evaluation of health care in the UK. It is one of our key themes that there are some long-standing conflicts about health care which need to be recognised as a backdrop to contemporary disputes. There are also some long-standing themes in analysis and evaluation which should not be re-presented as new simply because the terminology has changed and quasi-autonomous teaching hospitals are now quasi-autonomous Foundation Hospitals. Lastly, we have no doubt that it is possible to construct a range of plausible accounts of the history of health care in the UK (Carrier and Kendall 1977). What follows is one such plausible account.

# Part I

# Before the NHS

# Chapter 1

# Before 'new liberalism', the long history of the state and health care

> The National Health Service had its direct roots in the medical services of the Poor Law.
>
> (Hodgkinson 1967: 696)

We begin our history not only before the twentieth century, but also before the full impact of industrialisation and urbanisation was discernible. The reason for taking this longer-term historical perspective is that long-standing conflicts and divisions have influenced a number of subsequent developments in health and health care in the UK, at least in part because 'most of the basic characteristics of British medical practice were ... clearly in existence by 1900' (Stevens 1966: 11). The major state interventions of the twentieth century, National Health Insurance (1911) and the National Health Service (NHS) (1946), were constructed around the divisions within the medical profession and the voluntary sector which had existed in the nineteenth century. Furthermore, conflicts identifiable within late-nineteenth century health care played a part in how the interventions of the state were structured:

> The new Poor Law was thrust on England in an age of economic and social dislocation. The grave consequences of this upheaval were the mass of actual pauperism engendered and the migratory army of poor who were turned adrift to find livelihood and shelter in the new urban slums. Action for this chaotic flotsam and jetsam was inevitable, but fear was its conditioning agent; and national unrest made immediate legislation in the early thirties imperative.
>
> (Hodgkinson 1967: 1)

The origins of contemporary conflicts relating to issues associated with health and health care might plausibly be located in the development of the nation state rather than the establishment of a national health service. With the emergence of nation states and national economies, issues of poverty and destitution became matters of concern for governments, a concern, it has been suggested, connected as much with repression as with compassion (Bruce 1961: 23). In the UK we can identify the

Elizabethan Poor Laws (1598 and 1601) as indicators of this concern. In so far as ill-health was either a cause, or a consequence, of poverty and destitution, the activities of the Poor Law of 1601 (Poor Law) included some degree of care and support for sick paupers (Abel-Smith 1964: 3–4). The availability of even rudimentary health care was therefore an indirect consequence of a very limited form of public assistance; this meant also that such health care would be part of whatever conflicts would be associated with the subsequent development of this public assistance.

Some well-documented and enduring conflicts were between parishes, as Poor Law authorities, concerning the locality responsible for particular paupers (Bruce 1961: 3). These disputes between parishes were one indication that this system of public assistance was intended to expend minimal sums of public money to achieve broader social and political goals. It was also an enduring theme, and it was not surprising that the entire framework of parish-based relief should be the subject of particular interest and conflict in the early part of the nineteenth century when escalating expenditure generated concerns about its economic effects.

The resulting new Poor Law followed a Royal Commission and an Act of Parliament (Poor Law Amendment Act 1834) and has been widely identified with the liberal 'laissez-faire' ideology and the concept of 'The Liberal Break' (Doyal 1979: 142; Fraser 1973: Ch. 5; Gilbert 1966: 13–14; Thane 1982: 11). The core ideas of the latter included notions of individualistic freedom and self-help, and were essentially antithetical to anything more than minimal state intervention in areas broadly encompassed by the categories of economic and social policy. From this perspective the final decades of the old Poor Law had been an exercise in misplaced compassion involving excessive state expenditure on public assistance and excessive state intervention in social and economic affairs through the mechanism of 'outdoor relief'. The latter involved a situation in which many parishes had been party to the establishment of a range of 'allowance systems' supporting families in the community beyond the confines of the poorhouse.

The new order ushered in by the 1834 legislation was intended to proscribe the role of public assistance by a more precise delineation of who might be in receipt of such assistance. The principles underpinning the new Poor Law were not new, but were clearly intended to be more rigorously adhered to than had apparently been the case in the final years of the old Poor Law. The Poor Law had never sought to provide aid to all the poor, but its function of assisting only those who were completely destitute was now set down with greater clarity. The means by which such a minimal role could be maintained, whilst causing no offence to work incentives and the value of self-help, was the 'less-eligibility' or 'workhouse test'. Conditions within the workhouses of the Boards of Guardians, the new Poor Law authorities, were to be made less eligible than that of the lowest paid worker in the community and there was to be no poor relief offered beyond the confines of the workhouse. The framers of the Poor Law 'had assumed the individual to be poor because he was evil, and as such might be treated with a generous helping of salutary harshness' (Gilbert 1966: 26). The Poor Act 1834 was 'conceived for the welfare of the wealthy' (Hodgkinson 1967: 695).

The outcome was health care for the poor 'marked by a chilling and pervasive atmosphere of deterrence' (Brand 1965: 86), the intention being the maintenance of an ideal-type of minimal state intervention in health and welfare, an institution-based/less eligibility residual model. Almost the only thought from officials high and low was, 'reduce expenditure and save the rates'. Year after year, the Annual Reports congratulated the country 'that the cost of relief was diminishing when compared with the wealth and population of the nation' (Hodgkinson 1967: 65). Within 25 years, at least one medical practitioner would develop plans for a state medical service on an insurance basis (Rumsey 1856: 265–9), and within 50 years a President of the Poor Law Board would write that:

> the economical and social advantages of free medicine to the poorer classes generally, as distinguished from actual paupers, and perfect accessibility to medical advice at all times under a thorough organisation, may be considered as so important in themselves, as to render it necessary to weight with the greatest care all the reasons which may be adduced in their favour.
>
> (Hodgkinson 1967: 332–3)

Thus, subsequent developments and the trend away from the model embodied in the new Poor Law were anticipated by professionals and managers in the nineteenth century, although this trend would be accompanied by continuing conflicts about its desirability. The new Poor Law was intended also to provide a more efficient system of administration. A smaller number of larger Poor Law authorities were established. Boards of Guardians replaced parishes, and there was to be more central control through the Poor Law Commission. This may represent one of the earliest examples in British social policy of the tendency 'to seek administrative solutions to problems that are basically economic or techno-logical' (Brown 1972: 132). It would certainly not be the last occasion on which larger units of administration and more central control were seen as the most appropriate reform.

If one of the intentions of the new Poor Law was to limit what medical assis-tance it might offer in terms of quantity and quality, then it might be said to have done a service to those sick paupers for whom it was providing relief! The limitations of contemporary medical education, medical practice, and hospital care, in the first half of the nineteenth century, have been well documented. For hospitals the 'most notorious and persistent of ... controversies centred upon the question of whether [they] actually killed more people than they cured' (Harris 1979: 287). Medical education was rudimentary, although improving through the adoption of scientific findings into the curriculum. Practice was commercial not social in orientation, and therefore not rationally distributed to match needs, and hospital care varied in quality, distribution, and successful outcome for the patient (Eckstein 1958: 15–16; Stevens 1966: 23).

The operation of the new Poor Law did not altogether accord with the aims of its advocates. There is evidence of a considerable continuity of personnel and practices between the pre-1834 and post-1834 situations with the relatively limited powers of the central Poor Law Commission providing ample opportunity for local variations in the scale and standard of provision (Brand 1965: 82; Thane 1982: 12; Abel-Smith 1964: 47 and 50). After 20 years of operation the vast majority of paupers were on outdoor relief (Fraser 1973: 48), one indication that the new Poor Law might have constituted some sort of response to rural destitution but could hardly be made to work at all for the poverties of industrialism.

The new Poor Law was coming under pressure from two closely related factors. The first was the doubling of the population of Great Britain between 1801 and 1851, and again between 1851 and the outbreak of the First World War. Alongside this there was the movement of the population from rural to urban settings. The second factor was the social conditions in these urban settings, the new industrial towns and cities, dramatically demonstrated by Chadwick and others (Brand 1965: 2–21; Hodgkinson 1967: Ch. 17). These factors formed the basis of the initial case for specific state intervention in health care made by the 'public health movement', an intervention that could claim some support from those who favoured policies to minimise public expenditure on health and welfare:

> [Sickness] ... destroys a man's capacity for labour, and if he has failed to make timely provisions (or if wages are too low to do so) he is at once pros-trated, when sickness overtakes him, and has therefore of necessity to look for help to others. Whilst therefore adhering in their entirety to the principles of the Poor Law Amendment Act, we may yet admit that medical relief is in its nature, not only the least objectionable of all modes of relief, but it is within reasonable limits admissible and in the existing state of society, even necessary.
>
> (Nicholls 1854, quoted in Hodgkinson 1967: 59)

> [A] ... hell of depression and misery and hopeless degradation. Foul odors, vermin, vile food, drunkenness and promiscuity were the chief by-products of its depauperate and crowded existence: crime and disease were but the inevitable psychological and physiological responses.
>
> (Mumford 1940: 12, on the industrial slums of
> Victorian England)

> With the steadily mounting population came the new sanitary problems and mounting urban deaths. 'Laissez-faire,' still the favourite nineteenth century watchword, provided no solution.
>
> (Brand 1965: 1)

> To apply the prevention principle to the new social problems necessitated a new type of activity. Departure from 'laissez-faire' was inevitable.
>
> (Hodgkinson 1967: 621)

The Vaccination Act 1840 was an indicator of a potential conflict between the ideology that was intended to underpin the social policies in the first half of the nineteenth century and the social problems of the period. This piece of legislation provided for free vaccination to all who applied for it without reference to their circumstances. Vaccination was the first of the free health services provided by the legislature on a national scale. A beginning in positive health measures had been made, and it was administered through the channels of the Poor Law (Hodgkinson 1967: 31).

However, this identification of a social problem with a forthcoming administrative response can suggest that health reforms of the time logically followed the identification of 'public concerns' (Paulus 1974). It can easily be forgotten that this expansion of state intervention was extremely contentious at the time. Cholera scares seem to have been 'of great service to the advancement of English sanitation', reformers being well aware that this fear of cholera could be used to good effect to enact changes that had more impact on other threats to the public health (Brand 1965: 45), but support for reform 'waned with the passing of ... [each] ... epidemic' (Brand 1965: 2) and was anyway not sufficient to convince the leader writer in *The Times* who argued that the population might wish to take their 'chance with cholera and the rest' rather than be 'bullied into health' (*The Times*, 1 August 1854), As one commentator was to observe subsequently, it was not until a considerable time after the passage of the Public Health Act 1848 that 'that there was a general conviction that it might be better to suffer the compulsion of being kept alive than to enjoy the privilege of being allowed to die in an epidemic of fever' (Wilson 1938: 21). Such attitudes are one explanation of the delay in getting effective public health legislation on to the statute book.

The marked differences between death rates in urban and rural areas were being documented by the Registrar-General in the 1830s, yet it was 1848 before the first Public Health Act was passed. This has been identified as one of the earliest examples of state control over the lives of individuals in a predominantly laissez-faire society (Doyal 1979: 142), although it was permissive legislation and had a limited impact. Almost a quarter of century would pass until a comprehensive and mandatory piece of legislation was placed on to the statute book (Thane 1982: 40) and there would be graphic evidence after its enactment of a failure to use the resulting statutory powers effectively (Gilbert 1966: 28–9). If there were a necessary logic to public health legislation, it was a logic that took many years to be accepted by the government. The 'public health problem' of Britain's industrial cities had claimed many victims between the emergence of the 'objective evidence' collected by government civil servants and the acceptance of the need for action by the politicians in government. To identify a problem did not necessarily mean that a state-supported solution to eliminate that problem would be the 'rational response'. This is a further indication that the wide ranging consensus around the necessity of this form of state intervention, which is taken for granted today, was the subject of considerable conflict at the time.

In the period over which the government edged painfully slowly towards putting effective public health legislation on to the statute book, the modern medical profession emerged, at least in so far as its legal status is concerned. The latter was confirmed by the Medical Act 1858, the passing of which can be seen as the culmination of another conflict, that between the members and supporters of 'traditional professional groups', the apothecaries, physicians, surgeons and their professional associations, and those other individuals who aspired to the status of medical practitioner. The latter were a significant group in numbers at least. There were 30,000 individuals who recorded their occupation as 'doctor' who can be set against the 11,000 qualified physicians listed in the 1845 Medical Directory. Following the 1858 Act, the Poor Law Board would demand that all Poor Law medical officers should be registered and should possess a legal qualification to practise both medicine and surgery, actually requiring them to obtain better professional training than some practitioners in private practice (Brand 1965: 88).

The success of 'personal health care practitioners', surgeons, physicians and apothecaries, in attaining a professional status legitimated by the state makes an interesting contrast with the long drawn out and controversial battle to place effective public health legislation on to the statute book. The UK had effective 'professionalization of health' legislation before it had effective 'public health' legislation, although health professionals were significant campaigners for public health reform (Brand 1965: 2 and 10.) In terms of 'functions' for society, that is to say, meeting 'the needs of an industrial society', the potential of public health reform was demonstrable when that of personal health professionals was dubious. Indeed, the relative significance of public health and environmental measures by comparison with personal health services has been a continuing theme in much subsequent epidemiological literature (McKeown 1976). Whilst being active advocates of continuing public health reform from the country-wide requirement for their appointment in 1872 (Brand 1965: Ch. 6), public health professionals have continued to experience a status that appears to be inversely (and some would say perversely) related to the contribution they have made to the health and well being of the urban populations of industrial societies.

There has always been a widely held distinction between meeting individual medical need, and protecting society at large from the indivisible costs of large-scale disease, for example, cholera or typhoid, through public health services. This distinction may reflect the difference between the perceptions of medical care and health held by the lay public on the one hand, and the public health professions on the other hand. The former may be unaware of the invisible public health base of individual health status and may see only personal health services as responsible for their freedom from sickness, illness and disease. If public health issues had become somewhat less contentious in the latter half of the nineteenth century, it should not be presumed that this situation applied to state provision of personal health services. Nonetheless, by 1900 the British state was an important source of health care. Public health issues made a contribution to this change as local authorities were first empowered to build their own hospitals under section 37 of

Table 1.1 The number and size of county asylums 1827–1900

| Date | Number of county asylums | Number of patients | Average number of patients per asylum |
|------|--------------------------|--------------------|---------------------------------------|
| 1827 | 9 | 1,046 | 116 |
| 1850 | 24 | 7,140 | 297 |
| 1860 | 41 | 15,845 | 386 |
| 1880 | 61 | 40,088 | 657 |
| 1900 | 77 | 74,004 | 961 |

Sources: Goodwin 1989: 43; Scull 1979: 198; Jones 1972: 357.

the Sanitary Act 1866. These powers were further consolidated with the passing of Disraeli's Public Health Act in 1875 which permitted local authorities to build 'hospitals or temporary places for the reception of the sick' (Pinker 1966: 78). By 1900 there would be almost 1,000 isolation hospitals and other institutions under the public health service, although only two local authorities had used their statutory powers to open their own general hospitals (Stevens 1966: 34–5; Pinker 1966: 78; Parker 1965: 29).

Another dimension of state intervention in the first half of the nineteenth century was the building of asylums. The County Asylums Act was passed in 1808. However, it gave only permissive powers to Justices of the Peace to raise county rates for the building of asylums, and by 1827 only nine county asylums were in operation (Jones 1972: 88–90).

For much of the nineteenth century many 'persons of unsound mind' remained under the care of the Poor Law authorities and by the end of the 1860s the ratio of workhouse to county asylum residents (the insane) was still 2.29:1 (Hodgkinson 1967: 575 and 590). The reasons for the non-utilisation of the 'specialised asylum system' included some that would be familiar to twentieth-century reformers. These were separate authorities for the asylum and the workhouse, with separate budgets and no particular reason to co-operate. In addition, the interests of the ratepayers were well served by confining 'pauper lunatics' in the cheaper environs of the workhouse regardless of their needs for 'specialist care' (Scull 1979: 213–19). This position was changed by the 1874 legislation for Grant-in Aid for pauper lunatics. The sum involved was four shillings per head, and it gave an incentive, previously lacking, for the Poor Law authorities to transfer their paupers out of the workhouse and into the asylums (Jones 1972: 160–1).

It was really in the last quarter of the nineteenth century that the segregation of mentally ill people became more marked. There were now two and half times as many county asylums and over five times as many asylum residents as there had been in 1850 (see Table 1.1). The key role of the asylum was confirmed in statute by the Lunacy Act 1890, by which the new local authorities (county councils and county borough councils created by the Local Government Act 1888) were required to build and maintain asylums, alone or under joint agreement with a neighbouring authority (Jones 1960: Ch. 2).

Parallel to the development of the county asylums was a growing concern for the numbers of the mentally ill confined in private institutions, the 'private madhouse', or in ordinary private households, the 'single lunatic'. This concern related not only to the quality of care received by such people but also to the danger that they might be wrongfully detained, perhaps for ulterior reasons. The Madhouse Act 1828 covered not only private madhouses, but also all subscription hospitals with the exception of Bethlem, and involved the establishment of inspection by statutory authority and a more detailed form of certification of patients designed to obviate the possibility of illegal detention. The Lunacy Inquiry Act 1842 established, for a period of three years, the Lunacy Commissioners, who were empowered to carry out inspections of all asylums and madhouses. This was followed by the Lunacy Act 1845, which established a full-time inspectorate, with duties of inspecting, licensing and reporting. As part of its provisions 'a more detailed form of certification was devised ... [which] ... increased the legal safeguards against wrongful detention in each case' (Jones 1972: 147). Subsequently, there appeared to be a divergence of professional and public views of mental illness. The Lancet Commission suggested that 'patients labouring under mental derangement should be removable to a public or private asylum as to a hospital for ordinary diseases, without certificate ... the power of signing certificates of lunacy should be withdrawn from magistrates' (Jones 1972: 167). The 'public view' was perhaps reflected by the popularity of novels such as Charles Reade's *Hard Cash* (1863) and Wilkie Collins's *Woman in White* (1869) in the plots of which wrongful detention in 'private madhouses' played a key role (Jones 1972: 161–4; Taylor and Taylor 1989: 12). If this was indeed the 'public view', then it lent support to a 'legalistic' approach and the need to safeguard individuals against wrongful detention in asylums. This approach was represented in statute by the Lunacy Act 1890 which, as well as confirming the key role of the asylum in mental health services, also introduced 'every safeguard which could possibly be devised against illegal confinement' (Jones 1960: 40). There was also, at the end of the nineteenth century, a rapid expansion of beds in private nursing homes. This expansion provoked both public and professional concerns about the costs and standards of care within this new private sector. As with private madhouses, demands were made for its regulation (Abel-Smith 1964: 189 and 192–4):

> The voluntary hospital found its origin in medieval piety, and grew in later centuries through the philanthropy of laymen and doctors. The eighteenth century particularly saw the establishment of hospitals to give medical relief to the sick poor, but unlike developments on the Continent they depended on charity and not on public provision.
>
> (Hodgkinson 1967: 195)

In nineteenth-century Britain, voluntary institutions appeared well placed to meet the health care needs of the nation with limited recourse to state intervention. The predominantly middle-class and upper-class tradition of philanthropic, charitable activity was represented by the voluntary hospitals (Abel-Smith 1964: 4). A small number of these hospitals were well endowed with historical tradition and resources. Others were of more recent origins, forming part of the extensive establishment of new hospitals that had taken place in Britain between 1700 and 1825 when 'one hundred and fifty-four new hospitals and dispensaries were established as charitable institutions' (Stevens 1966: 14; Eckstein 1958: 15; Woodward 1974: Chs 2 and 3, and 36). Similar developments took place in other European countries (Abel-Smith 1976: 3–8).

Whilst these philanthropic institutions were not always held in the highest esteem, for example the hospital riots at Manchester and Paisley (Eckstein 1958: 16), there was the apparent potential within the voluntary hospital system to meet a wide range of health care needs for a broad spectrum of the population. Throughout Europe the voluntary hospital tradition involved providing care largely free of charge to the poorer sections of the community. This was partly attributable to the charitable origins and aims of these institutions, but was also linked to the position of many of them as institutions for teaching and research, for example, 85 per cent of London's general hospital beds were in teaching hospitals in 1861 (Abel-Smith 1964: 41). Interesting cases for teaching and research were as likely to be found amongst the poor as the rich, and the former were not well placed to object to their status as teaching subjects. The costs of the institutions were also minimised by having to pay nothing more than a modest honorarium for medical services. Appointments in such institutions were sought after as the basis for a reputation, the latter serving to obtain remuneration from a private practice that might well be conducted elsewhere for example, Harley Street in London, 'charitable work became the key to fame and fortune' (Abel-Smith 1964: 19, 6–7; Baggott 1994: 75; Stevens 1966: 14, 15 and 17; Woodward 1974: 23).

There were limitations to the scale and scope of voluntary hospital provision. The principal source of finance for these hospitals came from the subscriptions paid by individuals, parishes or towns. This provided a sound resource base for the hospitals even if it did lead to concerns that some institutions were less than accurate with their statistics, as competing institutions sought to attract subscribers, an early example of the limitations of simple, crude statistically-based league tables (Woodward 1974: 139–42; Abel-Smith 1964: 39–40). However, this system also meant that the sick person had to find a subscriber who was willing to certify that the person in question was a proper object of charity (Woodward 1974: 18, 38 and 39). This was the only way of gaining admittance to a hospital unless the prospective patient had been involved in an accident or had symptoms which needed immediate relief (Woodward 1974: 39). The scope of this philanthropy fell some way short of the 'universal stranger' (Titmuss 1970: 238), since worthy objects of charity frequently excluded servants, apprentices and, of course, paupers. The net result was that entry into hospital 'was bounded with many restrictions, which narrowed the section of the population for which the medical facilities were available' (Woodward 1974: 40 and 43; Abel-Smith 1964: 14–15 and 36–40).

Furthermore, whilst the need for 'interesting cases' and alternative sources of medical remuneration provided a rationale and a means to maintain the tradition of free hospital care for the poor, they also limited the contribution made by voluntary hospitals to identifiable needs for health care. It was a general feature of charity in nineteenth-century Britain that it was highly localised (Thane 1982: 21), and this was true of the voluntary hospitals. The range and scope of their provision was linked to the range and scope of private practice (Stevens 1966: Ch. 4). Voluntary hospitals could only lay claim to be adequate providers of the nation's hospital care in the more affluent or the densely populated parts of the country. They were established 'principally in the capital and in the main provincial centres of population' (Woodward 1974: 144). 'The voluntary hospitals, due to their geographical distribution, were available only to a small portion of the working population' (Gilbert 1966: 304). As well as this significant spatial limitation, 'the voluntary movement never became more than marginally involved in the needs of the chronically sick' (Pinker 1966: 72). This was in part a consequence of the focus on 'interesting cases' linked to teaching needs and professional prestige (Abel-Smith 1964: 45). It was also linked to fund-raising, for example, the more acute the cases admitted, the greater were the number of inpatients that could be treated in a given number of beds during the year. Such statistics were valuable for appeal purposes (Abel-Smith 1964: 39). It appears that the rules of admission to the voluntary hospitals 'were generally designed to exclude the chronic sick and the cases which might prove troublesome in one way or another' (Woodward 1974: 45):

> These exclusions link to the already mentioned public health problems of industrialisation and urbanisation. As more epidemics raged across Britain's large and growing cities, more and more hospitals were excluding the victims.
> (Abel-Smith 1964: 45)

The beginnings of state education in Britain can also be related to the limitations of voluntary institutions. Pilot surveys in four large cities ordered by Forster, Vice-President of Education in Gladstone's first Ministry, found less than 10 per cent of their population in schools, and Edward Baines, an advocate of voluntarism in education provision was forced to write, 'I confess to a strong distress of government action, a passionate love for voluntary action and self-reliance but now as a practical man I am compelled to abandon the purely voluntary system' (Fraser 1973: 80). In what seems like an almost inevitable parallel with the development of state intervention in education, the public authorities assumed a responsibility for 'what was left undone by charity' and private enterprise (Abel-Smith 1964: 45; Thane 1982: 41).

The epidemics associated with urbanisation, the restricted scope of voluntary hospital activity, and a combination of parsimony and permissive mental health legislation, had an impact on the health care activities of the Poor Law authorities. The Poor Law Amendment Act 1834 was intended to ensure that state intervention in health and welfare would be minimal. Alongside the failure to control outdoor relief (see above) can be recorded a failure to distance the state from any form of personal health services. The 14,722 beds in voluntary hospitals in 1861 can be compared with the 50,000 beds in the workhouses as recorded by the Poor Law authorities (Pinker 1966: 73 and 75). By 1891 the public sector was providing 2.88 beds per 1,000 of the population while 1.02 beds per 1,000 of the population were in voluntary hospitals (Pinker 1966: 70). It was the Poor Law authorities which accommodated 'the bulk of the sick children, the mental cases, the skin conditions, those with epilepsy, tuberculosis and venereal diseases and the unexplored mass of the chronic sick' (Abel-Smith 1964: 49). Medical care therefore began to be provided as an addendum to economic deprivation. Paupers 'housed' for reasons of destitution, turned Poor Law institutions into Poor Law infirmaries catering for the poor and the sick. A different set of institutions, administered by men not of the social elite which ran the voluntary hospitals (Abel-Smith 1964: 63), and employing a separate group of doctors, were becoming 'the real hospitals of the land' (*The Lancet Commission Report*, p. ix, quoted in Abel-Smith 1964: 64). 'The Poor Law institutions had become the first public hospitals' (Hodgkinson 1967: 451), and an important precedent had been set in that 'the poor had gained the right to institutional care when they were sick' (Abel-Smith 1964: 65).

The consequent duty of the state to provide hospitals for the poor received its first formal acknowledgement in the Metropolitan Poor Act 1867 (Ayers 1971: 1). The scene was set for 'the development of a poor law hospital service' (Pinker 1966: 75) in so far as increasing proportions of 'sick paupers' were located in workhouse sick wards and more significantly in separate Poor Law infirmaries. In 1904, new hospitals were accounting for 44 per cent of total expenditure on new Poor Law building (Abel-Smith 1964: 204). Between 1891 and 1911 the number of beds in separate infirmaries rose by 338 per cent (Pinker 1966: 76). The trend towards 'specialist' provision was also discernible in the building of asylums and the subsequent relocation of 'pauper lunatics' already noted. Much of the separate provision within the Poor Law remained of variable and often minimal quality, especially in rural areas, and the majority of the sick paupers remained in unclassified institutions, nursed by aged convalescent and feeble-minded paupers (Brand 1965: 96–8; Abel-Smith 1964: 212–15). However, in some parts of the country, notably in London through the Metropolitan Asylums Board, a publicly funded hospital system was emerging under the aegis of the new Poor Law. When the Public Health (London) Act 1891 removed the power of Poor Law authorities in London to charge patients with infectious diseases, 'every citizen in London had become entitled to free treatment from the Metropolitan Asylum Board'. This developed into 'one of the largest and most effective hospital systems in the world, while operating nominally as a branch of the Poor Law' (Abel-Smith 1964: 126–7; Brand 1965: 95).

As Poor Law infirmaries improved in quality they became effectively the general hospital for the community, notably where voluntary hospital provision was limited (Abel-Smith 1964: 206). They also began to acquire some other character-istics of the voluntary hospitals. Some were potentially problematic, for example, a preference for the acute sick over the chronic sick. Others were an integral part of the emergence of 'modern health care' in Britain, with the Poor Law infirma-ries making a substantial contribution to the development of nurse education and training (Abel-Smith 1964: 154 and 206–11; Hodgkinson 1967: 556–72). Thus, the whole character of the Poor Law infirmaries was beginning to change. '[The] development was in complete contrast to the whole philosophy upon which the Poor Laws were based' (Abel-Smith 1964: 132). That Poor Law infirmaries, local authority hospitals and county asylums might be deemed necessary at all, given the existence of an extensive network of voluntary hospitals, is indicative of one reason for the changing role of the British state in health care provision. That the state should get drawn into a more central role in the direct provision of personal health services might be attributable to a conflict between *the reality* of the scope of health care that could be provided through voluntary institutions, and *the aspira-tions* of those who would continue to argue for the health and welfare functions of the state to be constrained within a residual, deterrent system of public assistance represented by the new Poor Law.

By the mid-nineteenth century the asylum and prison were 'places of first resort' (Cohen 1979: 609). Part of the background to the development of policies for community care in the NHS (see Chapter 7) was the development of institutional care before 1900. Generally, we can characterise the situation as one in which the appropriate response to a range of social needs and social problems was seen as investment in forms of specialised institutional care, prisons, industrial and reform schools, children's homes and, as we have noted above in new voluntary hospitals, the county asylums and the new Poor Law hospitals. These changes would later be categorised as a trend in the 'social organisation of deviance' (Scull: 1979) and could be linked to a number of factors. Obvious structural factors include indus-trialisation and urbanisation of which one example would be the 'public health problem'. A further example would be the suggestion that the 'mentally and physically handicapped can more easily take some part in agricultural work than in the more demanding occupations characteristics of industrial society' (Parker 1975: 20). Similarly, the increases in the nineteenth century in the rates of 'known persons of unsound mind' per 1,000 of the population and 'the rate of insanity per ten thousand people' (Jones 1972: 356; Scull 1979: 225) might be attrib-uted to the social and psychological stresses inextricably linked to the dramatic changes associated with industrialisation and urbanisation. There could be a link to the operation of the capitalist market economy and the 'laissez-faire' ideology that dominated the British policy agenda for much of the nineteenth century. Specialist forms of institutional care could be seen to respond to identified needs and problems in a mode that interfered least with the 'free play of market forces', better to remove the disabled and destitute from their communities entirely, than to support them in their own homes and so distort the workings of the labour market, hence the principle of 'indoor relief'.

Three other rather general themes can be identified. First, the extent to which this new 'social organization of deviance' represented a rational-bureaucratic approach to 'social problems', the 'scientific' identification and categorisation of separate groups, for example the young offender from the adult offender, the mentally ill from the physically ill. Second, the extent to which this process was inextricably associated with the development of 'specialist bodies of knowledge' and the development of professions, most obviously in the development of specialist hospitals and especially in relation to the development of asylums and the asylum doctors (Abel-Smith 1964: 22–6). Third, and certainly linked to professionalisation, the extent to which the process of institutionalisation developed its own inherent dynamic as the building of the institutions created a need for more institutions by formally identifying and establishing a 'new response' to a range of 'social problems'. This perspective does not necessarily contradict the idea that certain social problems may have become more significant with industrialisation and urbanisation, but it does add the other dimension with which we have become increasingly familiar, the 'submerged iceberg' effect in which previously unmet or differently met need is 're-directed' towards a new, or newly accessible, service.

Two other possibilities follow from the 'submerged iceberg' effect. One is the extent to which social and economic changes were constraining the ability of families and communities to sustain their caring roles, creating a new 'institutional population' for which care had to be provided. An alternative, at least for people with mental health problems, is that their needs were previously ignored or neglected in the late eighteenth and early nineteenth centuries (Jones 1955: 1–2). The latter point also alerts us to what might be rather clumsily labelled as 'trans-institutionalization' by which the 'new state institutions', for example the asylum, removed people from the old state institutions, for example the workhouse. In addition, part of the growth of publicly-financed institutions (the county asylums) was replacing private provision (private madhouses and single lunatics confined in ordinary houses). The growth of publicly-financed asylums should not be taken to represent simple increases in the institutionalisation of the mentally ill, but partly a transfer of individuals from other, possibly less satisfactory, forms of institutional confinement. Certainly, the twin policies of creating infirmaries and seeking to eliminate outdoor relief played their part in increasing the institutionalisation of the sick during the nineteenth century (Abel-Smith 1964: 86). This 'trans-institutionalization' might be deemed a form of 'progress', alerting us to a further perspective on the new institutions, that they did, in certain respects, improve the circumstances of some groups. Later policies for community care would be significantly hampered by, for example, the building of large institutions 10 to 20 miles out in the countryside around London (Maxwell 1990), and these locations can easily be said to represent a 'social organization of deviance' that relocates social problems away from the public gaze (out of sight, out of mind). On the other hand, these rural locations were also a response to the then current theories of disease (especially the miasmic theory). Furthermore, whilst it may have been unfair to refer to 'palatial workhouse infirmaries' (*British Medical Journal*,

9 February 1884, quoted in Abel-Smith 1964: 149), there is the case that 'infirmary treatment was often a considerable improvement on the normal housing
conditions of the poorer classes' (Brand 1965: 99), that the inmates were often
better fed, better clad, better housed and better cared for than they were before
their admission, and 'better than the great mass of working classes who earn
their own living' (Abel-Smith 1964: 64). Certainly, some of the new institutions
represented improvements in quality of care by comparison with what had gone
before (Abel-Smith 1964: 200–1), 'rescuing' some of those they contained from the
'worse havens' of 'privatised institutional care' (Heywood 1965 on baby-farming)
or the 'ultimate safety-nets' of the nineteenth-century prisons and workhouses. It
is also probable that the 'batch living' of institutional life was a less unfamiliar and
devaluing experience in the middle of the nineteenth century than it would have
been even in the middle of the twentieth century. These new socially segregated,
geographically-isolated institutions must not automatically be presumed to be
obviously the wrong solution to a wrongly perceived problem, despite attracting
the epithet of 'warehousing' in the latter half of the next century.

If the expansion of the charitable/philanthropic voluntary hospital sector
could in the end meet only some of the nation's need for hospital provision, this
was equally true of the community health services made available through the
voluntary associations of the working-class mutual aid tradition, the Friendly
Societies. As with voluntary hospitals, a similar growth in voluntary health
insurance institutions took place in other European countries (Abel-Smith 1976:
8–11). In Britain, membership of Friendly Societies was already 10 per cent of the
population in 1804 (Abel-Smith 1994: 68) and it continued to grow throughout
the nineteenth century. By the turn of the century, Friendly Societies had at least
seven million members, over four times that of trade unions, and they were the
largest exclusively working-class organisations in Britain, estimated to include half
the adult male population (Abel-Smith 1994: 68; Gilbert 1966: 166; Thane 1982:
29). Most of these societies provided medical benefit, principally the payment
of sickness benefit and the services of general practitioners (GPs) under contract
to provide medical services to their members (Thane 1982: 28–9). As with the
voluntary hospitals, the Friendly Societies appeared to have considerable potential at least to meet the non-hospital health care needs of the working-classes. But
like the voluntary hospitals, the reality was less encouraging for those who wished
to see significant state provision of health care rendered unnecessary by the scale
of provision by voluntary associations. Never:

> ... were the weaker and more helpless elements of the working class success-
> ful in effecting a system of lasting consolidated societies. For generally, weak
> physical constitutions resulting from low wages, malnutrition, bad housing
> and squalid and filthy environments entailed an increase in disease, and
> therefore multiplied the claims for sickness benefits on a society which would
> obviously be impecunious

(Hodgkinson 1967: 236).

Thus the Friendly Societies made 'no appeal whatever to the grey, faceless lower third of the working class' and 'Friendly Society membership was not for the crossing sweeper, the dock labourer, the railroad navvy' (Gilbert 1966: 166–7). Instead, membership was 'the badge of the skilled artisan', 'the elite of the working-class (Honigsbaum 1989: 4). Furthermore, few societies admitted both men and women. Most women earned too little to pay their own contributions and few working-class families could afford double contributions (Thane 1982: 29, 30). If the health care needs of those unable to afford Friendly Society membership were met at all it might be through the outpatient department of a voluntary hospital, if location and circumstances permitted. More often it would be the Poor Law infirmaries and dispensaries that were the major providers of health care for women and children. More dispensaries appeared after the Metropolitan Poor Act 1867 (Brand 1965: 87 and 98–9; Hodgkinson 1967: Ch. 7). This 'elaborate systematisation of outdoor medical relief' put sick paupers within reach of:

> medical attendance far superior to that accessible to the lowest grade of independent labourers, but even placed sick paupers in the Metropolis, without loss of liberty, in a position equal to that of the superior artisan subscribing to a good provident dispensary.
>
> (Webb and Webb 1910, quoted by Hodgkinson 1967: 426–7)

Neither the personal nor the public health problems of an industrial and urban society seemed to be satisfactorily resolved by activities and institutions embodied in the 'Liberal Break' philosophy of 'laissez faire', personal initiative, voluntary associations and an institution-based, less-eligibility model of minimal state welfare.

Thus it was apparent in the last 30 years of the nineteenth century that the concept of a 'less eligibility' Poor Law was being compromised, first, by substantial variation in provision, especially between larger cities and elsewhere (Brand 1965: 106), second, by the principles applied by Poor Law medical officers in granting medical relief (Abel-Smith 1964: 64 and 206) and, third, by the standards attained by the best Poor Law infirmaries. Given the latter, the problem, as the framers of the 'less eligibility' principle might have predicted, had become one of moderating the use of nominally Poor Law institutions by the 'non-poor' (Abel-Smith 1964: 218). If there was a conflict between the Poor Law ideology and at least some Poor Law provision, there was potentially another one between that ideology and demands for even better provision. The argument was that a 'system of public relief deliberately made hideous for its recipients could not long outlast the grant of universal franchise' (Gilbert 1966: 15). However, if there was a conflict between the ideology formally underpinning the Poor Law, the reality of what the Poor Law authorities were making available in their areas, and the demands that might follow an extension of the franchise, these were not the only, even if the most significant, points of conflict within the pattern of health care provision in late nineteenth-century Britain.

There was the continuing significance of the long-standing divisions and related conflicts within the medical profession (Brand 1965: 147–8; Stevens 1966: 11–33; Woodward 1974: 4 and 27–8; Abel-Smith 1964: 2–3 and 116). The training and registration of the medical practitioners had been formally unified and their professional status legitimated by the Medical Act 1858. Nonetheless, the separate traditions of physicians, surgeons and apothecaries were still clearly represented in the division between community-based GPs and hospital-based specialist practitioners, GPs and consultants. This division was reflected in the different voluntary associations, with Friendly Societies employing GPs, and the specialist hospital doctors working in the voluntary hospitals. It remained a potential source of conflict within the profession because of the differential financial rewards favouring private practice (Abel-Smith 1964: 108–17 and 143–7), and indeed this division can be seen as one contributory factor in the maintenance of free voluntary hospital care in Britain at a time when 'pay hospitals' were developed in many other countries (Abel-Smith 1964: 137). The emergence of the referral system, by which the GPs had the patients and the specialists had the hospital beds, ameliorated the potential for conflict over remuneration by ensuring that the former played a role in the process of access to hospital care (Stevens 1966: 32–3; Honigsbaum 1979: Ch. 1).

There were potential sources of conflict between the medical profession, the state and the voluntary sector. Both the growing involvement of the state (through the Poor Law medical services) and the voluntary associations (through the Friendly Societies) were seen as threats to notions of professional autonomy and clinical freedom. Both Poor Law authorities and Friendly Societies sought to exercise detailed control over those medical practitioners under contract to them, raising the spectre of lay control over the profession (Brand 1965: 85–7, 94 and 102; Abel-Smith 1964: 60–2, 71 and 91; Honigsbaum 1989: 5). In addition, both the medical and emerging nursing profession found themselves in conflict with the Poor Law authorities over what they perceived as inadequate standards of care, the Poor Law medical officers becoming 'increasingly vocal on the need for reform in Poor Law medical care' (Brand 1965: 85; Abel-Smith 1964: 71–3). The level of remuneration was also a cause of complaint (Brand 1965: 88). On the other hand, contractual work undertaken on behalf of the Poor Law authorities and the Friendly Societies provided a relatively secure source of income for many members of the medical profession not linked with eminent voluntary hospitals and the more lucrative forms of private practice (Abel-Smith 1964: 214–5; Titmuss 1968: 233–8). The threats and merits of Poor Law and Friendly Society were inextricably linked. It was the employment and other costs of their medical practitioners, for example, prescribing, that led the Poor Law authorities and Friendly Societies to seek to exercise such close control over them. By contrast, the management environment of the voluntary hospitals was altogether more amenable to notions of professionalism. Governors were 'careful not to question the clinical judgement or examine the quality of the work of any of the doctors … unless they were forced to do so' (Abel-Smith 1964: 33). An altogether lighter touch was deemed appropriate for the eminent specialists working for mere honoraria!

Whilst the relationship between voluntary hospitals and their medical practitioners appeared relatively harmonious, the activities of the former, in terms
of the provision of largely free hospital services brought that sector into conflict
with both GPs in private practice and the Poor Law authorities. The GPs saw the
outpatient departments of the voluntary hospitals as a threat to their livelihood in
so far as the referral system was not universally applied at this time (Abel-Smith
1964: 104–8). The Poor Law authorities also found these outpatient departments
conflicting with their attempts to restrict access to free treatment within the Poor
Law, as one Guardian explained:

> When the attempt was made to extract a contribution from a patient with a
> broken arm before treatment the man might use some very coarse expression
> to us and walk out of the room. He goes straight to the London Hospital,
> where he gets treated for nothing.
>
> (Abel-Smith 1964: 131)

Even in the nineteenth century there were disputes about costs and the need for
cost containment (Abel-Smith 1964: 35), and by the end of the century the voluntary hospitals were finding it difficult to maintain the hospitals at the standard
to which they aspired. In particular, the cost of providing nursing care was rising
(Abel-Smith 1964: 134). The establishment of the Hospital Sunday Fund and
Hospital Saturday Fund, two national organisations to raise money for the voluntary hospitals, was a further early but clear indicator of the association between
'modern medicine' and 'escalating costs'. Also, more fundamental conflicts can
be discerned at this time by which new ideas might threaten the future of existing
political parties or perhaps of the political system itself. In the Trafalgar Square
riot of 8 February 1886, the old humanitarianism died in a spasm of terror. The
poor were no longer to be pitied and to be helped from Christian generosity. They
were now a menace to be bought off. What, it was asked, can the governors of
the nation do to prevent the poor from using their franchise to overturn a society
based on capitalist wealth (Gilbert 1966: 32 and 19)? The response to these conflicts would be a significant factor in further changes in health care for 'as it turned
out, the defence against socialism was social legislation' (Gilbert 1966: 19).

Thus there is a long history of state involvement in health care which can be
traced back at least as far as the origins of social assistance via the Poor Laws.
The state was a major provider of health care by the end of the nineteenth
century, via institutions such as asylums, hospitals and especially Poor Law infirmaries, 50 years before the establishment of the NHS. Some of the growing
activities of the state in the nineteenth century involved public health issues for
which state involvement is now taken for granted but which proved very contentious at the time. The growing activities of the state in the nineteenth century
also involved the search for better organisations (the new Poor Law authorities
(Boards of Guardians) and new local government (county councils and county
borough councils) following the Poor Law Amendment Act 1834 and the Local

Government Act 1888). There was significant growth of major voluntary institutions, the voluntary hospitals and the Friendly Societies. The growth of both voluntary and state institutions involved investment in, and a significant role for, various forms of institutional care, for example, Poor Law infirmaries, voluntary hospitals and county asylums. The resulting mix of voluntary and state institutions also involved much health care provided free at the time of need, for example voluntary hospitals. Nonetheless, there were major issues of equity of access to health care and the differing standards of health care received between social groups, regions and categories of medical condition. There were also concerns about escalating costs and the need for cost containment. The mix of health care institutions included private institutions (private nursing homes and private madhouses), which generated concerns about standards of care and calls for better regulation.

There were conflicts involving the medical profession (the legal standing of which was established by the Medical Act 1858) and the mix of voluntary and state institutions providing health care before 1900, such conflicts existing long before there was any significant discussion of a national health service. Unless the state and the organisations representing the professionals could agree upon the role of each in defining and meeting health care needs, with their subsequent administrative, economic and ethical consequences, then any relationship between them was bound to be full of conflict rather than complementary and consensual.

# Chapter 2

# From 'new liberalism' to the 'pre-war near-consensus'

The period immediately before the First World War was one of dynamic and extensive social policy reform. This is principally associated with the Liberal Governments of 1905–1914 and involved changing policies and provision in areas of child care, special needs education, employment services, income benefits for the sick and unemployed, maternity services, mental handicap, old age pensions and especially health care. The latter included the introduction of school health services, identified as one of two innovations that marked the beginning of the welfare state in Britain (Gilbert 1966: 102) The health care changes in this period both extended local government involvement in matters of health and at the same time introduced the concept of social insurance. The legislation introducing the latter has been described as one of the 'most expensive, the most ambitious, and the most controversial' of the social welfare reforms associated with the 1905–1914 Liberal Governments (Gilbert 1966: 289):

> Steps had to be taken to lighten the load of the poor lest the poor take violent steps to lighten the load of the rich.
>
> (Abel-Smith 1959: 351)

> As a working-class revolution resulting from poverty and unemployment had appeared to threaten the social structure in the eighties, so national physical deterioration became a clear danger after the Boer War, not only to the structure of domestic society, but to the very existence of Great Britain as a world power.
>
> (Gilbert 1966: 85)

The 'Liberal welfare reforms' can be related to a number of conflicts. First, there was the potential conflict between the Government and interest groups whose circumstances, especially financial circumstances, might be adversely affected by the Liberal welfare reforms. This was most obvious in relation to the proposed introduction of a state-regulated system of compulsory health insurance which developed into a classic exercise in pressure group politics. Second, there was the potential for conflict on party political lines. In particular, what was the political motivation of the 'Liberal welfare reforms?' Were the social reformist aspirations of the 'New Liberalism' associated with a concern to head off the political threat of the newly emergent Labour Party whose first Members of Parliament sat in the House of Commons following the General Election of 1905?

Third, the reforms became the focus of debates which pointed up potential conflicts (and perhaps contradictions) within the dominant ideologies of the time, especially those which combined a commitment to imperialist ideals abroad and a minimal state at home. Over the period 1893–1902, the official rate of Army rejections was of one in every three men examined by a recruiting officer and at least one Army general 'estimated that 60 per cent of men who volunteered were unfit for military service' (Brand 1965: 138). The latter statistic, relating specifically to Manchester in 1899, was publicised in White's book *Efficiency and Empire* (1901). Of a similar order was the conclusion in Rowntree's 1901 study of living conditions among the working-classes in York which could indicate that at least one-half of the manpower in England would be unavailable for military duty. These concerns gained a wider currency with the contemporaneous experience of the South African (Boer) War when 'rumours of ... widespread weakness and positive physical disability' (Gilbert 1966: 60) combined with revelations about ill-educated officers to generate an interest in 'national efficiency'. The noun 'efficiency' could take many qualifying adjectives. There could be political, educational, commercial, industrial, and above all, physical efficiency. The quest for national efficiency, therefore, gave social reform what it had not had before, the status of a respectable political question. Imperialism and the 'condition of the people question' became linked (Gilbert 1966: 60–1) and the particular interest in physical efficiency gave a special emphasis to the *physical* condition of the people and a particular resonance to social reforms relating to matters of health and health care.

Fourth, the Liberal welfare reforms can be set in the context of class conflict and the potential, real or imagined, for social unrest and even revolution. Socialist ideas could be perceived as dangerous to the political system as a whole, rather than just one identified political party within the system. Indeed, the whole social, economic and political order of capitalist, industrial societies might well have been seen to be threatened by the arrival of a workers' party, whose social and economic demands bridged the gap between the workplace and the home through the collectivist ideals. From this perspective, social insurance and the other social reforms of this period become not so much the means of saving the Liberal Party from the threat of the Labour Party, but of 'delivering Britain from the socialist solution to poverty' (Gilbert 1966: 451). Lastly, and perhaps most fundamentally, the Liberal welfare reforms can be seen as part of a long-running conflict between individualist and collectivist ideas and associated themes relating to the relative roles of the state, professionals and voluntary institutions.

Against this backcloth of interrelated conflicts linked to ideologies, interests and power, we can trace the particular conflicts of the health care reforms. Although hardly seen as the stuff of revolutionary politics, the school health services, health visiting and social insurance were to become important precursors of the National Health Service (NHS). The first two shared a focus on the perceived health needs of children and were to be provided through local government. They were introduced in a relatively uncontentious manner. The third involved a new form of taxation and a new principle of entitlement, a service partially financed by and accessed through what were termed insurance contributions. To implement this concept of social insurance, a new set of administrative arrangements would be put in place and the latter in particular can now be seen as providing a foretaste of the conflicts that would be engendered around the involvement of the state in bringing health care to a wider population.

## Health services for children

The introduction of a school health service was a rather muted affair; a surprising outcome for a new personal health service given the conflicts surrounding the establishment of public health legislation. This may be attributed to its origins in the Education (Administrative Provisions) Act 1907 which authorised the introduction of school medical *inspections* rather than a school medical *service*:

> Even this authorization was buried among more than a dozen other clauses dealing with uninteresting and involved housekeeping details of State school administration ... [thus] ... the medical service grew unnoticed and quietly from ministerial order.
>
> (Gilbert 1966: 117)

The wording of the relevant clause allowed local education authorities 'to make such arrangements as may be sanctioned by the Board of Education for attending to the health and physical condition of children educated in public elementary schools' but the entire debate on this clause occupied less than 20 pages in *Hansard* (Gilbert 1966: 130–1). Some advocates of inspection anticipated and hoped that medical inspection would reveal such a volume of ill-health that subsequent advocacy of a school medical service would be difficult to resist. The recent Report of the Committee on Physical Deterioration (29 July 1904) indicated that the former was a possible outcome. Its recommendations noted the importance of both environmental health reforms and a system of school medical inspection. But the attitude of the Conservative Government to this Report was significantly influenced by considerations of money. Prime Minister Balfour had told Anson curtly that so far as children's welfare was concerned he 'could be as sympathetic as he liked, but there would no increase in the rates' (Gilbert 1966: 95).

After the election of the Liberal Government in 1905, there were still issues to be resolved, such as disagreements about how such treatment should be administered and paid for, without making incursions into the income of private medical practice, replicating the stigmatising means testing of the poor law, or imperilling the financial and administrative independence of the voluntary hospitals. In the end, medical treatment provided by local education authorities became the norm with over 75 per cent of authorities making such provision by 1914 (Gilbert 1966: 156).

## Health visiting

In the same year that local government acquired the powers to develop school medical services, the development of health visiting services was facilitated under the Notification of Births Act 1907 (Parker 1965: 27). Local authorities were acquiring health service powers and duties beyond those most directly linked with the 'public health question', a trend that would continue so that a local government health service would be reasonably seen as the cornerstone of a national health service when the format of the latter became the subject of serious discussion (Chapters 3 and 4).

## Social insurance

Meanwhile, another model of health service administration was established. Its introduction generated significantly more conflict than the issues surrounding the school health services and health visiting. This was the concept of social insurance, to be inevitably linked with the concept of socialism, and which was embodied in a scheme to which the label National Health Insurance (NHI) was attached as part of National Insurance legislation which also introduced unemployment benefits.

Under Part I of the National Insurance Act 1911, manual workers and all others with incomes under £160 per annum were required to pay contributions to an approved society. Contributions were also required from their employers and there was a contribution to the scheme from other forms of taxation. In return for these contributions, insured persons became entitled to a limited cash benefit in sickness, to the services of a general practitioner (GP) and to a pharmaceutical benefit. There were optional additional benefits which Approved Societies were entitled to provide and the principle of free choice of doctor was enshrined in the Act. The Act did not directly affect the hospitals except through the provision for the care of tuberculosis patients. The latter operated partly through the new national insurance scheme, a sum being made available for expenditure on sanatorium benefit, and partly through central government grants for the construction of new accommodation (Abel-Smith 1964: 238–9; Brand 1965; Honigsbaum 1989).

The establishment of NHI in the UK can be seen as part of a trend apparent in a number of European countries in which voluntary health insurance, offering extensive but partial provision of community GP-based health care for working-class men, was supplanted by compulsory health insurance in which the services of GPs were extended to most working-class men. However whilst discernible as a common trend in a number of industrial societies, and indeed coming some considerable time after similar developments in other European countries, this introduction of a social insurance based, limited health service (it excluded hospital care) for a limited section of the population (it excluded all children, most working-class women, and men in non-manual occupations) generated considerable conflict. This related particularly to the position of potentially powerful interest groups whose circumstances, especially financial circumstances, might be adversely affected by the introduction of NHI.

These groups included the doctors, another common factor with the establishment of the NHS. Another group, to be of limited political consequence 35 years later, has been described as 'the single most powerful vested interest encountered by the social reformers of the New Liberalism' (Gilbert 1966: 165). This vested interest was the Friendly Societies, whose membership and activities had grown significantly during the latter half of the nineteenth century (see Chapter 1), and which had a long tradition of political conservatism and hostility to all government activity, despite its predominantly working-class membership. A state social insurance scheme appeared to pose a very real threat to their continued existence as providers of voluntary health insurance.

This opposition of the Friendly Societies was contained by enabling them to administer the Government's scheme as Approved Societies, a device employed in other countries and which significantly reduced the administrative costs of establishing a new state scheme. But the political and administrative advantages of this manoeuvre merely brought the Government into conflict with the medical profession and the industrial insurance companies. The former were opposed to being permanently consigned to the control of Friendly Societies in a Government health scheme. The latter saw their lucrative insurance business threatened by the potential expansion of their competitors as part of a government scheme. In the end the conflict was contained by two administrative devices.

First, the requirements for the Approved Societies, which were responsible for the day-to-day management of NHI, were constructed in such a way that industrial insurance companies, in addition to Friendly Societies, could qualify to administer the scheme on behalf of the Government. The industrial insurance companies had forced 'a virtual remodelling of national health insurance to permit their entry into the scheme', and achieved a 'great ... victory over the Government and over their colleagues in the Friendly Societies' (Gilbert 1970: 108). This arrangement lasted until Beveridge destroyed the veil of 'administrative rationality' that had eased the establishment of NHI. Second, a system for contracting with and paying the GPs was devised that avoided direct control by the Approved Societies. The latter solution was to survive the establishment of the NHS and several reorganisations of that service to become one of the more durable political compromises in British social policy (Klein 1973: Chs 3 and 4). Neither for the first nor last time, opposition to government commitment to a health care programme in the UK was contained by political manoeuvring.

One impact of the NHI scheme was to reinforce the existing referral system when some voluntary hospitals refused to treat NHI patients unless they were referred by their NHI doctors. Hospital outpatient departments also began to turn away 'trivial cases' on the grounds that treatment could be obtained through NHI. Whilst this approach was beneficial to hospital budgets, it was a factor in diminishing the value of the hospital setting as the sole location for medical education and training. But perhaps the major impact was on those members of the medical profession who joined the new scheme. Given the publicly stated fears of state control, it is ironic that NHI doctors found their remuneration guaranteed (and for most of them increased), their autonomy preserved and their professional status enhanced (Klein 1973: 60–3). They were at last freed from what they had seen as the petty administrative control and scrutiny of the Friendly Societies. Indeed, the argument has been advanced that NHI in the UK 'saved the GP' and 'reinforced general practice at the very time that specialisation was threatening it' (Stevens 1966: 53). The NHI scheme was responsible for locating GPs in a secure and central position in British health care, with the status of independent contractors. Maintaining this status was to become a point of principle with the British Medical Association (BMA) in subsequent conflicts with government.

The result of the conflicts engendered by NHI, and the actions taken to accommodate and ameliorate these conflicts, was that the social insurance scheme that became law in 1911 'bore practically no resemblance to the plan originally conceived in meetings with the friendly society representatives in October 1908' (Gilbert 1966: 290). This serves as perhaps the first example of a recurrent theme by which the detailed arrangements of health care reforms are significantly restructured to accommodate the perceived interests of key groups (see Chapters 4 and 8).

The introduction of NHI can serve to demonstrate not only the potential of professional power, but also its limitations. The National Insurance Act 1911 found its way on to the statute book not by accident, but by determined government action. The detailed administrative arrangements of NHI were significantly modified to accommodate key interest groups. But the Government's major commitment was to introduce a system of compulsory health insurance. This was established and the BMA's attempt to continue its boycott of the new system ended with a large-scale desertion of its members to the new NHI 'panels' (Eckstein 1955: 347; Lindsey 1962: 9), a trend to be repeated in 1948 and the early 1990s. The establishment of NHI marked another stage in a long-term trend in the UK and other industrialising societies by which significant changes were taking place in the relative roles of voluntary institutions and institutions of the state (Approved Societies, local government and poor law authorities) in the provision of health care.

The availability of GP services under NHI was subsequently extended. In 1919, the scheme was expanded to cover workers earning up to £250 p.a. 'bringing to 14 million the total of people within its orbit' (Hennessey 1992: 123). By 1940 it was estimated that 40 per cent of the population were covered by the scheme (Stevens 1966: 53; Fraser 1973: 184), but the latter figure concealed a major gender variation. For those aged between 14 and 64 years, the scheme covered 77 per cent of all men but only 39 per cent of women (Titmuss 1963: 213). Thus despite this extension, NHI remained true to its origins in providing a GP service primarily for working-class men. It continued to exclude most women and most forms of hospital care. At the same time, it bestowed the status of 'panel patient' on its recipients which, whilst being some way removed from the overtly stigmatising status of 'sick pauper', could embody a discriminatory and divisive approach when GPs also had private patients (Webster 1988: 27; Timmins 1995: 107). Lastly, 'the absence of integration and co-ordination among the thousands of participating units made the scheme expensive, inefficient and unwieldy' (Lindsey 1962: 10–11). Drawing more of the population into the NHI scheme was one of two modest extensions of state welfare activity in the nation's health care between the wars. The other strand of growing state intervention was the embryonic local government health service, the framework of which was certainly discernible by the 1930s.

## Municipal health services

In 1913 the Mental Deficiency Act required local authorities to appoint Mental Deficiency Committees whose responsibilities included the provision and maintenance of suitable institutions. The Maternity and Child Welfare Act 1918 made grants available to local authorities to improve their maternity services, infant welfare clinics and health visiting (Parker 1965: 28). In 1920, tuberculosis sanatoria became a responsibility of local authorities to enable the Approved Societies to meet the cost of increased capitation fees payable to NHI doctors (Gilbert 1970: 269–70). There was continued expansion of provision in local authority institutions which by 1921 provided nearly 22 per cent of the beds in England and Wales (Pinker 1966: 65). By 1936, local authorities had an obligation to provide, or at least finance, an adequate midwifery service and the power to provide a home help service (Parker 1965: 32). This was in addition to their other powers and obligations to employ health visitors, to provide a school health service and to undertake their long-standing public health responsibilities.

In addition, local government was a major provider of hospital care (see Chapter 1). Local authorities had inherited hospitals built by the nineteenth-century sanitary authorities. There were further piecemeal additions to this stock of fever hospitals and other sanatoria. Local government also retained responsibility for the treatment of mental illness in the asylums which were also a local government responsibility. The treatment of mental illness and the care of mentally ill people had been seen as something quite separate from physical illness and the care of physically ill people, and had also been seen as posing particular issues with regard to certification and detention (Chapter 1). In 1918, the Report of the Board of Control recommended that there should be treatment for a limited period without certification and that general hospitals should develop sections for the early diagnosis and treatment of mental illness. In 1926, the Royal Commission on Lunacy and Mental Disorder reported, and argued that there was:

*Table 2.1* The number and size of mental hospitals 1900–1948

| Date | Number of mental hospitals | Number of patients | Average number of patients per hospital* |
|------|----------------------------|---------------------|-------------------------------------------|
| 1900 | 77 | 74,004 | 961 |
| 1910 | 91 | 97,580 | 1,072 |
| 1930 | 98 | 119,659** | 1,221 |

Sources: Goodwin 1989: 43; Scull 1979: 198; Jones 1972: 357.

Notes:
* Still known as asylums before the Mental Treatment Act 1930.
** This figure rose to 147,546 in 1950.

> no clear line of demarcation between mental and physical illness ... a mental illness may have physical concomitants, probably it always has ... a physical illness, on the other hand, may have and probably always had mental concomitants, and there may be many cases in which it is a question of whether the physical or the mental symptoms predominate.
>
> (Jones 1960: 109)

The Commission also commented that the keynote of the past had been 'detention' and the keynote of the future should be 'prevention and treatment', and recommended that funds be made available for community care. In 1929, the Wood Committee recommended that greater use should be made of all forms of community care. 'Hospital regimes' did begin to change with the development of open wards, parole and day hospitals, night hospitals and outpatient treatment (Jones 1960: 128, 166–9 and 173–5; Roberts 1967: 26–9). However, these moves towards community care were paralleled by continuing increases in the numbers of mental hospitals and the number of mental hospital patients (see Table 2). The Mental Treatment Act 1930 made provision for voluntary treatment and by 1938 the proportion of voluntary admissions to mental hospitals was 35 per cent (and became 59 per cent by 1948) (Jones 1972: 256; Goodwin 1989: 45). After the Act the 'asylums' became known as mental hospitals.

A most significant change had been the Local Government Act 1929 which implemented a proposal of the Reconstruction Committee (Haldane) set up by Lloyd-George in 1917. The Act left the Poor Law on the statute book, but abolished the poor law authorities (Boards of Guardians) and transferred all powers, duties, buildings, personnel and paupers to county councils and county boroughs. The result was the potential for the establishment of a general municipal hospital service. By 1935, local authority health services 'accounted for about 60 per cent of expenditure in organised health care in Britain' (Webster 1995: 1584):

> [By 1938] From being a largely unorganised group of institutions mainly used by the infectious sick, the local authority hospital service had become a

reasonably well organised and diversified system based on county and county borough authorities

(Pinker 1966: 108)

Even more significantly, there was in place not only extensive local government *hospital services*, but a broad range of municipal *health services* (Webster 1988: 5–10). There was considerable scope for the development of a more comprehensive and co-ordinated set of health services located within the framework of local government. The circumstances were a model scenario for further modest, incremental extensions of state intervention in health care via both NHI and local government in line with any perceived pressure in that direction from the electorate (Timmins 1995: 109). Furthermore, these developments appeared to provide two potentially complementary means by which the state could intervene whilst leaving intact the established traditions of voluntary hospitals and substantial private medical practice.

## The voluntary hospitals

That the [voluntary] hospitals have fallen on evil days is known to all. The reason is two-fold. One is that the prices of all the commodities a hospital has to buy ... have increased. The other reason is that the investigation and treatment of diseases are becoming increasingly complex ... there is hardly a year but some new method of diagnosis or treatment makes it necessary to incur fresh expenditure. Almost without exception every (voluntary) hospital in the country is facing increasing difficulty in carrying out its work

(Dawson Report 1920: para. 82)

There was certainly pressure from some quarters to do something at this time about the organisation and finance of health care in the UK. This may be partly attributable to an emerging conflict within the voluntary hospital sector between the principles of voluntarism and the perceived need for modern hospital services. Whilst further expansion of poor law hospital services and their incorporation into local government complemented the acute focus of the voluntary hospitals, the latter were finding it increasingly difficult to meet needs even within their own narrowly defined sphere of competence. Medical advances were increasingly associated with escalating medical costs indicating a seemingly inevitable conflict between the scope of voluntary contributions and charitable bequests on the one hand and the needs of modern hospital services on the other. Between 1913 and 1920 contributions to the funds of voluntary hospitals rose by 67 per cent, but their expenditure rose by 138 per cent (Lindsey 1962: 14). The medical advances are illustrated by the account of a well-known provincial hospital which undertook less than 600 X-ray examinations in 1918 and was undertaking approximately 20,000 per annum by the 1940s. In the same hospital, pathological examinations multiplied by a factor of 33 and blood counts by a factor of 50 between 1927 and 1947. One source estimates that voluntary hospital spending was 640 times greater in 1947 than it had been in 1900 (Lindsey 1962: 24–5). These escalating costs associated with advances in medical technology were taking the voluntary hospitals up to and beyond the limits of philanthropy. It was no longer possible to sustain the standards of hospital work associated with the most eminent institutions without recourse to a much more substantial reliance on patient charges, some form of government funding or a combination of the two (Abel-Smith 1964: 303; Honigsbaum 1989: 16).

Payments by patients had formed 5 per cent of the income of London's voluntary hospital income in 1890. This had become 10 per cent just before the First World War, 40 per cent by 1931 and 50 per cent by 1938 (Abel-Smith 1964: 149 and 404; Webster 1988: 4, for similar figures for England and Wales). Between 1921 and 1938, total income from charitable donations doubled, and investment income also doubled, but income from fees and patient contributions increased fourfold (Harris 1979: 290). The Hospital Saving Association by which individuals sought to meet some of these new costs associated with hospital care, was set up in London in 1922, had 62,000 members by 1924 and 650,000 members by 1929. There were 300 similar schemes in place across the country by 1930. The character of the voluntary hospital sector was changing dramatically. They remained non-profit making but were losing some of their philanthropic features. With these changes another potential conflict loomed as the medical profession sought to change the terms under which they worked for these institutions. If the hospitals were charging fees for services should not some of this income accrue to their doctors?

Alongside the incremental changes in NHI and local government, and the crises in the costs and character of the voluntary hospital sector, there is clear evidence that the issue of health care reform was now firmly on the political agenda and not just a matter of private debate between the profession and the existing health care institutions. A series of reports and associated recommendations emerged from a variety of sources throughout the inter-war period.

## Recommendations for change

The Reconstruction Committee set up by Lloyd-George in 1917 recommended the abolition of the Board of Guardians, with all arrangements for the sick and infirm to be met through Public Health Committees. By 1918, the Labour Party was committed to the concept of a free national health service under democratic control centrally and locally. The voluntary hospitals would be merged into this system which would embody the principle of free choice of doctors. In the light of subsequent conflicts between the profession and a subsequent Labour Government, it is interesting that a spokesman for the BMA was reported to have expressed gratification at how much the Labour Party and the BMA were in agreement (Abel-Smith 1964: 285–7).

An early case for extending state intervention was made in the Dawson Report (1920). This can be seen as a precursor to the debate about rational management and arrangements for the equal distribution of health care which were to be an enduring point of discussion and conflict once the NHS was established. The Report is important for what it had to say about the organisation of health services and has been described as 'revolutionary' (Abel-Smith 1964: 290) and 'widely taken as the blueprint for a modern comprehensive health service' (Webster 1988: 241). It included the following statement:

> The changes which we advise are indeed necessary because the organization of medicine have become insufficient and because it fails to bring the advantages of medical knowledge adequately within the reach of the people. This insufficiency of organization has become more apparent with the growth of knowledge and with the increasing conviction that the best means of maintaining health and curing disease should be made available to all citizens. Such considered combined efforts to yield the best results must be located in the same institution.
>
> (Dawson Report 1920: para. 3)

The key recommendation was to create a series of neighbourhood preventive and curative services including those of GP, dentist, pharmacist, nurse, midwife and health visitor, and to base these services in a Primary Health Centre. Groups of Primary Health Centres should be based upon a 'Secondary Health centre dealing with cases of difficulty requiring special treatment staffed by consultants and specialists or by GPs acting in a consulting capacity' (Dawson Report 1920: 9–11). For Dawson and his colleagues the 'dominant purpose' underlying their recommendations was 'providing the best services for the health of the people' (Dawson Report 1920: para. 17), and their report was given a good press and well-received by the BMA (Abel-Smith 1964: 292–3). However, the political climate of the time was not propitious (Abel-Smith 1964: 298 and 301), and Dawson's guiding principle that 'the best means of maintaining health and curing diseases should be made available to all' was consigned to the 'world of medical utopias' (Webster 1988: 19).

Dawson raised the issue of the conflict between delivering medical care to the population through essentially nineteenth-century administrative means, protected by nineteenth-century guild-like professional concerns, and the twentieth century growth in scientific knowledge. This mismatch between a delivery system and the content of health care was to produce a long drawn out debate about whether or not a centralised service with decisions made in the Ministry should affect all parts of the UK. Dawson's insight has retained its general validity. A mismatch between scientific medical advance, public expectations and a well-funded and rationally administered system was to remain an enduring source of potential conflict.

The Cave Committee (1920–1921) anticipated the increasing role of patient contributions in the finances of the voluntary hospital sector but also recommended temporary support from public funds. Parliament responded with a grant half of that recommended by the Committee (Ministry of Health 1921). In

1924, Lord Knutsford recommended that all voluntary hospitals and Poor Law infirmaries should be placed under one local management arrangement with financial support in the form of large grants from the Ministry of Health (Abel-Smith 1964: 321).

The Royal Commission on National Health Insurance reported in 1926 and concluded that the scheme was working reasonably well. Both majority and minority reports recommended extending the coverage of NHI in terms of population (dependants) and health care, for example, dental care. However, the minority report not only identified the limitations of NHI already referred to, but judged the insurance principle to be an unsound method of financing medical services, concluding that ultimately medical benefits would have to be financed from public funds (Gilbert 1970: 276 and 281). A professional view was represented by the BMA's proposals for a *General Medical Service for the Nation* published in 1930 and reissued in a revised form in 1938. Key recommendations included the extension of NHI to dependants of insured persons but the emphasis was on the provision of more health care, such as maternity services, rather than extending those sections of the population eligible to receive such health care. An income limit of £250 per annum would be retained (BMA 1930). This would have the desirable effect, from the point of view of the profession, of maintaining the clinical autonomy associated with voluntary hospital work, whilst introducing remuneration for doctors in these institutions. It was intriguing, if somewhat prophetic, that the medical profession anticipated that the remuneration of voluntary hospital staff would introduce no more supervision over their activities than was the norm when they were practising as essentially unpaid professionals. Under this proposal, private practice would of course remain extensive for the more affluent members of society whose incomes took them beyond the upper limits of NHI (Abel-Smith 1964: 348–51).

The revised 1938 report continued to emphasise the need to pay all hospital staff, and also contended that there should be no GP services in hospital outpatient departments, the latter being the latest expression of the GP's fear of any system that enabled their prospective patients to seek out an alternative service to their own or an alternative mode of access (other than GP referral) to more specialist services (BMA 1938). In between the two versions of the BMA's report, a Voluntary Hospitals Commission (British Hospitals Association 1937) sought to draw public attention to both the value of the existing voluntary hospital system and for the need for co-operation between competing voluntary and local government hospitals. This identifies one theme in the developing debate about health care reform, the need for a rationalisation of the fragmented and somewhat haphazard assemblage of health care institutions that constituted health care in the UK before the NHS.

Arguments for change were given added weight for some commentators since the arrangements gave ample opportunity for enormous variations in service provision in different parts of the country. Whilst there is some evidence that public sector hospital provision did compensate to some extent for the vagaries in the voluntary hospital sector (Powell 1992a, 1992b), the overall effect was of profound regional disparities as indicated by per capita measurements of GPs, consultants and hospital beds (Eckstein 1958; Lindsey 1962: 7 and 15). The NHI system compounded this problem through the system which allowed the Approved Societies to make available additional medical benefits, for example, home nursing, subject to their finances being in a satisfactory state. But many urban societies were in a parlous financial situation attributable to variations in the incidence of industrial diseases and unemployment; these societies were not in a position to provide any additional benefits (Eckstein 1958: 29).

This was paralleled by significant variations in indices of health status. For example, infant mortality rates (IMR) in places like Glasgow and Jarrow were much higher than those for Surrey and Oxford. Jarrow's IMR was four times the rate in Oxford in 1936 (Briggs 1978: 448; Fraser 1973: 185–6). A rather dramatic inverse care law appeared to be in operation by which those parts of the country which appeared to have the greatest need were also most deficient in health care facilities. Around the related themes of efficiency and equity it was possible to construct a powerful case for health care reform for Britain's 'remarkably inefficient and inadequate set of services' (Eckstein 1958: viii). There was 'duplication, competition, lack of co-ordination' (Webster 1988: 391). The problem was how to fund the health care of the state, by taxes, rates, or contributory insurance, and the place of voluntary hospitals. There is evidence that the profession, the voluntary hospitals and successive governments recognised this. However, in an obvious parallel with early debates about NHI and school health services, it was less clear whether any degree of consensus about the need to 'do something' could be carried over into the more detailed discussion of what form that 'something' should take, and there were disagreements over the role of local government, the future of voluntary hospitals, and the contributory principle.

By the end of the 1930s, after a long period of discussion, a number of ideas had crystallised on the need for reform and redefinition of medical services (Stevens 1966: 53). The period covered by this chapter involved significant changes in the relative roles of voluntary institutions and institutions of the state (Approved Societies, local government and poor law authorities) in the provision of health care. There was the establishment and expansion of NHI and the provision of a broad range of municipal health services. But there was also a case for further changes in provision that involved a partial NHI scheme that excluded children, non-earning wives, the self-employed, many old people and higher paid employees, and which operated alongside other services whose scope and effectiveness depended on the wealth of each area, the political initiative of different local authorities, the 'provincial patriotism and parochial jealousies' (Eckstein 1958: 71) of a 'system' whose finances depended on 'the donations of the living and the legacies of the dead' (Abel-Smith 1990: 11). There was 'no hospital system' but rather a collection of individual hospitals 'criss-crossed, separated and enclosed by local government boundary barriers, legal, residential and occupational barriers, medical category and financial barriers' (Titmuss 1963: 143). Outcomes included a 'disjunction between municipal and voluntary hospital sectors ... [and] ...

unevenness of provision, especially of hospital resources' (Webster 1988: 20 and 12; Lindsey 1962: 14 and 17). In addition, those parts of the country which appeared to have the greatest need were also most deficient in health care facilities. The period covered by this chapter provides further evidence of the conflicts actual and potential which have characterised health care developments in the UK.

First, and perhaps most readily identified and understood, there are the conflicts associated with the broad macro debates about the role of the state in health and welfare. NHI represented a commitment to guaranteed access for a substantial proportion of the population to a state regulated form of health care based upon a stable system of finance, and without a means test. Any proposal or action, such as NHI, which takes the role of the state beyond a less-eligibility model of minimal state welfare has the capacity to generate conflicting questions, such as, for whom should the state provide, on what conditions and at what standard, and to encounter opposing interests, especially those of non-state welfare institutions, such as Friendly Societies and private insurance companies.

Second, emerging particularly from the more detailed social and political histories of state health and welfare developments, there are the conflicts engendered by the micro debates about administrative details. Any outcome that leaves the state with a significant role in providing health care is likely to provoke ongoing and quite fierce conflicts over the organisational and financial arrangements of these state provided health services. Once the relationship between the state and the medical profession is formalised, this encourages debates on resources, remuneration and redistribution. It is impossible to avoid conflict in discussions of these areas.

Third, there was the conflict between the past successes and contemporary roles of the poor law authorities. As we noted in Chapter 1, the latter had become important providers of health care at least in part through the limitations of the voluntary institutions. But despite the standard of its better health care facilities, the Poor Law could not escape the success of past legislators and administrators in creating its indelible association with the stigmatising status of pauper:

> When the welfare state began to grow, practically all the vast nineteenth century apparatus of parochial relief had to be abandoned lest it taint the new reform measures.
>
> (Gilbert 1966: 22; Lindsey 1962: 10)

If governments were to take seriously the concept of extending and improving the public provision of health services, they would have to look to some administrative arrangement clearly differentiated from the poor law authorities. The transfer of poor law health care to local government in 1929 represented one such administrative arrangement. However, both the unsuitable nature of many old Poor Law institutions, and the continuity of individuals and ideologies between the old Poor Law Boards of Guardians and the new local authority

Public Assistance Committees, restricted the potential of the new arrangements (Abel-Smith 1964: 369–70).

Fourth, the quite wide-ranging consensus about the need for health care reform yielded limited action in part because there was less agreement about the details of reform, but also because successive inter-war Governments 'practised ruthlessly the dogma of traditional public finance and were meeting the economic crisis with rigid economy on public expenditure' (Abel-Smith 1964: 298; Gilbert 1970: 302–3).

Lastly, we can note the enduring theme of the conflict between traditional concepts of voluntarism, voluntary organisations financed by voluntary contributions, and the generally accepted needs of a modern health care system. By the inter-war period it was apparent that the voluntary tradition could not be maintained even in the context of significant but narrowly defined forms of hospital care. 'The voluntary hospitals had become primarily trading concerns and only secondarily charitable institutions' (Abel-Smith 1964: 402).

Taken together, our first two chapters provide considerable evidence of wide-ranging conflicts relating to health care and its provision before any government had made any commitment towards anything resembling a national health service. But in addition to the material on health inequalities linked to class and geography, and major scandals relating to infant mortality, maternal mortality and child health, there was evidence, however, of increased public expenditure on health (Webster 1990: 142). There was certainly considerable interest in health care reforms, but this was understandable when inter-war health policy was dominated by strict Treasury discipline, an inclination to evade problems until public outcry made further evasion impossible, the use of investigative committees and commissioners to delay action, a minimum legislative response with maximum reliance on permissive powers, strict control of new services to give the impression of adequate response to need while actually providing services only on a token basis, a failure to distribute services according to need, and lastly a preference for services maximising the growth of medical bureaucracies, even when this involved inefficient use of resources (Webster 1990: 143). State intervention in health care changed significantly during this period, taking the role of the state well beyond a less eligibility model of minimal state welfare. By the end of this period the state (notably local government) was a very significant provider of health care, such as social insurance, local government hospitals and other community health services. The number of mental health institutions (asylums/mental hospitals) and inpatients had also continued to increase and there was a limited but growing interest in various forms of less institutional care. As a result of these developments there were significant changes in the relative roles of voluntary institutions and institutions of the state as health care providers. The Liberal welfare reforms can be seen as providing the context for the state to become involved in providing a wide range of services which addressed the major issues of childhood nutrition, maternity care, unemployment and sickness benefits, and old age pensions. They also involved providing health care coverage to insured male workers although not their dependants. This policy (the National Insurance Act 1911) was to become the platform upon which the modern NHS was built (Chapters 3 and 4). These reforms gained some impetus from concerns about 'national efficiency', particularly 'military efficiency'.

Once the relationship between the state and the medical profession had been formalised, it encouraged debates on resources, remuneration and redistribution and on the organisational and financial arrangements for state-provided health services. It was impossible to avoid conflict in discussions of these areas. The issue of escalating costs remained an ongoing issue in the provision of health care (and was posing particular problems for the voluntary hospitals). There remained major issues of equity of access to health care and the standard of health care received between social groups, regions and categories of medical condition. Those parts of the country which appeared to have the greatest need were also most deficient in health care facilities. There were concerns about the efficiency of the way health care providers were organised, with proposals being made for their rationalisation. Despite this interest in health care reform it yielded limited action in part because of the economic policies of inter-war governments. There was also a near consensus about the need for further reforms in health care provision, although there was much less agreement about the details of reform. By the end of 1939, however, there may have been a sense that any resolution of the problems of British health care would not form part of a political agenda since the nation was involved in an altogether more significant conflict. In the event, quite the opposite occurred, and questions of the quality, distribution and responsibility for health care were to form part of the wartime political agenda, in particular the purposes for which the war was being fought. As a result, the nation's health services became the core of the reconstruction of civil society in the immediate aftermath of the Second World War.

# Chapter 3

# War, Beveridge and health care

We reach a ... [further]... stage in our ascending scale of interest. Not only was it necessary for the State to take positive steps in all spheres of the national economy to safeguard the physical health of the people; it was also imperative for war strategy for the authorities to concern themselves with that elusive concept 'civilian morale.'

(Titmuss 1963: 81–2)

Wartime commitment to planning and interwar crisis exposed the instability and inappropriateness of the ramshackle edifice of medical services.

(Webster 1988: 16)

An initial judgement might be that total war in Europe would consign the arguments over health care reform to a forgotten corner of the political agenda for the duration of an altogether more substantial and dramatic set of conflicts. But governments who wage war are forced to consider the implications for the health of combatant troops, veteran services and the civilian population. It is no surprise that many of the descriptions and analyses of the modern National Health Service (NHS) raise the intriguing question of the relationship between total war and the development of universal health care. The connection between military conflict and changes in health care can be traced back at least as far as the Crimean War, including the changes in the nursing profession that flowed from Florence Nightingale's experiences of military hospitals. Public concern was generated by publicising the primary role of preventable disease rather than battle as the major cause of military mortality (Brand 1965: 137). Subsequently, the experience of the Boer War confirmed the potential threat to the armed forces of preventable conditions such as enteric fever and dysentery (Brand 1965: 140; Trombley 1989: Chs 7 and 8). In addition, problems of military recruitment during the Boer War provided a focus for the concerns about 'national efficiency' that underpinned some of the Liberal welfare reforms, particularly the development of the medical inspection of children in schools (Chapter 2). This concern re-emerged with the continuing rejection of recruits on health grounds during the First World War. A parallel inter-relationship between war and welfare was the inflation associated with the First World War, subsequently identified as one factor in pricing the least well off out of the housing market, precipitating rent control and contributing to the end of working-class house building as a profitable enterprise (Fraser 1973: 168). Lastly, war had a significant impact on the financial fortunes of the key voluntary institutions involved in health care. The voluntary hospitals and the Approved Societies emerged from the First World War in a significantly improved financial situation (Abel-Smith 1964: 282; Gilbert 1970: 263–5).

This theme, linking war and social policy, was explored in a well-known essay by Richard Titmuss, from which one of the opening quotations of this chapter is taken, and in his classic, *The Problems of Social Policy* (1950). Both texts include the argument that the scale and intensity of war had stimulated a growing concern about the quantity and quality of the population. As the nature of warfare changed so the scope of public concern broadened to include 'the health and well-being of the whole population and, in particular, of children, the next generation of recruits' (Titmuss 1963: 78). With the Second World War, a war in which Britain depended on the contribution of nearly all its citizens, we arrive at the situation where 'the war could not be won unless millions of ordinary people were convinced that we had something better to offer than had our enemies, not only during, but after the war' (Titmuss 1963: 82). The significance of this was recognised in the famous leader in *The Times* – a compelling contrast with the comments from the same source on public health (Chapter 1):

> If we speak of democracy, we do not mean a democracy which maintains the right to vote but forgets the right to work and the right to live. If we speak of freedom, we do not mean a rugged individualism which excludes social organization and economic planning. If we speak of equality, we do not mean a political equality nullified by social and economic privilege. If we speak of economic reconstruction, we think less of maximum production (though this too will be required) than of equitable distribution.
>
> (*The Times*, 1 July 1940)

In these circumstances, the relevance of pre-war debates about health care was not only retained but enhanced. Health care reforms would be in line with *The Times*'s clarion call, even if past experience of conflict between the government of the day and the medical profession would suggest they might be difficult to achieve. Even without these broader concerns, the perceived inefficiencies of the hospital sector of the health services were of immediate concern in planning for the likelihood of significant civilian air raid casualties (Eckstein 1958: 86–7). The solution to the haphazard and extremely variable quality of existing hospital services was a significant degree of central government control and expenditure through the Emergency Medical Services (EMS). In a sense, the hospitals were temporarily nationalised (Lindsey 1962: 19; Abel-Smith 1964: Ch. 26; Eckstein 1958: Ch. 4). The effects of the EMS had 'almost the proportions of a revolution' (Webster 1988: 24). Extensive investment was needed to bring the poorest quality institutions up to a reasonable standard involving the addition of at least 50,000 beds, the installation of 1,000 completely new operating theatres and the ordering of 48 million bandages, dressings and fitments. The estimated number of artery forceps now required represented over 30 years' previous demand for the whole country. Specialised treatment centres were also established and the ambulance service was improved (Eckstein 1958: 48; Abel-Smith 1964: 426; Titmuss 1950: 83; Lindsey 1962: 19).

The experience of the EMS added weight to the arguments that existing provision was both inefficient and inequitable, and made credible the concept of a national plan for health by demonstrating 'what the central government could accomplish through planning and financial assistance' (Lindsey 1962: 19). The deficiencies of many hospitals also became 'visible' for the first time to London-based doctors redeployed to the provinces (Abel-Smith 1964: 436; Harris 1979: 290) and middle-class patients who had not used certain services before (Eckstein 1958: 98). Furthermore, the poor physical state of many urban children also became 'more visible' with the evacuation of children (Packman 1975: 21). The public expenditure on health services and the public and professional experiences of using and providing such services, added considerably to existing arguments that the patchwork quilt of local government and voluntary provision which constituted the British hospital services was far from adequate to meet the health care needs of the population.

Meanwhile, reports on the future of Britain's health services continued to be issued in wartime Britain. In 1939, *The Lancet* appointed Dr Taylor to produce a plan. This recommended a National Hospital Corporation to take over all hospitals and run them on a regional basis with full-time salaried staff but minimal lay control (Abel-Smith 1964: Ch. 27). The following year the Socialist Medical Association produced a plan for a unified medical service organised on a regional basis with a salaried service. In the same year the British Medical Association (BMA) set up a Medical Planning Commission (Honigsbaum 1989: 36–7), and in 1941 a group of younger doctors and health service workers created Medical Planning Research through the columns of *The Lancet*, fearing that the age and background of the members of the Medical Planning Commission would lead to reactionary and unrepresentative conclusions (Abel-Smith 1964: Ch. 27). This activity was one indication that a state of total war was not considered inconsistent with a concern for the issues associated with health care reform. A most dramatic example of this continuing concern was the announcement in October 1941 by the Ministry of Health that the Government was committed to establishing a comprehensive *hospital* service after the war, including the intention that appropriate treatment would be available to all who needed it (Honigsbaum 1989: 28–9; Hennessey 1992: 134). This announcement did not stem the flow of reports and recommendations. In 1942, the BMA published the report of its Medical Planning Commission. The Commission was against local government control and a full-time salaried service, and in favour of forms of organisation with strong medical leadership and representation. A regional hospital service was favoured with health centres as the focal point for general practice. The Commission also favoured the retention and expansion of National Health Insurance (NHI) to cover approximately 90 per cent of the population (Lindsey 1962: 28–30) but in September 1942 the annual representative meeting of the BMA decided that provision should be made for the 'whole of the community'. Two months later the report of the Medical Planning Research group also supported a health service available to the whole community. They recommended a free health service as part of a comprehensive social security scheme with generous cash benefits, to be run by a national corporation operating through eleven regions. However, the espousal of the principle of universality by the BMA and the Medical Planning Research group was to be overshadowed by a more widely publicised advocacy of universality, including health services for the whole of the community (Lindsey 1962: 30–1).

The statement of a reconstruction policy by a nation at war is a statement of the uses to which that nation means to put victory, when victory is achieved. In a war which many nations must wage together as whole-hearted allies, if they are to win, such a statement of the uses of victory may be vital (Beveridge Report 1942: 171 para.459). The Battle of Alamein began on 23 October 1942 and was concluded on 10 November 1942. A week before the battle began, questions were being asked, as usual, in the House of Commons. On 15 October 1942 the Prime Minister was asked about the possibility of transferring the Elgin Marbles to the Greek government for restoration to their original site after the war. A question was also asked about placing disabled ex-servicemen poultry-keepers in the same category as the blind respecting supplementary rations for their flocks. Sandwiched between these was an innocuous sounding question, 'Is the Postmaster General in a position to say when the Beveridge Report on Social Insurance will be made available to the House?' (House of Commons 1942: cols 805, 1229, 1633 and 1762).

Beveridge was 60 years old when he was asked to chair the Manpower Requirements Committee of the Production Council in July 1940. Like many other people, he never got on with Ernest Bevin and was moved sideways to the innocuous, almost soporific sounding, inter-departmental committee on social security and allied services (Honigsbaum 1989: 35). His brief was to tidy up the fragmented social security system of the day, to disentangle Victorian and Edwardian social security legislation and administrative rules in preparation for post-war reconstruction, and to make recommendations to the wartime coalition Government.

What Beveridge found was a haphazard piecemeal social security system in which seven government departments administered cash benefits. For example, he found that Workmen's Compensation was administered by the Home Office, unemployment insurance by the Ministry of Labour, NHI by the Ministry of Health, non-contributory old age pensions by Customs and Excise, contributory old age pensions by the Ministry of Health, Supplementary Pensions by the Unemployment Assistance Board, war victims' benefits by the Ministry of Pensions and the civilian widows', disabled and orphans' benefits by the Ministry of Health. In addition, all benefits were funded differently, Workman's Compensation by the employer, war pensions, non-contributory old age pensions, and unemployment assistance by the taxpayer, public assistance by the ratepayer, and health, unemployment and old age insurance split between employee, employer and the state. Furthermore, the size and scope of the benefits varied. The whole system was beset by overlap and duplication. Children and the aged were missed out. Inequalities and anomalies abounded. As for medical benefit, this was provided by a panel system, excluding dependants and open to those only below a certain income limit:

> Again and again witnesses pressed spontaneously and independently for measures which became the main policy proposals of the Beveridge Report, namely, family allowances, full employment and a universal health service.
>
> (Harris 1977: 414)

The main idea behind the report was that there would be a single national insurance scheme, administered by a single department, and which would be 'universal' in its coverage, meaning that all members of the population would be potential contributors (via national insurance contributions) and potential beneficiaries (via national insurance benefits) for the contingencies identified as the major causes of poverty. Three principles underpinned the Report's recommendations. These were that, first, proposals for the future should not be restricted by the consideration of sectional interests. Second, that social insurance should be seen as one part of an attack upon want 'in some ways the easiest to attack' (Beveridge Report 1942: 6, para. 8), whilst still leaving the giants of disease, ignorance, squalor and idleness to be addressed. Third, that social security must be achieved by co-operation between the state and the individual. The principles underpinning the Beveridge Report were to be supported by three assumptions, that 'no satisfactory scheme of social security can be devised' without children's allowances, policies for maintenance of employment and 'Assumption B', comprehensive health and rehabilitation services for prevention and cure of disease and restoration of capacity for work, available to all members of the community (Beveridge Report 1942: 120, para. 301). It is this latter, a 'comprehensive health service' in the language of Beveridge's report, which was both the great promise of what the British population could expect, and, at the same time, the 'Achilles Heel' of the health service, depending as it did on finance, politics and the law. The history of the health service has been one of attempting to meet this high ideal, whilst constrained by financial and other socio-political and legal factors:

> Provision for most of the many varieties of need through interruption of earnings and other causes that may arise in modern industrial communities had already been made in Britain on a scale not surpassed and hardly rivalled in any other country of the world. In one respect only of the first importance,

namely limitation of medical service, both in the range of treatment that is provided as of right and in respect of the classes of persons for whom it is provided as of right, does Britain's achievement fall seriously short of what has been accomplished elsewhere.

(Beveridge Report 1942: para. 3)

A comprehensive national health service will ensure that for every citizen there is available whatever medical treatment he requires, in whatever form that he requires it, domiciliary or institutional, general, specialist or consultant, and nursing and midwifery and rehabilitation after accidents ... the service itself should ... be provided where needed without contribution conditions in any individual case

(Beveridge Report 1942: paras 426/427)

Six key concerns can be identified in the Beveridge Report. There are concerns with the relationship between social security and the health of individuals, families and communities; with administrative rationality; with comprehensive coverage; with services free at the point of consumption; with future demand and cost; and with the philosophy of a national health service.

On the relationship between social security and health, Beveridge was particularly critical of the existing scheme of Workmen's Compensation which he regarded as an especially ineffective provision for the rehabilitation of injured workers (Beveridge Report 1942: 38, para. 80). This serves as a particular example of the role of comprehensive health and rehabilitation services in the prevention and cure of disease and restoration of capacity for work, and the extent to which expenditure on effective health care contributes to containing the costs of the social security system, by minimising expenditure on unmet needs for health care.

The Report was critical of the 'the anomalies and overlapping, the multiplicity of agencies and the needless administrative cost' of existing administrative arrangements. Beveridge's preference was for 'co-ordination, simplicity and economy' (Beveridge Report 1942: 15, para. 29) and, accordingly, he recommended the ending of that seemingly essential element of the political settlement which had established NHI, the Approved Societies (Chapter 2). 'Experience and evidence together points the way to making a single Approved Society for the nation' (Beveridge Report 1942: 15, para. 29). Beveridge was also to recommend the 'separation of medical treatment from the administration of cash benefits and the setting up of a comprehensive medical service for every citizen, covering all treatment and every form of disability under the supervision of the Health Departments' (Beveridge Report 1942: 15, para. 30 and para. 106). For all practical purposes the social insurance principle, which was to be retained as a key principle of the social security reforms, was abandoned so that 'all classes will be covered for comprehensive medical treatment and rehabilitation and for funeral expenses' (Beveridge Report 1942: 10, para. 19, iii).

This advocacy of comprehensive coverage was clearly an important element in the Report given the degree of popular support it seemed to command. Although with hindsight it can be readily identified as a continuation of existing trends, government acceptance of this proposal would constitute a significant shift beyond the stated commitment to some sort of national hospital service. In addition the 'separation of medical treatment from the administration of cash benefits and setting up of a comprehensive medical service for every citizen, covering all treatment and every form of disability' (Beveridge Report 1942: 48, para. 105) might have implications for the organisation of health care that could not be accommodated by incremental changes to the resourcing of, and relationships between, existing health care providers. The recommendation that there will be 'comprehensive medical treatment, both domiciliary and institutional for all citizens and their dependants which ... will be without charge on treatment at any point' (Beveridge Report 1942: 14, para. 28) can be represented as continuing a well-established British tradition (Chapter 1) but also as a challenge to the emerging pattern of financing hospital care in the voluntary sector (Chapter 2).

A comprehensive health service largely free at the point of consumption has potentially profound implications for the demands that might be placed on such a service and the resulting costs of maintaining the service. This potentially explosive problem was to be at least partially ameliorated by developing 'a health service which will diminish disease by prevention and cure' (Beveridge Report 1942: para. 437). This accords with a subsequent comment by Titmuss that:

> Among all the ideas of the 1930s and 1940s which led to the creation of the Health Service the one which increasingly dominated the mind of the public and the profession alike was the idea of prevention
>
> (Titmuss, 1963: 140)

Thus the outcome of a better health service could be a healthier population that would have less need for health services and make fewer demands on social security benefits available for sickness and disability. This assumption can be related to both the existing evidence of an inverse care law, areas with the worst health services had the worst health (Chapter 2) and to a widely held view that improved personal health services have a simple and explicit relationship with improved health status.

Philosophically, Beveridge's plan for social security was in his words 'first and foremost a method of redistributing income, so as to put the first and most urgent needs first, so as to make the best possible use of whatever resources are available' (Beveridge Report 1942: 170, para. 457). It was also about 'balancing arguments and equities, comparing desires and resources' and devising 'methods of making all the immense good that has been accomplished into something better still' (Beveridge Report 1942: 20, para. 40):

> The greatest public acclaim was given to the proposal which was outside the Report's field.
>
> (Calder 1971: 611)

> Probably few members of the Government, least of all Churchill, guessed the impact which the Beveridge Report would make on the public mind.
>
> (Foot 1975: 407)

Beveridge's Report had been generating considerable controversy before its publication. One Member of Parliament (MP) had been critical of the 'powerful interests who are already trying to prejudge and sabotage the report in advance'. He was referring to the Approved Societies, which administered sickness benefit under the existing NHI scheme. Industrial insurance companies were responsible for 100 million policies a year in 1941, bringing in a total of £74,000,000 per year. Forty per cent of this went in management expenses. These policies were sold to the poor who often got into arrears, and once in arrears, there was the possibility that their benefits might lapse and their investment lost (Gilbert 1966: 319–26). Parliamentary grumbles continued over the Report until the parliamentary debate in the House of Commons on 17 February 1943. The flavour of these grumbles gives us some idea of how contentious the Report was. For example, *The Daily Telegraph* reported Beveridge as saying his Report 'would take us half way to Moscow'. Beveridge made a short and mild disclaimer in the newspaper. Other MPs were more concerned with leaked proposals to abolish 'free doctoring'. Others insisted that what was required in addition to Beveridge's proposals was 'a statutory minimum wage'. Large numbers of Labour MPs pressed the Postmaster-General continuously from September to November (1942) about the Report and all raised their own particular topics of importance. For example, would it contain proposals to reform old age pensions? A further series of parliamentary skirmishes took place concerning the leak of the Report to the press before it was considered by Parliament and the question was raised as to whether the BBC was using it as propaganda by broadcasting its contents to 'all parts of the world'. Bevan and Shinwell were furious with Anthony Eden for the press leak, 'If this practice goes much further, debates in this House will be rigged by private interests'. Eden gave an undertaking that in future the House would receive its policy papers before the press (House of Commons 1943: cols 1613–94).

The Report, with the somewhat uninspiring title of, *Social Insurance and Allied Services*, was made available to the general public in December 1942 (Beveridge Report 1942). People lined up outside the shops of His Majesty's Stationery Office to buy the Report, forming what one commentator has termed 'the most significant queues of the war' (Calder 1971: 609). A brief official summary of the Beveridge Report was issued and the combined sales of the full report and the summary reached 650,000.

Within two weeks of its publication, a Gallup Poll discovered that 19 out of 20 people had heard of the Report and nine out of ten believed that its proposals should be adopted (Calder 1971: 609; Barnett 1986: 29).

There was little doubt that the proposal that after the war Britain should have not just a comprehensive *hospital* service, but a comprehensive *health* service was quite firmly on the political agenda, despite the other pressing concerns of wartime Britain. A head of steam had built up politically to force the coalition Government to accept the recommendations of the Report almost before they were published. In February 1943 the House of Commons debated the Report (House of Commons 1943: cols 1613–2050). The Government announced that it welcomed the concept of a reorganised and comprehensive health service which would cover the people as a whole and include institutional treatment.

The debate included some unequivocal statements of support for Beveridge's proposals, especially as they related to a national health service. In particular, the Minister for Reconstruction addressed the House as follows:

> Freedom from want when people suffer adversity whether through lack of work, sickness, accident, disablement, loss of breadwinner or old age, seem to me to be our first human task, a further step to be taken along the road to prosperity to ensure the fulfilment of freedom from want means there must be hospital rehabilitation and medical services. I do not regard charges for these services crippling, but as an investment which will yield a rich return in human life ... efficiency and happiness. We must pay a price for such desirable ends ... state medical services should be expanded and brought within the reach of a wider public, even though the financial cost of such services is not yet calculable ... the poor demand that in health services they have the right to the best that is possible, therefore it comes to a question of finance.
>
> (House of Commons 1943: cols 1623–4, per A. Greenwood)

Replying for the Government the Lord President of the Council, Sir John Anderson, described the Report as one of 'great ingenuity', 'high idealism' and 'practical realities', promising that the Government would follow general lines of development laid down in the Report. He went on to describe the expenditure involved as 'formidable', but also said governments would not be deterred by doubts as to finance. He recognised that a comprehensive health service 'implies a reorganization of existing services ... [into]... one unified and comprehensive service'. And by comprehensive he meant:

> a service covering the people as a whole, no one left out and inclusion of institutional treatment to be administered by the Health Department not the Ministry of Social Security ... the object is to secure through a publicly organized and regulated service that any man woman and child who wants it, can obtain easily and readily a whole range of medical advice and

attention through the general practitioner, the consultant, the hospital and every related branch of the profession's up to date methods, the cooperation of public authorities, voluntary hospitals, voluntary agencies and the profession towards one common end.

(House of Commons 1943: cols 1655–78)

Before concluding, he also noted the need to ensure that 'professional interests must be amply and properly safeguarded and most important of all a free choice of doctor'.

The debate that followed generated a range of comments and observations, such as, 'a large sum on income tax would be acceptable. If people want a scheme, they should pay for it during their lifetime'. It was left to the Chancellor of the Exchequer, Sir Kingsley Wood, to remind everyone of the financial consequences of implementing Beveridge. In stating the Government's priorities after the war as housing, education and civil aviation, although he was in favour of Beveridge, he commented, 'generous hearts do not foot bills ... the financial aspect should be considered and weighed ... we should not hold out hopes that we are not able to fulfil'. On the question of a comprehensive health service, he said, 'Before we come to a final conclusion, we must obviously have regard to the costs and other claims that will be made upon us' (House of Commons 1943: cols 1825–38). Others in the debate made the same point, referring constantly to costs against high ideals. Some attacked the Government for placing implementation of the Report above other priorities. Our 'national defences are more important than this report' and 'housing must occupy a leading position in our post war considerations'.

Commander King Hall of the Brains Trust, an MP, detected a deliberate lukewarm attitude by the Government towards the Report because of the financial implications which he described as follows:

He, the Chancellor of the Exchequer, reminded me of a man who says to you, 'I hope you will spend a weekend with me, but of course my wife may die before you come, or the trains may not be running, or we may be invaded, or a tree may fall down and block the road,' after all those provisos you come to the conclusion that, after all, the man is not very keen on your spending the weekend with him.

(House of Commons 1943: cols 1765–916)

On the third day of the debate, 18 February 1943, Bevan, Griffiths and Shinwell moved an amendment to challenge the implementation of the Report in its current form, mainly because the Government of the day would not give an undertaking to create a Ministry of Social Security (Campbell 1987: 127). The Home Secretary thought there would be a serious constitutional and parliamentary issue if the amendment was carried. The Lord President of the Council committed the Government of the day, broadly speaking, to the principles of the Report. The amendment was defeated and the Report was supported in the House of

Commons being described as a 'landmark document' and a 'great state paper' (House of Commons 1943: cols 1964–2050).

The philosophy of this 'great state paper' was, in somewhat literary language, to 'slay' those five giants, want, squalor, idleness, ignorance and disease. The programmes for this would be, national insurance, a housing policy relying on council housing, full employment, secondary education for all, the Education Act 1944, and a health service. A modernised social security system was Beveridge's main concern and this was to be the decisive break with nineteenth-century methods of relieving poverty and twentieth-century struggles with the consequences of unemployment. A health service was seen by Beveridge as being a necessary partner in supporting a modernised social security system.

With the House of Commons debate and the Government's announcement of support for a comprehensive health service, the final stages of the policy-making process leading to the establishment of the NHS had begun. In this process the impact of the wider military conflict would be moderated and the conflicts which had been manifested in previous debates about extending state intervention in health care would assume a new significance. Beveridge's proposals for a comprehensive health service reflected current thinking in the medical profession and the Ministry of Health (Harris 1977: 429; Stark Murray 1971: 56). There was professional support for reform, but within parameters set by the profession. In moving the discussion towards the details of a comprehensive health service the Government might wish to redefine these parameters:

> What happened in 1942 … [was]… very simple; up to that time, planning for medical reform had been predominantly a professional enterprise and a paper enterprise. Now the government had shown its willingness to act on paper schemes, the possibility of reform became more concrete and imminent. Moreover the responsibility for reform was about to pass into the hands of the laymen, and worse into the hands of politicians and bureaucrats. Anxiety now gripped Tavistock Square.
>
> (Eckstein 1958: 132; note: the headquarters of the BMA is located in Tavistock Square)

In reviewing the final stages of the processes leading to the establishment of the NHS, we are entering a particularly well-documented phase in its history, and one in which issues of conflict and consensus have perhaps been most widely discussed. Most commentators agree that at this time the emphasis of professional interests changed. The medical profession had contributed to placing health care reform on the pre-war agenda and the profession's own wartime activities, such as the Medical Planning Commission, and experience, for example EMS, reinforced a considerable professional commitment to reform. But with the publication of the Beveridge Report and the wartime government's commitment to a national health service, the BMA 'lost its passion for reform' (Lindsey 1962: 39–40) and 'began to act as a trade union … in the hope of obtaining the most favourable terms of service' (Abel-Smith 1964: 459; Campbell 1987: 166). This meant that the conflict with the medical profession followed a rather predictable pattern in which support for general principles is replaced by concerns about, and often outright opposition to, the detailed proposals (Brand 1965: 15, for the medical profession and sanitary reform in the nineteenth century).

The final outcome seems often to have been the passing of the legislation despite professional opposition, for example, the Public Health Act 1872 (Brand 1965: 18) and the National Insurance Act 1911 (Chapter 2). One interesting outcome was the growing unpopularity of Beveridge amongst members of the medical profession, despite Beveridge's clearly stated view that both the medical profession and the voluntary hospitals should be involved in discussions relating to the detailed arrangements for the new national health service (Beveridge Report 1942: 169, para. 453).

A month after the Beveridge Report was published, the Ministry of Health drew up its own outline of possible legislation. Charles Webster's authoritative book, *The Health Services since the War, Volume 1* (1988) shows this outline to have contained the key principle, a service free at the point of use. This is evidence that senior civil servants in the Ministry had already accepted the idea. They had also considered the idea that charges for the hotel costs associated with hospital care might be necessary, along with national insurance and Exchequer 'support' as the main source of finance. With reference to the organisation of the NHS, the 'Ministry view' was that representation of local authority and the key medical interests would be essential in discussions concerning the implementation of the scheme, as well as its future administration.

The coalition Government's first attempt to take forward the process of reform was the never officially published 'Brown Plan', named after the then Minister of Health (March 1943). These proposals resembled earlier plans produced by the National Association of Local Government Officers and the Society of Medical Officers (Willcocks 1967: 24). It was influenced by a local government perspective, but perhaps also by a relatively apolitical 'civil service perspective' in which the pre-war significance of municipal health services (Chapter 2) led to a proposal for a unified health service based on regional local government units, despite predictions that this could generate considerable professional opposition (Webster 1990: 202). The voluntary hospitals would be utilised (and therefore at least partially financed) by the new national health service, but would not be nationalised. GPs would be employed in a full-time salaried service. The Plan was discussed with interested parties and was clearly opposed by the BMA both in principle and in detail. For the BMA, a universal scheme would destroy the private income of doctors. Both voluntary hospitals and doctors refused point blank to consider being run by local authorities, and for GPs to work for government-funded health centres would restrict professional freedom. Only the Socialist Medical Association approved. These were but opening shots in 'the war' to come, and the Minister spent the rest of the year listening to the conflicting views of various pressure groups before being replaced in December 1943 by a new Minister of Health, Henry Willink.

In February 1944, the first official publication emerged. This was the White Paper, *A National Health Service*, and it included a commitment to 'divorce the care of health from questions of personal means or other factors irrelevant to it' (Ministry of Health 1944: 47) and the idea of a comprehensive health service (Ministry of Health 1944: 9 and 47). In other respects, its proposals were simple and conservative, and included no references to the Beveridge Report (Webster 1988: 55). The White Paper proposed a local organisation for the new service based on joint local authority areas. The new organisation would take over municipal hospitals and lay down the conditions under which voluntary hospitals would contribute, in return for which they would receive grants towards part of the cost of patient care. Financial support for voluntary hospitals was uncertain. It marked 'the first detailed attempt to achieve a marriage of what were probably two incompatibles, the independence of the voluntary hospitals and a co-ordinated hospital service' (Willcocks 1967: 63; Abel-Smith 1964: Ch. 27).

Under this scheme the GPs would be under contract to a Central Medical Board, with remuneration in the same format as NHI. However, doctors working in health centres would be salaried, and the Central Medical Board were to have the power to refuse doctors the right to practise in over-doctored areas and to compel new doctors to work in poorly-served areas. In the House of Commons, Willink identified four principles of the proposed NHS, it would be comprehensive, there would be complete freedom for doctors and patients to use the service, there would be democratic responsibility through Parliament and local government and there would be the use of expert and professional guidance to ensure the best performance of the new service (Lindsey 1962: 36).

The White Paper received an 'enthusiastic parliamentary reception' (Eckstein 1958: 139) but Dr Charles Hill, the popular radio doctor, used the *Daily Express* to suggest such a plan would stop people getting advice from their own doctors. The BMA was still not satisfied with the Government proposals, especially any form of salaried service for GPs, the location where doctors could or could not practice and the significant role for local government. Two weeks after the White Paper was published, the Secretary of the BMA was reported as regretting both the absence of a corporate body at the top of the service and that the Government had been unwilling to dilute a democratic principle by including, in the public interest, some non-elected professional expert members in the joint authorities. A subsequent BMA poll recorded that 53 per cent of those polled were against the White Paper and 78 per cent against the control of hospitals by the proposed joint authorities (Eckstein 1958: 148; Honigsbaum 1989: Ch. 7). The medical profession's antagonism towards local government was proving a major impediment to reaching agreement. A leader in *The Times* commented that the medical profession appeared to have 'willed almost all the ends and rejected almost all the means'. A Political and Economic Planning Report was to characterise the doctors' approach as 'an evasion of the responsibilities of democratic citizenship' (Abel-Smith 1964: 467). Webster concludes that because the White Paper was 'neither a declaration of firm policy, nor a presentation of alternatives for adjudication by interested parties' it resulted in 'further destabilising negotiations' (Webster 1988: 44) rather than a swift transition to legislation.

By the early summer of 1945, the Minister had assembled the elements of an alternative plan (the Willink Plan) of 'nightmarish complexity embracing elements from all previous plans (Webster 1990: 130). This introduced a two tier system of regional and area planning authorities made up of equal local authority and voluntary hospital representation. Municipal hospitals would remain under local government control. Health centres were relegated to 'experimental status', and the powers of direction previously proposed for the Central Medical Board would disappear. Local administration of GP services would be undertaken by a modified version of the existing NHI committees. The right to 'sell practices', taken away by the White Paper, was reinstated. The major medical organisations were now happier.

But the Willink Plan was never officially published. With the surrender of Germany, the Second World War was coming to an end and a General Election was to take place in August 1945. The result was an overwhelming victory for the Labour Party, the Party with the most unequivocal commitment to a range of social policy reforms, including the implementation of the recommendations set down in the Beveridge Report (Morgan 1984b: 183). Britain had its first Labour Government to hold an absolute majority in the House of Commons and there was a new Minister of Health, Aneurin Bevan:

> The war ... inevitably brought about the end of the old medical system, both by the shortcomings it revealed in it and the attitudes towards medical reform which it engendered.
>
> (Eckstein 1958: 83)

> [One] ... of the lessons of the war, as a citizens' war, was the popular demand for the abolition of the poor law; of ineligible citizens; of personally merited disease; of inequality before the best ascertained laws of health.
>
> (Titmuss 1968: 241)

The hesitant steps towards a more comprehensive and accessible health service in the first half of the twentieth century were epitomised by the passing of the National Insurance Act 1911 and the subsequent concerns published in successive reports in the 1920s and 1930s, the latter indicating a broad if somewhat ill-defined consensus around the need for further reforms in the organisation of health care. The experience of war appeared to confirm and reinforce that consensus. The 'efficiency' arguments were even clearer as the demands of war-time exposed even more clearly the deficiencies of the pre-war system. The 'equity' arguments were also strengthened by concerns about social justice associated with the 'levelling effect' of war (Lindsey 1962: 23). Political pressures on government intensified when the public reaction to the Beveridge Report confirmed the strength of public opinion in support of social policy reform, including health service reform and key interest groups (especially the medical profession) remained in favour of reform, at least until the Government made a substantial response to the arguments and interests in favour of reform.

Once there was a tangible government commitment to establish a universal, comprehensive health service, there were indications that the consensus around generalities concealed conflicts about details, especially where the interests of the medical profession were concerned. This is a constant theme of this book, that few conflicts spring from original and unconsidered concerns. Often they are adaptations, amendments and attempts to address the unresolved problems of earlier periods. In some cases these were perceived or conceptualised as problems that would reappear to challenge the claim of the UK to be providing the modern comprehensive, adequate and universally available health services in which its legislators, professionals and public believed.

Beveridge was 'embarrassed when people referred to him as the creator of the NHS, insisting this term could only be applied to the Labour Minister of Health, Aneurin Bevan' (Harris 1977: 459). Nonetheless, it is difficult to consider the state of affairs in the current British NHS without assessing the significance of the Beveridge Report upon the development of the NHS. This significance relates to the values, the administration and structure, and the financing of today's NHS. Beveridge's chief concern was to rationalise the social security system. The right to medical care of those defined in need by qualified professionals was a crucial, but supplementary, concern. At no time was Beveridge involved in the policy discussions of the wartime coalition Government or the post-war Labour Government; and at no stage can he be seen as personally responsible for any great social policy statutes of this period, the Family Allowances Act 1945, the National Insurance Act 1946, the National Health Serve Act 1946 and the National Assistance Act 1948, but:

> the main structure and many of the principles of the welfare legislation of 1945–48 were those which Beveridge had laid down in 1942. In devising these principles Beveridge's role has been mainly that of a synthesizer and publicist rather than that of an innovator and it is difficult to claim that he had made any inherently original contribution to subsequent social policy. But, nevertheless, it was Beveridge who interpreted the main stream of public opinion and transformed an incoherent mass of popular feeling into a blueprint for social reform.
>
> (Harris 1977: 448)

The importance of the Beveridge Report for a future NHS lay in its refusal to restrict itself to a simple tidying up of the Poor Law legacy of cash benefits. Instead, Beveridge's biographer describes the scope of his enquiry as a 'radical interpretation' of his terms of references, going beyond a concern with cash benefits to other policy areas, especially medical treatment. He adopted a comprehensive conception of medical treatment, that is, comprehensive in scope and universally available to all (Harris 1977: 387). The philosophical issue of providing a service to meet health care needs without a test of means and free at the point of use was the final significant break with Poor Law thinking, and can be seen as completing the changes set in motion by the Liberal welfare reforms earlier in the century.

But this concept of a universal, comprehensive national health service was to bring open conflict when there were attempts to put into operation Beveridge's ideas for a health service, in the immediate aftermath of the Second World War. Some would also say that Beveridge laid the basis for expectations of health care for all citizens, but in the face of growing financial restraints and reluctant Treasury support, such expectations, as well as professional views of problems of equity, were bound to produce conflicts, even if the protagonists claimed that they shared the same purposes.

Thus the war-time experience appeared to confirm and reinforce the pre-war 'near-consensus' around the need for further reforms in the organisation of health care. Reports on the future of Britain's health services continued to be issued in wartime Britain with notable contributions from sections of the medical profession. The 'efficiency' arguments were made clearer due to the demands of war-time. In particular, planning for the civilian air raid causalities confirmed concerns that existing hospital provision was both inefficient and variable in quality. The resulting need for the better organisation of the hospital sector led to a significant degree of central government control and expenditure and the Government made a commitment to establish a comprehensive *hospital* service after the war (1941). Concerns for 'civilian morale' during the war and the com-mitment to post-war reconstruction policies were both likely to confirm existing concerns about the inequities in the organisation and delivery of health care. The public reaction to the Beveridge Report (1942) confirmed the strength of public opinion in support of health service reform. The principles underpinning the Beveridge Report were to be supported by three assumptions. These were full employment, family allowances and a comprehensive health service available to all members of the community and provided where needed without contribution conditions in any individual case. The Report was concerned with better forms of organisation and finance. The recommendations included ending the central role of social insurance (NHI) and any role for the Approved Societies in health care. The recommendations also posed a challenge to the emerging pattern of financing hospital care in the voluntary sector.

The Government also made a commitment to the principles of the Beveridge Report and the establishment of a comprehensive *health* service after the war (1943). It was assumed that the costs of the new service might be partially ame-liorated because the outcome of a better, more efficient, more equitable health service would be a healthier population that would have less need for health services. The support of the medical profession for general principles was replaced by concerns about, and often outright opposition to, the detailed proposals.

# Chapter 4

# Political parties and pressure groups

> I have examined the … [NHS]… Bill and it looks to me uncommonly like the
> first step, and a big one, towards National Socialism as practised in Germany.
> (Dr Alfred Cox, former Secretary of the BMA,
> quoted in Timmins 1995: 119)

Discussing the new social measures, Mr Bevan said that the 'slight conflict over
the National Health Service never worried him very much because, as a credulous
idealist, he knew the truth would survive, and that as the medical profession came
to know its provisions they would support it. The Act was not based upon contributions, and every individual had equal rights to the scheme, whether insured
or not. He paid sincere tribute to the voluntary work of hospitals, but said that
private charity could never be a substitute for organised justice' (4 July 1948,
Webster 1991: 123–4). The context for the remainder of this policy-making process were the struggles of the 1945–1951 Labour Government to carry out its
reconstruction policy for post-war Britain. The National Health Service (NHS)
moved to centre stage in this, it having become the most popular of these reforms
(Calder 1971: 611) ahead of nationalising the commanding heights of the economy. The task facing the Labour Government, with an inheritance of pre-1945
thinking on the structure, was to move from Beveridge's recommendation for a
comprehensive and universally available service to an administratively practicable
service philosophy and funding of medical care.

The first major obstacle in the way of turning the ideal into the feasible was
the power of the deeply entrenched professional interest groups, especially the
doctors who were able, until the National Health Service Act 1946, to control
the size of patient lists, the sale of practices and where doctors would be allowed
to practise (Willcocks 1967; Webster 1988). The administrative problem related
to the traditional points of conflict between bureaucracy and professionalism
and between democracy and professionalism, and the doctors' fear of the loss of
clinical freedom. The administrative compromises of National Health Insurance
(NHI) had resolved the former with regard to the Friendly Societies and the
doctors (Chapter 2). The poor law authorities, in the form of the Boards of
Guardians, and, after 1929, local government, represented elements of both

these conflicts, and neither had been resolved to the satisfaction of the medical profession prior to 1945 (Chapters 1 and 2). This was a particular dilemma given the crucial role of local government in existing health care (Chapter 2). A means had to be found to integrate professionals into a governmental bureaucracy without raising professional opposition whilst at the same time making the health care system accountable to the political process. Bevan's mission, as the new Minister of Health, was subsequently described as persuading 'the most conservative and respected profession in the country to accept and operate the Labour Government's most intrinsically socialist proposition' (Foot 1975: 104). The economic problem was the potential conflict between the aim of providing a universalist, comprehensive health service of a good standard and that of containing health costs to a reasonable level, and how to finance the system in such a way that certainty and sufficiency of funds could be guaranteed.

There were three related sets of debates, discussions and negotiations, between Bevan, the Labour cabinet and the doctors; between Bevan, the Parliamentary Labour Party and the Conservatives; and between Bevan and the teaching hospitals. Each was characterised by two sorts of conflict, the first about ideology, the role of the state in potentially dominating a free profession, and the second, about the administrative procedures that would be tight enough to guarantee an equitable distribution of scarce and valued medical care, yet loose enough to allow a professional discretion to remain unfettered within financial boundaries set by Parliament, and the minimum administrative regulations necessary to assure medical care to the population based upon Beveridge's aspiration in paragraph 426 of his report (Beveridge Report: 1942).

Bevan's solution was to rationalise the health service by using the political tool of the day, nationalising 'the commanding heights' of health care, the hospital (Campbell 1987: 167). The operation of the Emergency Medical Service had exposed both the problems of a non-planned system and the potential for state planning. Herbert Morrison opposed this 'solution' in Cabinet, seeing it as an attack on local government hospitals, especially the London County Council (Morgan 1984b: 154–5; Hennessey 1992: 139; Campbell 1987: 169–70). The voluntary hospitals also opposed the idea but were weakened by the underlying frailty of their financial circumstances with 80 per cent of their income already being provided by the state. The Conservative Party was also opposed, led by the ex-Minister of Health responsible for the original White Paper.

A new White Paper (Ministry of Health 1946) and Bill were both published in March 1946. The Second and Third Readings of the Bill were in April and July of the same year. Bevan made an hour and a quarter speech including his famous comment in support of the 'rational planning' of hospital provision, 'I would rather be kept alive in the efficient if cold altruism of a large hospital than expire in a gush of warm sympathy in a small one' (Webster 1991: 62).

Although the Bill adopted most of the proposals of the Willink Plan (Willcocks 1967: 57), the Conservative opposition actually divided the House on the Third Reading, a division at this stage of parliamentary proceedings traditionally being one of opposition based upon objections to the principles of a Bill. The British Medical Association (BMA) tried to wreck the whole Bill, although there was support from 'medical peers' in the House of Lords (Lords Moran and Horder) because the future of the major voluntary hospitals was assured within the new NHS. This was indicative of the way Bevan had exploited old conflicts and divisions within the medical profession, those between specialist hospital doctors and general practitioners (GPs) working in the community (Chapter 1; Honigsbaum 1989: Ch. 13; Jenkins 1963: 240–1). The BMA was, in these circumstances, more effective at representing the views of certain sections of the medical profession, especially GPs. Bevan's proposals for the NHS offered considerable gains to hospital doctors and this weakened the position of the BMA, which then balloted its members: 41,000 were against, 4,000 were in favour. Bevan proceeded as planned but put forward a compromise in the Bill that a salaried service for GPs would not be introduced without further specific legislation. The BMA balloted again; this time there was a smaller majority against the Bill, and a fear of a debacle like that which followed the National Insurance Act 1911 with doctors rushing to join the new service (Chapter 2). There were two key reasons for the approach that Bevan had taken. One was political, the other administrative. Politically, he did it 'to universalise the best'. There had to be equal right of access to the best medical care regardless of income and residence. This was the 'egalitarian socialist' at work. Administratively, the existing 'system' was not a system. It was a hotchpotch of hospitals and community services. Sources of finance were neither sufficient nor certain. A national health service required national administration.

The new NHS had the following characteristics. First, income was guaranteed by national government with revenue derived from predominantly national rather than local taxation. Within the former, social insurance contributions (national insurance) would play only a limited role and would in no way determine entitlement to use the NHS. Second, and related to the financial arrangements, there would be only a limited role for local government in providing health care such as community nursing services, and employing doctors such as medical officers of health. Third, for doctors and their patients there would be the doctor of choice, free treatment at the point of use, and referral to the hospital by GPs. Fourth, GPs remained self-employed independent contractors (continuing the political compromise developed for NHI) (Chapter 2). They could work in groups and partnerships, own their own premises, receive capitation fees and give primary care, diagnosis and the rights of referral. Fifth, GP services would be administered by appointed bodies, Executive Councils, which would hold the contracts of GPs, dentists, pharmacists and opticians, with half the membership of these Councils being nominated by professional bodies. Sixth, for the hospitals there would be a predominantly two-tier system. Regional Hospital Boards, covering populations of approximately five million people, would employ the senior hospital doctors (the consultants) and aim to establish an equal distribution of this scarce professional medical manpower. Hospital Management Committees would run hospitals on a day-to-day basis and employ all other hospital staff. Not only local

| Special hospitals | Teaching hospitals | Non-teaching hospitals | Community and public health | The Family Practitioner services |
|---|---|---|---|---|
| | Governors | Hospital boards 330 hospital management committees | 175 local health authorities (counties and county boroughs) | 134 executive councils |

*Figure 4.1* Administrative structure of the NHS, 1948

authority mental hospitals but also local authority mental deficiency institutions were to become NHS hospitals. The latter was perhaps particularly inappropriate in terms of the needs of the individuals in those institutions (Ryan and Thomas 1980: 14–18; Townsend 1973: 208–9). The two-tier arrangement did not apply to a group of special hospitals which were to be directly administered by the Ministry, whilst teaching hospitals would retain considerable independence from both the Ministry and the Regional Hospital Boards and would be managed by their own Boards of Governors (see Figure 4.1).

Later commentators would be largely in agreement that the National Health Service Act 1946 was 'a rationalisation and redistribution rather than a great advance' (Willcocks 1967: 20; Eckstein 1958: 3) with an 'odd administrative structure, especially when viewed against early attempts at a simplified but comprehensive administration' (Willcocks 1967: 19–20). The medical profession is also sometimes portrayed as 'a winner' from the associated pressure group politics especially by contrast with those with administrative skills and those with property to offer, the latter losing their influence once the decision was taken to nationalise the hospitals (Willcocks 1967: 30–3 and 71; Honigsbaum 1989: 183).

The post-war Labour Government paid relatively dearly for the settlements that drew the profession into the NHS, but two points can be made. First, that the doctors were 'formidable obstacles to anything other than incremental change' (Webster 1988: 16). Second, that the limitations of the resulting compromise can be compared not only with more 'desirable' and 'radical' alternatives, but also with the widely recognised limitations of pre-war health care in the UK which was characterised by 'anachronism, administrative complexity, duplication, parochialism, inertia, stagnation' (Webster 1988: 1; Willcocks 1967: 21). Set against this, the potential of the NHS was considerable, even when handicapped by financial and organisational arrangements which owed so much to the demands of political expediency:

> On 5th July 1948 most of Britain's hospitals were taken into national ownership. Only three years earlier there had been hardly any advocate of such an extreme solution to the problems of hospital planning and hospital administration. The processes which led to this development came not from any doctrines of the Labour Party, which by 1945 was confining its proposals for

nationalisation to the industrial sector, but from aspirations of parts of the medical profession. Nationalisation seemed the only way by which consultants and specialists could achieve their principal objectives, adequate financial support for the hospitals in which they worked, the retention of private practice and an effective 'say' in the running of all hospital services.

(Abel-Smith 1964: 488)

There is clearly a case for seeing the establishment of the NHS as a location for a conflict between the state and an established professional group (Doyal 1979: 180). Furthermore, it is possible to suggest that the professional group gained greatly from that conflict, hence comments that the National Health Service Act 1946 was 'a doctors' measure rather than a patients' measure' (Eckstein 1958: 3). Evidence of the power of the medical profession in the establishment of NHI (Chapter 2) and in other countries (Alford 1975) lends weight to a perspective that emphasises the significance of professional power in 'welfare state developments'. The prestige of the medical profession, the private market for their skills outside the NHS, and indeed an international marketplace for medical expertise, can all provide plausible explanations for this example of professional power and influence. Sections of the medical profession were active as pressure groups and the plans for the health service changed with regard to administrative and financial arrangements. Indeed, it has been suggested that the 'NHS which was created in 1948 was very different from that which had been originally proposed in 1943' (Doyal 1979: 180), an exact parallel of observations made about the establishment of NHI (Chapter 2; Gilbert 1966: 290). The plans changed in ways which can be seen to benefit sections of the medical profession and on which the profession campaigned. As Willcocks notes, 'it is quite clear that the original Government aims like those of the victorious Labour Party of 1945 had to be progressively modified or eroded to meet the conflicting views of the groups most concerned' (Willcocks, 1967: 105).

This is perhaps most obvious with the role of local government in health care which was significantly diminished when both voluntary and municipal hospitals were nationalised. The democratic and bureaucratic challenge to professional autonomy represented by local government was eliminated, at least for most of the medical profession (Honigsbaum 1989: Chs 5 and 12). The nationalised system would inherit a management system much more like that of the voluntary than the municipal hospital system, one that placed considerable emphasis on clinical freedom (Abel-Smith 1964: 281; Gilbert 1970: 234). This was of course indicative of the long-standing sensitivities surrounding professional/managerial relations, elements of which were obvious in voluntary hospital management in the nineteenth century (Chapter 1) and which would remain controversial in the future. The system of merit awards to supplement salaries and the ability, not only to continue with private practice, but also to undertake this work in NHS hospitals via the pay-beds system, were further benefits accruing to hospital doctors under the NHS. It was this combination of attractive financial arrangements that would cause Bevan to make his famous remark with regard to the hospital doctors that he 'stuffed their mouths with gold' (Webster 1991: 219–22). Thus the hospital doctors gained a good deal. Voluntary hospital doctors gained pay with little diminution in autonomy. Local government hospital doctors gained more pay with more autonomy. The introduction of the NHS improved the circumstances of hospital doctors significantly, in much the same way as the introduction of NHI improved the position of most GPs (Chapter 2; Abel-Smith 1964: Ch. 29; Campbell 1987: 168–9).

In addition, the most prestigious hospitals, the teaching hospitals, were afforded a special administrative and financial status within the NHS. They were to be financed directly by the Ministry, enabled to retain their pre-NHS endowments and given considerable managerial autonomy, a situation they would lose in subsequent NHS reorganisations but would regain with the introduction of an internal market including an opportunity (60 years later) to seek NHS Foundation Trust status. Perhaps less surprisingly the financial and administrative arrangements introduced for the NHI GP system were carried forward into the NHS GP system. Nonetheless, a case could be made both for a salaried GP service and for more consumer and/or community representation within these organisational arrangements. The latter would be significantly diminished by comparison with arrangements for NHI.

The tripartite structure of the new NHS was constructed around long-established divisions within the medical profession, retaining elements of the NHI arrangements for GPs in the NHS; continuing the employment of medical officers of health by local government, and making separate arrangements for hospital doctors. In so doing, the new Service replicated, within a state health service, the organisational divisions of Victorian Britain, the Friendly Societies, the sanitary authorities and the voluntary hospitals. The tripartite structure can also be seen as part of a broader trend of the demunicipalisation of state welfare. Local government involvement in social security was ended at this time.

The coalition and Labour Governments, especially the latter, were committed to a universalist and comprehensive health service. There was substantial support from sections of the medical profession for the '90 per cent solution' proposed by the Medical Planning Commission in 1942 (Chapter 3). This envisaged an NHI system extended to cover hospital care for approximately 90 per cent of the population – the richest 10 per cent remaining outside state schemes to sustain private practice (Willcocks 1967: 34 and 45–8). As with NHI, the government of the day may have made significant adjustments to professional interests on administrative matters, but it retained the key principles of the proposed reform. Furthermore, whilst the diminution of local government involvement in health care may have suited professional interests, it also served the interests of those in central government who wished to keep a close control over public expenditure on health and welfare.

The establishment of the NHS, like the establishment of NHI (Chapter 2), was part of a wider set of social policy reforms introduced by the war-time coalition, but principally by the post-war Labour, Governments. These included secondary education for all, universalist social security policies, following the 1942 Beveridge Report, housing and town planning legislation and the Children Act 1948. These reforms have attracted a range of descriptions from the 'creation of the welfare state' to the 'final shaping of the welfare state'. Many of the reforms, including the health care reforms, attracted considerable support, reflecting a wartime and sometimes pre-war 'political consensus or near-consensus' (Briggs 1978: 448; Barnett 1986: 33). It has been suggested that the particular achievement of the Labour Government was to put the wartime plans into effect 'with none of the qualifications about attractive schemes which turn out to be economically impossible', to quote a 1942 memorandum of Winston Churchill (Bruce 1961: 26):

> The National Health Service has been easily the most widely publicised and the most widely criticised of all the projects undertaken by the post-war Labour governments
>
> (Eckstein 1958: 1)

> The whole attitude of the Leader of the House, seconded by the *Minister of Health* ... is to offend, wound, injure and provoke those over whom they have got so great a Parliamentary majority ... the treatment which has been meted out to us, and which has already produced party antagonism, bitter as anything I have seen in my long life of political conflict.
>
> (Winston Churchill, 6 December 1945)

Churchill was speaking in the House of Commons in support of a Motion of Censure in which His Majesty's Government were said to be 'neglecting their first duty ... [including] ... the drastic curtailment of our swollen national expenditure' (House of Commons 1946: cols 2530, 2531 and 2534).

Thus the NHS came into existence in an atmosphere of conflict. This conflict was generated by the strong ideological commitment of the post-Second World War Labour Government, and the opposition of the Conservative Party and some sections of the medical profession, to what were perceived as a thoroughly socialist aspiration; a health service, universally available, comprehensive, centrally planned and free at the time of need. In addition, there were some long standing and deep-seated grievances within sections of the medical profession resulting in the new Labour Government being 'exposed to the full blast of a campaign which had been gathering momentum since 1911' (Webster 1990: 199). In spite of these well-documented conflicts (especially where administrative details were concerned), the establishment of the NHS owed a great deal to an emerging near-consensus about the need for health care reform (Klein 1983: 2–7; Briggs 1978: 448). Furthermore, the establishment of the NHS cannot be separated from the wider range of social policy reforms enacted by the war-time coalition and post-war Labour Governments; these reforms being in part a product of the way in which the Second World War was fought by Britain (Eckstein

1958: 133). It can also be seen as 'an important part of the post-war settlement between capital and labour' (Doyal 1979: 179) and, as such, a further episode in the class and ideological conflicts which prefigured the Liberal welfare reforms (Chapter 2).

'In many respects the National Health Service extended and developed practices which had been built up over many generations', and it could be viewed as 'no more than a stage in the evolution of the nation's social services and in particular that:

> for a century or more, medical care in Britain had been regarded ... as a responsibility for which the community should in some form provide. It was this heritage of shared opinion which was responsible for the widespread acceptance in Britain of what others chose to call 'socialised medicine.'
>
> (Abel-Smith 1964: 500 and 502)

There seems little doubt that what was put in place by the post-war Labour Government was influenced in its administrative detail by professional interests; and that the process by which this influence was exercised represents a classic example of both pressure group politics and interest group conflicts. The outcome has been described as a 'victory of tactical considerations over administrative and political logic, coherence and consistency' (Klein 1983: 22). However, the resulting organisational compromise would endure for a quarter of a century and might therefore claim to be an effective one although it was to pose significant problems for a co-ordinated approach to community care (Chapter 7), and the development of non-medical approaches to the needs of people with learning difficulties. However, it was acceptable to key groups, especially the more influential and powerful sections of the medical profession. But if professionally-based pressure groups disputed the detail, there is also little doubt that the principles of the NHS were 'accepted by the vast majority of the British people' and the profession 'could not deny public opinion' (Abel-Smith 1964: 500). It may be this considerable and consistent degree of public support which explains why the NHS has retained governmental support for so long.

The establishment of the NHS has to be set in a contemporary and recent historical context of a wide-ranging and well-established consensus as well as the broader historical contexts of class conflict and cultural continuity. It serves as a classic example of the interrelationship between the themes of conflict, consensus and continuity in the provision of health care in Britain:

> The Service has scored considerable popular success, to the point indeed, where, ten years after its inception, it seems to be accepted as an altogether natural feature of the British landscape, almost a part of the Constitution – so that it is now good politics not to let the Labour Party take all the credit for it.
>
> (Eckstein 1958: 2)

This was one of a number of post-war social policy reforms based on the political notion of equal shares, which structured the 'establishment of the welfare state' and the 'post war settlement between capital and labour' in which labour receives its social wage through state welfare services. Whilst this intense period of social policy initiatives seems to justify some general use of the label 'welfare state', the constituent elements of the 'post war settlement' were not of equal status or lasting effect, and the NHS can be conceived as more radical in its implications than other changes implemented at the time. For some, the National Health Service Act 1946 was 'one of the most unsordid and civilised actions in the history of health and welfare policy' (Titmuss 1968: 208). For others, it may be 'misleading to think of the NHS as a social welfare measure at all', but rather more 'an organizational rationalisation to combat inefficiencies and inadequacies' (Eckstein 1958: viii).

Certain aspects of the new service proved to be controversial right from the start, especially those concerned with the professional issues of doctor/patient relations, state regulation, remuneration of doctors and the relationships between the centre and local administration of the service. The role of the medical profession and the setting up of the NHS has served as a classic example of pressure group politics and most commentators agree that they played a leading role in shaping at least some of the decisions about the organisation of the new NHS (Eckstein 1958: 4). There seems a rather obvious link between the observation that 'the only person not represented round the Minister's table was the patient' (Willcocks 1967: 33) and an outcome in which the nationalisation of the hospitals is identified with 'the aspirations of parts of the medical profession' (Abel-Smith 1964: 488). The doctors emerge as perhaps the major beneficiaries of the introduction of the new Service (Titmuss 1968: 241) and an organisational structure which owed 'more to the opinion of the doctors than to political and public opinion' (Titmuss 1968: 235).

Most of the medical profession were committed to some kind of health care reform. In particular, the most powerful and influential section of the profession worked in those hospitals that were most involved in the 'voluntary health care crisis'. Given recognition of what they saw as important factors, the maintenance of clinical freedom within hospitals and the ability to sustain private practice, these doctors (in the voluntary hospitals) were quite likely to be supportive of increased state intervention in health care, if that intervention could resolve the 'health care crisis' that most concerned them, without compromising their 'clinical freedom'. Despite the heated debates surrounding the National Health Service Act 1946, the original objectives of the Service as contained in the White Paper (Ministry of Health 1944) nevertheless appeared, in the longer run at least, to command a large measure of support from the public, politicians, and the professionals so that, 'by the mid-50s the NHS was protected by a broad consensus embracing all social classes, both political parties, all but an eccentric fringe of the medical profession and all others employed by the Service' (Webster 1988: 389–90). The passage of the legislation is of more than symbolic importance. It institutionalised for the first time a 'free' health care service, publicly funded with unrestricted access providing a comprehensive range of services. At 'the time of its creation it was a unique example of the collective provision of health care in a market society' (Klein 1983: 1) and despite:

> the many compromises involved in the course of converting the plan devised in 1943 into the Service inaugurated in 1948 the NHS was at that time and has remained the most ambitious, publicly provided health service to be established by a major Western democracy
>
> (Webster 1988: 397)

There is continuity between Beveridge's analysis and values and the political commitment and initiative which translated Beveridge into policy. From 1948 onwards the policy was being translated into action, but with the change of government in 1951 there was a potential conflict of, rather than a continuity of, values. However, political expediency, if nothing else, would require successive Conservative governments to persist with the concept of a national health service. The difficulties were to be 'the finance and funding' or how to provide an economically effective and efficient service; and 'the delivery system', how to administer and manage such a Service.

The organisational and administrative details of the new Service were influenced by professional interests and the process by which this influence was exercised is a classic example of pressure group politics. The power of the doctors as a pressure group might be attributable in part to the markets for medical expertise outside the NHS in the UK and outside the UK, as well as their prestige as a well-established professional group. The details which could most obviously be attributed to professional influence were:

* the self-employed independent contractor status for GPs (continued from NHI, Chapter 2);
* the special administrative and financial status afforded to teaching hospitals;
* a hospital management system that placed considerable emphasis on clinical freedom (more like that of the voluntary than the municipal hospitals, see Chapter 1);
* a limited role for local government in providing health care and employing doctors.

The resulting organisational compromise owed much to the demands of political expediency, but still compared favourably with the widely recognised limitations of pre-war health care. The independence of the voluntary hospitals had been weakened by their financial circumstances, with 80 per cent of their income being provided by the state. Virtually all of them would be nationalised.

The other key characteristics of the new Service would be:

- income guaranteed by national government and paid for out of general taxation;
- no role for social insurance contributions (national insurance) in determining entitlement to use the Service;
- free treatment at the point of use/time of need.

Despite the conflicts associated with the establishment of the NHS the objectives of the Service appeared to command a large measure of support from the public, politicians, and the professionals. In his capacity as Minister of Health in the new Labour Government, Bevan had no doubt about the social and integrating purpose as against the political and economic value of the NHS:

> Society becomes more wholesome, more serene, and spiritually healthier, if it knows that its citizen have at the back of their consciousness the knowledge that not only themselves, but all their fellows have access, when ill, to the best that medical skill can provide. But private charity and endowment, although inescapably essential at one time, cannot meet the cost of all this. If the job is to be done, the state must accept financial responsibility.
>
> (Bevan 1978: 100)

> The fifth of July 1948 was one of *the* great days in British history … it was a day that transformed like no other before or since the lives and life chances of the British people.
>
> (Hennessey 1992: 143)

# Part I

# Conclusions

Our first four chapters described developments in health care provision before the NHS was established on 5 July 1948. There was a long-standing recognition that health care was the responsibility of the community in some form, including the continual presence of at least some state involvement over the period reviewed. The expansion of philanthropic and mutual aid voluntary associations in the nineteenth century played a key role in the development of health care.

The historical role of voluntary associations also provided evidence of the limitations of a reliance on altruism and mutual aid as the means of providing health care. Despite their considerable merits as providers of good quality hospital care to those who would be unable to purchase such care in a private market, Britain's voluntary hospitals were limited in their coverage both to certain areas of the country and to certain areas of health care. The major mutual institutions of nineteenth century Britain, the Friendly Societies, were also limited in their coverage of the population.

There were significant changes in the relative roles of voluntary associations and the state in the provision of health care. The state had become a major provider of health care by the end of the nineteenth century, 50 years before the establishment of the National Health Service (NHS). The Liberal welfare reforms represented a particularly intense period of changes in social policy (e.g. the introduction of old age pensions) and health care in particular (e.g. the introduction of National Health Insurance (NHI)). Some commentators have identified these reforms as representing the 'beginning of the welfare state'.

Between 1900 until the establishment of the NHS there was a continuing role for voluntary hospitals as well as for the Poor Law institutions. NHI was established and expanded with a significant role for mutual-aid organisations with an increasing range of local government health (especially hospital) services, so that local government was a significant provider of health care by the 1930s. However, the voluntary hospitals were facing mounting financial problems, the Poor Law could not escape the success of past legislators and administrators in creating its indelible association with the stigmatising status of pauper, the NHI scheme excluded children, non-earning wives, the self-employed, many old people and higher paid employees and the scope and effectiveness of municipal health services depended on the wealth of each area and the political initiatives of different local authorities.

The three major concerns were about equity of access to health care and the standard of health care received between social groups, regions and categories of medical condition, the persistence of inequalities in health such that those parts of the country which appeared to have the greatest need were also most deficient in health care facilities, subsequently to be labelled the 'inverse care law', and the efficiency with which health care providers were organised.

In particular, the voluntary and local government hospitals provided an arbitrary patchwork quilt of services of varying degrees of efficacy, separated and enclosed by financial, legal, medical, residential and occupational barriers and categories. By the outbreak of the Second World War (1939), despite the state being a significant provider of health care, there was also quite a wide-ranging consensus about the need for health care reform, although less agreement about the details of reform.

From 1939, the war-time experience appeared to confirm and reinforce the pre-war 'near-consensus' around the need for further reforms in the organisation of health care. In particular, 'efficiency' concerns were even clearer as the demands of war-time exposed even more clearly the deficiencies of the pre-war system, and 'health care equity' and 'health inequality' concerns were strengthened by wartime concerns about social justice and a growing commitment to the twin goals of minimising inequalities in health and access to health care. As a result, questions of the quality, distribution and responsibility for health care were to form part of the war-time political agenda, in particular the purposes for which the war was being fought. As a result, the nation's health services became the core of the reconstruction of civil society during and in the immediate aftermath of the Second World War.

The first new commitment of the war-time government was to establish a comprehensive *hospital* service after the war (1941). In the following year, one of the key recommendations in the Beveridge Report (1942) was the provision of comprehensive health services available to all members of the community and provided where needed without contribution conditions in any individual case. Political pressures on government intensified when the public reaction to the Report confirmed the strength of public opinion in support of social policy reform, especially health care reform. The second post-war commitment of the government was to establish a comprehensive *health* service after the war (1943).

The original objectives of the Service as contained in the White Paper (Ministry of Health 1944) were to bring health care to the entire population of the UK and to provide preventive, curative and rehabilitation services paid for out of general taxation so that they would be free at the time of need. This institutionalised for the first time a 'free' health care service, publicly funded with unrestricted access providing a comprehensive range of services. Once established (on 5 July 1948), the NHS became the most ambitious, publicly provided health service to be established by a major Western democracy. The Service came into existence in an atmosphere of conflict, including opposition from the Conservative Party as well as sections of the medical profession. However, the objectives of the Service appeared, in the longer run at least, to command a large measure of support from the public, politicians, and the professionals. By the mid-50s the NHS would be protected by a broad consensus embracing all social classes and all political parties.

Like the Liberal welfare reforms, the establishment of the NHS was also part of a wider set of social policy reforms (e.g. major changes in social security) introduced principally by the post-war Labour Government. These reforms, based on the political notion of equal shares, were said to have structured the 'establishment of the welfare state'. The NHS can be seen as more radical in its implications than some of the other changes implemented at the time.

The post-war social policy reforms had a very significant impact on the role of local government in health care. Previously, local government had been mostly acquiring new welfare responsibilities, especially in the area of health and community care, for example, the asylums or mental hospitals and other specialist hospitals, the school health service, health visiting, domiciliary midwifery and the poor law medical services. After the war, local government became a net loser of services with a much diminished role, in the new NHS.

The post-war social policy reforms also had a significant impact on the role of non-state organisations as service providers. Before the war, growing state involvement in health care and other areas was linked with a major role for non-state institutions as direct service providers (e.g. the Friendly Societies and insurance companies, the voluntary hospitals). At the same time as the role of local government was diminished so a similar fate befell these organisations. The most significant change following the Beveridge Report was the exclusion of Friendly Societies (as Approved Societies) from any administrative responsibilities within the NHS and the nationalisation of the voluntary hospitals.

Once the relationship between the state and the medical profession had been formalised, it encouraged debates on resources, remuneration and redistribution and on the organisational and financial arrangements for health services provided by the State. It was impossible to avoid conflict in discussions of these areas. There was professional opposition to NHI, focusing more on financial and management arrangements than the principle of state regulated social insurance. There was professional support for radical health care reforms in the 1930s and early 1940s, but this dissipated into fractious opposition to organisational details about the administrative arrangements for the new NHS (1946–1948). Such details were important for the representatives of the medical profession as they sought to minimise lay control over their activities. Professional influence was most obviously represented in the resulting tripartite administrative structure, maintaining the relative autonomy of the teaching hospitals, limiting the role for local government and keeping the independent practitioner status of general practitioners.

Even in the nineteenth century there were disputes about costs and the need for cost containment (Abel-Smith 1964: 35). The issue of escalating costs remains an ongoing issue in the provision of health care. The economic problem for the NHS was the potential conflict between the aim of providing a universal, comprehensive health service of a good standard and that of containing health costs to a reasonable level. However, it was assumed that the outcome of a better, more efficient, more equitable health service would be a healthier population that would have less need for health services.

# Part II

# The NHS, July 1948–May 1979

# Part II

# Introduction

Part II of the book reviews the NHS over its first 30 years of existence. It covers the following Governments:

1945–1951   Labour.
1951–1964   Conservative.
1964–1970   Labour.
1970–1974   Conservative.
1974–1979   Labour.

These Governments were led by eight Prime Ministers and over this time there were 15 Ministers of Health.

The history of the National Health Service (NHS) is dominated by five themes, efficiency, equity, community care, organisational reform and improving the health status of the population. All these themes had figured in discussions about health and health care before the NHS was set up and had formed part of the arguments being put forward in favour of health care reform before 1939. There had been long standing concerns about the efficiency of the way in which the various health care providers operated, especially the lack of co-ordination and planning. Chapter 5 reviews the search for efficiency and planning. The pre-NHS mix of voluntary and state institutions had also involved major issues of equity of access to health care and the standard of health care received between social groups, regions and categories of health care. In addition, those parts of the country which appeared to have the greatest need were also most deficient in health care facilities. Chapter 6 reviews the search for equity.

In the nineteenth century, there was investment in various forms of institutional care (hospitals, asylums, Poor Law infirmaries) but before the establishment of the NHS there was also a growing interest in various forms of less institutional and community health care. Chapter 7 reviews the search for more community health care. The organisational and administrative details of the NHS had been the subject of considerable conflict in the period leading up to the establishment of the Service. The resulting tripartite structure was to be identified as an obstacle to planning, greater efficiency, a more equitable distribution of health care and developments in community health care. Chapter 8 reviews the arguments that were advanced for changing this structure and the organisational changes that were introduced in the 1970s.

Part I shows that escalating costs had become an ongoing issue in the provision of health care, posing particular problems for the voluntary hospitals. Would it be possible to provide a universal, comprehensive health service of a good standard and at the same time contain health costs to a reasonable level? In the period leading up to the establishment of the NHS, the hope had been expressed that an efficient and equitable health service could be developed that would diminish disease and disability (Beveridge Report 1942: 105, 158 and 162). This outcome might provide a partial resolution to the issues of costs and cost-containment. This relationship between the nation's health care and its health is referred to in both Chapters 5 and 6 and discussed in greater detail in Chapter 9.

# Chapter 5

# The search for efficiency and planning

There had been long standing concerns about the efficiency of the way in which the various health care providers operated, and the demands of war-time had exposed even more clearly the deficiencies of the pre-war system. In particular, planning for the civilian air raid casualties confirmed the view that existing hospital provision was both inefficient and variable in quality. It also indicated the potential for national and regional planning as a means of remedying perceived deficiencies in service provision (Chapter 3).

After the establishment of the National Health Service (NHS), there was certainly evidence of 'more efficient' use of hospitals. With the closure of smaller hospitals and the concentration of beds in larger units, the number of patients treated increased. This was accommodated by an increase in the number of cases treated per available bed, reflecting a shorter average length of stay in hospital (Allsop 1984: 83), and part of a wide-ranging trend towards the de-institutionalisation of a range of health and social care activities (Chapter 7). These changes suggested it would be best to use expensive hospital resources more intensively. This could be facilitated by co-ordinated planning of hospital and community-based health care, general practitioners (GPs) and community nurses, so that, for example, continuing care could be provided in the community when it no longer needed to be provided in hospital. Such planning seemed feasible now that there was a *national* and *comprehensive* health service and seemed to be one obvious means by which a more efficient allocation of resources could be achieved to replace the haphazard nature of pre-NHS health care. To what extent was the goal of a more efficient, better planned health service achieved in the first 30 years of the NHS?

Peace-time planning proved difficult to realise, at least in part for political reasons, but there was evidence of it, most obviously with the publication of the Hospital Plan (Ministry of Health 1962). The Plan recognised that as capital spending on hospital building increased, sums being allocated should be based on the principles of priorities in bed usage for particular patient groups, coupled with an overall pattern of development of services throughout the Regions. It aimed to establish bed norm provision in the main specialities and ensure that all Regions met these norms. It also introduced the concept of the District General Hospital of 600–800 beds serving a population of 100,000–150,000 and proposed extensive investment in new hospitals. It was intended to provide 'a *rational* basis for the development of the hospital services' (Allsop 1984: 55, emphasis added). However, despite this evidence of efficiency and planning, it was apparent that the NHS was not the paragon of 'rational planning' hoped for by its advocates at the time of its inception.

First and most obviously, 14 years had elapsed between the establishment of the NHS and the publication of the first major NHS plan. Second, it was a *hospital* service plan not a *health* service plan. There was a community care plan published the following year, but close inspection revealed that to be little more than a collection of rather disparate local plans rather than a genuinely complementary exercise to match the Hospital Plan (Mittler 1965). The origins of some of the subsequent concerns about community care can be traced back to this time. It was the Hospital Plan that contained the first official projection of a reduction of mental hospital inpatient beds, but it was far from clear that the projected increases in community mental health services contained in the local authority health and welfare plans were sufficient to offset the effects of the projected decreases in inpatient services contained in the Plan (Chapter 7). This failure to bring together hospital and community health service planning was perplexing, given the potential contribution of the latter to supporting the existing trend towards a more efficient use of hospital resources. From a community health perspective the Plan could be viewed as evidence of the continuing dominance of the hospital sector and of acute medicine in the NHS (Allsop 1984: 55). Third, these rival plans were the products of different parts of the 'tripartite' organisational structure and they could be taken as further evidence of the limitations of this structure, especially for the development of effective health service planning (Chapter 8). Fourth, the rebuilding of teaching hospitals was given priority in the Plan, because of the need to expand medical education, and within that priority the emphasis was on the cheaper option of expanding existing institutions. As a result, there was significant investment in the London teaching hospitals. This did not advance the development of a more equitable distribution of health care (Chapter 6). This investment was the 'cheapest' way, in the short run, to remedy deficiencies in medical education (Abel-Smith 1990: 13). Despite the hopes and aspirations of its founders, 'rational planning was a late arrival in the NHS and when it came it was with a partial (hospital-based) and flawed (emphasis on London teaching hospitals) plan'. The sort of 'rational planning', population-based and priority-led, for which advocates of a national health service might have hoped was not in place until after 1974 (King's Fund 1987: 1). This was after two further changes of Government (Labour 1964–1970 and Conservative 1970–1974; Chapter 6). What happened to the vision of an efficient, rationally, nationally planned service between 1948 and 1974?:

> It is not only possible, but sensible to regard ... [the planning of health care] ... with what one might call pragmatic ... imperfectionism. That surely is what the present state of the health service demands.
>
> (Eckstein 1958: 283)

After its first ten years of operation it was the view of one American commentator that opposition to the state planning of the NHS was misguided. But the problems of planning in the 1950s were exacerbated by the inheritance upon which the Service was based. There was virtually no tradition of planning or planning expertise to draw upon (Chapters 1 and 2). Also, the tripartite organisational structure of the Service grew out of the political conflicts associated with the establishment of the Service (Chapters 3 and 4). We have already noted that one means of getting a more efficient health service might be through planning community health care developments in order to facilitate the more efficient use of hospital-based health care. This could enable the earlier discharge of patients who no longer needed 24 hours a day inpatient care. But the tripartite organisational structure separated hospital and community health services. Another potentially significant contributory factor to the more efficient deployment of health care within the community was better communication, and co-operation between medical and nursing services, for example, enabling GPs to work as a team with district nurses. But the tripartite organisational structure separated community-based medical practitioners (GPs) from the community-based nurses (domiciliary midwives, district nurses and health visitors), with the latter working for local authority health departments. This political compromise gave every appearance of hindering rather than helping the planning process (Chapter 8). The tripartite organisational structure was in part a function of professional power and influence, and planning was not facilitated by professional power and influence. 'The medical profession, particularly GPs, have always fought against anything smacking of direction of labour' (Buxton 1976: 35).

There was a change of government in 1951 and Conservative Governments would remain in power until 1964. They held state planning to be anathema, given their avowed aim of 'liberating the economy' from those war-time controls that had been retained by the post-war Labour Governments. Churchill, with his 'Set the People Free' slogan, pursued tax cuts in 1952, 1953 and 1954, and reduced public expenditure was the means by which this was to be achieved. There were recommendations for charging fees in secondary schools, charges for school meals and health service charges. Charges that were introduced in the NHS were for dentures in 1951 and for spectacles and prescriptions in 1952 (Abel-Smith 1990: 12). There was a reduction in capital expenditure on hospital building. By late 1951 the number of posts in health management had been frozen, especially clerical and administrative posts, following Treasury demands for a 5 per cent reduction in non-medical and nursing staff. By the end of 1952, Ministerial control was absolute with senior medical staff establishment having to be approved by the Minister himself (Glennerster 1995: 75–7).

The first major report into the new service commissioned by the new Conservative Government was concerned about its 'present and prospective cost'. The question was how to limit 'the burden on the Exchequer' through the 'effective control and efficient use of ... Exchequer funds'. It was a report on *the cost* of the NHS and it was apparent that containing the costs of the new NHS was firmly on the political agenda (Guillebaud Report 1956). Indeed, Aneurin Bevan was said to have seen the establishment of the committee as a 'partisan resort to expose and isolate the service as the most extravagant feature of the welfare state and one which any prudent government must curb or curtail' (Foot 1975: 212). In fact, the Guillebaud Report gave the NHS an 'economic clean bill of health' with no evidence of waste or extravagance. Indeed, the analysis undertaken for the Committee by Abel-Smith and Titmuss concluded that 'capital expenditure in 1952/3 was at a third of the rate of 1938/9' (Abel-Smith and Titmuss 1956: 138) and the Committee concluded that a major capital programme was required immediately (Guillebaud Report 1956). However, for the NHS the 'age of austerity' would continue throughout the 1950s, sustained as much by an ideological commitment to the 'public burden model of state welfare' as by pressing economic circumstances. This model of welfare holds that increased expenditures on programmes like the NHS diminishes economic welfare, with deleterious effects for rich and poor alike (Titmuss 1968: 124–25). The cost of the NHS as a percentage of gross domestic product would fall 'from 3.51 per cent to 3.24 per cent in the mid-1950s' (Briggs 1978: 449).

Lastly, it was the Treasury view that the new NHS charges noted above were merely the necessary first steps towards tighter financial control within the health service (Webster 1988: 137 and 182). For the Treasury, the dominant view was less likely to be 'can we afford an *unplanned* NHS?' and rather more likely to be 'can we afford *any sort of* NHS?' These concerns had some basis in the discrepancy between widely held expectations of the costs of the new NHS and the reality of its costs, for the new Service faced some relatively short-term but nonetheless significant resource issues when it was established. First, there were increases in staff numbers and pay levels, the inevitable result being an unforeseen escalation in staff costs in the hospital sector. Second, there was a significant backlog of pent-up demand. This had partly 'accumulated during the war and its uneasy aftermath ... most vividly depicted by the demand for spectacles, dentures, hearing aids and other postponable adjuncts to better health' (Titmuss 1968: 153). But it also represented something of longer-standing than the hardships of wartime. This backlog followed years in which many in the population had ignored and neglected their own health needs when faced with services 'marred by the taint of charity, less eligibility, minimum standards ... heavy handed bureaucracy ... social discrimination and the indignities of the poor law' (Webster 1988: 15; Titmuss 1950: 514). As such, this backlog represented an immediate and profound restatement of the case for a universal health service; to be remembered along with the queues to buy the Beveridge Report (Chapter 3). But it also provoked immediate concerns about the cost of the new Service and it was soon clear that the issue of financing the NHS was 'never to be unimportant again' (Briggs 1978: 448):

Financing the NHS was an instant and persistent headache

(Hennessey 1992: 143)

Even in the nineteenth century there had been disputes about costs and the need for cost containment (Chapter 1). The issue of escalating costs became an ongoing issue in the provision of health care posing particular problems for the voluntary hospitals (Chapter 2). The economic problem for the NHS was going to be the potential conflict between the aim of providing a universal, comprehensive health service of a good standard and containing health costs to a reasonable level. The political implications of this fundamental dilemma were acknowledged in 1948 by Bevan when he observed that 'we will never have all we need' (Foot 1975: 209). This problem reflected the growing significance of factors that had begun to undermine the finances of voluntary hospitals towards the end of the nineteenth century (Chapter 1), indicating that their pre-war financial crises (Chapter 2) were the result of something fundamental about health care in industrial societies, a seemingly endless escalator of rising costs. The key factors were demographic trends, medical advances, rising expectations and the complex relationship between health and health care.

It is an established demographic fact that most industrial societies have increasing numbers of elderly people, the 'greying' of the population. Amongst this group there exists a greater number than ever before of frail, elderly people, the 'old old', whose need for health care is markedly higher than the rest of the population, but also higher than that of people in the 65–79 age group. The main cause of this demographic trend has been identified as declining mortality among all age groups, testimony to both medical and non-medical interventions as well as the long-term downward trend in fertility (King's Fund 1992a: 71). Given that the more serious and more chronic health care problems for this age group constitute a significant proportion of hospital discharges and hospital inpatient days, the implications for the costs of any health care system are dramatic. Furthermore the 'old old' (those aged 80 years and over) have an even more significant impact on the demand for, and organisation of health care, there being marked increases in chronic illness and disability in this age group compared with those aged 65–79, including significantly greater use of domiciliary, GP and community nursing services (Phillipson 1990: 57–9).

These statistics show demographic trends that explain why existing hospital resources are largely taken up with the health care needs of the older members of society, although such projections tend to discount other factors, including medical advances (see below). Nonetheless, there was no doubt that the demographic profile of industrial societies was changing with associated changes in the disease profile as 'chronic degenerative diseases and cancers ... replaced acute infectious diseases as the primary causes of disability and death in Britain' (King's Fund 1992a: 70). This linked combination of demographic trends and the changing spectrum of disease could be seen as key factors pushing up the costs not only of the NHS, but of health care systems throughout the industrialised world.

Health care systems throughout the industrialised world also experienced a continuing growth in new forms of medical intervention and the development of new therapeutic methods; and most involved additional expenditure. For example, during this period medical technology dramatically improved with the introduction of procedures that could be life-saving or improve the quality of life. Dialysis, CAT scanners, and transplantation were three obvious examples. At the same time, the development of new therapeutic methods for treating and preventing infection with antibiotics as well as stabilising people with long-term chronic illness, such as the use of chlorpromazine for those with mental health problems, became commonplace and no longer were novel procedures. Such innovations had a cost-push effect and led to demands from clinicians to use the latest therapies and interventions on behalf of their patients, and in the name of scientific advance and progress.

The publicity surrounding medical advances was almost certainly a contributory factor in raising public expectations about what the service could and should deliver. An assumption of optimum standards was built into the aims and expectations of the Service, and Bevan had observed that 'expectations will always exceed capacity' (Foot 1975: 209). By 1969, a Labour Secretary of State for Social Services was identifying a 'revolution of rising expectations' that extended from physical goods to education and health (Crossman 1969: 5–7). Subsequent evidence indicated that 'public attitudes to health and health care are changing ... people are becoming more discriminating about what health care offers' (King's Fund 1992a: 70).

The growth of modern biomedicine closely paralleled a significant improvement in the health status of populations in relatively affluent, industrial societies. There were dramatic decreases in the death rates for common infectious diseases and other conditions in the twentieth century (see Table 5.1).

*Table 5.1* Standardised death rates (per million) from certain diseases: England and Wales

| Diseases | 1848–1854 | 1971 |
| --- | --- | --- |
| Bronchitis, influenza and pneumonia | 2,239 | 603 |
| Tuberculosis (respiratory) | 2,901 | 13 |
| Scarlet fever and diphtheria | 1,016 | 0 |
| Whooping cough | 423 | 1 |
| Measles | 342 | 0 |
| Smallpox | 263 | 0 |
| Infections of ear, pharynx, larynx | 75 | 2 |
| Cholera, diarrhoea, dysentery | 1,819 | 33 |
| Typhoid, typhus | 990 | 0 |
| Convulsions, teething | 1,322 | 0 |
| Syphilis | 50 | 0 |
| Appendicitis, peritonitis | 75 | 7 |
| Puerperal fever | 62 | 1 |

Source: McKeown 1976: 33–7.

At the same time, there were dramatic changes in health care. In place of hospital care of dubious value (Eckstein 1958: 15) and deficient medical education (Stevens 1966: 23), there were a range of improvements in relation to diagnostic techniques, chemotherapy, radiotherapy, organ transplantation and other forms of surgical intervention. So one plausible outcome of spending more money on improving our health care ought to be improvement in the health status of the population as a whole. Further evidence for this relationship was derived from the 'inverse care law' by which communities with poor health care facilities had poor health status. This appeared to confirm the close link between standards of health care and the health status of particular populations and thus the potential for a more efficient health service to have a marked impact on the health status of the population as a whole. The resulting lower demand on health care resources held out the possibility of stable, or even decreasing, costs for the new service (Campbell 1987: 180–1). However, the view that a more efficient health service would have a marked impact on the health status of the population as a whole increasingly came to be challenged, most notably by McKeown. His appraisal of important medical advances left 'little doubt that their impact was much smaller than is generally supposed' (McKeown 1976: 92). It was becoming apparent that the relationship between health services and the health of the nation was a more complex one (Chapter 9 summarises these arguments). A more efficient and effective health care system did not translate simply into either improved health status for the population as a whole, or reduced costs for that system.

Before the NHS was established, there had been long-standing concerns about the efficiency of the way in which the various health care providers operated, especially the lack of co-ordination and planning. War-time planning indicated the potential for national and regional planning as a means of remedying perceived deficiencies in service provision. With a *national* and *comprehensive* health service such planning seemed a feasible means by which a more effective and efficient allocation of resources could be achieved. However, such planning was delayed for many years and when it came it was with a partial (hospital-based) and flawed (emphasis on London teaching hospitals) plan. This lengthy delay was caused by the initial lack of planning expertise, the tripartite organisational structure of the Service, which hindered rather than helped any planning process, and the fact that state planning was little favoured by much of the medical profession and the 1951–1964 Conservative Governments. Despite the limitations of NHS planning and the concern with cost containment, there was evidence of more efficient use of hospitals. The tripartite organisational structure was changed in 1974 (Chapter 8) and by 1976 a formal system of population-based and priority-led planning was in place (Chapter 6). In addition, the issue of escalating costs had become an ongoing issue in the provision of health care before the NHS, and it was concerns about costs and cost-containment that tended to dominate the NHS agenda. Concerns about escalating costs were fuelled by the discrepancy between the expectations and the reality of the costs of the new Service based in part on some significant resource issues immediately after its establishment, such as increases in staff numbers and pay levels and significant backlog of pent-up demand. The longer-term factors contributing to escalating costs were demographic trends, medical advances and rising expectations. It was clear that every UK Government after 1948 would have to deal with medical advances, demographic changes, public expectations and financial shortfall in order to meet these constant pressures.

# Chapter 6

# The search for equity

When the National Health Service (NHS) was being established, one of its more clearly stated goals was the pursuit of a more equitable allocation of health care resources (Klein 1983: 25). As Aneurin Bevan explained in the House of Commons when presenting his Bill, the intention was to 'universalise the best'. The Service inherited profound inequalities in service provision. Health care equity issues had not been resolved by the growing state intervention in health care before the NHS. There were wide variations in both local government health services and the range of benefits provided by the Approved Societies under the National Health Insurance (NHI) scheme (Chapter 2). The result was that the pre-NHS mix of voluntary and state institutions had involved major issues of equity of access to health care and differences in the standard of health care between social groups and regions. Equity of access was also linked to concerns about the persistence of inequalities in health since those parts of the country which appeared to have the greatest need were most deficient in health care facilities (Chapter 2). There were also issues relating to the standards of health care received by different categories of patients. The latter were clear before the twentieth century and were linked to the different patient profiles of the voluntary and local government (Poor Law) hospitals. Doctors working in the former had more prestige and higher status (Chapter 1).

To what extent was the goal of a more equitable health service achieved in the first 30 years of the NHS? Pursuit of this goal would rest significantly on removing financial barriers to access and distributing resources equally across the country. There was evidence in the early years of the operation of the service that it had significantly improved the access of elderly people to services in ophthalmology (Titmuss 1968: 78), but there was also a growing recognition by the mid-1960s that higher income groups tended to make more effective use of the Service (Titmuss 1968: 196). Meanwhile, resource allocations between areas and between hospitals, primary and community care, and local authority services altered only marginally between 1948 and 1976 (Carrier 1978: 119). This problem was not confined to the NHS and it became recognised that the pursuit of 'territorial justice' was a more intractable problem than many had realised. 'Territorial justice' described the situation where variations in service level matched variations in need, 'to each area according to its needs' (Davies 1968). For the NHS, one writer coined the label 'the inverse care law' to indicate the persistence of a situation in which 'the availability of good medical care tends to vary inversely with the need of the population served' (Tudor-Hart 1971). This was an early illustration of the likely consequence that would flow from 'territorial injustice', namely the awareness of what would be increasingly referred to as 'the postcode lottery'.

With regard to different categories of health care there appeared to be growing evidence of these inequalities persisting. This was especially the case from the late 1960s onwards as a series of scandals and crises drew attention particularly to the quality of provision for the elderly and people with mental health problems or learning disabilities (Martin 1984), and the label 'Cinderella services' was attached to this part of the NHS. A particular focus for concern was the long-stay institutions which seemed to be providing poor quality care in settings that were increasingly felt to be expensive, unnecessary and stigmatising. The perceived failings of these institutions would give a further boost to the case for developing community care (Chapter 7).

Why was there so much less progress than anticipated in developing a more equitable health service? First, it was hoped that the elimination of explicit financial barriers to the utilisation of health care would have a profound impact on equity of access. However whilst the 'free play of market forces' may have been significantly moderated with the introduction of a universal health service that was largely 'free at the point of need', the 'free play of social forces' (Pinker 1971: 188) generated persistent evidence of the inability of some social groups to make effective use of the NHS. Second, it was presumed that distributing health care resources more equally would involve a continuing commitment to the sort of planning introduced during the war (Chapter 3), but comprehensive population-based and priority-led planning was not established until the mid-1970s (Chapter 5; King's Fund 1987: 1). With regard to the earlier major hospital planning exercise a detailed reading of the 1962 Plan indicated significant investment in London. The traditionally well-endowed areas such as central London maintained their position within the NHS (Benzeval et al 1991: 26), with the Plan doing little to redress the imbalance of resources between central London, the Home Counties and the rest of the country. The result was that nearly all the 12 London undergraduate teaching hospitals were rebuilt on their existing sites or only a few miles further out from the centre. While the population of central London declined and there was a rapid growth of population beyond the green belt, London's teaching hospitals were expanded, all within easy reach of Harley Street (Abel-Smith 1990: 13). Third, the emphasis on cost-containment contributed to the limitations of post-war planning (Chapter 5). With regard to distributing resources more equally between areas and different types of care, a pattern of resource allocation based on historic cost-budgeting meant that all areas benefited from increasing resources, but at the same time simply underwrote and perpetuated the inherited pattern of inequalities. The additional resources needed to begin the process of removing inequalities between areas were not considered affordable.

Fourth, we have noted already the potential significance of professional opposition to planning (Chapter 5). In addition, there seemed to be differences in professional prestige and resources attached to particular categories of health care. These categories relate to different types of care, different groups of patients and different sorts of need.

Before the NHS was established there was evidence of the 'unwillingness of trained nurses to care for cases of chronic sickness' (Abel-Smith 1964: 210) of the Poor Law hospitals and doctors to refer their 'burdensome' patients elsewhere, as well as the superintendents of the infirmaries in London being remarkably successful in keeping out the 'aged and infirm' patients (Abel-Smith 1964: 206). The Royal Commission on the NHS would conclude that perceived biases of the NHS in favour of hospital-based intervention in episodes of acute health problems, and the relative neglect of preventive measures, may be at least partially attributed to the interests of a range of health and social care professions (Royal Commission on the NHS 1979: Ch. 6). We have attempted to represent something of these different interests in Figure 6.1.

If resource allocation was influenced by professional prestige, this would indicate that, for example, community-based care for people with chronic mental health problems may be relatively less well resourced than hospital-based services for people with acute physical health problems.

Lastly, long-standing concerns about what was now being labelled 'the inverse care law' were linked to the hope that a fairer health service would have a marked impact on inequalities in health status. However, it was becoming increasingly apparent that the relationship between the utilisation of health care and health status was a complex one. Providing good quality health care on a universal basis at little or no cost to service users did not translate simply into a diminution in ill-health and did not ease the problem of escalating costs (Chapter 5). From this it followed that the relationship between the NHS and inequalities in health would not be straightforward. Any successes in the pursuit of equity in health care would not translate simply into a diminution in health inequalities.

| High status categories | Low status categories |
|---|---|
| Physical health problems | Mental health problems |
| Hospital-based | Community-based |
| Curative | Caring |
| Curative | Preventive |
| Curative | Health-promotion |
| (Health restoration) | |
| Acute health problems | Chronic health problems |
| Life-saving | Terminal care |
| Disease | Disability |

Figure 6.1 Perceived status of health problems

After 1974, the NHS had a new organisational structure which was somewhat more amenable to effective planning (Chapter 9), and a formal planning system was in place by 1976 (DHSS 1976c; Butler and Vaile 1984: 109). At the same time, more active policies were pursued by the 1974–1979 Labour Government to redress spatial disparities and to redirect the balance of resources in favour of the 'Cinderella' areas. Between 1975 and 1977, the Government published five important policy documents which proposed to alter the traditional pattern of resource allocation. Whilst the public expenditure White Papers (HM Treasury 1976, 1977) laid down a pattern of future expenditure that would stabilise capital investment and contain the rising revenue costs in the NHS, the Priorities documents (DHSS 1976a, 1977) faced the question of redistributing resources in favour of neglected client groups, children, elderly people and people with mental health problems or learning difficulties. The Report of the Resource Allocation Working Party (RAWP) began the process of equalising resources going to similar client groups in different regions throughout England (DHSS 1976b). Both the RAWP and Priorities documents can be seen as outcomes of a long process of discussion about the planning, organisation and administration, and, ultimately, the justification of the NHS as the major means of providing health care to meet the needs of the population. Subsequently, the Secretary of State for Social Services was to endorse a commitment to what he called 'positive discrimination', and to follow it up in circulars related to the Court Report on child health services (Carrier 1978: 119). The terms of reference for the RAWP involved a commitment to 'a pattern of distribution responsive objectively, equitably and efficiently to relative need. The Working Party identified their underlying objective as securing 'through resource allocation that there would eventually be equal opportunity of access to health care for people at equal risk', and to this end identified the criteria for need which they suggested had been largely ignored in existing resource allocations. These criteria included population size and composition, morbidity, and relative cost (DHSS 1976b: paras 1.6–1.9).

The problems faced by the Working Party related especially to the quality, complexity and sources of information. This included finding reliable indicators of ill health. For the latter, the RAWP's formula involved using the Standardised Mortality Ratio as a measure of morbidity. This, and other aspects of their approach, attracted a good deal of criticism (Carrier 1978: 124–35). The policy implications of the RAWP were clear, a significant redistribution of resources away from the Regional Health Authorities (RHAs) of Oxford RHA, South-Western RHA and London. The latter attracted particular criticism as the analysis that showed the Thames RHAs had more resources relative to the populations that they served, also confirmed that much of this over-provision was focused geographically upon Inner London, and functionally upon the group of services known as Local Acute Hospital Services and, in some districts, upon other services as well, such as those for the mentally ill and handicapped (King's Fund 1987: 3). Furthermore this *over-provision* of acute hospital services in inner London was combined with the *under-provision* of community health services in the same areas, an example of the limitations of past planning and the complex challenges of planning for more equitable services in the future (Chapter 12) Also, there was evidence that variations within regions were even more significant than those between regions (Buxton and Klein 1975).

The 1976/77 allocations to RHAs were based on the first RAWP report (DHSS 1975a). The Secretary of State would subsequently claim that he was taking a 'middle course' in his response to the final RAWP report, in which all regions would receive 'real increases' in their allocations with the equalisation of resources recommended by the RAWP being phased in over a ten-year period. In addition to the proposed reallocation of resources between regions it was proposed that similar principles of redistribution should, as far as possible, be applied to allocations at area and district levels (HM Treasury 1976). However, 'planning for territorial justice' was difficult. The NHS had an abundance of *quantitative* measures of health care *inputs* and it seemed likely that the more significant variations in such inputs, such as numbers of health professionals employed by a service, represented some variation in service quantity and quality. However, the pursuit of a finer degree of territorial justice required 'worthwhile' measures of spatial variations in health care needs to be set against *qualitative* measures of health care *outputs*. This argument would be deployed with particular force following the RAWP initiative (below) with calls for more research into the relationship between revenue inputs and patient care outputs (Barr and Logan 1977). The issue would remain relevant in the 1980s when more systematic use would be made of performance indicators, which would provide some information on outputs but 'none about outcomes', and which would remain 'silent about the question of quality' (Klein 1995a: 145).

The Priorities documents (DHSS 1976a, 1977) acknowledged the RAWP principles and some of the difficulties that might flow from operating them, alongside their own projections for increased spending on the 'Cinderella services'. Of course, it was the RAWP principles that had the most direct impact on resource allocation, even if they were intended to work over a full decade. The Priorities principles had less tangible outcomes, leading to the understandable observation that 'in practice the language of norms and objectives turned out to be merely the vocabulary of exhortation', although even critics had to note that there was evidence of the priorities being incorporated in the allocation of resources (Klein 1983: 128). The second Priorities document, *The Way Forward*, also noted the issue of social class inequalities, reporting that a Working Group on Inequalities in Health had been set up by the DHSS (DHSS 1977: 29). The report that emerged two years later (Black Report 1980) was to become politically contentious. Work was completed as the Conservative Government took office in 1979 and few copies were published. The interpretations used by the Report were disputed by the then Secretary of State, Patrick Jenkin (Chapter 10). One outcome was a resurgence of interest in the whole area of social divisions, social inequalities and health.

The history of health services from the establishment of NHI in 1913 until the establishment of the NHS in 1948 was one of state financed and regulated medical care being supplied to limited, clearly designated groups of the population. The historians of the pre-1948 period suggest that services were deficient in coverage and that provision was unequal, when judged by the criteria of social class, geographical distribution and categories of health care. The health needs of the population were met more by the chance of living in an area well-endowed with public health services, voluntary teaching hospitals, or enough panel doctors per head of population than by any rational planning criteria of matching population health care needs to available medical care resources. In addition, the inequalities in health care provision were matched by inequalities in health. It was these circumstances that underpinned what we have labelled the 'equity' arguments that formed part of the case for the NHS (Chapter 2). The 'search for efficiency' and 'rational planning' (Chapter 5) would play a part in the 'search for equity' but the basic principles of the service, an optimum standard service available to all citizens (universalist) funded by taxation rather than user charges (free), were seen as making a crucial contribution to minimising these inequalities. The attempt to plan the equitable distribution of NHS resources to reflect identified priorities brought up both old and new conflicts. We have already noted the potential conflict between the concepts of 'rational planning' and 'professional autonomy'. This would inevitably be heightened when the priorities involved a reallocation of resources away from the more professionally prestigious locations (urban-based teaching hospitals) and categories of health care. The resulting professional opposition might be assuaged by moderating the policies, introducing them over a lengthy time period, or providing the resources to limit the impact on the 'non-priority' areas. Concerns about cost containment seemed likely to rule out the latter leaving a potential conflict between the Priorities documents and the RAWP principle of a more equitable distribution of resources. A conflict of this nature might be resolved through 'a massive reduction in acute services' (Klein 1976: 983) but this would exacerbate professional opposition. Thus there was less progress than anticipated in developing a more equitable health service for all these reasons. It was also becoming apparent that the complex relationship between health care and health status meant that any successes that were achieved in the pursuit of equity in health care did not necessarily translate into a lessening of health inequality. Whilst improving the access to and utilisation of health care remained a reasonable aspiration for the NHS, the other dimension of the 'inverse care law' (inequalities in health) might persist due to a combination of historical and current social and economic circumstances. 'Health care equity' would be only one of these circumstances.

The new organisational structure, from 1974, was somewhat more amenable to effective planning and the 1974–1979 Labour Government actively pursued policies to redress spatial disparities (RAWP) and to redirect the balance of resources in favour of the 'Cinderella' areas (the Priorities documents). At the same time, it was becoming clear that achieving 'territorial justice' was a complex task. There were more measures of inputs than of outputs and problems relating to the sources of information, the quality of information and the complexity of information. In addition, it became apparent that variations *within* regions were even more significant than those *between* regions.

# Chapter 7

# The search for more community health care

Constant recurring theme in all debates about the National Health Service (NHS) has been the definition, location and potential of community-based health care. In Chapter 1 we noted a growing commitment to various forms of institutional care, including investment in new institutions. But some of the new institutions (the county asylums) were also pioneering outpatient facilities in the latter part of the nineteenth century (Roberts 1967) and community health care was certainly not a new phenomenon. Indeed, there existed long-standing traditions represented by community-based medical practitioners (general practitioners (GPs)) community-based nursing staff and pharmacists in high street chemist shops. Community-based nursing staff included the long-established provision of health visiting, district nursing and domiciliary midwifery. There was the later development of community psychiatric nursing, and we noted the growing interest in non-institutional alternatives in the mental health services in the inter-war years. Lastly, there has always been an enormous volume of informal caring devoted to the care of the terminally ill and those with major disabling conditions as well as the immense quantity of minor childhood ailments that are effectively contained and cared for within families. The latter was represented by relatively unchanging statistics indicating that most reported illness is dealt with by community-based GPs, nurses and pharmacists.

Since the establishment of the NHS there had been a clear trend towards a different, more intensive use of expensive hospital resources. This could be facilitated by community-based health care (GPs, community nurses) and at this time a considerable political consensus began to build up around the desirability of the further development of community care policies (Walker 1983: 157). This related especially to developing provision for certain categories of need where there would, in the end, be little or no place for large, socially segregated, geographically isolated institutions. This included the network of county asylums/mental hospitals.

For people with mental health problems, this would involve a trend away from provision based exclusively on the 'mental hospital', with the development of a range of services including outpatient, and day-patient care, community nursing, social work support, day centres, hostels, and group homes. For elderly people, this would involve a similar trend away from provision based in what were often old Poor Law buildings, with the development of a range of services – health visiting, home help, care attendants, social work support, day centres and 'sheltered housing'.

However, this trend away from the institution-based services was not universal. Certain rather important events in life (birth and death) were tending to be 'institutionalised' with much greater proportions of births and deaths occurring in hospitals rather than at home, especially since the Cranbrook Report (1959) with regard to maternity cases. There were also variations in the active pursuit of meeting different categories of need. In the mental health services, the case for community care was being advocated before the NHS was established, but only became a priority for children and adults with learning difficulties following the publication of the White Paper, *Better Services for the Mentally Handicapped* in 1971 (DHSS 1971b).

Nonetheless, we can identify with a degree of certainty that, first, a political and professional consensus was emerging around the desirability of the further development of community care, and, second, there was an increasingly widespread advocacy of, and requirement for, more community-based provision in policy documents and legislation. These policy documents included the community care plans of 1963 (Ministry of Health 1963) and the *Better Services* White Papers of 1971 and 1975 (DHSS 1971b, 1975b). The legislation included the National Assistance Act 1948, the Mental Health Act 1959, the National Assistance (Amendment) Act 1962, the Health Services and Public Health Act 1968 and the Chronically Sick and Disabled Persons Act 1970 (Walker 1982a: 14–20; Jones 1983: Ch. 6).

## The end of the asylum

> There they stand, isolated, majestic, imperious, brooded over by the gigantic water tower and chimney combined, rising unmistakable and daunting out of the country-side, the asylums which our forefathers built with such immense solidity.
>
> (Powell 1961)

Local government was the major provider of mental health services before the NHS was established. With the setting up of the NHS all the local government mental hospitals (previously asylums) were nationalised and became part of the NHS. They were transferred to specialist hospital authorities as part of the tripartite structure and the role of local government was now restricted to mandatory duties with regard to the initial care of patients and their removal to hospital with only permissive powers with regard to prevention, care and aftercare. In 1955, the Royal Commission on the Law relating to Mental Illness and Mental Deficiency was established; they reported two years later (Royal Commission on the Law Relating to Mental Illness and Mental Deficiency 1957). The recommendations included the introduction of new legal terminology (i.e. mentally ill, psychopathic, severely subnormal), inspectorate functions to be taken over by the Ministry of Health and the establishment of Mental Health Review Tribunals to take over the functions of investigating wrongful detention. It was proposed to end the special designation of mental hospitals.

The Royal Commission also recommended the legal confirmation of two established trends. First, that patients should be admitted to hospitals in the same way as to other hospitals (compulsory detention would be used only where treatment was deemed necessary for personal or public safety but was refused). Second, that no patient should be retained as a hospital inpatient when that patient has reached the stage at which he or she could return home if he or she had a reasonably good home to go to. At that stage the provision of residential care would become the responsibility of the local government. The subsequent Mental Health Act 1959 led to the provision of community care becoming a duty for local authorities (Jones 1960: 191) However, neither the Royal Commission nor the Act led to any changes in the organisational arrangements (the tripartite NHS) that had already been identified as a hindrance to policies of community health care (Chapter 5). Furthermore, the Act 'provided no additional resources to facilitate the development of community care services' (Goodwin 1989: 41).

The first plans to run down the mental hospitals (which were in most cases the old asylums) came with the publication of the Hospital Plan in 1962 (Ministry of Health 1962). It projected a significant decrease in mental illness beds available per 1,000 population by 1975, with an increasing proportion of this decreasing number of inpatients being located in the psychiatric units of the new District General Hospitals (Maynard and Tingle 1975: 152–3). However, between 1962 and 1970, a period over which the Hospital Plan proposed a 43.3 per cent reduction in mental hospital beds, the actual reduction was only 14.88 per cent (Maynard and Tingle 1975: 156), and by 1975 when it had been expected that 13 mental illness hospitals would be closed, only one large hospital had been closed in England and Wales.

Despite this very slow process in reducing mental hospital beds, there was evidence of discharged mental hospital patients left without help and 'sensational stories of psychiatric hospitals dumping their patients in the streets are regularly cropping up in the national and local press' (*New Society*, 22 July 1976: 184; Ball 1972: 241). The term 'careless community' was being used to describe the circumstances that faced those decanted or diverted from the traditional asylum (Harrison 1973). This outcome may not have surprised those contemporary critics of the Hospital Plan who had suggested that it 'dismissed too lightly the increasing proportion of the elderly in the population' and that the Plan was 'slightly unrealistic in considering the 1954–59 period as normal; when it was, in fact, a stage of sudden advance whose pace could hardly be maintained', and in failing to take account of 'the probability that rehabilitation programmes had been directed at those long-stay patients who seemed the most hopeful prospects' (Roberts 1967: 43; Tooth and Brook 1961).

In 1968, the Report of the Chief Medical Officer said that District General Hospitals would totally replace the old mental hospitals, assuming that community services and geriatric services provided full support. But it was noted subsequently that the Hospital Plan had 'made no directive as to what level of provision in the community should be, but simply assumed that the local authorities' plans would be carried out' (Maynard and Tingle 1975: 156). NHS, personal social services and local government restructurings had been under discussion since the mid-1960s. The outcome of these restructurings was a new pattern of two-tier local government, with responsibilities for all aspects of the personal social services, and an NHS completely separate from local government with responsibilities for all health services. These restructurings tried to make a reasonably clear distinction between medical and non-medical areas of work, the latter to be the responsibility of the new Social Services Departments. However, problems arose because there were bound to be overlaps and difficulties in making this distinction in the care of people with mental health problems. (Chapter 8 has a more detailed review of these changes.)

In 1975, the Government published a new White Paper, *Better Services for the Mentally Ill* (DHSS 1975b). This paper laid down norms of provision, attempting to match resources to needs. It included the observation that 'the hallmark of a good service for the mentally ill is a degree of local co-ordination' (DHSS 1975b: 10) and that 'joint planning of health and local authority services is essential' (DHSS 1975b: 86). The latter comment highlighted yet again the significance of inter-organisational co-operation, especially given that 'it is not easy to draw an exact line between the functions of day centres ... (managed by local authority Social Services Departments) ... and those of day hospitals ... (managed by the NHS); nor to define precisely the point at which mental infirmity is severe enough to be beyond the scope of residential care' when the locus of responsibility would shift from the Social Services Department to the NHS (DHSS 1975b: 34 and 39). The White Paper principles were endorsed in the Priorities documents (DHSS 1976a, 1977). The former committed a rising proportion of NHS and personal social services budget to outpatient, day-patient and day-care service, although the latter moderated the increase somewhat.

## The case for more community care

There are four themes which made the case for the development of community health care: (a) 'public burden'; (b) 'efficiency'; (c) 'needs'; and (d) 'rights'.

The 'public burden' theme was simple and straightforward. It rested on the inability to afford to maintain and staff some of the large institutions. In particular it was noted that it was becoming increasingly difficult 'to staff isolated institutions in an age when few people are prepared to make a career in residential work' (Brown 1977: 195; Williams Report 1967).

The 'efficiency' theme also concerned costs, but focused on the relative costs of forms of care along the institutional/community care continuum. The

*Table 7.1* Comparative costs of institutional and community care

| Type of care | Average cost of mental handicap |
| --- | --- |
| Hospital inpatient care | £6,000 pa |
| Hostel place | £1,500 pa |
| Day-centre place | £1,200 pa |

Source: DHSS 1981c.

comparisons set out in Table 7.1 serve to illustrate the point but were preceded and followed by similar calculations (Boswell and Wingrove 1973: Ch. 6; Audit Commission 1986).

The implication of these figures seemed clear. For the same budget, more people could be helped by using non-institutional settings. This became an especially powerful argument when it was complemented by the needs case.

The 'needs' theme could be sub-divided into four inter-related dimensions. The first of these is the growing evidence of 'over-institutionalisation' with researchers consistently concluding that a substantial proportion of the existing 'institutional population' did not need to be placed in such institutions 24 hours a day, seven days a week, and (for some of the residents) for many weeks or even years. The early research produced quite dramatic figures. Only 15 per cent of mental illness inpatients needed to be hospital inpatients (McKeown et al 1958). In the 1960s, 1970s and early 1980s, various sources were still concluding that at least 30 per cent of elderly people, people with mental health problems and people with learning difficulties were located unnecessarily in forms of institutional care (McKeown 1967; Gilderdale 1971; DHSS 1972d; Durkin 1972: 7; DHSS 1981c).

Another dimension is that this identification of 'over-institutionalisation' was itself related to changing (especially professional) perceptions of the needs of individuals who had traditionally been viewed as 'suitable cases for long-term institutional care'. This was especially related to developments in geriatric and psychiatric medical and nursing care, the so-called 'pharmacological revolution' (Jones 1972a; Martin 1984: 2; Jones 1983: 226). For people with learning difficulties:

> the work done in the hospitals and elsewhere ... has demonstrated that even the severely handicapped have previously unrecognised capabilities for the development of manual and other skills and varying degrees of social independence if they receive the necessary stimulus and appropriate education and other forms of training.
>
> (DHSS 1971b: 19)

The third dimension is that alongside this growing recognition of the potential for new forms of support, and the identification of 'over-institutionalisation', there was a growing concern that the traditional institutions were an inappropriate setting in which to meet the needs of their residents. Certain dimensions of this problem could be observed in Goffman's classic definition of the 'total institution' as a place where, 'all aspects of life are conducted in the same place and under the same single authority ... inmates typically live in the institution and have restricted contact with the world outside' (Goffman 1961: 17–18).

This 'restricted contact' with the outside world was seen as increasingly problematic now that many of the services identified their rehabilitative and/or curing roles, in addition to their traditional long-term caring roles. Traditional forms of institutional care had not facilitated 're-entry' into the wider community, indeed the barriers involved in the transition from the 'total institution' to 'normal society' were well recognised for a range of individuals previously living (and working) in, for example, the armed forces, children's homes, mental hospitals and prisons.

The fourth dimension in the 'needs' theme related to the distinctive qualities of the 'total institution' which were seen as not simply limiting the 'need-meeting' capacities of the services based there, but also of 'creating needs'. This argument was probably first used most effectively for the mental health services with the concept of 'institutional neurosis' (Barton 1976), in which the adjustments made to the distinctive qualities of institutional life were seen to generate their own psychiatric (behavioural) problems. Subsequently, the 'dependency enhancing' effects of residential care for older people was noted (Walker 1982b) and a dramatic TV documentary, *Silent Minority*, produced in the UN Year of the Disabled Person, made a graphic case for the difficult and disturbing behaviour of young people with learning difficulties being a function of their institutional confinement rather than a rationale for that confinement (Evans 1981). It can be seen that a particularly effective case for community care could be assembled around the twin themes of 'efficiency' and 'needs'.

The 'rights' theme was perhaps the last theme to get onto the political and professional agendas. The disabling effects of institutional care, noted above, clearly had implications for the rights of inmates. If institutions do indeed 'create needs' and in certain respects 'disable' their residents, this is not just 'a problem for professionals' who might be presumed to be meeting needs and minimising dependency, although Illich (1976, 1978) has claimed that professionals themselves disable the lay person and deny individual autonomy. This 'disabling effect' can be seen as an affront to the rights of the individuals concerned, and could no longer be easily justified. The point was made with increasing force for the different groups who had been most subject to the 'institutionalisation of social problems' in previous years. 'There is no deliberate policy of punishment on the part of institutions but unfortunate side effects develop if a child is removed from the nuclear family and, although the policy is to care for the child ... the outcome is inevitably detrimental to the recipient' (Tutt 1974: 48).

There is evidence in many cases of loss of contacts with relatives and friends without the substitution of social relations with fellow residents. There is the restriction of occupational activity and evidence of loneliness and apathy, by comparison with people of comparable age and physical condition outside. Quite apart from the deplorably low standards of amenities, there is also the organisational rigidity of institutional life which inevitably creates severe problems of adjustment and integration for residents from diverse backgrounds. Many old people are dismayed at the interruption of a lifetime's routines, loss of contact with locality and family and reduction of privacy and identity. The closer a residential institution approximates in the scale, privacy and freedom of the private household, the greater the qualified expression of contentment (Townsend 1973: 218). 'In ensuring that handicapped people are able to enjoy similar living standards as those enjoyed by non-handicapped members of the community the question becomes one of whether this can be accomplished in an isolated institutional setting' (Jaehnig 1979: 9).

Another dimension of the 'rights' theme, is the growing awareness of, and concern for, the stigmatising effects of institutional care. This became more obvious when policies of rehabilitation were hampered by cases of discrimination against ex-long-stay hospital patients. More generally, it could be seen to reflect the extent to which life in a traditional institutional setting was increasingly a devalued and devaluing experience. In his account of 'total institutions', Goffman contrasts 'batch living' with 'a meaningful domestic existence'.

Total institutions are also incompatible with another crucial element of our society, the family. Family life is sometimes contrasted with solitary living, but in fact the more pertinent contrast is with batch living, for those who eat and sleep at work, with a group of fellow workers, can hardly sustain a meaningful domestic existence (Goffman 1961: 21–2). What is perhaps missing from Goffman's evocative phrasing, is the sense of the social and economic changes that made this contrast much more marked and poignant for individuals in the latter half of the twentieth century by contrast with the impoverished and impoverishing 'batch living' that was imposed on many working-class households by the social and economic conditions of nineteenth-century Britain. This concern with the 'citizenship rights' dimension of the traditional institutional services was taken up most obviously in concepts of 'normalisation' and 'social role valorisation' in services for people with learning difficulties and the campaign to reform the Mental Health Act 1959 (Gostin 1975). Policies for community care became 'a move to provide disadvantaged and disabled people with services in settings which everyone in the community values, as a way of establishing or re-establishing fulfilled lives' (Heginbotham 1990: 43).

The third and final dimension of the 'rights' theme became a major political issue from 1968 onwards with the first of a depressingly lengthy series of enquiries into the neglect and ill-treatment of long-stay residents of a variety of institutions, especially, but not exclusively, NHS hospitals (Martin 1984; Robb 1967). Life in our traditional institutions was not only probably disabling, and certainly devaluing. It was also potentially dangerous. When attempts were made to identify those factors that seem to precipitate abuse and neglect, they included staff who were poorly paid, poorly trained and overworked; inadequate amenities; and powerless inmates (Beresford 1978: 700). In many respects, these characteristics could serve as a description of many of the settings bequeathed from the 'institutionalisation of social problems' before the NHS was established. The concern with the disabling, devaluing and dangerous aspects of institutional life could serve as a basis for the right for a non-institutional life. 'All people should have the right to live within the community, contribute to it and benefit from it, and simply be a part of it, except in very rare circumstances' (Brown 1977: 195).

## The problems of developing more community health care

We have seen that a persuasive, and indeed quite powerful, case for further developments in community health care could be assembled around the themes of 'efficiency', 'needs' and 'rights'. Yet despite this the history of these developments was problematic and controversial. The 1962 Hospital Plan contained the first official projection of a reduction of mental hospital inpatient beds, but it was far from clear that the projected increases in community mental health services contained in the local government health and welfare plans (Ministry of Health 1963) were sufficient to offset the effects of this projected decrease in inpatient services (Chapter 5).

Community care services were not immune from the cost implications of demographic trends. Indeed, larger numbers of elderly people were the major client group in terms of policies for community care and hence the phenomenon of needing more resources merely to sustain current standards and services was as marked for community care as for other aspects of health and social care (Heginbotham 1990: 46–7).

Continuing the theme of cost containment, the persuasiveness of part of the case for community care was perhaps counter-productive. The combination of the 'efficiency' and 'needs' cases suggested the potential to develop a more acceptable, accessible and effective set of services with limited additional expenditure, because of the savings that would accrue from redistributing resources from expensive and unnecessary institutional care, into cheaper, more effective and less institutional alternatives. There were a number of problems with this seemingly 'free lunch' in which everyone would benefit and there would be no losers.

First, the scale of 'over-institutionalisation' was such that the initial development of community-based alternatives often involved rather modest expenditure, given the limited dependency of the individuals who were diverted to non-institutional settings. This almost certainly exaggerated the 'cheapness' with which successful community care policies could be pursued with more dependent people.

Second, many calculations advanced as part of the efficiency case, underestimated the full range of services needed for successful community care policies (e.g. building and planning regulations for access and mobility, labour regulations for discriminatory employment practices) and hence the costs of the latter. In many respects there is no excuse for such miscalculations since the point had been made quite forcibly many years ago that to scatter the mentally ill in the community before we have made adequate provision for them is not a solution, in the long run not even for HM Treasury. Considered only in financial terms, any savings from fewer hospital inpatients may well be offset several times by more expenditure on the police forces, on prisons and on probation officers; more unemployment benefits masquerading as sickness benefit; more expenditure on drugs; more research to find out why crime is increasing (Titmuss 1961: 106).

Third, it was in the nature of the 'total institution' that substantial savings from their reduced role would only accrue when they were completely replaced by a new continuum of community-based services. The 'efficiency savings' associated with community care were therefore significantly long term rather than short term. In the shorter run, the NHS might well be 'burdened' with sustaining a dual track of 'old fashioned institution-based provision' and the 'new community-based services'.

Fourth, the circumstances of the long-stay residents of the older institutions would figure in the arguments for a more equitable health service (Chapter 6). In this case, there was a failure to recognise the needs of the more dependent residents and the role played by their less disabled co-residents in caring for them, hence the profound implications of the transfer of the latter to the community. This may well have contributed to creating some of the factors that were to pre-cipitate successive long-stay hospital 'scandals' as fewer staff coped with fewer, but more demanding, long-stay patients.

Fifth, one result of the 'scandals' was that the NHS was faced with the argu-ment that current and capital expenditure on the traditional long-stay institutions should actually be increased to remedy the worse deficiencies identified in the 'scandals', and to provide for the increasingly dependent residents who remained in this setting. There was a sound case, relating to both 'needs' and 'rights', for responding to these calls for more expenditure, but this could exacerbate concerns about the costs of developing community care. The development of certain types of community health care for certain groups of patients (including those with mental health problems) might have limited professional prestige and professional support (Chapter 6, especially Figure 6.1).

The tripartite organisational structure of the Service (Chapters 3 and 4) sepa-rated hospital and community health services and was a barrier to joint planning. Thus policies for community care were not facilitated by organisational and financial arrangements. There had never been effective mechanisms by which the efficiency gains that might accrue from a run-down of traditional institutions (run by one part of the tripartite structure) would be transferred to those services that were to be developed as part of policies for community care (run by another part of the tripartite structure and also beyond the NHS). In virtually all cases the resulting scenario was that the traditional institutional provision was being eliminated too swiftly by comparison with the development of community-based alternatives. This was perhaps most marked in the mental health services. At this time a key Government document had to admit that 'by and large, the non-hospital resources are still minimal' (DHSS 1975b: 14).

Despite a 'political consensus' about the importance of community care, con-flicts around the interpretation of the concept meant that it lacked clarity and operational effectiveness. In supporting 'community care', different groups and individuals may have been, and may still be, supporting different concepts of 'community care'. The most obvious distinction was that between care *in* the community and care *by* the community. The former has been described as 'concerned with the provision of care by *paid* social services workers *in* the community ... (rather) ... than *by* the community' (Walker 1982a: 4, emphasis added). The latter is taken to refer to the 'provision of help, support and protection to others by lay members of societies acting in everyday domestic and occupational settings' (Abrams 1977: 125). Whilst it may be impossible to envisage care in the community unsupported by care by the community, or vice versa, there was clearly potential for significantly different policies for community care to be developed around these concepts and a considerable potential for conflict. In particular, different policies for community care could have radically different implications for public expenditure. Compare the resources required for maintaining small-scale but good quality institutional care alongside large-scale, good quality care *in* the community with the resources required for the total abandonment of institutional care alongside a reliance on care *by* the community.

The new commitment was to provide good quality community care. Whatever standards had been set by the nineteenth-century institutions, they were in many cases not providing good quality residential care by the second half of the twentieth century. Therefore the policy was not just about switching resources between different modes of service delivery but about significant changes in service standards and philosophy (e.g. normalisation). The resources 'tied up' in old, poor-quality institutional care might not always be sufficient to develop new, high-quality community care. Perhaps most significantly, the needs and rights cases for community care had been developed initially in relation to existing 'institutional populations'. However, they were increasingly seen to have a wider significance, for the needs and rights of those 'beyond the institution'. This was quite clearly expressed in the White Paper, *Better Services for the Mentally Handicapped* in 1971. It was this White Paper that proposed the first significant decline in the inpatient population for people with learning difficulties. Despite this policy for community care starting *only in 1971*, the same document noted that 'about 80 per cent of severely handicapped children and 40 per cent of severely handicapped adults, and a higher proportion of the more mildly handicapped, live at home' (DHSS 1971b: 4).

The message from this, and community-based surveys on disability, seemed clear. Despite previous extensive investment in new forms of institutional care (Chapter 1), this investment may have had only a relatively marginal impact on the activities of the newly revealed and vast army of informal carers, a view that had already been partially confirmed by the research that indicated, for example, that most of the older people in residential care had limited access to informal carers, whether families or friends (Townsend 1973). If the needs and rights of those beyond the institutions were to be taken seriously it would require more resources than would be released through the recognition of the efficiency case for community care. Furthermore, a new set of needs and rights now entered the equation, those of the informal carers. A number of concerns had been expressed before the Mental Health Act 1959 was enacted. McDougall had encapsulated a number of these when observing that 'community care … a fine-sounding phrase … can be an almost intolerable burden on individual husbands, wives or parents involved' (McDougall 1959: 229). Almost 20 years later it was noted that 'virtually no help' was available to those caring for other people at home (Brown 1977: 199). Whilst the needs and rights of the carers were certainly not necessarily in conflict with those of the cared-for, they were not necessarily always compatible.

So more accessible and acceptable community-based services would reveal more and more of a previously 'submerged iceberg' of unrecognised and unmet need (Goodwin 1989: 47) as service-providers become aware of those 'beyond the institutions' who had managed 'out there' by themselves, or with support from informal carers. It is this, perhaps more than anything else, which swept away the 'free lunch' model of community care. Given uncertainties about the numbers and contributions of informal carers relating to various trends (e.g. the scale and intensity of needs; separation, divorce and the reconstitution of families; the participation of women in the labour market), it seemed that the resource implications of 'good community care' were not such that they could be readily accommodated only through the resources still 'tied up' in traditional forms of institutional care.

Lastly, in so far as the impact of a combination of cost-containment policies and an unhelpful administrative infrastructure contributed to widely perceived failings of 'community care', then perhaps the rights (and needs) of two other groups could be identified, the 'institutional' and the 'community' population. The dismantling of traditional institutional care, with insufficient attention (or resources) committed to less institutional alternatives, had its greatest impact on the most vulnerable and most dependent individuals. The generality, and indeed validity, of the arguments for community care could conceal variations in the circumstances of different client groups, children in care, people with learning difficulties, mentally ill people, and of individuals within these groups. It was clearly never part of the case for community care that all forms of residential care would be abandoned. The research on over-institutionalisation was at times startling but never indicated that 100 per cent of those surveyed could be cared for in non-institutional settings. Yet at times local policies seem to have come close to this scenario. In these circumstances, the rights and needs of the most dependent individuals are clearly at risk, raising questions of whether the right to a non-institutional life should be complemented by the 'right of asylum' (Parry-Jones 1987: 411) or the 'right to protection' if, as was noted many years ago, 'our society is increasingly unwilling to accept responsibility, socially and financially, for those who do not recover quickly and who do not conform to our expectations of medical productivity' (Titmuss 1961: 108). The right to long-term nursing care (as part of the NHS) might be another essential element in getting the balance 'right' between institutional and community care.

## Conclusions

A growing commitment to various forms of institutional care nonetheless recognised long-standing traditions of community health care, with recognisable 'community care' policies also being developed in the nineteenth century. In addition, there has always been a large, unquantifiable and unrecognised volume of informal caring taking place in households up and down the country. Since the establishment of the NHS there was a clear trend towards a different, more intensive use of non-community facilities for a wide-range of health problems but this may have concealed to some degree the need for further developments in community health care. Considerable political and professional consensus began to build up around the desirability of these further developments, the case for which could be well-founded on the needs and rights of a significant number of potentially vulnerable people of all ages. In particular, the concern with the disabling, devaluing and dangerous aspects of institutional life could serve as a basis for the right to a non-institutional life.

Despite this consensus, the further development of community care policies proved problematic and controversial. In particular, it became apparent that the range and costs of services needed for successful community care policies had been underestimated. Reasons for this included demographic trends and the initial development of community-based alternatives often involved misleadingly 'modest' expenditure. In the shorter run it would be necessary to sustain a dual track of 'old fashioned institution-based provision' as well as the 'new community-based services', and in addition, there was a case for increased expenditure on the 'old-fashioned institution-based provision' for the increasingly dependent residents who remained in that setting.

It also became apparent that there were other needs and rights to be considered such as informal carers and those needing community care who had not been living in the institutions and who found themselves with little or no support. Recognition of these 'other needs and rights' would involve additional costs to those factored into some of the early estimates of the costs of developing more community health care. Lastly, we should note that policies for community care were not facilitated by the organisational arrangements for health and social care before 1970 when these arrangements began to be changed. This will be discussed in the next chapter.

# Chapter 8

# The search for better organisation

The organisational structure of the state's involvement in health care has been the subject of conflict at least since the introduction of National Health Insurance (NHI) in 1911 (Chapter 2). With the establishment of the National Health Service (NHS), it became a major focus for political debate in which a considerable degree of political consensus around the general case for reform dissolved into conflicting views about the details of the reform, especially the organisational details. The outcome, as virtually all commentators seem to agree, was a political compromise in the form of the so-called tripartite organisational structure of the NHS (Chapters 3 and 4). This structure was to prove problematic for planning (Chapter 5), the search for equity (Chapter 6) and for further developments in community care (Chapter 7).

Whilst 'tripartitism' appeared to be a key concept in the organisational structure established in 1948, the major three way division into general practitioner (GP), hospital and local community health services was further complicated, first, by slightly different organisational arrangements in England and Wales, Northern Ireland and Scotland, and second, by different organisational arrangements for non-teaching, special and teaching hospitals.

Under these arrangements, the NHS was administered by more than 500 separate units, based both inside and outside local government, servicing areas which were not necessarily coterminous one with another. The situation was especially complex in London, where the boundaries of four regional hospital boards converged on a point in central London and where there were located a large number of teaching hospitals managed separately from of those boards. These teaching hospitals had illustrious histories (St Bart's going back to the eleventh century), possessed high status and were staffed at the highest levels by the elite of the medical and surgical professions. One relatively early judgement on these administrative arrangements was that the NHS presented 'a large area of irrational administration' (Eckstein 1958: 82), a consequence of the Bevan compromise with the medical professions to ensure their co-operation in the setting up of the Service in 1948.

## Organisational problems

This 'irrational administration' was problematic at all levels of health care delivery and not just in London. It was a hindrance to basic day-to-day administration and the management of a range of theoretically complementary services (Parker 1965: 86–93). It was a threat to continuity of care, especially for the many patients who would become the responsibility of more than one branch of the service, an area that assumed greater and greater significance with the trends towards more efficient use of hospital resources and the development of primary and community health care. Lastly, it made the concept of health service planning very difficult to realise even without the other issues already identified in Chapter 5.

The division between those services inside and outside local government was especially problematic. There were at least four areas of difficulty. First, there were different financial bases, most obviously the separate system of local government taxation (rates, community charge and council tax). Second, different cultural contexts, the NHS had two main professions while local government had many professions and a bargaining environment with political control subject to elections. Third, there were different structural arrangements. The NHS was hierarchical and was controlled by one central government department while local government was not hierarchical, county and district councils being independent of one another, and was responsible to several central government departments. Fourthly, there were different procedures and time planning systems (Thomas and Stoten 1974: 65–9).

These problems were recognised from the beginning of the Service. One possible solution was the development of health centres which had been advocated in 1920 in the Dawson Report (Chapter 2). Health centres had the potential to promote liaison and co-operation between key health professionals. They could be a work-base for GPs, community nurses and some hospital-based doctors whose outpatient clinics could be relocated to the centres. They certainly afforded the opportunity to give some patients a less fragmentary experience of health care delivery by providing a single, major location for much of their health care. In the event, very few health centres were built until the mid-1960s. The reasons are familiar and relate to some of our enduring themes of conflict. First, investment in health centres required capital expenditure and hence a conflict with concerns for cost-containment. Second, health centres were to be built and managed by local government and hence a conflict with concerns about professional autonomy, and the perceived threat of local government to that autonomy (Chapters 3 and 4; Hall et al 1975: 285; Campbell 1987: 179; Webster 1988: 393). Thus it was not surprising that the Government did not respond positively to the suggestion made in 1951 in the Association of Municipal Corporation memoranda to the Select Committee on Estimates (enquiring into the Hospital Service) that the organisational problems of the NHS would be ameliorated by making the whole service a local government responsibility (Parker 1965: 78), taking us back to an earlier dispute between Morrison and Bevan (Chapter 4).

## Proposals for reform

Organisational problems were recognised by the Guillebaud Committee (1956) especially with regard to services for elderly people and the maternity services. However, the Committee suggested that it would be too disruptive to attempt any major changes at that time and emphasised the need for greater co-operation between the different parts of the Service. Subsequently, a separate committee was established to look at the maternity services identifying the need for greater clarity about the respective roles of different parts of the service (Cranbrook Report 1959).

That circumstances might be more amenable to organisational reform was signalled by the publication of the Porritt Report (1962). This was a report from a non-governmental, predominantly professional committee, and it recommended the unification of most of the NHS under Area Health Boards, although the teaching hospitals would retain their separate status (Watkin 1978: 134–6). By this time, the case for reform could be based on identifiable trends and policy initiatives. These included early discharge schemes in the maternity services, the attachment of nursing staff to general practice; and the commitment to develop community-based mental health services (Abel-Smith 1978: 35–7). In the event, 12 years would pass before the service was reorganised, a time-scale that was at least partly indicative of the continuing political sensitivity surrounding organisational issues in health care. There were also changes of government in 1964, Conservative to Labour, and again in 1970, Labour to Conservative.

This restructuring of health care was also part of a broader agenda of change in state welfare. The case for organisational changes in health care was paralleled by similar debates relating to the personal social services. These services had a similarly fragmented structure, although in this case mostly within local government. Once again the move away from traditional institutionally based services (children's homes, residential care for elderly people) to community-based services (day-care for under-fives, home helps) was seen to be hindered by the division of service responsibilities between different departments. The Seebohm Committee was established in 1965 to review the personal social services. At the same time, concerns were expressed about the overall structure of local government which consisted (outside London) of unitary authorities based on cities and large towns (county boroughs) and a two-tier system in the more rural areas (county and district councils). In response to these concerns a Royal Commission on Local Government in England (1969) was established.

Thus when the Government made its first pronouncements on a possible organisational restructuring in health care in what became known as the First Green Paper (Ministry of Health 1968), it had already set in train parallel reviews to restructure the personal social services and local government. The potential for discontinuities and contradictions in this situation were all too obvious. They were made more so with the publication of this First Green Paper, since its central proposal for unifying the NHS under 40 to 50 Area Health Boards mooted the possibility of these Boards taking responsibility for local authority health and public health responsibilities, and more significantly that the Boards might be incorporated in the new local authorities to be established following the publication of the Redcliffe-Maud Commission. But the Redcliffe-Maud Commission had not been required to examine the implications for the NHS of any recommendations they might make (Abel-Smith 1978: 38). The first tangible contradiction in this process soon appeared. The Seebohm Committee reported soon after the publication of the First Green Paper and recommended a different division between health and social care to that contained in the latter. Seebohm proposed that key services located in the local authority health departments would move to a new local authority social services department rather than the new Area Health Boards (Seebohm Report 1968).

Between the First and Second Green Papers (1968 and 1970) the Government reassured the medical profession that the 'new NHS' would not be part of the 'new local government' and took steps to implement most of the recommendations of the Seebohm Committee to the evident satisfaction of most of the social work profession. The Second Green Paper (DHSS 1970) confirmed that new Area Health Authorities (AHAs) (of which there would now be about 90) would be outside local government, but there would be enhanced potential for NHS/local government co-operation through 'coterminosity', the new AHAs would match the new local authorities proposed by the Redcliffe-Maud Commission (Royal Commission on Local Government in England 1969).

The simplicity of the First Green Paper was also modified. Whilst the chain of authority would run directly from the Secretary of State to the AHAs, there would be regional health councils with a mainly advisory role and there would be Family Practitioner Committees to administer the GP services on behalf of the AHA. Given the key role of regional authorities for hospital consultants, in the non-teaching hospitals their contracts were held at the regional level (Chapter 4), and the long-term commitment of GPs to their own distinctive organisational arrangements, these additions to the simple Area Health Board model seemed like the beginning of a reassertion of the priorities and interests that had shaped the original 'tripartite' compromise of 1948.

Lastly, the Second Green Paper contained a commitment to what might be called 'the professional principle' (DHSS 1970: 10, para. 31). All that was social work-related would remain in local government as part of the new Social Services Departments; all that was medical- and nursing-related was to move outside local government into the reorganised NHS. As aspects of the old tripartite division disappeared, most obviously between hospital- and community-based nursing services, a new and even clearer health and social care division was being established. Indeed, the outcome of the 1974 reorganisation was a more clearly delineated administrative, financial and professional division than at any previous stage in the history of post-war health and community care policies (Carrier and Kendall 1995: 17). For some writers this signalled the end of the specialised mental health services (Jones 1972a: 34; Jones 1983: 218–34).

After the change of Government in 1970, three further documents were published by the new Conservative Government. A Consultative Document (DHSS 1971a) and a White Paper (DHSS 1972b) set out the Government's proposals for England, with separate documents setting out the similar proposals for Wales and Scotland. Crucially, a set of Regional Health Authorities (RHAs) were reintroduced in a direct line relationship between the Secretary of State and the AHAs, leading to a concern that 'RHAs based on RHB areas and staff will perpetuate the hospital orientation of these authorities' (Draper et al 1976; Abel-Smith 1971). The AHAs were to be coterminous with the new county councils and metropolitan districts and were to be introduced by a reorganisation of local government in 1974 (a different arrangement to that which had been proposed by the Redcliffe-Maud Commission). A statutory duty to co-operate via Joint Consultative Committees was incorporated in the relevant legislation and there were to be joint consultative committees to facilitate this local government/NHS co-operation. But the new pattern of local government was not suitable for aspects of health services (especially hospital) management and planning. The result was that most AHAs created a sub-tier of health service management in the form of District Management Teams (DMTs). Districts also formed the focus of Community Health Councils (CHCs) intended to represent the views of consumers.

A further document specified aspects of the internal management arrangements (the Grey Book) (DHSS 1972c), notably the concept of the DMT as a consensus forming team of equals, a model that was to attract subsequent criticism in the first Griffiths Report (DHSS 1983). The 'management team' approach had some basis in previous organisations. The arrangement that in England there would be no line management between the DMT and their area counterparts, but instead they would be directly accountable to the AHA, was more novel. This sophisticated relationship was peculiar to England and many felt it was unworkable. In Wales, Scotland and Northern Ireland, things were arranged in a more straightforward manner, with a direct line relationship between area officers and their district counterparts (Watkin 1978: 147).

Following the National Health Service Reorganisation Act 1973, the new restructured NHS came into effect on 1 April 1974, the same day as the new restructured local government system. Of course, the latter generated significant upheaval for many of the new local authority Social Services Departments which had been operational for only three years at the time of this restructuring.

## 1974 NHS restructuring, an evaluation

We have already identified some of the major concerns expressed at the time about this restructuring, notably the separation of related NHS and personal social services with a particular impact on a new health and social care divide, and the management and organisational problems of AHAs, for example divisions into districts. However, the changes introduced in 1974 generated an even wider range of criticisms, at least some of which were to be repeated with regard to subsequent major managerial and organisational reforms. Criticism was directed at the manner or style in which the reorganisation was carried out. This was not a peripheral issue. The quality of care provided by the NHS rests on the skills of its personnel and such matters as their commitment to the service. If a reorganisation is carried out in such a way as to seriously undermine staff morale, it may well have an effect on the quality of service given by staff, and its impact might be quite substantial and quite long lasting. One particular comment was that the restructuring was carried out too quickly. This is debateable since the reorganisation took place in 1974, while the first Government document on reorganisation (First Green Paper) had appeared in 1968. How then could the reorganisation have been undertaken too speedily? The real issue appears to be not speed of reorganisation, but that the conflict generated by the First Green Paper which was unacceptable, especially to the medical profession. A combination of medical politics and party politics (in the form of a change of government in 1970) meant that the reorganisation actually took place only about 18 months after the relevant legislation.

Another question was whether the reorganisation was too ambitious. It was intended to be much more than an amalgamation of different types of health authorities. In particular, the restructuring aimed for a more co-ordinated management and operation of interlocking services, particularly those requiring interaction between hospital and community, more critical evaluation of current resource use, clearer lines of managerial accountability, with responsibilities decentralised as far as possible, subject to guidelines from higher levels and performance monitoring, more clearly articulated arrangements for participation by the professions in management and planning, and more sensitivity to user interests, particularly as institutionalised in CHCs (Brown 1979: 161–2). In addition, there was the more general problem of the new health and social care divide, between the NHS and the personal social services. This particularly affected community care and those services which were concurrently being identified as priorities (Chapter 6). The latter all suffered a 'double handicap because responsibility is divided and both sides have more attractive uses for their money' (Brown 1979: 207). Exchequer money was made available for schemes to be jointly financed by health and local authorities (Abel-Smith 1978: 49) but understandably local authorities were not always willing to support schemes whose long-term implications were greater expenditure for them and reduced expenditure for the NHS.

There is little doubt that the gains from the changes were more modest than might have been anticipated and hoped for at the time of the publication of the Porritt Report (1962) or the First Green Paper (1968). This was in part due to the continuing health and social care divide, but also to changes that had taken place since the First Green Paper. These changes had lessened the significance of some of the concerns that provided the rationale for organisational change. These included the emergence of the 'community health team' of GP, district nurse, health visitor and domiciliary midwife. This was further facilitated by the Health Services and Public Health Act 1968, which enabled local authorities to arrange for cross-boundary visiting to patients on the list of GPs working in their area. By 1972, 70 per cent of health visitors and 68 per cent of home nurses were working in association with GPs (Mays et al 1975: 191). The amelioration of administrative divisions between GPs and community nursing staff, one of the few tangible achievements of the 1974 restructuring, had been rendered largely irrelevant before the restructured service came into operation. Furthermore, researchers were identifying administrative structures as only part of the problem. Differences in professional perspectives allied to a lack of resources were perhaps more significant barriers to identified desirable service objectives (Brown 1972: 132; Scammells 1971). This places a value on organisational restructuring but implies there is a danger of presuming that too much can be achieved through these means.

## Reorganising the reorganisation

Given the controversy surrounding the changes introduced in 1974, it is unsurprising that attempts were soon made to modify structures, especially given a further change in government in 1974. The new Labour Government was quick to do something about its criticism of the undemocratic nature of the new NHS with the publication of *Democracy in the NHS* (DHSS 1974). This proposed changes in the composition of AHAs and RHAs, plus a number of changes relating to CHCs. The Secretary of State's decision on these proposals, following submissions by interested parties, was made in July 1975. In the following year, joint financing money was made available after the initial failure of the statutory requirements for local government and the NHS to co-operate with one another. However, the sums involved were modest (1976/77, £8 million, 1978/79, £32 million) and the new scheme ran into similar difficulties. No scheme was ever better intentioned, but joint funding demonstrates the difficulty of creating inter-organisational working when the contributing organisations have different objectives, political environments and modes of working to reconcile (Royal Commission on NHS Research Paper 1 1978: 59; Booth 1981).

## Conclusions

The organisational structuring of the state's involvement in health care had been the subject of conflict at least since the introduction of NHI (1911). The establishment of the NHS (1948) involved the tripartite organisational structure with the Service being administered by more than 500 separate administrative units. This organisational structure was to prove problematic for continuity of patient care and planning (Chapter 5), developing more equitable health care (Chapter 6) and further developments in community care (Chapter 7). These organisational problems were recognised even by the Guillebaud Committee (1956), the main concern of which was the finances of the NHS. A further decade would elapse before a government published a consultation document on this issue (Ministry of Health

1968). This First Green Paper was part of a broader agenda of organisational change involving the personal social services and local government. Personal social services changed in 1971 (establishment of Social Services Departments) with local government and health service reorganisations following in 1974. In the end, the health service reorganisation involved five major government documents, two produced by the Labour Government in 1968 and 1970 and three by the Conservative Government, one in 1971 and two in 1972.

The reorganised NHS attracted a number of criticisms suggesting that the Service was over-bureaucratic, top-heavy with managerial hierarchies and undemocratic, and that it involved a new and significant health and social care divide. In 1974, the new Labour Government made some changes to the undemocratic aspects of the new structure. Commentators have also identified a series of fallacies in relation to the 1974 reorganisation, with a wider significance for future organisational reforms. These were:

- the 'unitary fallacy' (Brown 1972);
- the 'administrative solution' fallacy (Brown 1972);
- the 'single best solution fallacy' (Draper et al 1976); and
- the 'institutional change fallacy' (Royal Commission on the NHS, Research Paper 1 1978).

Although the organisational gains from the 1974 restructuring were modest they were sufficient to support a more sustained and systematic pursuit of the goals of equity and efficiency and provided more scope for comprehensive planning than the 1948–1974 tripartite structure.

# Chapter 9

# The search for better health

(The death rate) ... is in truth the sum of the influences of an almost infinite number of causes, all of which require to be duly considered and allowed for before any useful comparison can be made.

(Bristowe and Holmes 1863: 513)

We can buy human life. Each country, within certain limits, decides its own death rate.

(Sand 1935, quoted in Titmuss 1950: 535)

A more efficient and fairer health service does not by itself deliver better health, moderated health care costs or reductions in health inequalities (Chapters 5 and 6). What are the reasons for improved health status in industrialised societies? McKeown demonstrated that for many causes of death (with the notable exception of smallpox) the proportionate fall in the standardised mortality rate which could be attributed to specific personal health care innovations was relatively modest, the largest fall coming before such innovations (see Table 9.1).

Table 9.1 Death rates of the introduction of specific measures

| Cause of death | (A) Fall in Standardised Death Rate (SDR) between 1848/51 and 1971 | (B) Year when specific measure became available | (C) Fall in SDR by 1971 after introduction of specific measures | (D) C as a % of A |
|---|---|---|---|---|
| Tuberculosis (respiratory) | 2,888 | 1947 (streptomycin) | 409 | 14.16% |
| Measles | 342 | 1935 (sulphonamide) | 50 | 14.6% |
| Bronchitis, pneumonia and influenza | 1,636 | 1938 (sulphonamide) | 531 | 32.4% |
| Smallpox | 263 | Before 1848 (immunisation) | 263 | 100% |

Source: McKeown 1976: 52.

Indeed, given that the factors reducing death rates might be presumed to remain active after the introduction of the specific measures, for example, streptomycin for tuberculosis, McKeown concluded that the reduction of the death rate attributable to immunisation and therapy was less even than these figures suggested. Mortality from all diseases was declining before, and in most cases long before, effective procedures became available (McKeown 1976: 53). For McKeown, improvements in diet and advances in public health would explain the fall in mortality rates as plausibly as medical innovations:

> We owe the improvement not to what happens when we are ill, but to the fact that we do not so often become ill; and we remain well, not because of specific measures such as vaccination and immunisation, but because we enjoy a higher standard of nutrition and live in a healthier environment.
>
> (McKeown 1976: 94)

This general link between quality and quantity of food intake on the one hand, and general levels of health on the other, was accepted by the World Health Organization when it concluded that 'for the time being an adequate diet is the most effective "vaccine" against most of the diarrhoeal, respiratory and other common infections' (WHO 1973). This perspective applied particularly to developing societies, but was also applicable to the pattern of disease in the more affluent societies. For example, Burkitt identified 12 'common and serious diseases of the western world', including coronary heart disease, cancer of the large intestine, appendicitis and diverticular disease of the large bowel. He labelled these 'diseases of modern economic development' because they were 'rare or unknown in communities little touched by Western civilisation, and Western dietary customs in particular' (Burkitt 1973: 141). Given other conclusions that, for example, 'most cancers are due to environmental factors' (Doll and Kinlen 1972), the contribution of health care to the health status of the population was being seriously questioned in relation to both historical and contemporary evidence.

The complexity of the relationship between health and health care was illustrated by other evidence. This included the so-called 'submerged iceberg of sickness in society' (Last 1963), the label attached to the substantial volume of treatable illness in the community identified by researchers but not recorded in the routine record keeping of health service professionals. Health surveys in the more affluent sections of the world 'have noted that as much as 90 per cent of their apparently healthy subjects had some physical aberration or clinical disorder well worthy of treatment' (Robinson 1973: 34). This indicated, amongst other things, the imperfect relationship between individuals with treatable conditions and health care systems, even ones like the National Health Service (NHS) where some of the more obvious barriers to access and utilisation, charges and stigma, had been much reduced in significance.

Subsequently, McKeown's conclusions were subject to further critical appraisal (Szreter 1988) and debates continued around the relative contribution of different elements in the environment, for example, nutrition or pollution, especially the benefits and dangers to health of individual items within these elements, for example, different foodstuffs. Nevertheless, the general argument that the environment has a major impact on health status was widely accepted, consigning personal health services to a limited role in improving the health status of the population. Part of this healthier environment could be attributed to the epidemiological tradition from Snow to be followed by Semmelweis, Pasteur, Koch, Erlich and Salk. This has certainly had an impact in terms of preventing and alleviating human misery, disability, disease and death. But other factors take us beyond the 'medical tradition' with, for example, analyses which focused on improvements in the quantity and the quality of milk supplies in urban areas (Beaver 1973), on controlling the adulteration of food (Paulus 1974) and the transport system, and therefore the knowledge of civil engineers rather than doctors (Szreter 1988).

The arguments put forward by McKeown and others reasserted the significance of environmental factors for health status first developed in the public health movement in the nineteenth century. It accorded with the conclusion that the country was far healthier in 1948 than it had been ten years earlier (Briggs 1978: 448), testimony to the impact of a range of social policies deployed in the Second World War and especially those targeted at children (Titmuss 1950). It also emphasised the inter-sectoral approach to social policy that was a feature of the Beveridge Report for whom the NHS was but one part of a broader programme of social policy reform (Chapter 3). This is relevant to discussions about the scale and scope of a health care service concerned with the prevention of disease and the alleviation and cure of sickness. In particular, it leads us to a more realistic assumption about what the NHS or any other health care system can achieve. It is certainly not the only or even the major factor improving the health status of the population. In a similar vein, it cannot be the only or even the major factor in reducing inequalities in health status between different areas and social groups.

On this reading, a main aim for the NHS could have been that of a partnership between scientific knowledge and humane ethics in pursuit of four goals. First, individuals could be kept out of the health care system by emphasising the impact on health status of socially produced conditions and the importance of prevention. Second, once individuals enter the health care system, evidence-based health care should be diffused in as equitable and sensitive a manner as possible (Chapter 6). Third, persons should be enabled to return to their 'normal environment' as soon as possible (Chapter 7). Lastly, if individuals are unable to return to 'normality', then the most sensitive and 'caring' setting for their future should be planned with and by the individual and their potential carers. These issues would be reviewed by the Royal Commission on the NHS in 1979.

## The case for evidence-based health care

To what extent was the operation of the NHS based on the diffusion of evidence-based health care? This could be linked to the concept of the 'submerged

iceberg of illness' already mentioned, and especially that the diagnosed characteristics of some 'ill' and some 'healthy' people are not widely different. The
problem then becomes one of discovering the point, or points, on the distribution
at which therapy begins to do more harm than good. One solution to this problem
is randomised controlled trials (RCTs) to test the hypothesis that 'a certain treatment alters the natural history of a disease for the better' (Cochrane 1972: 20).
Cochrane's conclusion was that many procedures were being applied were not
soundly based on evidence drawn from RCTs. Furthermore, there was available
evidence to question, for example, variations in the length of hospital stays and
treatments advocated or used in relation to such conditions as ischaemic heart disease and mature diabetes. Some of his most devastating criticisms were directed at
ear, nose and throat departments, where he concluded that:

> we have two therapies which are probably effective in limited spheres; the
> first (tonsillectomy) is probably effective for only a small percentage of the
> cases operated on at present and has a definite mortality, but it is an urgent,
> dramatic therapy and is still rather fashionable. The other (audiological)
> is probably effective in improving the quality of life in some of a defined
> group of the population; it is dull, smacks of a local authority service, is not
> nearly as fashionable and serves the elderly. The first is applied inefficiently
> because it is too widely applied; the latter is applied inefficiently because it is
> under-applied.
>
> (Cochrane 1972: 63)

He was even more critical of psychiatry, concluding that it uses a 'large number
of therapies whose effectiveness has not been proven. It is basically inefficient'
(Cochrane 1972: 60).

Cochrane's themes continued to be pursued and supported, and later evidence
continued to show that there remained considerable scope for focusing NHS
activities more explicitly on an evidence-based medicine relying upon sound medical research, and the communication of these research results to all NHS doctors
(Fries et al 1993, for a presentation of this argument; Yates 1987; National Audit
Office 1987; Frankel and West 1993; Sackett and Rosenberg, cited in Bayley
1995).

It should be noted that the approach advocated by Cochrane and others does
not necessarily provide an opportunity to significantly diminish public expenditure
on health care by focusing much more precisely on those activities with proven
efficacy. Some of the evidence supported increased activity and expenditure, for
example, in relation to audiology services for elderly people, and reducing social
class inequalities in the use of health services (Cochrane 1972: 61–3 and 75).
However, evidence-based practice may provide the case for what might be termed
a 'reasonable' basis for cost-containment. The 'wasteful use of diagnostic tests
and the excessive use of X-rays, and unnecessary intervention, including unnecessary surgery' appeared at this time to be a more common attribute of more

market-driven health care systems, especially the private insurance and private market system in the USA (Abel-Smith 1976: 62). So a health service modelled on NHS principles might have the greatest potential to make progress towards a model of evidence-based medicine as well as evidence-based cost-containment. However, this approach would not be taken forward systematically in the NHS until after 1997 (Chapter 11).

## Conclusion

The relationship between health services and the health of a nation is a complex one. The health of more affluent nations like the UK has improved over a period of 150 years, but it was a set of factors operating largely *outside* the boundaries of the health services that played a crucial role in this improvement. *Within* the boundaries of health services it was the public health rather than the personal health dimension that had contributed most significantly to improving the health of the nation. This did not mean that there was a conflict between health and health care, or that it was necessary to choose one rather than the other. It did mean that policies for better health must involve substantially more than policies related to health care delivery, as indicated in the Beveridge Report 1942.

Earlier assumptions that 'better' arrangements for health care might deliver savings in the costs of health care delivery were shown to be erroneous. It was perhaps beyond the powers of the NHS to ameliorate the persistence of many 'health problems,' including many health inequalities, to any significant degree. However, it had become more apparent that there might be considerable scope for focusing NHS activities more explicitly on evidence-based medicine.

# Part II

# Conclusions

> When the Service began to operate in 1948 it … inherited the debts of a decade of sacrifice and neglect, financial poverty and disorganization.
>
> (Titmuss 1963: 153)

> The National Health Service is heading for the bankruptcy court … and we are facing bankruptcy because of the Utopian finances of the Welfare State.
>
> (*British Medical Journal*, 2 December 1950)

The professional and political opposition that accompanied the establishment of the National Health Service (NHS) made it seem likely that it might not survive for 30 years, especially with the change of government in 1951 from Labour to Conservative. Its survival may have owed a great deal to its popularity with the general public.

A key question was whether it would be possible to provide a universal, comprehensive health service of a good standard and at the same time contain health costs to a reasonable level. Certainly, the NHS came into existence in a most inauspicious time. The period has become known as 'the age of austerity' in which raw materials were rationed, there was competition for infrastructure schemes for council house and school building, and the pound sterling was devalued. Indeed, it has been suggested that without a loan negotiated with the USA 'the welfare state … would not have been possible' (Morgan 1984b: 151). When the Korean War led to increased defence spending, the Treasury sought economies in housing and the NHS. Within 21 months the first cash-limit was introduced into the NHS. Charges were introduced for dentures in 1951 and for spectacles and prescriptions in 1952 (Abel-Smith 1990: 12), it was the Treasury view that such charges were merely the first steps towards tighter financial control within the health service (Webster 1988: 182).

The NHS also revealed an underestimation of medical care need which placed the new Service under increasing financial pressure from 'day one'. Medical advances and the provision of more accessible and acceptable services would increase further the potential volume of treatable illness confronting the Service. Expectations rose in terms of both what the Service could achieve and the manner of its delivery. The Service also had to contend with increasing demands associated with demographic changes. Successive governments found themselves in a situation where additional expenditure was necessary merely to enable the Service to maintain the standard of service expected by doctors, patients and the general public. Increases in costs were inevitable, cost-containment became a dominant theme and from the early years of the Service the pattern of increasing demand became a characteristic feature of NHS discussions.

One means of containing costs seemed to be the planning of more effective and efficient allocation of resources facilitated by having a national and comprehensive service. Professional power and influence, combined with political concerns about the shortage of doctors, played a role in both delaying and limiting the scope of NHS planning. Population-based and priority-led planning was delayed until 1976.

Other hopes for cost-containment rested on the idea that an improved health service might diminish the need for health care by producing a healthier population. Sufficient resources for such a service might be afforded in part by reducing the incidence of disease and disability (Beveridge Report 1942: 105, para. 270 (3), 158 para. 426 and 162, para. 437). This provided part of the rationale for the NHS with the 1944 White Paper implying a 'causal relationship between the provision of medical services targeted against illness and the reduction of ill-health' (Seedhouse 1987: 146).

However, the relationship between the nation's health services and the health of the nation was more complex than this. It was certainly the case that the health of more affluent nations, like the UK, had improved over a period of 150 years, but the social and economic circumstances of the nation were a significant influence on its health status so that the demands for health care and the costs of health services might be only marginally influenced by the way these services were organised. From a simple equation attributing improvements and variations in morbidity, to improvements and variations in health care, a more complex picture had emerged. Differences in morbidity between different parts of the country might be the result of 'age/sex differences, socio-economic differences, physical aspects of the environment, or merely an artefact of differences in the availability of general practitioners (GPs) and the preparedness of patients to consult them about the iceberg of untreated illness' (Buxton 1976: 25).

The relationship between health status and health care was complex, influenced by social divisions, lay/professional relationships, and attitudes towards health and sickness.

But if the widely shared assumption in the Beveridge Report (regarding health care costs) was misplaced, another assumption, that many 'health problems' were beyond the powers of the NHS to ameliorate to any significant degree, was proved correct. This point would be made by the Black Report (1980) and later publications such as the Health Education Council's *The Health Divide* (1987) and the King's Fund's *Tackling Health Inequalities* (1995b), which would emphasise the significance of social security and housing policies for improving health and moderating inequalities in health.

Having a more efficient and equitable health care system did not translate simply into improved health status for the population as a whole, fewer inequalities in health status between locations and social groups, or reduced costs for the health care system. It was unrealistic to expect the NHS either to eliminate the health inequalities that had so disfigured pre-war society or to deliver stable or declining health care costs.

Another debate that came to the fore in these years was that of 'institutional care' versus 'community care', which represented two ends of a continuum. Policy and practice as advocated, enacted and interpreted was subject to variation not only by category of need but also by location, the latter sometimes, and sometimes not, justifiable by variations in local circumstances. In the context of this continuum, advocates of '100 per cent institutional care' or '100 per cent community care' were in a minority, and the 'practical reality' was that different aspects of health care were located somewhere between the ends of the continuum throughout the twentieth century. Given a commitment to make more intensive use of some hospital resources (Chapter 5) and the growing awareness of the limitations of some forms of institutional care, there was a case for the further development of community health care. Nevertheless, community care has always had to 'fight its corner' for resources and recognition as the appropriate location of care for many of the conditions presented by patients over the years.

The trend towards policies for community care discernible by the middle of the twentieth century represents important changes in terms of a restructuring of ideologies of, and resources for, caring. The quest for community care had three major themes. First, the *concept* of *community*, and its operational consequence, *care*, were highly valued ideas for several decades, but were unmatched by either a firm agreement on their meaning, or the economic support to give a reality to either their potential beneficiaries, carers, or citizens at large. An early warning of this theme was given by Titmuss in 1961 (Titmuss 1968: Ch. 9). Second, the political response has always lagged behind the policy support for such concepts. Third, the result of these gaps between valued intentions, policy support and political responses has been a distrust of the relocation of the populations of institutional care, the latter being seen as a nineteenth-century reasoned response to the 'social problems' of the time, but unmatched by the same response required in a modern society. Thus, an ambiguous conceptual basis, an under-resourced policy and an ill-prepared, and in some instances prejudiced, citizenry unintentionally combined to produce a lack of faith in what is assumed to be a widely shared commitment to supporting those with conditions requiring that very care summarised by the conceptual 'baggage' of community care.

The limitations of the 1948 organisational 'tripartite' structure were a product of accommodating conflicts. Action to ameliorate these limitations, for example the development of health centres, was delayed because of similar and additional conflicts. Despite the problems of this tripartite structure 'one need only to glance at the state of the old medical system ... (i.e. pre-NHS) ... to see that there ... (had been) ... a record of considerable improvement' (Eckstein 1958:

283). Nevertheless, the delay in remedying these organisational shortcomings would hinder policies for both a more equitable and a more efficient health service, and exacerbate the inevitable difficulties of recasting the balance between institution-based and community-based health and social care.

Twenty years would pass before a government published a consultation document on this issue (First Green Paper) initiating a five-year period of debate and discussion culminating in the National Health Service Reorganisation Act 1973 and the introduction of a new organisational structure in 1974. This new structure was soon to attract as much criticism as the previous system, this time for being over-bureaucratic and top-heavy with managerial hierarchies. It was also seen as affording rather limited gains in terms of organisational change. One part of the previous organisational division between hospital and community care went, with the virtual elimination of local government health responsibilities and the transfer of community health hospital services to Area and Regional Health Authorities, an outcome that had been predicted by Herbert Morrison (Honigsbaum 1979: 176). The administration of GPs remained largely separate via Family Practitioner Committees. Lastly, an earlier reorganisation of personal social services within local government had created (in 1971) Social Services Departments with major responsibilities for developing community-based services for elderly people and people with mental health problems and learning disabilities. The result was that policies for community care were still hampered by what was to become known as the health/social care divide. Health care services (e.g. home nursing and day-hospitals) were to remain the responsibility of the NHS. Social care services (e.g. home helps and day-centres) were to remain the responsibility of local authority Social Services Departments.

In his study of the reorganisation, Brown suggested that 'even if some restructuring ... is a necessary condition for better management and planning, it is by no means a sufficient condition' and he concluded that perhaps it is 'often better to live with some disadvantages than to incur costs of major change to secure improvements that may turn out to be illusory' (Brown 1979: 163 and 202). Lastly, Abel-Smith reminded us of the parallels with the organisational arrangements put in place in 1948 – noting that, once again, what 'eventually emerged was inevitably a compromise between conflicting interests' (Abel-Smith 1978: 41). Although the organisational gains from the 1974 changes were modest, they were sufficient to support a more sustained and systematic pursuit of the goals of equity and efficiency (King's Fund 1987: 1). It was argued that there was now more scope for 'rational planning' as it became feasible to look coherently at problems of allocation (Brown 1979: 162–3 and 196) and issues of equity were pursued with the Priorities (DHSS 1976a) and Resource Allocation Working Party (RAWP) (DHSS 1976b) documents. The implication was that a structure had been established that offered more scope for comprehensive planning than the previous system (Chapter 5).

The pre-NHS mix of voluntary and state institutions involved major issues of equity of access to health care and the standard of health care received between social groups, regions and categories of medical condition. These health care equity issues had not been resolved by growing state intervention in health care before the NHS, since there were variations in the services and benefits provided. These health care equity issues were also linked to health inequality issues since the areas with the greatest need were also most deficient in health care facilities. The pursuit of a more equitable allocation of health care resources was a clearly stated goal of the NHS, to be achieved by removing financial barriers (no user-charges) and distributing resources more equitably across the country. However, higher income groups continued to make more effective use of health care services and the pattern of resource allocation increased resources to all areas but did not equalise their distribution.

It was the 1974–1979 Labour Government which actively pursued policies to redress spatial disparities (RAWP) but it became clear that achieving 'territorial justice' was a complex task. There were more measures of inputs than of outputs, and problems relating to the sources, the quality and the complexity of information. In addition, it became apparent that variations within regions were even more significant than those between regions. Another focus of concern was the quality of provision for elderly people and people with mental health problems and learning disabilities, especially for those in long-stay institutions, the 'Cinderella areas'. It would be the perceived failings of these institutions which would give a further boost to the case for developing community care. Once again, it was the 1974–1979 Labour Government which sought to redirect the balance of resources in favour of these areas (the Priorities documents), but in 1976 cuts were imposed on public expenditure in the UK (Glennerster 1995: 167). This was not an auspicious moment to attempt a more active pursuit of some of the original goals of the NHS.

Within three years a Conservative Government was elected which seemed likely to be more interested in questioning those original goals. Previous (notably Conservative) Governments had tried to enable pursue those goals effectively, and it seemed that the search for savings in the use of resources might extend some way beyond the closure of a few hospitals and units. In particular, a renewed commitment to the public burden model of welfare was anticipated. This was despite the historical evidence which did not lend any straightforward support to this concept. When post-war British state welfare expenditure was put in a comparative context, post-war British Governments emerged as consistently low spenders, especially with regard to Britain's frugal expenditure on health care. In the comparative context of the countries of the Organisation for Economic Co-operation and Development, the most striking point is the over-simplification of the public burden model. It did not fit with what was known about relative economic performances of different societies. High spenders on state welfare and more specifically high spenders on state health care programmes had coped very well with the so-called 'public burden' and consistently outperformed lower spenders on health and welfare in terms of the conventional measures of economic growth (Harris 1990: 181; Wilensky 1981).

# Part III

# The NHS, 1979–2010

# Introduction

Part III reviews the more recent history of the National Health Service (NHS). Chapter 10 covers the Conservative Government's 19 years, 1979–1997, and Chapter 11 covers the 14 years of Labour, 1997–2010.

These Governments were led by four Prime Ministers, and over this time there were 13 Ministers of Health. These chapters discuss the key changes associated with these Governments. In particular, we have, where appropriate, endeavoured to illustrate the continuing relevance of the themes in health care history identified in Parts I and II.

The Conservative governments were especially concerned about the level of public expenditure and cost-containment would be an important aim. The search for better ways of organising the Service continued including a major management inquiry (DHSS, 1983) and a major White Paper (DoH, 1989a), the latter leading to the introduction of an 'internal market'. There was also a major report on community care (Griffiths, 1988). With primacy given to economic and financial considerations, traditional ideals of coherent planning towards meeting aims defined in terms of needs, would seem to be displaced by the ideal of remaining within budgets defined in terms of cash limits.

The Labour government elected in 1997 made the NHS one of the centre-pieces of its domestic policy agenda. There was a commitment to increase NHS resources and to build more hospitals. Key values, especially fairness and equity, were restated. The first White Paper of the new Labour Government reasserted faith in professional self-regulation, but the limitations of these arrangements were soon exposed by a series of cases which prompted the establishment of various committees of enquiry between September 1999 and January 2001, leading the Government to take a more significant role in regulatory matters.

# Chapter 10

# The Conservative years, 1979–1997: money, managers and markets

Let me make one thing absolutely clear. The National Health Service is safe with us.

> (Margaret Thatcher in a speech to the Conservative
> Party Conference, 8 October 1982, reported
> in *The Times*, 9 October 1982)

The NHS had become a bottomless financial pit.

> (Thatcher 1993)

In this country when you are ill they take your temperature, in other countries they take your credit card; while I'm in Downing Street that will never happen here.

> (John Major in a speech to the Conservative Party
> Annual Conference, 11 October 1996, reported in
> *The Independent*, 12 October 1996)

## Introduction

Changes in government have almost inevitably been associated with changes in social policies including policies on health, often based on manifesto promises. Significant changes, the introduction of National Health Insurance and the National Health Service (NHS), were associated with reformist, 'left of centre', governments. However, it has been suggested that alternate periods of Labour and Conservative Government in post-war Britain did not herald major changes in policy. The period was one of 'post-war consensus'.

The election of a Conservative Government in 1979, with Mrs Thatcher as Prime Minister, perhaps signalled the demise of this consensus. This is because the new Government was identified with a particular political ideology sometimes labelled the 'New Right' or 'radical right'. The 1979 Government believed in the virtues of the market, that the market is the best mechanism for producing and distributing resources. In particular, the market is seen as more efficient and more responsive to people's needs than state provision. There was an emphasis on individualism, the belief that the individual is to be seen as self-reliant and responsible for his or her own actions (Savage and Robins 1990: 5–6).

Although these themes have been identified with the 'New Right' they can be seen as very similar to the 'laissez-faire' ideology that was particularly influential during the nineteenth century. A belief in the virtues of the market and individualism implies a very limited role for state intervention in economic and social affairs. Commitment to this political ideology would seem to raise serious questions about the future of the NHS. These questions were to dominate the period 1979–1991 and the subsequent reforms would constitute the controversial policies of the 1990s. This is unsurprising because despite the idea of a 'post-war consensus', there had always been politicians and commentators who had questioned the concept of a national health service on the basis that health care needs of the population could best be met by the operation of a private market system rather than a government financed and regulated health care system. From 1979 there was a government in power which seemed to share this view.

## The Royal Commission

The first major Government publication on health care in 1979 was that of the Royal Commission. Although set up in 1976 by the Labour Government of the time, it reported to a new Conservative Government in 1979. The Commission endorsed much of the criticism of the 1974 reorganisation (Chapter 8) before concluding that it could recommend 'no simple, universal panaceas for the cure of the administrative ills of the NHS' (Royal Commission on the NHS 1979: 325). However, the Commission did make a series of detailed recommendations for organisational reform which included enabling Community Health Councils (CHCs) to have the right of access to Family Practitioner Committee (FPC) meetings, the transfer of Department of Health and Social Security (DHSS) accountability to Regional Health Authorities (RHAs), the establishment of a Select Committee on the NHS and a more flexible approach to administration. The Commission also in fact recommended the abolition of FPCs. It concluded that there was one tier too many in the NHS and that there should only be one management tier below the region (Royal Commission on the NHS 1979: 149, 307–9, 313, 324–5 and 327).

The Royal Commission strongly supported the concept of a national health service and the basic priorities of the Service. The Commission's brief had included the examination of the possibility of a greater reliance on insurance and charges as a means of financing the NHS. It rejected both, emphasising a point which was to be made with considerable force over the next decade, that by comparison with the health care systems of other advanced industrial societies, the NHS was remarkably cheap and by implication quite efficient (Royal Commission on the NHS: 334, especially para. 21.8). The Royal Commission also sought to clarify the objectives of the NHS, which it defined as being to:

(a) encourage and assist individuals to remain healthy,
(b) provide equality of entitlement to health services,
(c) provide a broad range of services to a high standard,
(d) provide equality of access to these services,
(e) provide a service free at the time of use,
(f) satisfy the reasonable expectations of its users and
(g) remain a national service responsive to local needs.

(Royal Commission on the NHS 1979: 9)

These aims accord, in part at least, with the well-known paragraphs in the Beveridge Report as well as the duty of the Minister as laid down in the National Health Service Act 1946 and subsequent legislation (Chapter 9). The implication was that there were a set of substantial purposes for the NHS, separate from the more ambitious goals of enhancing the health status of society as a whole or of particular groups within society (Chapters 5, 6 and 9).

## The continuing search for better organisation

In December 1979, a new Consultative Document, *Patients First* (DHSS 1979) was published. In that document, the new Government rejected the Royal Commission's proposal that RHAs should become accountable to Parliament, saying it was inconsistent with statutory responsibility and accountability to Parliament which the Secretary of State must retain. There was agreement regarding only one management tier below RHAs, and the Consultative Document included the proposal to establish District Health Authorities (DHAs) serving areas similar to existing 'health districts'. These DHAs would have boundaries coterminous with social services, housing and education and there would be management teams like those for the existing AHAs. Members of the DHAs would continue the NHS tradition of being appointed (by RHAs) with one-quarter local government nominees. Statutory joint consultative committees and the present arrangements for FPCs would continue but it was suggested that CHCs might be unnecessary in the new structure (DHSS 1979: 5–6, para. 10; 7, 9 and 12–14).

In July 1980, a circular (HC (80) 8) was issued confirming the proposals set out in *Patients First*. RHAs were to make recommendations on the new NHS structure to the Secretary of State by February 1981 (i.e. on the boundaries of the new DHAs) with the process of structural change to be completed by April 1983. It was anticipated that most DHAs would be in existence on or before 1 April 1982. CHCs were to be retained. This new administrative structure came into effect in 1982, with subsequent confirmation that the FPCs would be reconstituted as separate health authorities in their own right.

This process of organisational change was less contentious than those associated with the establishment of the NHS and the changes introduced in 1974. This may reflect the degree of consensus about the need for change, but also the absence of the ideas most likely to generate conflict, changing the independent contractor status of general practitioners (GPs) or enhancing the role of local government in health service provision. The most controversial aspect of the new organisational structure was the extent to which, after many years of debate and considerable investment of resources, another 'tripartite' organisational structure had been established with a major division between social care – the responsibility of local authority Social Services Departments – and health care – the responsibility of the NHS – with the latter divided into two by the continuing separate organisational and budgetary arrangements for GPs. The potential to develop effective policies for community care for elderly people, people with mental health problems and people with learning disabilities would continue to be hampered by these continuing administrative, budgetary and professional divisions between health and social care. The failure of the 1974 and 1982 reorganisations in this respect was to be the subject of a series of critical reports in the 1980s. These criticisms and the burgeoning social security budget for private sector nursing and residential care were key factors in drawing the Government into a set of community care reforms that paralleled those to be introduced in the NHS (DoH 1989a, 1989b).

## 'Safe with us'?

Despite the endorsement of the NHS and its basic principles by the 1979 Royal Commission, the new Government commissioned its own review of the financing of health care. This still officially unpublished 1981 review was intended to reduce the extent to which health services were financed by the taxpayer and involved examining a number of alternatives, including an almost total switch to private spending (Carrier and Kendall 1990a: 89). It seems likely that the Government was deterred from publishing the report because of its growing awareness of the enduring popularity of the NHS amongst the general public. Certainly, official government policy made no mention of a dramatic retreat from the concept of a national health service. The future of the NHS seemed reasonably secure and previous commitments to reduce inequalities in resource allocations to regions and to the 'Cinderella areas' were continued.

The year after the Royal Commission, another report, commissioned by the previous administration, was published (Black Report 1980). The Report confirmed the persistence of significant inequalities in health. It concluded that relative material deprivation was the most important factor in explaining the links between social class and health, thus confirming the significance of social and economic circumstances for health status (Chapters 5, 6 and 9; also Phillimore et al 1994; Power 1994; HSE 1996). The Report recommended that more information, research and effective planning of health and social care were necessary. In the tradition of the inter sector approach advocated in the Beveridge Report (1942), it also recommended increases in social security benefits to improve the economic circumstances of the most disadvantaged sections of the population.

In his Foreword to the Black Report, the Secretary of State, Patrick Jenkin, noted that the policy recommendations contained in the report could not be considered because they were too expensive. This seemed to indicate that whilst the government had abandoned the notion of eliminating the 'burden' of taxation associated with the provision of the NHS, it was very keen to moderate that 'burden' in various respects.

## Cost-containment 1: user charges

Perhaps the most obvious means by which the burden on the taxpayer could be diminished was by increasing the burden on the service user. Of course charges were not a new element in the 'free' NHS (National Health Service Act 1946; Chapter 4). Nonetheless, new charges were introduced, for example for eye tests, and well-established charges such as dental and prescription charges were increased by significantly more than the rate of inflation. Indeed prescription charges, which had remained unchanged throughout most of the 1970s, were increased by '40 times the rate of inflation' between 1979 and 1994 (Timmins 1995: 505). Despite these changes, the NHS remained the most prominent health care system in the industrial world that was least reliant on direct service-user charges as a source of finance, and less reliant than it had been in the 1950s and early 1960s (Klein 1995a: 162; Timmins 1995: 505).

## Cost-containment 2: a role for non-state health care

The view of the Conservative administrations from 1979 was that the NHS would cost less if people turned to non-state institutions for their health and social care, and accordingly the Government sought to encourage and emphasise the virtues of these alternatives to the NHS. Significantly, steps were taken to reduce sharply the role of the NHS in the provision of ophthalmic services. The result of this was High Street 'shop front' ophthalmic services. In a similar vein, the White Paper on services for elderly people contained an unequivocal statement that the advancement of community care would rely less on public provision and more on the community itself (DHSS 1981a) and the voluntary sector found itself drawn back into mainstream provision in areas such as day-care.

Previous attempts by Labour Governments to limit pay beds in NHS hospitals and control private hospital development were both abandoned. Supportive comments were made regarding private hospitals and nursing homes as alternatives to the NHS. In addition, the latter were to receive dramatically increased indirect support via the social security budget during the 1980s. This had the paradoxical effect of increasing government intervention in traditional forms of residential care whilst financial restrictions were placed on local government, which had significant responsibilities for developing the social care dimension of community care. The escalating costs of this 'policy accident' (Klein 1995a: 158) may have been one of the factors influencing the Government's subsequent commitment to reform policies for community care. It was certainly subject to criticism in the report of the Audit Commission (1986) along with organisational and other divisions identified previously (Chapters 7 and 8).

## Cost-containment 3: contracting out

The old theme of cost-containment was pursued by requiring health authorities to produce efficiency savings. Drug budgets were cash limited. Generic prescribing was proposed but after much heated discussion between representatives of GPs and the government, agreement was reached on a 'limited list' of drugs which could and those which could not be prescribed. Also, forms of resource management were introduced. The perceived advantages of the market were to be obtained by the introduction of contracting-out. Ancillary services were the main target (Klein 1995a: 160). Private sector firms would be given the opportunity to tender for contracts to provide catering, cleaning and laundry services, so called 'compulsory competitive tendering'. The theory was that the most efficient contractor would provide the cheapest tender and the NHS would benefit from cheaper and more efficient services. This was seen as an effective way of containing costs and bringing the virtues of private sector management into a large public sector organisation. However, it also led to a resurgence of trade union militancy in hospitals, reminiscent of the conflicts over 'pay-beds', understandable given that the 'price of successfully defending in-house contracts tended to be lower earnings and redundancies' (Klein 1995a: 161). However, this approach had its limitations. How could the virtues of private sector management be brought to those parts of the NHS that 'contracting out' could not reach? The answer was presumed to lie in a more fundamental reform of management arrangements within the Service.

## The search for efficiency and better organisations 1: managers

Prior to the 1980s the NHS had a range of management traditions. The self-employed GPs were largely left to manage their own workloads. Community and public health services were, until the 1974 NHS reorganisation, managed in a manner similar to other profession-based departments in local government. Within the hospital sector there had emerged a form of shared management by doctors, nurses and administrators based on a perceived need and demand for considerable professional autonomy, especially for the hospital consultants. This had its origins in the management style of the leading voluntary hospitals at the end of the nineteenth century (Chapter 4; Abel-Smith 1964: 68). This shared management approach was most obviously and formally recognised in the 1970–1974 Conservative Government's White Paper on NHS reorganisation (DHSS 1972b: 57). At regional, area and district levels, the NHS was to be managed by consensus forming management teams including doctors, nurses, treasurers and administrators (Chapter 8). Proposals for administrative restructuring indicated that the Government was interested in managerial reform within the Service, although it also restated the commitment to the appointment of teams of equals to co-ordinate activities in the new DHAs. In addition, the DHAs were required to organise their hospital and other services in consensus management units (DHSS 1979). At this stage it seemed that this managerial reform was to be left to the health authorities themselves to take forward.

But at a time when the new management units were still coping with the impact of this most recent reorganisation, and some DHAs were still in the process of appointing staff to their new unit management teams, the Secretary of State announced the establishment of an independent NHS management inquiry headed by Roy Griffiths. The inquiry team's key observation was that there was a 'lack of a clearly defined general management function throughout the NHS' (DHSS 1983: 11). To remedy this situation they recommended the introduction of a single general manager acting as a chief executive and final decision-taker to replace the consensus management teams. This commitment to general management was to be extended above and below the level of health authorities. As a well as a District General Manager for each DHA, there would be a general manager for every unit of management within the DHA. Each RHA would have a Regional General Manager and there would be a small management board at the centre, the Chair of which would have the general management function at a national level.

The Government's commitment to the appointment of general managers regardless of discipline involved a significant move away from the previously stated principles (1972 White Paper and 1979 Consultative Document) that some NHS professionals should be exempted from managerial hierarchies and others should be managed by their fellow professionals. It implied that health care managers should manage efficiently, using management skills which might be applied with equal effectiveness in public or private sector organisations. It might also be seen as a vindication of the view expressed by the medical superintendents of the old London County Council that in every government hospital, clinicians must be answerable to someone (Honigsbaum 1979: 171). Professional groups, health authorities and the House of Commons Social Services Committee expressed their reservations on this occasion, and there were requests for pilot schemes to evaluate the costs and benefits of the new ideas (Carrier and Kendall 1986: 206–13). However, such reservations and requests were ignored as the new general managers were appointed with great speed.

The Government went into the next General Election (May 1987) seemingly confident that the reforms it had put in place, culminating in the introduction of general management, had provided the basis for a more efficient NHS and that no new major reforms were required. However, there was evidence of pressure building up for further reforms before the General Election. Whilst the Government may have claimed that its focus on efficiency was intended to benefit the patients, the latter seemed increasingly sceptical of the outcome. The view seemed to be gaining ground that the Government's cash limits were leading to 'real cuts' in services. The results in some cases appeared to be inefficiencies, consultants apparently told not to work to prevent their Units from overspending their cash limited budget. The needs-led approach, for which there was certainly widespread support, seemed to be clearly at risk if hospitals were closing specialist units for seriously ill children, for example Guy's Hospital Special Care Baby Unit, and some teaching hospitals were refusing to accept patients from outside their boundaries without some form of payment from the patients' health authority (Carrier and Kendall 1990a: 90). By September 1987, it was being reported in the press that health authorities might be making their biggest round of ward closures and deferred developments for at least four years. By mid-November, many hundreds of beds had been taken out of service. The growing perception that the Service was in serious financial difficulties was given further confirmation in December 1987 when the Presidents of the three senior Royal Colleges, the surgeons, the physicians, and the obstetricians and gynaecologists, issued a statement warning that the NHS had 'almost reached breaking point'. It was at this rather inauspicious time that the Government published its White Paper on primary care. This proposed more spending on family doctor services, paid for in part by new and higher charges. It included measures to introduce more competition between GPs, tougher monitoring of their work, more preventive and health promotion work, and more information and consumer choice for patients (DHSS 1987).

The mounting public and professional concern in the latter half of 1987 eventually drew a response from the Government. According to Nigel Lawson (1993), a private dinner with Mrs Thatcher in January 1988 to discuss the Budget included the proposal for a review of the NHS. The basic way the NHS was financed was thought to be correct. It was thought to be working well, but the object was to make it better (Lawson 1993, quoted in Glennerster 1995: 204). Subsequently, in a TV interview, Mrs Thatcher announced the creation of a Ministerial Working Group (mainly composed of Treasury Ministers) to review the NHS. During the period in which this review was undertaken, the Resource Allocation Working Party (RAWP) formula was modified to take account of social deprivation in the inner cities, the Griffiths Report on community care was published but seemingly ignored by the government (Griffiths 1988) and much was written about the state of the Service by professional pressure groups and academics. The House of Commons Social Services Committee also produced three reports while the review was in progress. The First Report recommended that the government should make good the acknowledged (by the DHSS) shortfall in the funding of pay and price inflation for 1987–1988 (Social Services Committee 1988: xix). The majority of the submissions received by the Committee were in favour of retaining the NHS in its existing form. The Committee's own recommendations included no basic changes in the funding of the NHS and some limited experimentation with internal markets (Carrier and Kendall 1990a: 91).

## The search for efficiency and better organisations 2: markets

The review was eventually published in January 1989 as the White Paper, *Working for Patients* (DoH 1989a). It was prefaced with a personal statement unequivocal in its support for a tax-funded universal health service and billed by the Prime Minister as the most far reaching reform of the NHS in its 40-year history (DoH 1989a). Some three years earlier, an American health economist, Alan Enthoven, while reviewing the NHS on a six-month sabbatical stay with the Nuffield Provincial Hospital Trust, described the Service as approaching the New York traffic grid lock. The solution was to 'free it up' as a market of purchasers and providers (Enthoven 1985). Enthoven's model was accepted by the government, with the 'internal market' as a basis for the reform. Purchasers would be separated from providers, and capital charging on assets would be introduced to stimulate competition between NHS and private sector providers. The White Paper proposed self-managing NHS Trusts to run the larger hospitals as one such group of providers, almost a rediscovery of the autonomous management status of teaching hospitals within the NHS between 1948 and 1974 (Chapter 4) or perhaps the pre-NHS voluntary hospitals. GP services were to be brought into the internal market through direct allocation of budgets on a voluntary basis to larger general practices to enable the buying of certain hospital services. The DHAs would hold a budget to ensure the health of a defined population, identifying health needs, planning ways to satisfy them and ensuring the quality of the service. The 'ideal model' was of the DHAs (and the GPs) buying care from semi-independent hospitals, thereby creating a purchaser/provider split, retaining a public system of responsibilities, resources and regulation but disciplined by the operation of an 'internal market'.

In organisational terms, the review recommended the replacement of the existing resource allocation system (RAWP; Chapter 6) with one based on population weighted for age and the relative cost of providing services. The White Paper also contained proposals for the local governance of the NHS through management boards with no local authority representation and a restructuring of the Department of Health (DoH) into an NHS Policy Board taking strategic decisions, with an NHS Management Executive for the day-to-day functioning of the system. The separate Family Practitioner Authorities would become more managerially oriented and, for the first time, be subject to overall control by RHAs. A series of ten Working Papers were issued subsequently to the publication of the White Paper, filling in some of the detail absent from the latter. The proposed autonomous Trusts could take responsibility for both groupings of smaller hospitals and community-based NHS services. Similarly, smaller GP practices would be allowed to co-operate over budget-holding.

The publication of *Working for Patients* provoked a number of concerns about the operation of the internal market. Would hospital Trusts specialise in areas of greatest 'economic gain' and would the market ensure that these were appropriate to the needs of local communities? Might hospital Trusts tend to discharge patients to the community before it would otherwise be appropriate? Would budget-holding GPs have an incentive to get their patients admitted to hospitals as emergencies rather than straightforward referrals? Would people with costly problems of ill-health find themselves being treated by reference to the size of a

GP's budget and the accessibility of specialist hospital care, rather than by reference to their real care needs? Enthoven's comment on the White Paper was that he was 'very surprised by the lack of detail' in the proposals. Echoing the Research Reports on the 1974 reorganisation and many of the comments on the implementation of the Griffiths Report, Enthoven also considered the lack of pilot studies to be a mistake. 'I cannot understand why the Government did not choose to test their very promising ideas in a series of pilot projects' (Smith 1989).

This comment was repeated by the House of Commons Social Services Committee in May 1989. They said they attempted to find out more about the details of the proposals in three sessions of oral evidence with the Secretary of State. 'Those sessions, like the working papers, have raised more questions than they have answered' (Social Services Committee 1989: vii).

The House of Commons Social Services Committee noted the generally hostile reception given to the White Paper, both inside and outside the NHS (Social Services Committee 1989: vi). The British Medical Association warned of the dangers of fragmenting the NHS, claiming that concerns with costs might override the need for treatment, rejecting moves to involve managers in appointing consultants, and condemning GP budgets and hospital trusts. The Association of Community Health Councils deplored the disappearance of local authority representation from the smaller, management-orientated health authorities, criticising the change as a distancing of the service from the service-users (Carrier and Kendall 1990a: 95–6). Doubts about the wisdom of the basic principles of the White Paper and the manner of its implementation were further compounded and confused by its coincidence with negotiations over a new contract for GPs which followed on the publication of the White Paper on Primary Care (DHSS 1987). Set against the claim that 'there is nothing like a competitive market to motivate quality and economy of service' (Enthoven 1985: 43) were the concerns that 'in the context of health care, the evidence that exists to support this statement seems at best limited' (Mooney 1992). Would it be possible to capture the advantages of the free market, efficiency, and still safeguard equity in an 'internal market'?

Lastly, the political background to the NHS review could be fairly described as an exercise in crisis management. Its establishment was announced within eight weeks of a General Election in which the Conservative Party's manifesto had contained no indication that such a review would take place and within a fortnight of John Moore (Secretary of State for Social Services) dismissing rumours that any such action was intended. Government action, setting up the review, was a response to a perceived resource crisis in the NHS. For a major public service which operated for all of 21 months before its first cash-limit was introduced, the scenario was depressing if somewhat familiar. As it happened, any long-term conflicts associated with these reforms would not be the responsibility of a government led by Margaret Thatcher. By the time they were being enacted, a new Conservative administration with John Major as Prime Minister would face up to the consequences, good or bad, of these market-led reforms. In 1990, the National

Health Service and Community Care Act received Royal Assent and was implemented from April 1991. This Act implemented not only the reforms derived from *Working for Patients* but also those set down in a White Paper on community care, *Caring for People* (DoH 1989b). This was soon followed by the announcement of major job losses in two prominent NHS Trusts (Harrison and Wistow 1992: 123; Klein 1995a: 205). The Government ordered a 'steady state', indicating it was not prepared to countenance the political consequences of dramatic switches of contract by purchasers. The internal market was to be a managed or quasi market (Klein 1995a: 204; 1995b: 302).

## The search for more community health care

The extensive post-war efficiency gains recorded in the use of expensive hospital resources, 'patient throughput', were certainly facilitated by the contribution of community health care services (Chapter 5). For many patients, community social care services, for example home helps, also made an important contribution, and Government policy documents noted the impossibility of drawing a clear line between the role of NHS day hospitals and local authority day-care facilities (Chapter 7). Successive reorganisations of health and social care between 1971 and 1985 made limited contributions to creating a framework which was intended to facilitate, rather than hinder, the effective co-operation and co-ordination between health and social care agencies and professionals. Basic organisational and budgetary divisions were compounded by differences in professional and managerial cultures (Chapter 8). The Royal Commission on the NHS had recognised the attraction and logic of the transfer of NHS to local government, but advised against it at the time as there was no regional tier of local government. The Commission considered the transfer of the personal social services to the NHS an insufficient reform (if health, why not education and housing?) but also offered the slightly contradictory opinion that the system in Northern Ireland, where health and personal social services are combined in one agency, should be encouraged and further developed. They also rejected the transfer of client groups on the grounds that this would lead to intra-professional divisions (Royal Commission on the NHS 1979: 265–7). The Commission also expressed concerns relating to the contribution of general hospital units to the care of mentally ill people, observing that:

> some DGH units have been selective, either in their admission policies or about those for whom they would continue to care, and the mental hospitals have had to receive those patients whom the DGH units have thought were unsuitable in the first place, or whom they had failed to cure.
> (Royal Commission on the NHS 1979: 137, para. 10.57)

By 1981, there was further evidence that these tasks were not being successfully undertaken in many areas. In June of that year, a Government minister noted that 32 local authorities were still making no provision for mentally disabled people and seven provided no residential accommodation. The shift of the balance of care from the NHS to local authorities, and of resources to priority groups, was happening far more slowly than had been hoped for and intended.

The policy document *Care in Action* (DHSS 1981b) broadly confirmed the development of services as set out in the 1975 White Paper thus, 'The aim is for people to be able to use the services they need with the minimum of formality and delay, and without losing touch with their normal lives' (DHSS 1981a: 33). It stressed the need for accessibility, non-separateness, and co-ordinated and complementary services. On local authority provision, it noted that progress had been uneven and identified the aim to make satisfactory progress on closing those mental illness hospitals which were not well placed to provide a service reaching into the community and were already near the end of their useful lives.

In 1981, the Government also published *Care in the Community* (DHSS 1981c), addressing the issue of the long-stay population in all institutions, including those for elderly people and people with learning difficulties. The paper referred to four means by which resources might be moved from traditional hospital-based to community-based services. These were, first, extending joint finance arrangements; second, pooling funds for client groups and planning services jointly; third, transferring funds centrally from NHS to personal social services; and, lastly, concentrating responsibility for a client group on a single agency. If nothing else, *Care in the Community* recognised that the shift of the balance of care from the NHS to local authorities, and of resources to priority groups, was happening far more slowly than had been hoped. Subsequent guidance enabled the RHAs to make payments to local authorities in support of people moving out of NHS hospitals, and in 1983 the DHSS made available £19 million to fund a number of locally based pilot resettlement projects (Tomlinson 1991: 16–17).

Perhaps the most effective critique of community care policies, in terms of political impact, came with the Second Report of the Social Services Committee, *Community Care*, which included the following comment:

> We do not wish to slow down the exodus from mental illness or mental handicap hospitals for its own sake, but we do look to see the same degree of Ministerial pressure, and the provision of the necessary resources, devoted to the creation of alternative services. Any fool can close a long stay hospital. It takes more time and trouble to do it compassionately.
>
> (Social Services Committee 1985: xxii, para. 40)

The Committee went on to say:

> the Minister must ensure that mental illness or mental handicap hospital provision is not reduced without demonstrably adequate alternative services being provided beforehand for those discharged from hospital and for those who would otherwise seek admission.
>
> (Social Services Committee 1985)

The Committee also noted that:

> The concept of asylum has nothing inherently to do with large or isolated institutions. Asylums can be provided in a physical and psychological sense in the middle of a normal residential community; traditionally indeed, in the midst of a busy church. We must face the fact that some people need asylum.
>
> (Social Services Committee 1985: xvii, para. 26)

In November 1985, the Government published its response to the House of Commons community care report. It confirmed governmental commitment to the development of the integrated network of central policies and local services necessary for community care. In 1986 the first 'genuine' closure of a large mental hospital (that is, not used for other long-stay residents) involved Banstead Hospital in Surrey, but only by decanting its residual patients to Horton Hospital. Other closures would follow in the period up to 1989, and one such closure (Powick) was the subject of a specific DHSS development project to replace the local mental hospital (Tomlinson 1991: 42 and 47). The closure process for the hospitals in the Exeter area was regarded as particularly successful. The Exeter service prior to closure and reprovision has been described as representing 'the worst kind of picture of mental health care, the very antithesis of care in the community' (Tomlinson 1991: 57). However, by 1988 the new services for Exeter, based on community mental health centres and hostels for long-term clients, were judged to be working effectively and providing a better service than the previous regime (Beardshaw and Morgan 1990).

The next major national report on community care was published in 1986. This came from the Audit Commission which, reviewing a variety of community care schemes, concluded that all the successful schemes known to them involved 'a radical departure from the generally accepted ways of doing things'. In particular such schemes had at least six dominant features. First, the presence of strong and committed local 'champions' of change. Second, a focus on action and not just the bureaucratic machinery for change. This meant taking risks rather than focusing strictly on conventional procedures. Third, the existence of locally integrated machinery for service planning was identified as vital if the patient was not to fall between hospital provision and the enhanced social service responsibility for care.

A fourth feature, emphasised by the Audit Commission, was the partnership between statutory and voluntary organisations. The final two features identified by the Commission were a focus on the local neighbourhood and a multi-professional team approach (Audit Commission 1986).

At the same time, the Government announced the appointment of Sir Roy Griffiths to undertake another review, this time of community care. This announcement, following the Audit Commission's remarks, was a response, not to the good practices highlighted by the Commission, but to the Commission's criticism that the substantial sum of money spent on services for the care of people with mental health problems, people with learning difficulties and elderly people, estimated at £6 billion, was not being effectively deployed. Sir Roy Griffiths was also charged with investigating whether or not the structure of social security payments was having the effect of forcing people into residential care, instead of keeping them in their own homes supported by professional staff, an indication that its attempts to favour the private sector and relieve the 'burden' of the NHS was in one case simply shifting that 'burden' to another budget heading. In the end, it was the budget of a governmental bureaucracy, social security, not private enterprise, that was 'really providing' for those in long-stay nursing and residential care.

The Griffiths Report was published in March 1988 (*Agenda for Action*) and restated many of the themes of the Social Services Committee and the Audit Commission. 'Community care is a poor relation, everybody's distant relative but no-body's baby' (DHSS 1988: iv). His answer was to identify a key role for local government, in the form of Social Services Departments, as 'the designers, organisers and purchasers of non-health care services' (DHSS 1988: 1). To some extent, Griffiths was advocating an 'internal market' in community care, certainly a purchaser/provider split in which local authorities would be major purchasers rather than direct providers. As purchasers they would make 'maximum possible use of voluntary and private sector bodies to widen consumer choice, stimulate innovation and encourage efficiency' (DHSS1988: 1).

Griffiths also suggested there should be a 'Minister for Community Care' and a ring-fenced specific grant for community care services. His views on 'ring-fencing' could be taken as a further vindication of views expressed during the debates on the Mental Health Act 1959 (Chapter 7). Although there was a degree of consensus about what was wrong about the organisational infrastructure for community care policies, the Government was slow to respond to Griffiths' recommendations, perhaps because of the important role he assigned to local government (Evans 1994: 225). It was not until November 1989 that the White Paper, *Caring for People*, was published. This followed closely the Griffiths proposals. The role of local authority Social Services Departments would be crucial in enabling people to live in their own homes wherever feasible. Thus domiciliary, day and respite services were to be developed. The social security budget for private institutional care would be redirected to local authorities to enable them to fulfil this role. Services would include a 'flourishing independent sector alongside good quality public services' (DoH 1989b: 5). A later Government publication was to note that 'if implementation is to be effective, there must be close working links between all agencies, social services departments, NHS bodies, housing authorities and associations, voluntary organisations and social services providers' (DoH 1990).

In the same year, the Parliamentary Under-Secretary at the DoH, Stephen Dorrell, was confident that treating:

> a much larger proportion of mentally ill patients within the community ... and the move towards a smaller and more humane scale of treatment for those patients was clearly not a 'leap in the dark' ... (but) ... the result of a

shift in medical practice that had been fully considered and the implications of which will be properly followed up.

(Dorrell 1990)

The proposals were incorporated in the same legislation that introduced the 'internal market' into the NHS, the National Health Service and Community Care Act 1991, but full implementation was delayed until April 1993 and the problems of local government finance, that is, the poll tax issue, had been resolved. Furthermore, in one respect the situation was not changed. Even after *Caring for People*, the long standing division remained between health authorities, as purchasers of health care, and local government, as the lead agency for social care.

## Managing the internal market

The goals of the internal market model were hardly new. They included better care that produces better outcomes for patients, better access and greater patient satisfaction, less costly care and hence more care and more responsive care with inevitably limited resources. But the conditions for operating a successful internal market were not nationally met in terms of market structure, accurate information and transaction costs, so it was not always apparent that health care purchasers would be able to use market structures to achieve these ends. Purchaser choices were often limited. Sometimes there were monopolistic providers locally and hence restricted leverage for improved provider performance. New suppliers came up against entry barriers. There were heavy capital costs and private competitors were deterred. The existing pattern of referrals might be retained with a value being placed on local convenience so limiting the willingness of patients to travel and use of distant providers. On the purchasing side, DHAs were monopolistic, but GP fundholders introduced an element of competition although raising concerns about the fragmentation of health care planning. There were information deficits, a major area of difficulty being that purchasers were especially dependent on providers for information. Other consequences appeared to be opportunistic behaviour by providers, inadequate contracts, and poor strategic decisions by purchasers. Of course the information problem was hardly new; there were pressures on hospitals to massage the statistics when they were competing for funds in the nineteenth century (Chapter 1; Woodward 1974: 139–42).

Concerns were also expressed about the increased numbers and associated costs of the managers of the new internal market. The numbers of managers rose by about 20 per cent between 1991 and 1996. There were also transaction costs involved in negotiating, managing and monitoring contracts. This process was time-consuming and there were additional information costs, accounting costs, management costs associated with long-term relationships between buyers and sellers plus transitional and start-up costs. This provided something of a paradox, given that the strongest advocates of a market approach were often those critics of the administrative costs associated with traditional bureaucratic modes of operation. Overall, it was a huge management agenda for both purchasers and providers. Switching from a non-market administered system to a managed market system with a million employees and a £40 billion budget meant that increased management costs were a natural corollary and a necessity (Klein 1995a: 205; 1995b: 320). From 1990, £70 million per annum extra was allocated to the NHS in England and Wales to bolster finance, personnel and information services (Audit Commission 1995: 2).

Since 1991, GPs had become involved in the purchasing process in a variety of ways, quite apart from fundholding (Glennerster et al 1996). The model of GP fundholding aimed to introduce competition on both the purchasing and providing sides of the internal market. In this case, patients would be able to choose 'between those who would purchase services on their behalf' (Glennerster et al 1994: 166). Concerns were expressed about a 'two-tier arrangement' in which unacceptable advantages might accrue to the patients of fund-holding practices especially over faster access to hospital services, an example of an equity issue being exacerbated in the new 'quasi-market'. Studies of fundholding found efficiency gains to be set against possible, although not inevitable equity losses, and that consumers lacked the knowledge and interest in choosing between practices (Glennerster et al 1994: 175 and 179; Klein 1995a: 239).

## How successful was the internal market?

That the reforms should be linked to, and probably initiated by, concerns about costs and their containment was unsurprising. Governments influenced by radical right ideology would readily presume that cost-containment will be especially problematic in the NHS since its finances continue to rely more significantly on general taxation than systems operating elsewhere in the European Community. The result is a system largely free at the point of use, and conventional economic analyses suggest that this would be a recipe for abuse and waste by consumers.

However, histories of the more competitive, pre-NHS, environment in British health care tended towards conclusions that it 'did not bring economy' but rather led to 'uselessly expensive administration', to 'waste' and to 'behaviour which had no discernible relevance to medical needs' (Eckstein 1958: 68; Gilbert 1970: 300).

Indeed, the limitations of markets in health care are now widely recognised and as the state-supported NHS became the dominant guarantor of such care in the UK, so the evidence showed that it provided 'a most efficient service ... a remarkably comprehensive service at a remarkably reasonable price' (Klein 1995b: 309) leading to the seemingly paradoxical conclusion that a universal, open access, free service making little or no use of conventional market mechanisms is more successful at containing costs than more market-oriented systems. At least part of this success may be attributable to a modest degree of planning, the Service's traditional role as a monopsonist with regard to health care personnel and the absence of complex systems for charging and billing individuals or organisations. But all of these features were now to be changed with the introduction of the 'internal market', and the revival of competitive elements in British health care generated a set of concerns rather similar to those expressed about the arrangements before the NHS was established.

In two national surveys of district general managers, they identified advantages with the purchaser/provider split clarifying the roles of each, a focus on health needs, more emphasis on quality issues, availability of better information and increased provider accountability. Market pressure may well have opened up and made visible long standing problems. But the restructuring, by changing provider patterns and closing hospitals, had involved significant social and political costs. More generally, inpatient numbers, day cases and outpatient attendances all increased, but we might have expected these trends with or without the quasi-market, since they were well-established before its introduction and are evident throughout the history of the NHS (Chapter 5). Furthermore, in 1990/91 NHS spending in real terms was increased by 2.8 per cent and in 1991/92 by 4.1 per cent. This coincided with the introduction of the quasi-market and the run up to the General Election of 1992. Proponents of an alternative explanation of the pre-*Working for Patients* crisis, that it was based on failure of resourcing rather than a failure in structure, could argue that the NHS would show signs of improvement, or at least a 'steady state', given appropriate resourcing. Lastly, the underlying trends of changes in medical science and medical practice continued. These changes, given appropriate funding which takes account of their resource implications, have the potential to lead to improvements for the health service-users. If the funding of the NHS also takes account of both 'medical inflation', inflationary pressures adjusted for the distinctive costs of health care, and demographic change, we would anticipate these improvements to be sustainable and not 'counter-balanced' by a loss of service-quality elsewhere 'in the system'.

Given that a 'rational' approach to resourcing had not been a consistent feature of government funding of the NHS, especially in the period leading up to the setting up of the review that led to *Working for Patients* (DoH 1989a), and given the ongoing influence of other long-term factors, for example changes in medical science, then anything resembling a definitive judgement on the reforms was inherently problematic. Perhaps the only clear conclusion that could be reached was that it was very difficult to assemble the evidence that the *general managed quasi-market* NHS was 'better' than either the *consensus team managed post-1974* NHS or the *historic cost budgeted tripartite pre-1974* NHS (Klein 1995a: 224, 230–1 and 236–40; 1995b: 309–10; Robinson and Le Grand 1994: 243). In the rather unlikely event that we might be able to state with some degree of certainty and precision the benefits that had flowed from the 'internal market', we would have to set those benefits against the costs involved in operating such a market. Another 'NHS cash crisis' linked to concerns over whether there had been, for the 1996/97 financial year, a 'real increase' of 0.1 per cent, or a 'real cut' of 0.3 per cent, in spending on health and personal social services (*The Independent*, 5 November 1996: 2), illustrated again the significance of the overall level of resources going to the NHS. It also lent support to a concern that 'the Tory reforms of the health service are now blamed for everything that goes wrong' (Abel-Smith and Glennerster 1995: 1).

In the end, the introduction of the 'internal market' at this time might be viewed as the latest, and most radical, attempt to reorganise the internal workings of the NHS by continuing the searches for efficiency and better forms of organisation (Chapters 5 and 8). Indeed, what the NHS Executive described as 'the final stage of the NHS reforms introduced in 1991' involved a conventional organisational restructuring in which the RHAs disappeared, to be replaced by eight regional offices of the NHS Executive, and DHAs and Family Health Service Authorities were to be merged to form new health authorities (NHS Executive 1993: 2). Some might see this as the long-delayed implementation of key elements of the First Green Paper (Ministry of Health 1968). This reform took place in parallel with the introduction of unitary local authorities across much of the country, one of the recommendations of the Royal Commission on Local Government in England (1969) (Chapter 8).

## The search for better health

In 1987, the evidence from the Black Report (1980) was updated with the publication of *The Health Divide* (Health Education Council 1987) which concluded that little progress had been made since the publication of the Black Report, and that higher levels of unemployment were now contributing more significantly to social deprivation. Since the conclusions and recommendations of the Black Report had not been welcomed by the government it is perhaps unsurprising that *The Health Divide* should record a rather similar picture.

Whilst the Government's reaction to the Black Report and *The Health Divide* might be seen as essentially ideological, an unwillingness to accept explanations that called for more government expenditure and more government intervention, there were other critiques of the Report. In particular, it was suggested that the apparent persistence, or even widening of health inequalities, might be a function of the limitations of the data, especially with regard to the inconsistent classification of social class over time (Illsley 1986). Furthermore, it was suggested that lower class status might for some people be a function of poor health and disability, rather than the other way round (Stern 1983; Wilkinson 1995; Judge 1995).

The themes of the Black Report and *The Health Divide* were replayed with the publication of *Tackling Health Inequalities: An Agenda for Action* (King's Fund 1995b). This showed death rates amongst the poorest groups to be rising for the first time in at least 50 years, with the widening of social inequalities and social divisions in the 1980s as a likely cause. The resulting policy agenda focused, like the Black Report, on incomes and housing plus action to diminish the incidence of smoking, such as advertising restrictions and tobacco taxes. Meanwhile, the Government's own *Health of the Nation* strategy (DoH 1992) largely ignored the relationship between poverty, inequalities and health in contrast to initiatives taken by governments elsewhere (Bayley 1995: 7).

## Conclusions

Cost-containment was an important aim, to be achieved through a more rigorous application of cash-limits, including the ending of GPs' open-ended budgets, so that all NHS spending was to be capped for the first time. In addition, there were efficiency savings, new and increased charges, and a marked unwillingness to enter into any new commitments like those advocated by the Black Report (1980) or which might have been anticipated in the White Paper on services for elderly people (DHSS 1981a).

The search continued for better ways of organising the Service, with particular emphasis on changing what had been introduced by the previous Conservative Government (1970–1974) (Chapter 8). DHAs were established by April 1982 with boundaries coterminous with social services, housing and education. In February 1983, the Secretary of State announced the establishment of an independent NHS management inquiry headed by Roy Griffiths. His report was published in October 1983 and recommended the introduction of single general managers in all levels of the NHS, replacing the consensus management teams (DHSS 1983). More radical reform followed with the White Paper, *Working for Patients* (DoH 1989a). In an 'internal market', purchasers would be separated from providers, and capital charging on assets would be introduced to stimulate competition between NHS and private sector providers. GP services were to be brought into this market through direct allocation of budgets on a voluntary basis to larger general practices to enable the buying of certain hospital services. The 'ideal model was of the DHAs and GPs buying care from semi-independent hospitals, thereby creating a purchaser/provider split, retaining a public system of responsibilities, resources and regulation, but disciplined by the operation of the 'internal market'. Advantages identified with the new purchaser/provider split included more emphasis on quality issues and the availability of better information, but the restructuring, by changing provider patterns and closing hospitals, involved significant social and political costs. In particular, the conditions for operating a successful internal market were not nationally met in terms of market structure, accurate information, and transaction costs. There were particular concerns about the 'two-tier arrangement' in which unacceptable advantages might accrue to the patients of fundholding practices with faster access to hospital services. This was one example of an equity issue being exacerbated by a market condition.

With regard to the development of community care, the shift of the balance of care from the NHS to local authorities, and of resources to priority groups, continued, but far more slowly than had been hoped for and intended. Sir Roy Griffiths was once again appointed to undertake a review. In his Report he identified a key role for local government as 'the designers, organisers and purchasers of non-health care services', but not as direct providers (Griffiths 1988: 1). As purchasers, they would make 'maximum possible use of voluntary and private sector bodies to widen consumer choice, stimulate innovation and encourage efficiency' (Griffiths 1988: 1). As with the period between 1948 and 1979, economic and financial considerations had remained paramount, but were given an added significance in the light of government concerns about the level of public expenditure and its impact on levels of taxation. In some respects, the Service was placed back in a political context not dissimilar from that following the change of government in 1951 (Chapter 5). However, it remained the case that concerns about the UK's expenditure on health care were not evidence-based with regard to comparative data. Britain's expenditure on health care was still frugal compared with other European countries, and all European countries were relatively low spenders by comparison with the USA (Hills 1997: 56–7).

Government policies towards the NHS between 1979 and 1997 had assumed a pattern recognisable in some other social policy programmes. The broad parameters of government responsibilities for health services remained unchanged and there was no explicit policy of transferring health care away from the NHS and into the private sector. But attempts were made to introduce 'private sector efficiencies' into the NHS by 'contracting out' services, bringing in a system of management modelled on the private sector and by introducing the quasi-market with the purchaser/provider split.

However, there was little prospect of testing the cost-containment virtues claimed for the quasi-market, and whether these virtues were being compromised by the well-documented cost-inflation qualities associated with more market-orientated health care systems. After four successive Conservative administrations there was a change of government.

# Chapter 11

# The Labour Governments, 1997–2010: reforms, resources and regulation

The NHS was a beacon for the world in 1948. It will always be safe with us. I want it to be better with us ... The values will remain ... I will never countenance an NHS that departs from its fundamental principle of health care based on need, not wealth.

(Tony Blair, speech to the Labour Party Conference, reported in *The Times*, 1 October 1997)

The arrival of the new Government in 1997 generated a range of responses regarding what should happen to the National Health Service (NHS). It was certainly assumed that a successful outcome for the Labour Party in the General Election would herald further changes in the funding and organisation, as well as the distribution, of health care throughout the NHS. It came as no surprise that the first Labour Government for 18 years would wish to emphasise its connection with the previous landslide Labour Government of 1945–1951, by making the NHS one of the centrepieces of its domestic policy agenda and making commitments to a set of principles not dissimilar from those on which the Service was originally based. The new Government's view of its immediate predecessors was clearly expressed by the Minister of State at the Department of Health (DoH), Alan Milburn. The previous Conservative Government had, he said, 'left the NHS in a mess ... (with) record waiting lists ... (which were) ... rising. (There was) ... huge pressure on emergency hospital care ... (and) widespread hospital and health authority deficits' (Milburn 1997: 22). At the end of September 1997, the Prime Minister's speech to the Labour Party Conference included a number of statements relating to the NHS. The speech was a balanced mixture of restated NHS values, while also taking the opportunity to reinstate the values thought to be have been subordinated to market forces during the years of Conservative Government. From the following April (1998), 'The two-tier NHS of the Tories will go for good ... (and that) ... (the)... hospitals will be built. Fourteen of them, the biggest hospital building programme in the history of the NHS. It will mean an extra £1.3 billion in 14 towns and cities; serving five million people. And as of today, it is 15' (Tony Blair, speech to Labour Party Conference, reported in *The Times*, 1 October 1997). The Prime Minister continued the speech by proposing

that money was 'not the only problem with health care in Britain'. While emphasising the importance of principle, he claimed that it was necessary to change the
methods of protecting that principle, without going down the road of privatisation
or the private market:

> The NHS itself needs modernisation and hard choices. We appointed the first
> Minister for Public Health because the health service should not lose millions
> every year because of avoidable illnesses like those from smoking. Barriers
> between GPs, social services and hospitals must be broken down. Hospitals
> cannot stand still. Increasingly, general hospitals will provide routine care,
> supported by specialist centres of excellence in treatment, research and edu-
> cation. GPs and nurses will do more of what hospitals used to do, often work-
> ing together on the same site in partnership with chemists, dentists, opticians
> and physiotherapists. New technology offers huge opportunities in the NHS
> and we haven't yet begun to seize them properly. We will get the money. But
> in return, I want reform. From next April, there will be up to ten specially
> funded Health Action Zones set up in Britain. Their remit to experiment with
> new ideas in the way health care is delivered, so that patients get a better deal
> from their health services for the 21st century.
>
> (Tony Blair, speech to Labour Party Conference,
> reported in *The Times*, 1 October 1997)

## The White Paper, *The New NHS*

A White Paper on the NHS had been scheduled for publication in the Autumn
of 1997 (NHS Executive 1997a), but it did not appear until 9 December 1997.
However, there were indications of the new Government's approach in a number
of publications and other pronouncements between 1 May and 9 December 1997.
At the NHS Confederation Annual Conference on 25 June 1997, the Secretary
of State for Health, Frank Dobson, announced his intention to set up a number
of Health Action Zones (HAZs). The purpose of such zones would be to bring
together all those contributing to the health of the local population, local authorities, community groups, the voluntary sector and local businesses in their work, to
develop and implement a locally agreed strategy for improving the health of local
people. Potential outcomes were ambitious. There should be improvements in the
effectiveness, efficiency and responsiveness of services. Longer-term aspirations
for HAZs indicated something of Government thinking on the future of the NHS,
a blurring of the distinction between secondary and primary care, co-operative
and complementary commissioning procedures, more health care needs met outside traditional acute hospital settings, a public health dimension to the work of
primary care teams with 'clinical effectiveness ... at the root of all that is done in
the NHS', These aspirations would find their objective presence in the 'system
reform' measures of the following decade.

In September 1997, 'priorities and planning' guidance was published, which included abandoning the internal market, new approaches to private finance initiative (PFI) and NHS pay and a revisiting of the Patients Charter. Public health issues and health inequalities were also identified as key areas for action (NHS Executive 1997c: para. 1), especially a ban on tobacco advertising and the development of smoking cessation services, and the creation of a new Food Standards Agency. The significance of information management and technology for the achievement of many of the Government's objectives was also noted (NHS Executive 1997c: para. 4). The NHS could make a significant contribution to the promotion of fairness and equity by acting to reduce 'the most significant local avoidable health variations between different areas, social groups, ethnic groups, and men and women' (NHS Executive 1997c: para. 10). Another aim was 'to develop a leading role for Primary Care in commissioning and provision of health care' (NHS Executive 1997c: paras 29A and 29E).

The White Paper was described in the Foreword by the Prime Minister as a 'turning point for the NHS' (DoH 1997:10). The needs of patients were to be central. The changes proposed in the White Paper were based on six 'important principles', some of which had been clearly flagged up in earlier documents (NHS Executive 1997c: para.2), and also followed on from the objectives of the NHS identified in paragraph 2.6 of the Report of the Royal Commission on the NHS (1979).

The six principles were fair access, excellence, local responsibility, promoting partnership, reducing bureaucracy and improving financial management. These principles structured subsequent 'system reform' developments in the Service. In particular, a major aim was to replace the 'misconceived' and 'divisive' internal market with 'integrated care' and a 'more collaborative approach' based on 'partnership and driven by performance' (DoH 1997: 2, 10 and 12).

To maintain the 1948 values, the Blair Government proposed reforms of the system of health care delivery and promised the resources necessary to ensure the improvement in quality required. This would remain the constant theme of the Labour Governments led by Tony Blair and Gordon Brown. While the values and system reform were to be peculiarly British, the promise of increased resources was to be benchmarked against the EU average for the proportion of gross domestic product (GDP) devoted to all health care, public and private:

> The Government has committed itself anew to the historical principle of the NHS: that if you are ill or injured there will be a national health service there to help; and access to it will be based on need and need alone – not on your ability to pay, or on whom your GP happens to be or where you live.
>
> (DoH 1997: 5)

This statement of principle was a reinforcement of traditional Labour values of equity for all in need of health care. An attempt was being made to convince the public that those values were to be maintained in a modernised form whilst taking into account the continued pressures on the cost of the Service associated with the long-term care of the elderly and scientific advances which impact upon clinical care (Chapter 5). The NHS should be comprehensive in its range of services which should be universally available to everyone. The aim should be to 'universalise the best' as Aneurin Bevan had stated in the House of Commons when presenting the 1948 Bill. *Ensuring fairness* related not only to recent concerns about financial equity between fundholding and non-fundholding general practitioners (GPs) (Chapter 7) but also to long standing inequities (Chapter 5) which has more recently been termed the 'postcode lottery'. Fair access was to be achieved by abandoning the internal market and devising a national formula to set fair shares for the new Primary Care Groups (PCGs), which would become Primary Care Trusts (PCTs), and by developing new evidence-based National Service Frameworks (NSFs) to ensure access to services of a consistent quality across the country.

There would be a rolling programme of NSFs setting out 'the patterns and levels of service which should be provided for patients with certain conditions', to ensure that patients 'will get greater consistency in the availability and quality of services, right across the NHS' (DoH 1997: 56, 57). There was an existing NSF for cancer care which had been set out in the Calman-Hine Report in 1995 (DoH 1995). The new NSFs were launched in April 1998 and the first covered paediatric intensive care, mental health, diabetes (1999). Subsequent NSFs covered coronary heart disease (2000), older people (2001), children and renal services (2004), long-term conditions (2005) and Chronic Obstructive Pulmonary Disease (2008). The Government proposed to address the unjustifiable variations in the application of evidence on clinical and cost-effectiveness and the failure to share best practice in part through two new bodies, set up in 1999, the National Institute for Clinical Excellence (NICE) and the Commission for Health Improvement (CHI). The aim of NICE was to produce and disseminate clinical guidelines. These were to be based on relevant evidence of clinical and cost-effectiveness, associated clinical audit methodologies and information on good practice in clinical audit (DoH 1997: 58). It was assumed this would lead to 'rigorous assessment of clinical and cost-effective treatments and … ensure good practice is adopted locally', with the potential to remedy the current 'uneven and unsystematic' take up of research findings on clinical and cost-effectiveness (DoH 1997: 9).

The deliberations and decisions of NICE were to become the subject of much debate especially when disappointed patients challenged the Institute over the denial of potentially 'quality of life' and even 'life-saving' drugs, therapies and treatments. Their refusal to fund new treatments was constantly criticised by the media. The decision regarding Herceptin, a drug for use in the treatment of breast cancer, seemed to be a high point in this debate. The Court of Appeal overturned the decision of the High Court not to fund the drug for a nurse with breast cancer (*R (on the application of) Rogers v Swindon NHS Primary Care Trust and Another* [2006] EWCA Civ 392, 12 April 2006). It probably left 'the law relating to the challengeability (sic) of decisions about NHS funding … more or less exactly where it was before' (Foster 2006: 558). The use of Herceptin was eventually recommended for use in 2010. NICE altered its draft guidance when the manufacturer submitted new evidence on the drug's effectiveness. Subsequently, there were other High Court actions by patients and drug companies over NICE decisions.

The aim of the CHI was 'to support the quality of clinical services at local level, and to tackle shortcomings'. It was to be a statutory body 'at arm's length from Government' and intended to 'offer an independent guarantee that local systems to monitor, assure and improve clinical quality are in place' (DoH 1997: 18 and 57–9). These arrangements were intended to 'offer an independent guarantee that local systems to monitor, assure and improve clinical quality are in place' (DoH 1997: 18 and 57–9). The Commission would later become the Commission for Health Audit and Improvement, and subsequently the Healthcare Commission (HCC), before being combined with the Commission for Social Care Inspection and the Mental Health Act Commission to form the Care Quality Commission (CQC) in October 2008.

The CHI was intended to enhance the patient experience through equity of *access* which would involve reducing hospital waiting times, introducing patient choice and extending the opening hours of GP surgeries, equity of *treatment* which would involve an emphasis on quality and clinical governance overseen and regulated by the CHI and equity of *outcome* which would involve the introduction of NSFs and the Care and Developmental standards set by the CHI. As with the renewed commitment to the principle of fairness, the Government was hoping that the new evidence-based NSFs would help to ensure transparency in the quality of care to be established right across the country. In addition, there were to be 'explicit quality standards in local service agreements' and a 'statutory duty for quality in NHS Trusts' (Health Act 1999, sections 18–25). The blueprint for ensuring quality was set out subsequently in *First-class service: quality in the NHS* (DoH 1998c).

All this was to be supported by a 'new system of clinical governance in NHS Trusts and primary care to ensure that clinical standards are met' (DoH 1997: 18, 57). It was hoped that professionals falling below the expected standard would be identified at the earliest possible moment with continuous professional development as a first-line defence in assuring the quality of service to be expected. One desirable outcome would be to make redundant the 'name and blame' culture which could lead to the involvement of the General Medical Council (GMC), and 'claim', that is, compensation approved by the NHS Litigation Authority. The objective was to replace this culture with a transparent and early reporting system where concerns about quality were raised within health service organisations. Evidence-based approaches (NSFs, NICE, and CHI to CQC) were intended to institute a sea-change in quality. Standards and quality would no longer be the monopolistic concerns of professionals, but the legitimate subject of debate by politicians and the public. A veritable Pandora's Box of ideas was thus created and would have the effect of placing medical care decisions and the organisation and finance of the NHS under the scrutiny of a 'quality' perspective. This was later to be systemised into an NHS Constitution.

## System reform – the search for efficiency and better organisations

> I want reform ... the NHS needs modernisation and hard choices.
>
> (Tony Blair, speech to the Labour Party Conference,
> reported in *The Times*, 1 October 1997)

The internal market in the NHS had been in operation throughout the 1990s, with constant criticism about a range of widely perceived problems, for example, lengthy waiting lists and waiting times, implicit rationing, community care deficiencies, the costs of bureaucracy, patients denied innovative treatments, a two-tier service based on fundholding and non-fundholding GPs, and 'postcode prescribing'. For at least some politicians, professionals, and patients, these problems could be at least partly, if not wholly, attributable to the Conservative Government's public expenditure programme, its ideological objections to traditional models of public sector professionalism and planning, and its preference for new public sector management in quasi-internal markets (Chapter 10). Thus a major aim of the Labour Government's first White Paper was to replace the 'misconceived' and 'divisive' internal market with 'integrated care' and a 'more collaborative approach' based on 'partnership and driven by performance' (DoH 1997: 2, 10 and 12). The Conservative policy based upon a market model of price would be replaced by a decision-making system which would be in place for the next ten years.

The 'system reform' as set out in the White Paper (DoH 1997) involved new institutional arrangements, setting up PCTs and Foundation Hospitals. PCTs would take over the commissioning of services. Patient choice would be introduced. Service delivery would be flexible. A more responsive and appropriate service would be made possible by a change in professional attitudes and working procedures. The service would promote partnership and local responsibility. Thus there was an emphasis upon raising quality and creating a cost-efficient service. The virtues of 'planning sensibly for change' were extolled and were to be facilitated by 'scrapping annual contracts' (DoH 1997: 15 and 68), which would be replaced by three- to five-year planning guidelines based upon the financial allocations from the DoH as a consequence of the recently introduced Comprehensive Spending Review. The White Paper included a commitment to 'a strong public voice in health and healthcare decision-making' with an expectation that health authorities would play a 'strong role in communicating with local people and ensuring public involvement in decision-making about the local health service' (DoH 1997: 29). This was contrasted with the internal market which 'made it hard for local people to find out what their local hospital was planning' and allowed GP fundholders to 'make significant decisions without reference to the local community' (DoH 1997: 11 and 15). Between 1997 and 2008, Community Health Councils were abolished and replaced by Patient and Public Involvement, which in turn was replaced by the LINK scheme in April 2008. The latter involved greater powers for local people to challenge local health care policies, alongside the powers given to the Oversight and Scrutiny Committees of local authorities to raise any matters of local significance regarding health care with their local primary care and acute Trusts.

*Local responsibility* involved a further and significant organisational reform by which 'for the first time in the history of the NHS all primary care professionals, who do the majority of prescribing, treating and referring, will have control over how resources are best used to benefit patients' (DoH 1997: 37). The intended outcome was that 'local doctors and nurses who best understand patients' needs ... (would) ... shape local services' (DoH 1997: 5). The new proposals drew on two by-products of the 'internal market', GP involvement in commissioning services and decentralising responsibility for operational management. The changes proposed the establishment of PCGs, later PCTs, throughout the NHS, involving all GPs and community nurses in each area. PCGs were to be developed around 'natural communities'. These would be coterminous with social services, and would typically serve about 100,000 patients, taking 'responsibility for a single unified budget covering most aspects of care so they can get the best fit between resources and needs' (DoH 1997: 19). PCGs would 'have a range of new powers to lever up standards and efficiency at local NHS Trusts and as a last resort to change provider if, over time, performance does not meet the required standard'. They would be representative of all GP practices in the Group, promote integration in service planning, have clear arrangements for public involvement, promote the health of the local population, commission health services for their population, monitor performance against service agreements and develop primary care and integrate it with other community health services (DoH 1997: 18, 19, 34, 36 and 37).

The new PCGs would take over fundholding in April 1999 and health authorities would, over time, relinquish the direct commissioning of services to the new PCGs 'as soon as they are able to take on this task' (DoH 1997: 27). At the time of the White Paper, it was recognised that one size does not fit all, and variation from area to area suggested that there should be four optional forms of responsibilities for PCGs:

Option 1:  to support and advise the health authority in commissioning care;
Option 2:  to take formal, devolved responsibility for managing the budget for health care in their area, as part of the health authority;
Option 3:  to become established as a free standing body accountable to the health authority for commissioning care; and
Option 4:  to become established as free standing bodies accountable to the health authority with responsibilities for commissioning care and the provision of community health services for their population.

With this final option, PCGs would become PCTs with full practice-based commissioning (PBC) responsibilities. All PCGs would begin at whatever point on the spectrum was appropriate for them, but would be expected to assume fuller responsibilities over time with an end-point in Option 4. These changes were to become extremely significant with the introduction of PBC from 2004 onwards and by 2007 PCTs were to assume sole responsibility for commissioning services. The provider arms of the PCTs were being prepared for 'business ready' and 'autonomous provider status' by the late summer of 2009, another form of internal reorganisation facing 'providers' with market forces for health service provision, for example with physiotherapy or sexual health service provision. In this context GPs would also advise their patients over the choices available for secondary care, with patients being able to select their acute care from a choice of four acute care hospital providers ('Choose and Book').

Existing NHS Trusts were expected to continue alongside Options 1–4, but would be accountable to the evolving PCG/PCTs. Before full implementation of Option 4, NHS Trusts would operate with a new stability through longer-term financial and commissioning arrangements with PCGs. The latter, however, would still be able change their local service agreement 'where NHS Trusts are failing to deliver'. It was clearly hoped that the latter would be infrequent given the 'new focus on quality' guaranteed in part through the clinical governance of NHS Trusts, involving senior health professionals more closely in designing service agreements. Both sets of organisations (existing NHS Trusts and the new PCGs/PCTs) were expected to contribute to developing the new Health Improvement Programmes. The NHS Trusts were also to be accountable to health authorities and were given a new statutory duty to work in partnership with other NHS organisations. The Trusts were obliged to publish details of their performance, including the costs of the treatments they offered (DoH 1997: 45, 46, 48, 49 and 53). The intention was to find a 'third way' of running the NHS, which would avoid what the White Paper termed the old 'stifling' top down centralised planning and control systems of the 1970s and the 'wasteful grass roots free for all' of the 1980s (DoH 1997: 10 and 27). This would be a system based on *partnership* and driven by *performance* (DoH 1997: 10, para. 2.2, emphasis added).

However, there was one element of continuity with previous forms of health care organisation from before the inception of the NHS in 1948. The independent contractor status of the GP was to continue in the 'new NHS' (DoH 1997: 35 and 40). However the 'system reform' involved significant extensions to the traditional roles of GPs, as well as organising the choice agenda for patients, they were now expected to take on a range of services which were to be devolved to primary care following the publication of *Our Health, Our Care, Our Say* in January 2006 (DoH 2006a).

## Resources

> The money will be there. I promise you that. This year, every year … we will get the money. Millions saved from red tape, millions more into breast cancer treatment already under new Labour.
>
> (Tony Blair, speech to the Labour Party Conference,
> reported in *The Times*, 1 October 1997)

Provision of resources is one of the longest-running issues for all health care, dating back at least to the end of the nineteenth century. Increasing costs and cost containment have been central to the NHS since the beginning (Chapter 4) and had posed major problems for the health care organisations preceding it, especially the voluntary hospitals (Chapter 3). A key conclusion of the Royal Commission on the NHS had been that the principles upon which the NHS was based seemed to be almost 'inherently efficient' by comparison with other health care systems, but this did not prevent resourcing for the Service becoming a politically sensitive issue for the previous Conservative administrations (Chapter 10). The new Labour Government was committed to remedying past deficiencies in NHS spending.

The Prime Minister's October 1997 speech referred to both cost savings and increased resources. Cost-savings were to be derived in the short run from the abandonment of the internal market and in the longer run from the programme of system reforms. It had become clear that there would be no scope for health authorities or NHS Trusts to 'relax their approach to achieving and maintaining financial balance, and improving value for money in the service' with the NHS Executive stressing that 'rigorous and rapid action to improve cost-effectiveness and efficiency will be essential if the NHS is to achieve an acceptable balance between patient care and financial stability'. Before the White Paper was published it was claimed that there would be an increase in real terms health funding by moving £100 million into patient care out of 'red tape', that is, by eliminating the bureaucracy associated with the internal market, and savings associated with reducing the number of health care providers. When the White Paper appeared it was explicit about the need for an *efficient* NHS, that the Service 'has to make better use of its resources to ensure that it delivers better, more responsive services for patients everywhere' (DoH 1997: 15).

The White Paper asserted that the abandonment of the internal market would yield 'big gains in efficiency' (DoH 1997: 9) with substantial savings, estimated at £1 billion over the lifetime of that Parliament, from greater organisational efficiency. Reference was made to the complex, time-consuming and wasteful bureaucracy of the internal market, associated with administering competition including fragmented decision-making, spiralling transaction costs, short-term and individual case contracting and the absence of strategic co-ordination (DoH 1997: 2, 4, 8, 13, 14, 19, 22, 38 and 72–4). Other identified 'internal market inefficiencies' included the artificial budgetary divisions between emergency care, waiting list surgery and drug treatments, and the limitations of the existing Purchaser Efficiency Index (PEI). The PEI was replaced in April 1999 by a new Performance Framework intended to focus on 'more rounded measures, health improvement, fairer access to services, better quality and outcomes of care and the views of patients, as well as real efficiency gains' (DoH 1997: 11, 14, 20 and 64–5). There were also organisational efficiencies and cost savings linked to cutting the number of commissioning bodies to as a few as 500 and capping management costs with a combined health authority and a PCG/PCT management cost envelope for each health authority area.

With the system reforms, aligning 'clinical and financial responsibility' for all professionals, in particular the teams of local GPs and community nurses working together in the new PCGs/PCTs, would deliver 'better value for money'. The intended outcome was a Service with treatment based on the best evidence of 'what does and does not work and what provides best value for money' (DoH 1997: 56). The two bodies, CHI and NICE, would by 'rigorous assessment of clinical- and cost-effective treatments … ensure good practice is adopted locally' (DoH 1997: 9). A national schedule of 'reference costs' was promised which would 'itemise what individual treatments across the NHS cost'. NHS Trusts would be required to publish and benchmark their own costs on the same basis. The intention was to make performance much more transparent and give health authorities, PCGs/PCTs and the NHS Executive a 'strong lever with which to tackle inefficiency' (DoH 1997: 19). Thus improved financial management would remain a constant theme in all future 'system reform'. Before the White Paper it was claimed there would be increased health funding in real terms, and the largest new building programme in the history of the NHS. As well as the 'system reforms' which, it was hoped, would create a more efficient Service and provide more resources for services to patients there was also the commitment to increase 'spending in real terms every year' (DoH 1997: 3 and 8).

## Reactions to the reforms

The Government's first initiatives on health and health care were generally well received. *The New NHS* White Paper was described as 'very positive', 'exciting', 'bold', 'brave' and 'imaginative', offering a vision for the future which is both 'radical' and 'right', promising an 'improvement in the fair delivery of health care' through 'empowering professionals, encouraging innovation, better informing the public, holding institutions to account through publication of standards' (Editorials in *The Guardian*, 10 December 1998 and *The Times*, 10 December 1997; Ham 1998a: 2; 1998b: 212; also the Director of Institute of Health Services Management and the Chief Executive of NHS Confederation, quoted in *The Guardian*, 19 December 1997).

The organisational changes which featured in *The New NHS* White Paper were well-received, in particular the 'sensible and welcome' process of bottom up evolution over five to ten years which eschewed the 'immediate big-bang introduction of untested reforms' (Dixon and Mays 1997: 1640; Glennerster and Le Grand 1997). Saying that the Government did not 'seek to enforce one model in every city, suburb and rural area', Frank Dobson recognised that different arrangements might suit different parts of the country (Hansard, Vol. 302 No. 85, 9 December 1997, col. 807). This included a different set of arrangements for Scotland (Secretary of State for Scotland 1997) although these did attract the criticism that they could represent a return to the old command and control approach (Parston and McMahon 1998: 213).

The gradualist introduction (via the four options) of PCTs was seen as a 'sophisticated concept' that will need 'time to bed in' with concerns expressed about the interest, the time and the managerial capacity of all GPs in relation to the commissioning process (Editorials in *Daily Telegraph*, 10 February 1997 and *The Independent*, 12 November 1997; also House of Commons 1997, col. 31, per Lord Howe). These comments indicated that there were management needs and costs associated with the new arrangements (Dixon and Mays 1997: 1640). The genuine concern with an over-bureaucratic public service might result in shifting the burden on to professional practitioners, given the complications surrounding contracting for hospital and community services. The intended significant downward pressure on management costs might limit the effectiveness of PCGs/PCTs and health authorities in undertaking their new roles in commissioning, planning, monitoring and regulating (Dixon and Mays 1997: 1639–40). There might be a tension between the new roles and the new institutions (PCGs/PCTs, NICE, etc) and the intention to generate significant savings in the administrative and managerial costs associated with the NHS.

With regard to the question of resources, there was the cautionary observation that 'studies carried out in the US have generally shown that very little of expected savings have occurred' (*Health Care Today*, October 1997, No. 50), and in January 1998 this periodical had the headline 'Managers question £1billion savings target', echoing the concerns of others that the proposed savings were 'ambitious and will not of themselves provide the additional resources the NHS will need' (Ham 1998b: 212).

## The search for better health and reduced health inequalities

The new Government signalled its interest in public health issues by appointing the first ever Minister for Public Health in England, Tessa Jowell. Her role was identified as developing 'a coherent strategy for public health' seeking to 'systematically engage the many arms of Government in delivering better health for the whole nation by taking action to address the root causes of ill-health' (NHS Executive 1997c: para. 5). The policy direction was now one of cutting across other government departments so that the multi-causal nature of ill-health could be dealt with at a strategic level. This included ensuring that local authorities and health authorities 'abandon the old pointless territorial disputes' (*Health Care Today*, October 1997, No. 50: 24).

A consultative Green Paper on Public Health was originally scheduled for publication in the Autumn of 1997 (NHS Executive 1997c: para. 8) but was preceded by a food standards White Paper which created what at least one newspaper referred to as 'one of the most powerful food watchdogs in Europe' (*The Independent*, 15 January 1998: 1, 'Foul food: can the Government protect us from killer bugs?'). The new Food Standards Agency was to report to the DoH not the Ministry of Agriculture Food and Fisheries. It was made up of a commission of 12 independent people backed up by advisory committees and several hundred civil servants. There was some disappointment that the Public Health Laboratory Service would not report directly to the new agency but the inclusion of advice and education on nutrition into the agency's remit was seen as recognition of food as a public health issue (James 1998: 416). The Green Paper eventually appeared on 5 February 1998 as *Our Healthier Nation* (DoH 1998b). The commitment was to 'integrate policy on public health, social care and the NHS so that there is a clear national framework within which similar service development can take place locally' (DoH 1998b: 55). The Government's public health strategy identified four priority areas for which 'realistic' but 'challenging' national targets would be set. These areas were heart disease and stroke, accidents, cancer and mental health. These were 'significant causes of premature death and poor health' and 'there is much that can be done to prevent them or to treat them more effectively' (DoH 1998b: 6 and 56–7).

The previous Government's health strategy, *The Health of the Nation*, had included targets, but its vision for health had been limited, mainly because of its reluctance to acknowledge the social, economic and environmental causes of ill-health (DoH 1998b: 57 para. 4.12). The position in the Green Paper was that the Government recognised 'that the social causes of ill health and the inequalities that stem from them must be acknowledged and acted on. Connected problems require joined up solutions' (DoH 1998b: 44). The Cabinet Committee of Ministers from 12 different departments showed a clear commitment to support 'the co-ordination of health policy across Government' and to 'apply health impact assessments' to 'relevant key policies' (DoH 1998b: 31–2). At the local level, the Government proposed placing on local authorities a new duty to promote 'the economic, social and environmental well-being of their area' (DoH 1998b: 44).

As with their first White Paper, the Government claimed to be pursuing another 'third way', this time between the 'old extremes of individual victim blaming on the one hand and nanny state social engineering on the other' (DoH 1998b: 5). The latter comment is interesting since New Labour's interest in public health sparked charges of the 'nanny state', pointing of course to one of the dilemmas in formulating policies for illness prevention and health promotion. The Minister for Public Health, Tessa Jowell, in an interview with *The Independent*, was clearly sensitive to these criticisms, noting that:

> it is important that we go with the grain of public enthusiasm and don't turn people off by being overtly prescriptive, ambitious or intrusive. This is not about creating a nanny state but it is founded on the belief that people should be able to make grown-up choices on the basis of information they can trust.
> (*The Independent*, 5 January 1998: 8)

Interestingly, the Government did not presume that the 'case of health' was self-evident and took the opportunity to elaborate on the 'overwhelming personal, social and economic case … for improving our health', that 'our own health and the health of our families and friends underpin our ability to enjoy life to the full' (the personal case), that everyone 'should have a fair chance of a long and healthy life' (the social case), and that to 'succeed in the modern world economy, the country's workforce must be healthy as well as highly skilled' (the economic case) (DoH 1998b 7, 9, 12 and 14).

The commitment was not just to improve the health of the population as a whole but also to narrow the health gap. 'This means tackling inequality which stems from poverty, poor housing, pollution, low educational standards, jobless-ness and low pay. Tackling inequalities generally is the best means of tackling health inequalities in particular' (DoH 1998b: 1,2 para. 1.12). So broader public policy measures, the Welfare to Work programme, the National Minimum Wage and an integrated transport policy, were clearly identified as essential to the 'New Public Health' (DoH 1998b: 29, para. 3.5; 37, para. 3.31; 46, paras 3.61 and 3.63). The Government also established an independent enquiry into 'the evidence base for action to tackle inequalities in health' (DoH 1998b: 5 and 53). There was recognition that the public health agenda for narrowing health inequalities was quite ambitious, especially since it is possible to target the more easily tackled health problems and end up widening health inequalities (DoH 1998b: 56 and 82). This commitment to the importance of public health and the multidisciplinary approach to health care, prevention, and health maintenance stimulated a number and variety of innovative approaches to make it a reality. Examples which attracted specific additional resources were the Schools Initiative and £300 million from the National Lottery for Healthy Living Centres. It was intended that the Consultation Paper would be followed by the publication of a White Paper on public health in the summer of 1998 (NHS Executive 1997c: para. 8) and a comprehensive strategy on reducing smoking later in 1998 (DoH 1998b: 22).

The Public Health White Paper, *Choosing Health: making healthy choices easier*, was eventually published at the end of 2004 (DoH 2004). In his Foreword, the Prime Minister emphasised the Government's commitment to 'fairness and equity, good health for everyone'. He said it was clear that 'the Government cannot, and should not, pretend it can 'make' the population healthy', but that it can and should 'support people in making better choices for their health' (DoH 2004: Preface). Whereas the Green Paper had emphasised the connection between public programmes and the effect of public health programmes on the long-term health of the population, the White Paper emphasised the economic contribu-tion public health could make to the resource problems of the NHS so that by 'preventing avoidable illness we can concentrate resources on treating conditions which cannot yet be prevented' (DoH 2004: 4), with particular emphasis on devoting greater resources to those parts of the population experiencing health inequalities.

## The search for more community health care

> More health care needs (can be) met outside traditional acute hospital settings.
> (Frank Dobson, 25 June 1997, at the
> NHS Confederation Annual Conference)

In 1997, the year the Labour Government was elected, the Audit Commission published another critical report on the balance between community and institutional care. There remained perverse incentives within current arrangements, including early discharge policies within NHS hospital services which could lead to inadequate rehabilitation and the transfer of patients to expensive nursing and residential care. If time and facilities were made available for adequate recovery and rehabilitation within the NHS, patients could go back into their own homes. Meanwhile, the local authority social care service retained an incentive to place individuals in residential care where residents might contribute all or some of the costs from the sale of their own homes (Audit Commission 1997). The Priorities and Planning Guidance published in September 1997 included a commitment to ensuring that 'old people, adults with a physical or learning disability, children and other vulnerable people with continuing health care needs are enabled through the NHS contribution to their care to live as independently as possible in their own homes or in homely settings in the community' (NHS Executive 1997c: paras 29A and 29E). It was also proposed to establish a Royal Commission on long-term care which was set up three months later, although this would remain an unresolved issue when Gordon Brown replaced Tony Blair as Prime Minister in 2007.

Many politicians and professionals were familiar with the obstructive and obdurate nature of the health and social care division put in place by the health and social service reorganisations of the 1970s (Chapters 7 and 8). The Government recognised that 'the effective delivery of community care requires co-ordinated provision of continuing health and social care services developed through partnerships between health, local authorities, housing, and other agencies' (NHS Executive 1997c: para. 29E). The Under Secretary of State in the DoH, Paul Boateng, announced that plans to close the remaining 35 psychiatric hospitals would be halted while a new system was put in place to ensure that adequate alternative care in the community was available (*The Times*, 13 September 1997). Frank Dobson said he wanted to start breaking down the 'Berlin Wall' between health and social care, noting that there were as many as 6,000–7,000 people in hospital who should not be there. Three areas for action were identified, first, local joint investment plans for continuing and community care; second, improving the content and process of multidisciplinary assessments; and, lastly, 'the development of health and social care services for older people which focus on optimising independence through timely recuperation and rehabilitation opportunities' (*The Times*, 13 October 1997, Secretary of State for Health).

The first White Paper had promised that the Government would 'ensure the NHS works locally with those who provide social care, housing, education and employment' (DoH 1997: 4). It also indicated a renewed faith in the benefits of coterminosity with social services (DoH 1997: 37) and a commitment to breaking down organisational barriers, forging stronger links between the NHS and the local authorities with 'a *new statutory duty of partnership* placed on local NHS bodies to work together for the common good' (emphasis added). This would strengthen the existing requirements under the National Health Service Act 1977 (DoH 1997: 11 and 26), giving the Oversight and Scrutiny Committees of local authorities the right to look carefully at the health policies of the local Trusts, in both primary and acute care (Local Government Act 2000; Health and Social Care Act 2001, sections 7–10). The Regional Offices with the DoH Regional Social Services Inspectorate were charged with monitoring local action to strengthen partnerships across health and social care and to review progress in areas such as continuing care and mental health (DoH 1997: 60). Closer working between health and social services was seen as essential to integrated health and social care resources so that 'patients get a seamless service' (DoH 1997: 27 and 71). If serious attention could be given to public health and preventive measures, many hospital admissions could be avoided. There was also an assumption that some hospital care might be 'unnecessary'. The over use of accident and emergency departments is still blamed on poor primary care and out of hours services. Other examples are repeat outpatient appointments at hospitals, and the clinical case for GPs carrying out minor surgery and overseeing in local primary care settings the treatment begun by the hospital. Dermatology services and services for diabetic patients could be maintained by GPs in the community without expensive hospital visits, although both conditions if misdiagnosed can have serious consequences for patients.

The redirection of services from hospital to community raised suspicions that financial constraints might be overriding clinical decision-making, an echo of the 1940s debates about state interference in professional judgement. PCTs attempted to counter this argument with the introduction of Referral Assessment Centres (RAC) through which non-urgent cases could be considered by local GPs who would decide if a referral to secondary care is necessary. The RAC would be funded by PCTs, and GPs would monitor their fellow GPs, a twin approach to controlling costs and refining clinical judgement, or, as some believe, rationing care.

## Regulation

In its first White Paper, the Government had reasserted a continuing faith in systems of *professional self-regulation* as 'an essential element in the delivery of quality patient services' (DoH 1997: 59). At the same time, it proposed to strengthen such systems, most notably the Health Service Commission, to be followed by the HCC and the CQC (DoH 1997: 56, 59). The autonomy of the medical professions and clinical decision making was virtually unchallenged until the revelations of the seriously professionally deviant behaviour of Drs Ledwood and Shipman. Dr Rodney Ledward, a gynaecologist, was struck off the Medical Register for serious misconduct, and the inquiry report, chaired by Jean Ritchie QC, said that poor management was partly to blame (Ritchie Inquiry 2000). Dr Shipman, a GP, was convicted of murdering 15 of his elderly patients, and the inquiry, chaired by Dame Janet Smith, found that he was probably responsible for more than 200 deaths and recommended changes to the GMC (Smith 2002–05).

Similarly, the institutional failings demonstrated in the Bristol Royal Infirmary by the Kennedy inquiry into paediatric and cardiac surgery (Kennedy Report 2001), and the discovery of body parts taken from deceased children at Alder Hay hospital, without the knowledge or consent of parents, also challenged the reputation of the Medical Profession (Redfern Report 2001).

These new scandals differed from those that had come to light in the 1970s and 1980s, which were associated with the long-stay chronic warehousing of the vulnerable, the old and the mentally ill (Chapters 5 and 7). Alongside raised expectations about new possibilities for innovative treatments, they provided a reminder that as research science opening up to the new public new possibilities and generated new expectations, there was always the possibility of new scandals. They also demonstrated failings in the regulatory regime under the auspices of the GMC. Public confidence was shaken by these events giving the Government a stimulus to take a much more significant role in relation to regulatory matters. Although these new scandals may have been the impetus to the regulatory regimes put in place since 1997, nevertheless the overall 'system reforms' of the NHS were bound to produce new ideas, lay as well as professional, about standards, clinical performance and the quality of clinical outcomes.

The new tools of regulation to assure quality (NSFs, NICE, HCC to CQC, and Patient Environmental Action Teams) were to break new ground by introducing into the NHS the managerial and bureaucratic dimensions of clinical decision making, resting upon a commitment to improving old and introducing new standards of medical care. For many years academic commentators had been writing about professional autonomy and independence resisting bureaucratic methods overseen by central government (Abel-Smith 1971; Alford 1975; Klein 2004; Weale 1998). The regulatory reforms introduced since 1997 would have been unthinkable in 1948 because of professional resistance and public distrust of bureaucracy.

## More resources and more reorganisation

In January 2000, Tony Blair promised to bring the funding level of the NHS, at that time 6.81 per cent of GDP, closer to the European average of 8.61 per cent within five years, an increase of about £10 billion a year. It was clear that this money would not come without conditions. There would have to be improvements in service quality. To this end, the Government planned a further reorganisation of the Service, and on 27 July 2000 *The NHS Plan: a plan for investment, a plan for reform* was published (DoH 2000). A major theme was the need for increased spending to enable capacity to be expanded and it reiterated that investment needed to be accompanied by reform. Specific targets were set to cut hospital waiting times, expand cancer screening programmes, enable patients to have a GP appointment within 48 hours, provide more consultants, GPs, nurses and health professionals, create extra hospital beds and new hospital buildings, and develop intermediate care to allow patients to recover before returning home. Nursing care, but not personal care, in nursing homes would be funded by the state. There would better training for NHS staff and the NHS would be enabled to use private facilities if appropriate. An independent panel would be set up to advise the Service on major hospital changes, such as closures. There would be greater patient choice and protection through patient representatives on Trust boards, and new contracts for consultants and GPs. The intended outcome of the NHS Plan was to change of the Service from a market-driven managed and under-resourced service to a quality-assured, patient-centred professionalism in a well-resourced service. It was clear that such a bold strategic direction would create operating dilemmas. First, would structural and financial repositioning conflict with clinical freedom and patient expectations? Second, would this agenda produce an over-regulated system in which implicit rationing would become explicit and economic criteria would dominate political and public discourse? Third, would the evidence-based research which demonstrated the importance of the non-medical contribution to health, the public health agenda, tobacco control, drug abuse, alcohol control, and the public health message, be subordinated to the concerns of those responsible for the funding and administering the Service?

It was hoped that the public would be reassured by the possibility of greater choice and shorter waiting times as well as the use of benchmarked quality and performance measures through NSFs, NICE and HCC/CQC. This overall emphasis on the quality of the service may be seen as the most dramatic and challenging engagement with the medical profession since 1948, with some unexpected difficulties. An example was the unrestricted consultant-to-consultant referrals. Hospital consultants had always taken it for granted that once a patient has been referred to them by a GP, they could refer that patient to more highly specialised 'tertiary care' colleagues without going back to the referring GP. This was a classic 'clinical freedom' issue, and had serious cost implications for PCTs. Unplanned and unscheduled cost pressures compromised the obligations of hospitals and PCTs to meet their statutory duties and balance their income and expenditure for the year. With the 'target culture' of reduction of waiting times, especially for cancer, the pressure on all parts of the system became intense. The overriding purpose behind the introduction of 'targets' was to shorten the time between GP diagnosis and 'Referral to Treatment' at the most appropriate acute hospital. This laudable aim has had some adverse consequences in that it may well have encouraged professionals to prioritise the waiting list and waiting times to the potential detriment of the quality of the treatment received. This unintended consequence has acted to denigrate the important criteria of the timeliness of treatment. Working to the target, especially in accident and emergency departments, has been in danger of putting the target of seeing 95 per cent of those attending to be treated within four hours of arrival above the importance of seeing patients according to professional need. However, it should also be said that the wait from primary care to a hospital consultant is now 18 weeks, whereas it was not uncommon to wait 18 months before 1997.

The Secretary of State, Alan Milburn, was gradually converted to a more market-like approach, and in 2002 he announced legislation to set up NHS Foundation Trusts (FTs) with a stronger statutory underpinning of independence than NHS Trusts had enjoyed up to this point. These FTs were to be rolled out gradually, encouraged but not imposed. They also remained subject to oversight by a new regulator, Monitor, which would have extensive powers to intervene. In addition, an NHS inspectorate, the CQC, and NICE had already been set up to recommend which treatments the NHS should and should not adopt, and to provide guidelines on best practice. Lastly, a fixed NHS price or tariff was developed for a range of hospital treatments which provided a standard currency for NHS treatment. The intention was to get NHS and independent suppliers to compete on quality and the structure of service. They were not to waste time, effort and money merely haggling over the price of treatments at the margin, as many fundholders had done after the 1991 reforms. The 1991 reforms had restricted patient choice because if the GP or health authority did not have a contract with the hospital concerned then a bureaucratic procedure would ensue which was not always applied consistently. The intention of the 2002 reforms was that eventually all trusts, including PCTs, would graduate to the new foundation status. This could be seen as representing 'a large step towards a health service that '... (would) be accountable to local communities, rather than to central government' as part of a 'larger shift towards a more pluralistic, consumer-oriented health care system' (Klein 2004).

In 2002, Gordon Brown, as Chancellor of the Exchequer, appointed Sir Derek Wanless, a former banker, to review the financial pressures on the NHS. His first Report was published in April 2002 (Wanless 2002). He found that the NHS had fallen behind EU spending by a cumulative £220 billion in 25 years. In his report, Wanless also asserted that the manner in which the NHS performed its everyday tasks could be made more efficient. Suggesting that the NHS should revise its skill mix was a key insight that would have both quality enhancement and efficiency consequences. Great store had already been placed on the development of the National Programme for Information Technology (NPFIT) as a way of streamlining these back office, but vital, functions. Wanless also emphasised the future role of modern technological innovation in communications in the NHS at a number of levels, diagnostic results through the rapid transmission of diagnostic results, rapid communication between acute Trusts and GPs, especially with regard to appointments. This latter was to be especially important with the 'Choose and Book' system coming online in 2004. The King's Fund commissioned a further report by Wanless in 2006 to review progress (Wanless and Forder 2006).

In the April 2002 Budget, the outcomes of the 2002 Spending Review were announced. In this, the NHS secured increases of 7 per cent per year in real terms between 2002/03 and 2007/08 as a result of the first Wanless Review. Subsequently, Klein (2004) described the commitment to increase spending on health care over a ten-year period to reach EU levels and to redesign the Service in the direction of patient-led demands, and away from supply side controls, as 'an ambitious process of self-transformation'. He concluded that it remained 'an open question whether the NHS will have changed sufficiently to cope with budgetary constriction ... (when the growth monies cease in 2008) ... and at the same time satisfy the expectations raised by the period of euphoric expansion'.

Later in 2002, the DoH published *Reforming NHS financial flows* (DoH 2002). This indicated the intention, over the next few years to move the NHS from being a 'monopoly provider of health services, run from Whitehall, to ... (one that would) offer a greater diversity and plurality of services for NHS patients'. To this end, a system of 'payment by results' would be gradually being phased over subsequent years with the aim of supporting 'patient choice by ensuring that diverse providers can be funded according to where the patients choose to be treated'. Early in 2003, the Secretary of State, Alan Milburn, acknowledged that Labour's strategy of introducing a 'plethora of service targets, inspection regimes, and national standards' had become counter-productive. He argued that 'the NHS cannot survive as a monolithic top down centralised system. Without greater diversity the NHS cannot be more responsive. Without responsiveness there cannot be public confidence. Without public confidence the NHS will not be sustainable' (Klein 2004: 939).

## The Labour Government perspective on health reforms

At the end of 2005, the Government set out its own interpretation of its health reforms (DoH 2005). They were described as a 'coherent and mutually supporting set of reforms, which together provide systems and incentives to drive improvements in health and health services, increased responsiveness to patients and help to achieve reductions in health inequalities' (DoH 2005: 9, para. 3.2). The 'framework of reforms' was said to rest upon 'four related streams of work' with the intended outcomes of 'better care', 'better patient experience' and 'better value for money'. The first of these two are quality issues and the third is an efficiency issue. These 'related streams' are described as 'transactional', 'demand side', 'supply side' and 'system management'.

## The transactional stream

The transactional stream reform was designed to force money to 'follow the patient' thereby emphasising the incentives given to the most efficient providers of health care. The stated aim of this 'stream' was reinforcing 'patient choice' and rewarding 'the good provider'. The main mechanism would be payment by results and this would be supported by the new NPFIT, a £13 billion project, in 2006. This was later acknowledged to be a very expensive mistake and work on it would be discontinued by the coalition Government. This payment by 'results' could be seen as payment by 'activity', and was the source of many disputes between Acute Trusts, FTs and PCTs. The disputes usually concerned the 'over-performance' of activity by hospital trusts going beyond the Service Level Agreements (SLAs) and contracts between the PCTs and the hospitals. Such disputes were responsible for PCTs forecasting in-year deficits, and hospital trusts maintaining that 'over-performance' was simply a managerial way of describing the meeting of professionally defined patients' needs. The 'price' of hospital procedures was based upon a constantly disputed tariff or price for a health-related group procedure with exceptions to the standard tariff for hospitals that provided highly specialist services. This was an extremely important issue for FTs and teaching hospitals.

## Demand side

Supporting the 'transactional' reforms were the so-called 'demand-side' reforms, emphasising the necessity for patients to have more choice of the timing, location, nature and type of treatment. The intention of the reform was to prevent 'patient exit' from the NHS by institutionalising 'choice and voice' – 'Choose and Book'. Anyone needing surgery could use a system to choose from up to five hospitals, and to pick the time and date of their first appointment. GPs had to offer patients the 'choice' of four or five secondary care providers in the NHS, including services provided by independent treatment centres. Clearly, by activating this latter choice, GPs might by-pass the traditional secondary care system and be responsible for injecting into the system a form of market discipline, at which even past Conservative Governments may have baulked. The aim was to encourage the independent sector to provide 15 per cent of care in the NHS. This was the orientation of *Our Health, Our Care, Our Say* (DoH 2006a). The mechanism for this arrangement was to be PBC whereby budgets were devolved to GPs and GPs would form consortia or clusters within their PCT areas when referring patients to secondary care. The purpose of these innovations was to devolve financial power to the GPs in order to give them leverage over the dominant secondary care providers. This may be compared with the attempt by Government to save money by shifting care from hospitals into primary care. It would place professionals and managers in the position of mediating between political prescription, legislative rights and 'inadequate resources'. The Government's intention was 'to create more knowledgeable, assertive and influential users of services', the 'challenging' patient, and whether this would lead to 'planning by decibels' or succumbing to 'the sharp elbows of the middle-class' is yet to be seen. However the policies to involve 'patient choice' were put in place. *Commissioning a Patient-led NHS* (DoH 2006b) required PCTs to publish an annual patient prospectus and to engage in patient and public involvement. Clearly, the overall aim was to provide arrangements that would reinforce and bed in the concept of patient choice and voice, so that demand-side concerns would take precedence over traditional supply-side concerns.

## Supply side

The supply-side reforms rested upon a belief that a pluralistic and diverse set of providers of health care would be more likely to adopt innovative methods of service-supply, thus providing a counterweight to traditional working practices. This commitment to encouraging flexibility in the NHS to meet patient needs was a serious challenge to the 'one-size fits all' in its traditional form and was clearly the highest risk set of reforms being undertaken. Those hospitals that could demonstrate to Monitor that they were financially sound with a 'robust business plan' could become FTs. The Government stated that by 2009 all NHS organisations would be FTs.

The independent sector would be encouraged to bid for NHS work. This involved both the private and voluntary sector and covered both hospital and primary care services. It was this feature of the reforms that attracted the most criticism. It was alleged that the NHS was being privatised and commercialised. There was also an attempt to encourage more flexible working practices and team working through personnel policies.

## System management

The system-management reforms were meant to ensure that technical and value questions were built into the 'new NHS'. The technical reforms concerned patient safety and service quality. The issues of MRSA and the attempt to impose national quality standards throughout the NHS were central to the system management reforms. The value issues revisited the traditional Labour Party reasons for introducing the NHS. To ensure the safety and quality of services, the role of the HCC was to be central, annually reviewing the self-assessment by primary care and other Trusts around core and developmental standards. As the system changed from a supply side/provider side orientation to a demand-led, commissioned set of services, disputes between PCTs and acute (secondary) hospital services became endemic whether it was through the primary care/FT hospital contract or the primary care/secondary care service level agreement. However, it may have been that politicians, managers and the professions were slowly adopting the view of the recently appointed (2005) NHS Chief Executive, David Nicholson, that relationships within the NHS between these major players must become more like dancing than tennis. He did not say whether he was discussing a sedate waltz or a more frenetic tango (*Health Service Journal*, 15 December 2005). The concern was to reduce the conflict and arbitrate between PCTs responsible for commissioning and hospitals responsible for secondary care funded by PCTs through the SLA and contract.

## From Blair to Brown

The Prime Minister's decision to end his term of office in 2007 coincided with the embedding of the reforms that would be difficult to disaggregate under a new administration. Chapters 13 and 14 describe the way in which the coalition Government set about this task. The first debate on the address of the tenth and final Queen's Speech of Tony Blair's Premiership was on health and education.

Within the debate, all the major issues which structured the contents of the Government's first White Paper (1997) were raised again by MPs as a judgement upon the success or failure of the modernisation agenda. The issues were the traditional concerns of MPs and their constituents, scarcity of resources leading to closure of services, the reconfiguration of services leading to threats of closing accident and emergency departments, the quality of individual Trust performance, and the unequal distribution of resources based on geography, popularly called postcode prescribing. The Secretary of State's response was that the NHS had experienced an unprecedented period of growth in financial terms, that quality was at the heart of the Government reforms and the systems reforms that had been put into place will ensure that patient needs will be met regardless of geography or social class. Reference was also made to the success in bringing down waiting times for hospital treatment. Tony Blair's final speech on the NHS was on the 61st birthday of the Service (30 April 2007), in this speech he emphasised the relative efficiency of the NHS compared with France, Germany and the USA, and was clearly proud of being associated with this increase in real resources that were going to the NHS in the opening decade of the twenty-first century.

## The Darzi Reports

At the end of the previous year (December 2006), an eminent professor of surgery, Ara Darzi, was asked to look at the health needs of Londoners. His Report, *Healthcare for London: A Framework for Action* (Darzi 2007b), was published on 11 July 2007 (Chapter 12). When Gordon Brown became the new Prime Minister in June 2007, he appointed Darzi Parliamentary Under Secretary of State in the DoH and asked him to lead the NHS Next Stage Review. Darzi emphasised the importance of quality, saying that 'this Review should be both clinically-led and evidence-based'. The final Report of the Review, *High Quality Care for All*, was published in June 2008 (Secretary of State 2008). The Report focused particularly on need to improve quality of health care and patient safety and was described by the *Financial Times* as 'the world's most ambitious attempt to raise the quality and effectiveness of an entire nation's healthcare'. In the foreword to the Review, the new Secretary of State, Alan Johnson, promised that power and control would be 'devolved to where it is most needed, to patients and the public and to front-line clinicians' (Secretary of State 2008). Frontline clinical staff were to be given more control over budgets, and every provider of NHS services would be required to publish Quality Accounts from April 2010. Allied to this commitment was the concern with ensuring that the NHS workforce would have the capacity to be committed to the quality agenda. Referring to clinicians, nurses, dentists and pharmacists, the paper emphasised the importance of education and training to provide satisfying careers in the NHS for professional and other staff, as well as the teamwork required to deliver quality care. Sir John Tooke's 2007 inquiry into modernising medical careers (Tooke 2007) was critical of the existing system and some of his suggestions were taken on board. The Next Stage Review emphasised the 'core principles' underpinning the expectations of clinicians, and focused on quality, promising a service that would be patient-centred and clinically driven, flexible and valuing people, promoting lifelong learning.

## The NHS Constitution

The month before the publication of *High Quality for All* (May 2008), the Prime Minister had indicated that the Government would be establishing an NHS Constitution and a draft version of this Constitution was published alongside this latest Darzi report.

Alongside this commitments made to quality and staff professional development in *High Quality for All*, the NHS Constitution had 'seven over-arching principles' and '37 rights and pledges' (*NHS Handbook*, 21 January 2009: 4–7). Five rights concerned access to health services, two covered quality care and environment, three rights referred to nationally approved treatments, drugs and programmes, five rights covered respect, consent and confidentiality, three covered informed choice, two about patient involvement in health care in the NHS and complaints and redress. There were also 13 staff rights which cover equal treatment of employment and six staff legal duties towards patients, other staff and their profession. These rights were contained in the Health Bill which was placed before Parliament on 15 January 2009. Although the final Report of the HCC (Health Care Commission 2008) finished on a positive note, it placed the NHS once again within the political fray, however much it was claimed that some subsequent reforms were based upon technical and value-free approaches. The problem was that the criteria for decision making on behalf of patients were contested and there was dissonance between public expectations, evidence-based health care, ethical considerations, and professional custom and practice, a problem which is ongoing.

As the period of Labour Governments (2010) came to an end the House of Commons Health Select Committee produced a highly critical report. In particular, it noted a growing view that commissioning as a whole had not lived up to its promise in the two decades since *Working for Patients* (Chapter 10). Concerns included increased managerial costs associated with the purchaser/provider transactions. PCTs remained mainly passive buyers of care rather than active shapers of services and the situation had been made worse by constant reorganisations and the high turnover of staff. At this stage, there was some indication that these concerns would be taken on board whichever Party or Parties formed the next government.

As a result of Labour's changes, the NHS had an in-built review of quality. It had major injections of funds year on year from 1998. It focused on reducing costs but in terms not only of efficiency but effectiveness of medical care. It was concerned with equity and recognised the importance of primary care through the renegotiated GP contract. Despite the language of demand and supply-side economics, choice and relationships with the private market, the NHS was still based upon meeting the medical needs of the individual rather than ability to pay.

This latter value had survived in the face of system reform and occasional public disillusion (King's Fund 2005: 6).

A survey of public attitudes in 2005 found that most people were happy with the NHS. Three-quarters of those in the survey thought the service was good or very good. Those who had visited an NHS hospital in the previous year came away with an even more positive view, a possible indication of service improvements. Main concerns were waiting times and booking appointments (16) and 92 per cent of those surveyed said that the quality of hospital service was more important than having a choice of hospital (14).

During the 2005 General Election, which resulted in the return of a third consecutive Labour Government, John Reid stated that:

> Our vision is of a responsive and quality health service that is free to all, not only to those that can afford it. Our aim is to ensure the NHS is not only a national health service, but also a personal health service for every individual. Today, in health as in every other walk of life, the public expect high-quality products, better services, choice and convenience. This means putting power in the hands of patients rather than Whitehall.
>
> (*Health Director*, 05/2005)

Many commentators maintain that real strides had been made in that decade in improving the performance of the NHS. At the NHS Conference in 2008, Donald Berwick, a former Administrator of the US Centers for Medicare and Medicaid Services, gave a lecture entitled *A transatlantic review of the NHS at 60*:

> In good faith and with sound logic, the leaders of the NHS and Government have sorted and re-sorted local, regional and national structures into a continual parade of new aggregates and agencies. Each change made sense, but the parade doesn't make sense. It drains energy and confidence from the workforce, which learns not to take risks but to hold its breath and wait for the next change. There comes a time, and the time has come, for stability on the basis of which, paradoxically, productive change becomes easier and faster for the good, smart, committed people of the NHS.
>
> (quoted in Thorlby and Maybin 2010: 11 and 214)

Simon Stevens, the Prime Minister's health policy adviser from 2001 to 2003, and DoH policy adviser to two past Secretaries of State, asked whether 'constructive discomfort' should be expected and would be of value to the NHS (Stevens 2004). He identified three broad phases to NHS reform since 1997. These were phase one, central direction (national standards and directives); phase two, financial investment and support (e.g. the work of the Modernisation Agency); and phase three, 'constructive discomfort' or 'edgy instability' (the introduction of market-style incentives to improve the quality and efficiency of care). The 'system reforms' that had been put in place were undoubtedly uncomfortable because they enforced new ways of funding services, new working relationships, the reconfiguration or abolition of certain services, the scrutiny of professional activity alongside the ever-increasing media attention and the resulting generation of perhaps unrealistic public expectations. He described the period 1998–2003 as 'England searching for the optimal policy mix to generate that constructive discomfort' to improve the NHS. The repositioning of the NHS was to encompass both old and new values. This was particularly so with regard to the legacy of ancient hospital buildings which needed to be rebuilt. The NHS building programme had been based upon a continuing use of a reworked PFI. This initiative was to provoke much critical comment in the ensuing years. For example, whether collaboration with the private sector, independent treatment centres and PFI schemes, would close the gap between public expectations and government (political) promises is given a decidedly negative answer by Pollock. She concluded that 'with each new insertion of private provision into the NHS the political clout of the private providers increases, and the dominant culture shifts further in the private enterprise direction, while the structures of national control are … (being) … progressively dismantled' (Pollock 2004: 80).

The 'third way' response was that to harness the private sector was to adopt a pragmatic view of state finances and their place within the fiscal system as well as within public expenditure context. The consequence of the above has meant that the concept of quality has moved beyond a concern dominated by professional-technical considerations and into the arena of public discussion. This has led to health authorities being accountable for the quality of health care within their geographical areas and not just the quantum of such care. This recognition that the quality of health care has moved beyond a concern with the allocation of resources by geography (postcode prescribing), gender, social class and ethnicity to an examination of what the public can expect from the components of medical care which in aggregate define 'quality' medical care may be the most important reform of the NHS in its 60-year history.

## Conclusions

On 23 May 2001, Tony Blair declared that the Government's priority 'was, is and always will be education, education and education' (speech to launch Labour's education manifesto, University of Southampton). However, future historians may well decide that 'NHS, NHS and NHS' was the more dominant social policy and public concern of his tenure. The Blair Governments' period of office was dominated by the belief in the continued existence of the NHS and its values, but also a commitment to a further period of change within the NHS, although the aim was to encourage 'evolutionary change rather than organisational upheaval' (Ham 2004). The Labour Governments were responsible for 'unprecedented increases in funding for the health service' (King's Fund 2005: 1) but it would be argued that these increases could only be justified by a programme of organisational reform and modernisation of health service structures. To this end, the new

Government abandoned the price-led purchaser/provider split and replaced it with a quality-led commissioner/provider split. A key commissioning role was to be associated with what would become PCTs. The focus was on integrated care for patients as a reaction against the fragmentation said to be associated with the market. The aim was to promote continuity of care and collaboration between different agencies and staff. The Labour Government inherited an NHS that 'remained marked by large geographic variations in the level and quality of the services available' (Klein 2004: 937). In a drive to achieve a more equitable NHS, clear national standards would be developed through the operation of NICE and the development of NSFs. The CHI (later HCC) was set up to monitor health service delivery and to provide regulatory inspection and assessment. The number of performance targets 'proliferated' and 'their use became central to the management of the NHS' (Klein 2004: 939). Subsequently, the NHS Plan and Delivering the NHS Plan could be seen as an attempt to move the NHS from a hierarchically managed to a regulated health care system.

Both the Wanless reports (Wanless 2002, 2004) supported a tax-funded NHS with a high value being placed on preventive services. The three traditional explanations of costs pressures in the NHS, the ageing of the population, the price of high-tech medical innovations and rising public expectations, were taken seriously, but also maintaining the quality of services in the NHS was be a substantial pressure on costs. Spending would have to rise to maintain this quality and this was accepted by the Government. There was a year-on-year growth of resources going to the NHS between 2000 and 2008 with an increase in the annual expenditure on the NHS from £42 billion per annum to £105 billion, which raised spending from 5.9 per cent to 8 per cent of GDP.

In reviewing the achievements thus far, the King's Fund concluded that the Government had met targets with regard to waiting lists and access to care, targets had also been 'broadly met' with regard to increases in NHS bed and staff numbers and that patients were generally 'very happy with their care'. Overall, the results of this audit were described as 'very positive' (King's Fund 2005: 2–6). The audit of the King's Fund also concluded that 'much of the improvement' was linked to 'central fiat and targets'. Klein's conclusion around the same time was that 'an ambitious process of self-transformation' was under way (Klein 2004: 937), but the King's Fund also noted that it was too early to say whether 'greater use of market incentives and regulation' will achieve 'the desired transformation'.

Tony Blair's commitment to move to European standards of resourcing, reaching the average EU standards was achieved. The price for having more money was a greater degree of regulation and accountability through performance measures and 'system reform' checks. These complemented the increases in the NHS budget which included FT contracts being placed as standard DoH contracts with national application and PBC. The goals of efficiency and value for money and evidence-based medicine were to be complemented by serious attention being given to public health and preventive measures and the centrality of primary care service in avoiding hospital. Thus the modernisation agenda of the NHS involved reinforcement of values, system reform, reconstruction and renewal of resources. Future performance would be assessed not only in relation to efficiency (the preoccupation of the Thatcher and Major Governments), but also health improvement, fair access, effective delivery, patient experience and health outcome (Ham 2004). Nevertheless, in 2004 Rudolf Klein suggested that the NHS was 'now suffering from an acute case of 'change fatigue' (Klein 2004: 937). Perhaps the last thing that was needed was more reorganisation. The Conservative and Liberal Democratic coalition Government that was elected in 2010 had nothing in either of their manifestos to suggest that any major structural reorganisation was intended.

# Part III

# Conclusions

The National Health Service (NHS) survived to its sixtieth year despite the General Election in 1979, which was won by a Government whose ideological position involved a commitment to reduce 'burdensome public expenditure on welfare'. However, there is some evidence to support the contention that the Government soon discovered that blanket condemnations of the 'welfare state', of the sort favoured by its supporters from the radical right, did not strike a uniform chord amongst the general public. A disinclination to vote for restrictions on private health care was not the same as a vote for abandoning the NHS. Reservations about public expenditure in support of unemployed people in times of fuller employment, were not necessarily associated with similar reservations about public expenditure on sick children in hospital.

Whilst the Government may have abandoned any notion of significantly diminishing a major social policy programme of public expenditure on health care, it did appear to have a growing commitment to replacing the traditional modes of public service administration and professionalism with a form of private sector managerialism. Whilst the emphasis on efficiency was far from new, it did seem to be taking a different form. The traditional ideal of 'rational' coherent planning to meet needs, for example the Priorities documents (Chapter 6), seemed to be displaced by a new idea of 'strong' managerial control to remain within cash limits. On the other hand, in its impact on the Service, this retreat from 'rational planning' was more rhetorical than real. The first effective NHS planning system was not introduced until 1976 (Chapter 5).

Given the continuing popularity of the NHS, the alternative was to bring the market into the NHS through compulsory competitive tendering, private sector management approaches and, most radically, the introduction of an internal market and the purchaser/provider split. Nevertheless, the White Paper which introduced the internal market was prefaced with a personal statement by the Prime Minister, which was unequivocal in its support for a tax-funded universal health service. There was a shift in Government thinking from conventional administrative reform in the 1980s, to an economic solution based on 'internal markets' the 1990s. Both modes were constructed to cope with the major problem confronting the NHS, escalating costs in the face of professionally defined need. This was a recipe for conflict with the professionals responsible for defining that medical care need, and with the public whose expectations are based upon a legitimate assumption of that need being met. It is not surprising that this managerial and economic ideology would come into conflict with the historically based expectation of a public service meeting legitimate public health care needs. In particular, and despite Government claims to the contrary, the imposition of the Government's cash-limits were seen as leading to 'real cuts' in services, with the growing perception that the Service was in serious financial difficulties. The state was changing from being the sole guarantor of finance and provider of care, with a small private sector of up to 10 per cent of the population covered by company schemes, to being a major source of finance with an internal quasi- or managed-market to deliver health care. The 1991 reorganisation of the NHS was introduced a compromise between a state monopoly and an equivalent free market. Although this was an attempt to replace state dominance with private market principles it had, within the first few years, settled down to a halfway house of state finance through general taxation and quasi-market relations in purchasing, administration and local assessment of need. Even that most radical of Conservative Prime Ministers, Mrs Thatcher, was unable to convince her Government, her party and the general public that a wholesale switch to a free market arrangement was preferable to the presumed drawbacks of state provision – monopoly, inflexibility and bureaucracy – the concerns of providers being more dominant than the interests of service-users. However, the introduction of the internal market and the refusal to enter into any major new policy commitments seemed to make the search for equity a relatively low priority. The Government's reaction to the Black Report (1980) and *The Health Divide* (Health Education Council 1987) could be seen as essentially ideological, an unwillingness to accept explanations that called for more Government expenditure and more Government intervention. As a consequence the Government's own *Health of the Nation* strategy (DoH 1992) largely ignored the relationship between poverty, inequalities and health.

The Labour Government elected in 1997 introduced a range of organisational reforms in the NHS during its three terms of office. While the volume of resources going to the NHS was increased significantly, this was combined with 'earned organisational autonomy' within a more rigorous regulatory framework. There were also new commitments to the introduction of patient choice, flexible service delivery and changing professional attitudes and working procedures. The intention was to provide a more responsive and appropriate service. The modernisation agenda of the Labour years were supposed to ensure that the NHS would remain the major provider of health care. In addition to the commitment to increase the resources going to the NHS, there was a restatement of the traditional Labour values of equity for all in need of health care underpinning the establishment of the Service, that health care should be available irrespective of financial status, geographical location, urban or rural, and health status, whether acute, chronic or long-term. This strategic reinforcement of founding principles was demonstrated by referring to operational arrangements concerning waiting times, access to general practitioners and hospital treatment. It was presumed, however, that this restatement and reinforcement of traditional values would need to be accompanied by modernisation and planning. Because of the concern with equity and outcome measures, the introduction of measurable targets and the reform of the regulation of standards were dominant features of this entire period. These tools of regulation were to break new ground by introducing into the NHS managerial and bureaucratic dimensions to clinical decision making, resting upon a commitment to improving old and introducing new standards of medical care. Legislation reinforced the importance of regulation through 'the duty of quality'. The outcome was that central government played a much more central role with regard to standards and clinical governance. This would have been unthinkable in 1948 and in all reorganisations and debates up until 1997. Like all previous post-war governments, the new Labour Governments remained committed to efficiency and value for money. However, the attitude to expenditure on the NHS appeared to be different to that which had prevailed between 1979 and 1997, in particular, the immediate commitment to raising 'spending in real terms every year' (DoH 1997: 3 and 8). Continuing widespread public support for the principles of the NHS was identified, which legitimised a further increase in spending on the NHS by a redistribution of public expenditure from other services. Indeed, it seemed politically feasible to deploy 'small, as opposed to huge, increases in taxation' to support the NHS. There was also the potential for medical advances to achieve desired outcomes more cheaply, for example more day surgery, a reminder that not all medical advance increases health care costs, and an easing of demographic pressures was projected, as the NHS had to respond to a much less dramatic increase in the number of people aged 85 years and over for the next decade.

A continuing value was placed on competition during this period (1997–2010). The Labour reforms differed from those of the preceding Conservative Governments in the sense that the continuing element of competition within the system – commissioning competition – was not a recipe for crude cost-cutting. This was because the agencies, for example Foundation Hospitals, have a 'quality' obligation in the form of 'clinical governance', as well as a 'value for money and financial stability' obligation. They operate in a more rigorous regulatory regime and there is patient empowerment of various sorts. Lastly, this continued use of a form of competition takes place within an overall increase in resourcing. Thus the years of Labour Government involved a repositioning of the NHS through reforms intended to take the NHS from a market-driven managerialism in an under-resourced service to a quality-assured, patient-centred professionalism in a well-resourced service. The manifestos for the next (2010) General Election contained yet more commitments to NHS reform from the three major parties. However, there was also evidence that there was some recognition that the time had come for a period of stability with no plans for any major organisational upheavals (Chapter 13).

# Part IV

# Case study

# Introduction

This part of the book is a case study, taking an historical perspective to London's health care provision and problems, posing some interesting problems of interpretation, represented by our opening quotations. These indicate that the health care needs of the capital city have been addressed by service quality which is in some respects superior and in other respects inferior to provincial provision. Some of the enduring qualities of the debates concerning health services in London have included the following.

First, the apparent disparity between the resources in London and the rest of the country, but also the disparities within London itself most graphically illustrated by the concentration of high quality acute hospital resources in a relatively small area in central London, a spatial and service inequality. Second, the role of the medical profession in influencing health service organisation will emerge as a potentially important theme in understanding changes (and the absence of changes) in London's health services. As the location, throughout the period under review, of the majority of the country's teaching hospitals, London has also been home to the major organisations of the medical profession (the British Medical Association, the General Medical Council and the Royal Colleges) and has been seen as the location of the medical establishment. As such, the doctors based in the London teaching hospitals have been seen as the most influential section of the health professions and, indeed, one of the most influential of professional groups. We have noted their influence on successive organisational arrangements for the National Health Service (Chapters 4 and 8). In this chapter we can concentrate more specifically on how well the health care needs of Londoners have been served by the organisational structures which owed a good deal to the views of at least some London-based doctors.

Third, London's health services provide good examples of the conflicts that have been an integral part of the development of health care in the UK, between the aspirations of professionals, politicians and the public and the limitations of essentially voluntary institutions, between the ideals of 'rational planning' and 'professional autonomy', between the concept of a national health service and the demands of private practice, between hospital and community-based health services and between territorial justice and centres of excellence.

# Chapter 12

# London, 1601–2010

Medical facilities were completely unorganised and virtually uncontrolled, except in the immediate vicinity of London.

(Woodward 1974: 2, referring to the late
seventeenth century)

The conditions in London hospitals appear to have been worse than those in provincial hospitals.

(Woodward 1974: 101, referring to the late
eighteenth century)

Urban poverty, especially in London, attracted more attention and alarm than that in the countryside, and poorer rural areas were last to receive adequate schooling, housing, sanitation or other services, not to mention adequate wages.

(Thane 1982: 8, referring to the late nineteenth century)

Well before the foundation of the NHS, the deep-seated nature of the problems facing London's hospitals was recognised by policy-makers and health care professionals … key elements of the (London) problem have remained entrenched for many years: a tribute to the power of the many interests involved.

(King's Fund 1992a: 25 and 35)

London was the world's largest city and the capital of the greatest empire during the period 1850–1930, when the emergence of biomedical science prompted the construction of hospitals throughout the industrialised world (King's Fund 1992a: 22). As we have seen, paupers had access to medical treatment by virtue of the Elizabethan Poor Laws (1598 and 1601) (Chapter 1) and in the first half of the eighteenth century, 50 of the 155 workhouses in Great Britain were in London (Woodward 1974: 4). By the 1780s, there were seven general hospitals in London contributing to a situation where there were as many hospital beds in London as the whole of the rest of England and Wales (Abel-Smith 1964: 4–5; Woodward

1974: 36). In 1861, there were three times as many beds per 1,000 population in London as there were in the provinces (Pinker 1966: 84). As well as having a significant proportion of the beds in voluntary hospitals, 35 per cent in 1861 (Pinker 1966: 81), London had a higher proportion of beds in public hospitals per thousand population, 0.76 per cent compared to 0.34 in 1891 (Pinker 1966: 90). It was also in London that 'the greatest improvements in furnishing hospital service to the poor' took place and by 1877 'only six London parishes housed their sick poor in mixed workhouses' (Brand 1965: 95; Abel-Smith 1964: 127). Finally, it was in London in the 1880s that the first demands for some system of hospital planning were voiced, this being partly attributable to the sheer volume of hospital resources in the capital (Abel-Smith 1964: 161).

Part of this considerable volume of hospital resources was a significant preponderance of teaching hospitals. By 1858, there were 12 London hospitals with medical schools and 80 per cent of the general hospital beds in London were in teaching hospitals (Abel-Smith 1964: 17–18). Furthermore, this considerable quantity of distinctive hospital resources was also associated with profound spatial inequalities within London itself:

> Thus, a voluntary hospital, it was thought, had to be within easy coaching distance from the centres of private consulting practice. Thus, where there were fewest poor was the greatest provision for them. Within a radius of a mile from the Middlesex Hospital there were eight general and twenty-six special hospitals.
>
> (Abel-Smith 1964: 161)

Those factors that led to a concentration of voluntary hospital resources in London and other major areas of population (Chapter 1), led also to a further concentration of those resources within London itself. In marked contrast to this concentration in Inner London, continuing care developed on the outskirts of London leading to 'the great concentrations of psychiatric and mental handicap hospitals in Hertfordshire and places like Epsom' (King's Fund 1992a: 22–3). All this posed particular problems for any notion of 'rational planning' of health care for London.

One such attempt to rationalise the provision of health care in London, at least for the poor, came in the form of the Metropolitan Poor Act 1867. This provided for the establishment of district infirmaries, formed by combined parish action, for the sick, infirm or insane. A Metropolitan Asylums Board was set up to 'superintend the new facilities' (Brand 1965: 87). Another historic precursor of more recent publications was the petition presented to the House of Lords on 29 July 1889 calling for an inquiry into 'the financial and general management and the common organisation of medical institutions … (and) … Poor law institutions for the aid of the sick in the Metropolis' (*Hansard*, House of Lords, Vol. CCCXXXVIII, 29 July 1889: col. 1548; Abel-Smith 1964: 163–5). A House of Lords Committee was set up, accumulating a substantial body of evidence before reporting in 1892 and 1893, the first of 17 enquiries into London's health care over a 100-year period (King's Fund 1992a: 27–9).

Some of the evidence taken by the Committee identified the need for co-ordination and planned development and the Committee recommended that a central board be set up, although with 'no statutory powers as regards the formal licensing of any hospital built, or about to be built'. However, the board would receive audited copies of accounts and statistics, report on proposals for new hospitals and hopefully 'have a powerful influence on preventing the building of useless hospitals' (House of Lords Select Committee on Metropolitan Hospitals, 1890–93, Third Report: cv and cvii, quoted in Abel-Smith 1964).

The report had no immediate effect. 'It was one thing to show that some central board was needed but quite another to get one set up, in view of the rivalry and jealousy of the different hospital authorities' (Abel-Smith 1964: 173). However, within five years of its publication, the recommendation for a central board was effectively implemented by the establishment of The Prince of Wales's Hospital Fund for London, to commemorate the sixtieth year of the Queen's reign (later The King Edward's Hospital Fund for London). 'What was impossible by any other means was achieved through the almost mystical influence of the monarchy' (Abel-Smith 1964: 182). Tasks undertaken by the Fund included the amalgamation of small hospitals 'by persuasion backed up by the promise of substantial grants'. By these means the three orthopaedic hospitals were amalgamated between 1903 and 1906, but it was only possible to get two of the five ear, nose and throat hospitals to amalgamate. In addition, money was given to enable two hospitals to move south of the River Thames. However when, in 1906, the Treasurer of St George's Hospital wanted to move the hospital from Hyde Park Corner, he could not gain the support of the governors. Whilst the Fund could perhaps prevent the situation getting worse, it could 'do nothing to plan a rational division of responsibilities between the voluntary hospitals and public infirmaries' (Abel-Smith 1964: 183–5).

In 1902, a plan was announced involving the establishment of a central medical institute in South Kensington to take over the teaching of the basic sciences to medical students from the medical schools. After a substantial sum of money had been collected the scheme was rejected by the Medical Faculty of the University due 'partly to jealousy of University and King's College' (Young 1968: 298).

At the time, the major social insurance measure of the New Liberalism was being enacted the characteristic London hospital was still a teaching or special establishment. By contrast 'in the provinces general hospitals were the more usual form of accommodation' (Pinker 1966: 82). Indeed, general hospital provision remained relatively limited 'and it was not until 1938 that general provision exceeded teaching provision in the metropolis' (Pinker 1966: 83). In terms of overall provision, the general disparity between London and the provinces (as measured by beds per 1,000 population) diminished in this period. By 1921, the amount of voluntary hospital accommodation was nearly 50 per cent higher than in 1891, but over the same time period the number of provincial beds had more than doubled. The gap continued to be narrowed during the 1920s and 1930s (Pinker 1966: 83–6). When the offices and institutions of the Poor Law were transferred to local government on 1 April 1930 (following the Local Government Act 1929) the London County Council (LCC) was in a position to take a systematic approach to its extensive range of hospital facilities, a total of 77,000 beds compared to the 14,000 in the voluntary hospitals within the LCC boundaries (Abel-Smith 1964: 368–73). 'It was the largest municipal hospital system in the world' (King's Fund 1992a: 24).

The London teaching hospitals figured in another planning initiative when they ran into financial difficulties in 1938 due to the rising costs of medical education and the growing demands for pay from hospital doctors (Chapter 2; Honigsbaum 1989: 16). It became apparent that the Ministry of Health wanted the LCC to resolve the problem and by so doing facilitate co-operation between municipal and voluntary hospitals, 'perhaps even force the closure of inefficient units'. In addition, the Ministry did not want to single out the London teaching hospitals 'since it was felt that London had too many medical schools' (Honigsbaum 1989: 16). In the event, no action was taken and the immediate financial difficulties of the hospitals were resolved by the introduction of the Emergency Medical Service (EMS) (Chapter 3). One indicator of the continuing dominance of London in certain areas of health care, and of the wider problem of territorial injustices in the distribution of health services, was the location of specialist doctors, more than one-third of whom were still based in the capital in 1939 (Stevens 1966: 3).

The administrative arrangements for the EMS in London paid particular attention to the interests of the voluntary hospitals. London was divided into ten sectors radiating from Charing Cross, each including a teaching hospital. This scheme 'enabled the teaching hospitals to preserve their natural catchment areas … but did nothing to promote co-operation among themselves or with LCC hospitals (Honigsbaum 1989: 17 and 171). When the Goodenough Committee was reviewing postgraduate medical education in London in 1944, they talked in terms of '*the* hospital authority for London' (Royal Commission on Medical Education 1968: 183, emphasis added) indicating the more 'rational' approach to health care organisation that might be anticipated when the National Health Service (NHS) was set up. This did not happen. The distinctive approach taken by the EMS in London was retained in the arrangements designed for London's hospital services when the NHS was established. The non-teaching hospitals would be administered by four separate Regional Hospital Boards (Honigsbaum 1989: 144). With London's 12 undergraduate teaching hospitals under separately-administered boards of governors, the scene was set for an administrative arrangement that could have been designed explicitly to prevent any significant amelioration of the problems that had been inherited by the new Service with regard to both resource allocation in London, and between London and the provinces. There seems little doubt that this administrative system was arranged to accommodate the concerns of those who staffed the London teaching hospitals (Honigsbaum 1989: 171). Not only was London carved into four hospital regions but:

> The bulk of the inner city acute services were provided by 12 undergraduate teaching hospitals and 14 postgraduate teaching hospitals, each of which had their own Board of Governors. In the regions which had their own teaching hospital, the problems of concerted planning did not pose major problems. But in London they were formidable.
>
> (Abel-Smith 1978: 36)

Given the distinctive history of health care in the capital, it was paradoxical that the commitment to 'rational planning' represented by the NHS should do nothing to facilitate the sort of London-wide health service planning that was long overdue.

As with the Service as a whole, the themes identified in Chapters 5 and 6 have a particular significance for what has happened to the health services in London. Alongside the *over-provision* of acute hospital services in Inner London there was the *under-provision* of community health services, a particularly graphic example of the failure to plan effectively for a more efficient and equitable health service.

The particular organisational structure bequeathed to London by the political compromises of 1945–1948 was a potentially major obstacle to such planning. To the universal problems posed by 'tripartism' (Chapter 6), were added the division of London between four Regional Hospital Boards and the presence within those regions, and particularly within London, of a larger number of relatively autonomous units associated with the teaching hospitals. Whether the Regional Hospital Boards would be able to carry out their functions of planning hospital and specialist medical services in these circumstances was questionable. A new pattern of local government was established for London in 1966 following a Royal Commission. But although the Commission had to take account of issues relating to local authority health services, they did not have to consider the rest of the 'tripartite' NHS (Royal Commission on Local Government in Greater London 1960). The subsequent Royal Commission on Medical Education (1968) criticised the arrangement where there were 30 separate hospital authorities in the territory of the four Metropolitan regions, each with its own finance and direct access to the Minister of Health. It did not, in the Commission's view, lead to either 'efficiency or to economy in the provision of clinical facilities for medical education', nor did this arrangement serve the needs of other areas of hospital and health care planning (Royal Commission on Medical Education 1968: 195 and 197).

We have already noted the significance of historic cost budgeting (Chapter 5) which led to NHS funding being significantly determined by the historical pattern of health service provision. The outcome was that traditionally well-endowed areas like central London maintained that position within the NHS (Benzeval et al 1991: 26). The 1962 Hospital Plan did little to redress the imbalance of resources between central London, the Home Counties and the rest of the country. The rebuilding of teaching hospitals was given priority in the plan, because of the need to expand medical education, and within that priority the emphasis was on the cheaper option of expanding existing institutions. The result was that:

> Nearly all the twelve London undergraduate teaching hospitals were rebuilt on their existing sites or only a few miles further out from the centre. While the population of central London declined and there was a rapid growth of population beyond the green belt, London's teaching hospitals were expanded all within easy reach of Harley Street.
>
> (Abel-Smith 1990: 13)

This continuing concentration of a particular set of health care resources in London was not matched by complementary community health services. London gained proportionately less than other parts of the country from the 'health centre boom' of the late 1960s and early 1970s (Chapter 5). The Royal Commission on the NHS later noted that the increase in health centres had been less rapid in conurbations generally, and that within that category Greater London appeared to be faring worse than other conurbations, for example, Greater Manchester (Royal Commission on the NHS 1979: 86–7). In 1968, the Royal Commission on Medical Education recognised the continuing pre-eminence of the London medical schools, which at the time were teaching nearly one-half of those graduating in medicine at British universities (Royal Commission on Medical Education 1968: 171). With so many medical schools in London in competition for funds, the Commission expressed themselves unsurprised that:

> despite much goodwill, each of the medical schools in London has found great difficulty during the past thirty years or so in attracting financial support comparable with that made available to other medical schools in other British centres.
>
> (Royal Commission on Medical Education 1968: 174)

The varied and accidental factors that led to the foundation of the 12 main London undergraduate teaching hospitals and their associated medical schools could not be expected to have produced a pattern of distribution of hospitals that would be appropriate for the purposes of modern medical education (Royal Commission on Medical Education 1968: 196–7). This, the Commission concluded, should not be allowed to continue. The general pattern of the London medical schools was 'no longer satisfactory' and the 'present number of separate medical schools in London is ... no longer desirable or ... possible'. The Commission identified the need for a 'comprehensive and rational plan for future development in London' without which 'rebuilding could involve waste of scarce national resources, not only of money but of human skill and effort' (Royal Commission on Medical Education 1968: 172, 175 and 177). The 'radical reorganisation' recommended by the Commission involved reducing the number of undergraduate medical schools in London by six through a series of amalgamations, for example,

St Bartholomew's Hospital Medical College with the London Hospital Medical College. Each of the new medical schools formed by these mergers would become a faculty of medicine of a multi-faculty university institution (Royal Commission on Medical Education 1968: 175 and 177–8).

When the Commission turned its attention to the organisation of postgraduate medical education, it found a similar situation. Major problems persisted, despite the lengthy consideration that had been given to the issues for at least a quarter of a century. The Commission's conclusion was that 'only a small minority of the postgraduate institutions and their associated hospitals are housed in reasonably modern and adequate buildings', another set of circumstances which 'clearly cannot be allowed to continue indefinitely' (Royal Commission on Medical Education 1968: 185). It was the Commission's view that the postgraduate institutes should for all academic, financial and administrative purposes become an integral part of the reorganised medical schools.

Lastly, the Commission also recommended that 'the teaching hospitals in England and Wales should be brought within the framework of administration of the regional hospital service' to be accommodated in London by having five rather than four metropolitan Regional Hospital Boards. If possible the boundaries were to be coterminous with local authorities. In an historical parallel with the central board proposed in 1892/93, the Commission proposed the establishment of a Committee for Medical Education in London which would take general responsibility for the implementation of all aspects of the complete plan for London (Royal Commission on Medical Education 1968: 198, para. 479; and 201).

The commitment to more equitable funding of the NHS represented by the Resource Allocation Working Party (RAWP) process (Chapter 5) involved an attempt to 'redress the imbalance created by historical patterns of funding by shifting resources away from London to the North and North-West (Benzeval et al 1991: 26). In fact, the implications of the RAWP approach were more complex than this since the same analysis that showed that the Thames Regional Health Authorities (RHAs) had more resources relative to the populations they serve than the rest of the country, also confirmed that much of this apparent over-provision was focused geographically upon Inner London. Functionally, this concentration was upon the group of services known as Local Acute Hospital Services and, in some districts, services for the mentally ill and handicapped (King's Fund 1987: 3). The result was resource allocation policies designed to re-allocate resources both *away from* the Thames regions *and within* the Thames regions, from central London to Outer London and the Home Counties.

The Royal Commission on the NHS (1979) reviewed the particular problems of health care in London. These included the high proportion of single-handed general practitioners (GPs) (almost twice the national average), shortages of nursing staff, and the use of GP deputising services (Royal Commission on the NHS 1979: 89, para. 7.57). The Commission concluded that in parts of London the NHS 'is failing dismally to provide an adequate primary care service to its patients' (Royal Commission on the NHS 1979: para. 7.58). Ameliorative policies and practices were recommended which included financial inducements to attract GPs and other health personnel to work in Inner London (Royal Commission on the NHS 1979: para. 7.62), health authorities giving priority to building health centres in 'health-deprived' localities (Royal Commission on the NHS 1979: para. 7.51) and experimenting with salaried appointments with reduced list sizes to attract groups of doctors to work in them (Royal Commission on the NHS 1979: para. 7.59). These concerns would remain a feature of subsequent reports on health care in London. The Commission suggested that teaching hospitals have not always taken appropriate responsibility for fostering and improving the quality of primary care services in their surrounding areas. The Commission recognised that the expenditure of health authorities in London was being adversely affected by the application of the RAWP formula, but urged the London RHAs to make additional provision for distributing funds for primary care services to inner city Area Health Authorities (AHAs) (Royal Commission on the NHS 1979: 89–90). They also noted a major longer-term failure of previous planning. This failure was that despite the recommendations of the Royal Commission on Medical Education (1968), little progress had been made in reducing the number of medical schools in London. Therefore, they concluded that 'there is still an excessive concentration of teaching and research facilities in London and more hospitals than its population needs' (Royal Commission on the NHS 1979: 274). The key recommendation of the Royal Commission concerning London was that an independent enquiry should be set up to consider the special health service problems of the capital. The latter were identified as including:

> the administration of the postgraduate teaching hospitals,
> whether London needs four RHAs,
> whether some special adjustment to the RAWP formula is required to take account of the high concentration of teaching hospitals in London and
> what additional measures can be devised to deal with the special difficulties of providing primary care services and joint planning in London,
> (Royal Commission on the NHS 1979: 282)

Despite the 1974 reorganisation, the Royal Commission on the NHS made further critical comment on the arrangements in London noting that 'problems arise through the lack of coterminosity which affects 12 out of 16 London AHAs' (Royal Commission on the NHS 1979: 325).

## NHS in London: 1979–2010

### The Conservative Years (1979–1997)

> There is no shared, positive vision of what London's health services ought to be like.
> (Maxwell 1990)

The London Health Planning Consortium (LHPC) had been set up towards the end of 1977. In 1980 the Consortium drew attention yet again to the concentration and fragmentation of acute speciality medicine and surgery in London and the continuing inadequacy of primary care in London (LHPC 1980). Meanwhile, the Flowers Report recommended the formation of six schools of medicine and dentistry out of the existing 34 schools and the integration of postgraduate institutes with general medical schools (Flowers Report 1980). Also in the same year, a Fabian Tract emphasised again the problems posed by the administrative arrangements for NHS health care in London (Carrier 1980: 31–4).

The following year, the LHPC published its major review of primary health care services in Inner London, chaired by Sir Donald Acheson (LHPC 1981). The report confirmed much of the analysis of the Royal Commission including the large number of single-handed GPs and GPs with small list sizes, unsuitable premises, a lack of support staff, problems of accessibility and availability of GPs and a lack of co-ordination with hospital services as well as poor medical education in general practice. One conclusion was that:

> in areas with major social problems the primary care services are less well organised to cope with the extra burdens involved in caring for patients in the community and many more people end up being treated in hospital.
>
> (LHPC 1981: 19; Jarman 1981: 2–4)

The report of the London Advisory Group chaired by Sir John Habakkuk was also published in 1981. Recommendations included reductions in acute beds to free resources for mental health services and services for elderly people, including more community-based provision (London Advisory Group 1981).

Between 1982 and 1989 the continuing effects of the RAWP policies were demonstrable in London with 62 smaller hospitals being closed in the London area between 1979 and 1987 (King's Fund 1992a: 30 and 32–3) and a reduction of 3,700 acute service beds in Inner London, a faster rate of decline than that experienced nationally. However, despite this reduction in bed numbers, specialist provision and medical staffing levels in teaching hospitals remained much as before, the reductions affected general medical and surgical beds, leaving specialist provision relatively unaffected (King's Fund 1992a: 30–1 and 52).

In 1987, the King's Fund published a report commissioned by the Chairmen of the ten District Health Authorities (DHAs) covering Inner London. It covered the planning period from 1983–1984 to 1993–1994 and its Foreword included the interesting observation that there was an absence of a systematic factual basis against which to judge the current concerns about London's health services being expressed by Health Authority members, NHS staff and the general public (King's Fund 1987: iii). Given this observation, one of the Report's central conclusions was perhaps less startling than it might otherwise have been, that:

it is not in fact possible to draw a coherent and comprehensive picture of inner London's future health services from the published plans of the four Regions, nor indeed from the unpublished documents to which we have had access.

(King's Fund 1987: iii and 1)

As well as providing a further reminder that 'the populations of districts in Inner London are relatively deprived compared with many other parts of the country', the Report also confirmed the long-expressed concern that the regional authorities, now the RHAs, had not been able to co-ordinate their approach to planning on a London-wide basis (King's Fund 1987: iii, 9). The Report's detailed analysis of the then current plans and trends was particularly disturbing. Substantial bed reductions had occurred in Inner London's local acute services prior to the planning period under review, and the then current RHA plans involved further reductions. These planned reductions were based on a projected decline in hospital admissions in Inner London. However, not only were the planned service reductions proceeding at an alarming rate, 74 per cent of planned ten-year bed reductions occurring within the first two years of the plan, but they were also yielding substantially less spending reductions than had been anticipated, only 34.5 per cent of the planned reduction in spending had been achieved by undertaking 74 per cent of the planned reduction in beds. Furthermore, this reduction in beds was taking place against a background of an *actual increase* rather than the *anticipated decrease* in hospital admissions, perhaps an indication of the continuing limitations of London's community health services and the social and economic circumstances of at least some inner-city areas. One conclusion was that:

either more than the planned reduction in local acute services would be required to release the required resources, or revenue reductions would have to be extended to priority services.

(King's Fund 1987: iii/iv and 12)

Given that effective investment in priority services was one policy which might facilitate the anticipated, but not yet realised, reduction in hospital admissions, there appeared to be considerable potential for an emerging 'crisis' in London's health services, combining both 'over-spending' and 'insufficient services'.

In December 1990, the King's Fund appointed a Commission 'to examine the future of acute health services in London' in response to a growing concern about the future of health services in the capital. Its terms of reference required it to 'develop a broad vision of the pattern of acute services that would make sense for London in the coming decade and the early years of the next century' (King's Fund 1992a: 15 and 104). The Commission's report on health services, medical education and research in London was published in June 1992. Its conclusions about policies during the 1980s were particularly scathing:

What has happened to the capital's hospitals since 1980 has been almost the worst of all possible worlds, acute specialities have retained their grip on the capital's hospitals. There has been virtually no redistribution of medical manpower away from central London despite the decline in bed numbers and little progress has been made in concentrating specialist resources into fewer, stronger centres.

(King's Fund 1992a: 58)

The key issues identified in the report were inevitably an updated statement of points identified in previous reports regarding the concentration of acute hospitals in central London. These were inadequate primary, community and continuing care, poor linkages between London's medical schools and the rest of London University, fragmented and inadequately supported specialist and clinical research units, ageing buildings and equipment and inadequate management and planning structures for London (King's Fund 1992a: 22, 26 and 34). Despite the operation of the RAWP criteria, and the very limited role played by London as a national referral centre, with exceptions for some hospitals, it was noted that around 20 per cent of all English hospital and community health services expenditure was devoted to London, which contained 15 per cent of the relevant population. This calculation excluded the expenditure on London's Special Health Authorities, which also had a largely London-based caseload. Health care in Inner London was costing 45 per cent more than the national average. Contributory factors to the latter would include a longer average length of stay in hospital and a marked difference between hospital costs in London and elsewhere (King's Fund 1992a: 9, 30, 45, 46, 48, 51 and 52).

Concerns about the effectiveness of this higher spending were related to a number of issues. First, competition between, and the duplication and fragmentation of, specialist expertise and equipment, for example four cardiothoracic surgery services, three renal units, three plastic surgery centres and three sites for radiotherapy services were operating within three miles of one another in south-east London (King's Fund 1992a: 63). Second, there was evidence that Londoners were dissatisfied with their health services (King's Fund 1992a: 9 and 42). Third, there were problems of access to standard hospital services for Inner London residents and to specialist hospital services for Outer London residents (King's Fund 1992a: 53, 69). Lastly, the overall higher spending coexisted with relatively lower spending on, for example, family health services and drugs, and:

much less comprehensively developed primary and community health services than other parts of the country ... with frail elderly and homeless people, and those with mental health problems ... (receiving) ... a distinctly poor service.

(King's Fund 1992a: 9, 54, 55, 56 and 69)

The continuing major role of London-based medical education – approximately one-third of all medical students in the UK were still being trained in London – was identified as problematic in terms of fragmented research efforts, poorly developed formal postgraduate training opportunities and the quality of educational opportunities offered in an environment where bed numbers had declined significantly and further significant reductions were planned. All this was despite 'a succession of policy recommendations urging closer association between the medical schools and the multi-faculty colleges of London University' (King's Fund 1992a: 10, 60, 61 and 64–6).

If much of this was familiar, if somewhat depressing, to readers of the Royal Commission Reports of 1968 and 1979, the new report was able to add a significant new dimension in terms of the impact of the NHS reforms. The high cost of care in central London, exacerbated by the introduction of charges for land and equipment, might very reasonably be assumed to lead to the possibility of quite dramatic and significant changes in the traditional flows of patients into Inner London. At the same time the new mode of funding health authorities as health purchasers (weighted capitation funding, Chapters 6 and 7) would reduce the resources coming to Inner London DHAs (King's Fund 1992a: 9 and 35). The implication was clear. The workings of the internal market would significantly extend the range and intensity of the potential problems for Inner London health services that had been identified in the previous Fund report on plans and trends (King's Fund 1987).

Before putting forward their proposals for reform, the King's Fund Commission identified changes in the social and economic context within which health care was delivered and which needed to inform plans for the future shape of health services in London and indeed throughout the UK. These included requests for improved information about health and involvement in choices about health care, a closer scrutiny of the quality of health care, including waiting times for operations and expert opinions. In addition there was evidence that well-established trends would continue as further developments in pharmaceutical and less invasive methods of diagnosis and treatment afforded the opportunity both to shorten even further the lengths of hospital stays, for example, day surgery, and to relocate activities which were currently taking place in outpatient and other acute hospital settings to primary and community health care. In addition, as the primary causes of disease and death changed and continued to change (from acute infectious diseases to chronic degenerative diseases and cancer) so the *management* of disability would become as relevant as *treatment* to the needs of patients and the aims of the health services (King's Fund 1992a: 10 and 71–4). Some of these trends posed particular challenges for London's health care, given the 'intense concentration of specialist units in inner London' and the long-standing and widely acknowledged limitations of primary health care in London (King's Fund 1992a: 52).

The interpretations of demographic, technological and social changes contained in the report led the authors to recommend what they termed a 'radical programme of investment and restructuring' to reshape London's health services (King's Fund 1992a: 9). The resulting strategy was an interesting combination of

familiar and less familiar suggestions. The key point had been made before, that
there needed to be:

> a major shift of services and resources from hospital-based to primary care.
> The aim must be to locate many diagnostic and investigative procedures, and
> much treatment and care, in primary and community health settings close
> to where Londoners live, where this can be reconciled with quality and cost
> criteria.
>
> (King's Fund 1992b: 3, para. 7.3)

Some of the supporting points reflected developments that had taken place since
the Royal Commissions of 1968 and 1979 including the handling of a high
proportion of planned acute interventions through dedicated day care facilities,
hospital-at-home schemes, and a wide-ranging role for primary health care practitioners, including convalescent and respite care, rehabilitation, care for people
who are dying, and for people experiencing mental health problems (King's Fund
1992a: 77). If the vision of health care in London in 2010 was radical but well-
founded in terms of evidence and judgements, the Report's attempt at 'costing
the vision' was more problematic. Most significantly for its acceptability to the
Government, the Report concluded that 'there is sufficient scope within the capital's existing resources to achieve a significant transfer from acute to primary care
without requiring additional funding for the NHS over the whole period' (King's
Fund 1992a: 87). As with other major shifts of resources towards primary and
community health care (Chapter 5), key assumptions concerned the potential
reduction in core speciality hospital beds (25 per cent) over a specified time period
(18 years) and the volume of resources released by this planned reduction (King's
Fund 1992a: 84–5 and Appendix 4). Given the previous experience in relation to
both national and London-based plans, such assumptions could be seen as unduly
optimistic. To carry forward the vision, the Report recommended the establishment of a Task Force to undertake the reshaping of services in London including
a £250 million primary and community care development programme to address
the current deficit in these services, encourage primary health care practitioners
to undertake aspects of treatment currently taking place in acute hospital settings,
and to involve Londoners in designing services to meet needs which they had
helped to identify. Other tasks identified for the Task Force included planning
the more rational disposition of specialist services, and the consolidation and
reorganisation of undergraduate and postgraduate medical teaching, involving
an overall reduction in the number of medical students trained in London (King's
Fund 1992a: 10, 89–91 and 95–6).

We have noted the problems posed by the 'internal market' for London's health
services. A further problem was the statutory financial targets for the new NHS
Trust hospitals, their External Financing Limit, their 'break-even' on income and
expenditure, and a 6 per cent return on capital. Meeting these targets would be
difficult with evidence that 'the more costly London hospitals have begun to lose

contracts for patient care to the cheaper provider units in the Home Counties' (Bartlett and Harrison 1993: 88). It was in this context that the Government commissioned (October 1991) and published (October 1992) the Tomlinson Report to 'advise on the organisation of, and inter-relationships between, the NHS and medical education and research in London ... focusing on the management action needed to resolve immediate and foreseeable problems in London' (Tomlinson Report 1992: 1). The essential questions to be answered were those posed many times in the past. Should London have so many acute hospitals (Tomlinson Report 1992: 8–19) and why is primary care in London of such poor quality (Tomlinson Report 1992: 20–30)? Tomlinson identified and reviewed the same issues as the King's Fund Report, recommending a managed rationalisation of hospital services in London in recognition that acute health services in London could be delivered equally well and cost-effectively from fewer sites and with fewer beds, especially when considering likely contracted activity levels. The latter was likely to involve a 'withdrawal of patient flows from outside Inner London as purchasers secure high quality, but cheaper, services locally' (Tomlinson Report 1992: 4). The answer was to close and merge several teaching hospitals (Tomlinson Report 1992: 32–8). As with the King's Fund, Tomlinson recognised the need to invest in London's 'comparatively undeveloped ... primary and community health care services' (Tomlinson Report 1992: 4). The Report recommended 'a gradual and systematic transfer of resources from the acute sector to community health ... and family health service budgets' (Tomlinson Report 1992: 9). The associated transitional costs were dealt with very briefly commanding only one, three sentence paragraph (Tomlinson Report 1992: 59). The Report noted the need to manage the reduction in demand for London's acute service in order to prevent chaos:

> If this change is not managed firmly and in certain cases urgently the result will be serious and haphazard deterioration in health services in London.
>
> (Tomlinson Report 1992: 3)

In other words the managed quasi-market would need to be complemented by a substantial degree of directive 'command planning' of the sort the NHS had been set up to facilitate (Tomlinson Report 1992: 12, para. 42; 15, para. 53; 16, para. 58; and 18–19, para. 65; Donaldson 1993: 22–34). The Report also revived an organisational device with a lengthy history:

> that NHS commissioning authorities ... should be coterminous ... (and) ... that health purchaser and local authority boundaries should be coterminous.
>
> (Tomlinson Report 1992: 45 and 19)

The Secretary of State promised to consult widely over the Tomlinson proposals before reaching firm decisions in early 1993 (Smith 1993a: x). The Report (along with those written by the King's Fund) generated considerable opposition from a disparate range of groups including the medical and nursing professions, manual and non-manual trade unions, community health councils and voluntary organisations such as Age Concern. The essence of the opposition was that both reports were wrong. They were rushed and were about 'rationalisation' rather than health care needs. Existing waiting lists were used as evidence that Londoners needed not only all their current services, but more services rather than enforced closures and mergers. Particular issues identified included the impact on the development of community care (Jowell 1993: 46–53), the future of clinical research (Green 1993: 63–76) and the ongoing post-RAWP debate about the measurement of variations in health care needs. For London, issues of continuing concern included the significance of transient populations and the health care needs of people from minority ethnic groups. In addition, there were reservations about the 'assumption that hospitals serving deprived populations can increase efficiency to the level of the top quartile of health providers' (Jacobson 1993: 43–4). Then there was the national picture. If the NHS needed more resources then London should not be penalised because the Government was not providing sufficient resources for the country as a whole.

In early 1993, the Government published its own proposals, *Making London Better* (DoH 1993), which concluded that 'no change in London is no option' (DoH 1993: 20). A House of Commons statement by the Secretary of State (16 February 1993) indicated that the Government proposals took account of the Tomlinson recommendations, of evidence submitted since that Report was published and also the informal consultations with the institutions affected by the proposals. *Making London Better* set out a strategic framework for London's health services with four main elements, developing higher quality, more accessible local community and primary health care services, providing a better balanced hospital service, on fewer sites, to meet the needs of London's resident working and visiting populations, rationalising and developing specialist hospital services to safeguard standards in patient care and medical education and research whilst securing value for money and merging free standing undergraduate medical colleges with multi-faculty colleges of the University of London for the benefit of medical teaching (DoH 1993: 3).

*Making London Better* confirmed the establishment of the London Implementation Group (LIG) as part of the NHS Management Executive (NHSME). The LIG would be responsible for overseeing and implementing the major programme of work following from the Tomlinson Report by working with existing health agencies in the capital (DoH 1993: 37). *Making London Better* confirmed that the criticisms of London's primary health care were accepted by the DoH and as a consequence it proposed the creation of a London Initiative Zone (LIZ) as a focus for new investment and new approaches to improve primary health care and community-based services in those areas of Inner London with high population needs (DoH 1993: 4–8). An additional £43.5 million was allocated in 1993–1994 to support primary care development plans in the LIZ with £170 million made available over six years for community and primary health care capital projects, £7.5 million over three years for voluntary sector schemes to reduce the need for hospitalisation or to enable early discharge and £10 million allocated to help tackle waiting times in London (DoH 1993: 35).

The overprovision of acute hospital beds and duplication of specialist services was also accepted (DoH 1993: 8 and 9). For the latter, a series of parallel but separate Speciality Reviews were ordered to be carried out to determine how the six specialist services, cancer, cardiac, neurosciences, plastic surgery and burns, renal and children's services, should be organised. Each review was to be led by an eminent clinician from outside London and a senior NHS manager from a health purchasing authority. The key aim was to reduce unnecessary duplication of specialist services and suggest a more rational disposition to provide a stronger service and academic base. The LIG would be responsible for providing medical project management, information, and drafting support to the teams.

*Making London Better* also identified some specific proposals. These included ending accident and emergency services at some hospitals, for example, Charing Cross, continuing proposed rationalisation, for example, University College Hospital and Middlesex, and indicating the uncertain future of St Bartholomew's (DoH 1993: 10–15). Unsurprisingly, given that to state otherwise might be seen as confirming the views of critics of the post-1979 Conservative administrations, it was concluded that the 'root cause of London's problems is not a lack of resources' (DoH 1993: 18).

The Speciality reports were published on 23 June 1993 following an 'extremely, some would say dangerously, tight timetable' (Maxwell 1994: 5). The reports were separate entities with recommendations in one speciality being made without reference to the position in other specialities. Therefore, no overall conclusion was published, or was possible. However, except for the report on plastic surgery all the reviews proposed to consolidate services in fewer centres. Thirteen London hospitals were to lose specialities, with services being concentrated in high quality centres for research and patient cover, two to three times their current size. Overall, half of London's tertiary services would disappear as separate entities. In a letter to all interested parties, the Chairman of the LIG stated that the speciality reviews were 'only one element in a complex jigsaw … they are independent advice to the Minister … not policy … and not for formal consultation' (LIG 1993; Dillner 1993). The proposals were condemned by the Royal College of Nursing and the Association of London Authorities, and amid Opposition protests in the House of Commons, the Secretary of State for Health would not commit the Government to implementing specific recommendations contained in the Reviews (*The Independent*, 24 June 1993: 2).

In October 1993, the Secretary of State announced that the existing 14 RHAs would be replaced by eight regional offices of the NHSME, North and South London would be covered by the North and South Thames offices. In March 1994, the Government reported that 'good progress was being made' in relation to London (DoH/OPCS 1994). But the following month there were press reports that a NHSME review of allocation criteria concluded that rather than being over-provided by £70 million, London was underprovided by £200 million

(*The Independent*, 29 April 1994). The implication was that current plans to reduce beds might be halted. Four months later (August 1994), a well-known health policy analyst argued that there should be no more overall acute bed reductions (Maxwell 1994: v). Maxwell's report concluded that whilst the overall case for change remained valid along the lines of the King's Fund and Tomlinson recommendations, current concerns and experiences underlined 'the difficulties of making changes on the scale proposed' (Maxwell 1994: 1). Progress on London's primary health care (notably in the LIZ) had been 'slow' but 'uncontroversial', but the proposals for acute hospitals services had proved to be very controversial with deleterious effects on nursing and medical morale, and public confidence (Maxwell 1994: 8–9). Against this background there were the unexplained rises in emergency admissions being experienced in London and elsewhere, and the arguments that London was not 'over-bedded' (Jarman 1993, 1994). Maxwell expressed particular concern about the scale of bed closures (2,500 before any major hospital closure occurs) and their piecemeal, unplanned nature, by implication, led by the internal market (Maxwell 1994: 11–13).

A month after Maxwell's report was published, the King's Fund published another report indicating that patients needing emergency treatment in London faced long waits before and after they reached hospital, and that there was no evidence to support claims that attendances at casualty departments are higher in London because of inappropriate referrals by GPs (*The Times*, 2 September 1994). In February 1995, the theme of a moratorium on hospital bed closures in London was pursued not only through an Opposition motion in the House of Commons but also in a report from the King's Fund (King's Fund 1995a; *The Independent*, 23 February 1995: 7). In the same month, a report commissioned by the Inner London Health Authorities was published. Its brief included 'examining what is happening to London's hospitals at the present time' and its overall conclusion was that 'London's acute hospitals are operating under very considerable pressure' (ILHACE 1995: 1 and 3). The following month, members of the London Health Economics Consortium were reported as concluding that 'there is no evidence to support ambitious targets for a reduction in hospitalisation' (*The Independent*, 6 March 1995: 2).

Meanwhile, the Government reported 'good progress' with medical school mergers in London and indicated that there would soon be an announcement relating to proposals for 'the reconfiguration of the acute hospital service in London' (DoH/OPCS 1995: 37). In April 1995, Virginia Bottomley, the Secretary of State for Health, came under unprecedented attack in the House of Commons from senior Tories, especially from Sir Peter Brooke, MP for City of London and Westminster and former Secretary of State for Northern Ireland, as she avoided making a Commons statement on this 'reconfiguration' which involved a string of London hospital closures (House of Commons 1995a: cols 1651–2). The changes involved capital investment of £400 million and a £210 million investment in primary care. In May 1995, the Opposition again asked the Government 'to halt the withdrawal of hospital services and moderate the pace of change' (House of

Commons 1995b: col 765) and in the subsequent debate there was much critical comment from London-based Conservative MPs (House of Commons 1995b: cols 789–92, 804–6, 813–15 and 837–8).

A few weeks after the election of the new Labour Government in 1997, on 20 June 1997 the Secretary of State announced the setting up of a London Review Panel, chaired by Sir Leslie Turnberg (the President of the Royal College of Physicians), to undertake an independent review of London's health needs. The resulting report was made available to the Government on 18 November 1997 but was not published by the Government until 3 February 1998 (DoH 1998a). The Panel stated that they had made 'proposals about how London's services can be planned equitably and rationally ... we believe ... our proposals are realistic and rational' (Turnberg 1998: 1). One of its most significant conclusions was that 'there is no evidence that there are more acute beds available to Londoners than the England average'. Indeed, the Panel's interpretation was that 'London probably has fewer beds available to its population than the average' leading to the intention that the 'rationalisations being proposed should not result in losses of beds overall' (Turnberg 1998: 19 and 1). This confirmed the views of those critics who had been suggesting that the policy option of resolving the problems of London's health services by a reallocation of resources from existing hospital services was increasingly suspect and contrasted with the conclusions and recommendations of the Tomlinson Report (1992) and *Making London Better* (DoH 1993). The Review Panel's different conclusions derived not only from more reliable data, but also from referral patterns from Outer London to Inner London providers that were in the opposite direction to those predicted by Tomlinson and that primary and community care alternatives to inpatient hospital care were not developing with the speed and quality assumed in the King's Fund (1992a) and Tomlinson (1992) Reports. The Panel's recommendations on organisational arrangements complemented the themes of the *New NHS* White Paper (DoH 1997), accurate management information systems, good collaborative work, public health strategies as part of the planning agenda, improved local strategies for public consultation, groups of GPs commissioning services for populations of about 100,000, the centrality of close working with local authorities and the value of coterminosity (Turnberg 1998: 1–2). Long-standing concerns were expressed. 'General practice still lags behind the rest of the country and, in some ways, appears to be getting worse', and long-standing priorities were reaffirmed as primary care, mental health and community health services (Turnberg 1998: 1 and 35). Another long-standing problem was addressed by proposing not only that the two Thames Regional Offices should enhance their working relationship, but that the longer-term aim should be 'a single London Regional Office' (Turnberg 1998: 1).

Given the view that there was not an excess of hospital beds in London, it was unsurprising that the Review Panel should call for a careful re-evaluation of existing proposals, for example, the closure of the Guy's Hospital Accident and Emergency Department. In terms of one of the highest profile elements in the debate about London's health care the Review Panel concluded that there was a 'continuing need for St. Bartholomew's Hospital to fulfil its service, teaching and research responsibilities' for several years yet, with a longer-term future as a base for certain tertiary services, for example, cardiac and oncology services (Turnberg 1998: 77).

In its response to Turnberg, the Government stated its determination:

> to ensure that all Londoners have accessible top quality local services in GP practices, clinics and their own homes, supported by specialist advice, care and treatment in hospital and community settings, with accident, emergency and ambulance services capable of meeting foreseeable needs.
>
> (DoH 1998a: 1)

They accepted the recommendations in the Turnberg Report and proposed a programme to implement them. This included building on 'the long-tradition of medical excellence at St. Bartholomew's Hospital' with a request that plans be developed for 'a specialist hospital providing cardiac and cancer services ... for implementation once the other changes in the East End have reduced the need for the wider range of services it now provides' (DoH 1998a: 1 and 18). The public expenditure implications were estimated at £140 million over the life-time of that Parliament, with £30 million targeted on these services in 1998/99. The Government also accepted the case for capital developments in each of the five recommended sectors of London (North, South-East, South-West, West and East) at an estimated cost of over £800 million (DoH 1998a: 1–2).

The complete acceptance of all the Panel's recommendations was an unusual event in British social policy. The challenge to the King's Fund (1992a) and Tomlinson (1992) estimates of the number of acute beds required was quite direct, and the commitment to rebuild was an example of placing planning rather than the market at the centre of decision making. The complete acceptance of every recommendation in the Strategic Review demonstrated quite clearly the combination of political power with an ideological commitment to a historically favoured geographical sector, in which clinical excellence through concentrated specialist services and research appeared untouchable. The recommendations were accepted by the new Government, and included organisational change in the form of one strategic authority for London. The new authority (NHS London) was established on 1 July 2006.

In the autumn of 2006, NHS London commissioned a further review of health services in London by Professor Sir Ara Darzi. The first stage of this review was published in March 2007 (Darzi 2007a) and the final report in July 2007 (Darzi 2007b). This was a wider review than both Tomlinson and Turnberg, covering not just medical schools and hospitals, but the entire health network of London with primary care at its centre. The report included a comment that London's previous five SHAs were 'not configured to lead the pan-London improvements envisaged' (Darzi 2007a: 2). Its main concern was with the health needs of Londoners and the health outcomes that could be expected from investing in quality services. After the publication of the final report, Darzi was quoted as saying that the:

> three major themes are to improve access, quality and safety, and the staying healthy agenda to address inequalities in London. There is no set of new policies that will create havoc, it's clinically driven to improve access, quality and safety.
>
> (*Health Service Journal*, 12 July 2007: 5)

The reports noted the considerable achievements of recent years, reduced waiting lists, shorter waiting times in accident and emergency departments and for routine operations. But they also stated that health services in London were still not serving certain groups as well as they could. The groups identified were those with life-threatening short-term illnesses, the smaller number suffering from more serious illness, such as stroke or heart attack and those with major injuries. The conclusion was that persisting with the status quo in London was not an option (Darzi 2007a: 11) and that continuing with the old ways of doing would be unaffordable under all but the low-growth scenario (Darzi 2007a: 39). This conclusion was a clear, if unintended, forerunner to the political debate which followed the General Election of 2010 around the 'reconfiguration proposals' or 'cuts', 'privatisation' and 'any willing' or 'qualified provider' (Chapters 13–15).

Darzi's view was that there had been a lack of focus on the specific challenges facing health care in London. The changes envisaged in London-specific strategic documents, most notably the 1998 Report by Lord Turnberg, had not been fully implemented. Much of the Turnberg Report continued to be relevant, with its emphasis on the rationalisation of major hospital services on the one hand, supported by the development of high quality community care on the other. Of its major recommendations, only the suggestion that London did not need to reduce its acute inpatient beds, had been proved obsolete by health care developments.

Darzi's Reports wanted to see improved care 'from cradle to grave' based on five principles for change identified as:

1. universal services focused on individual needs and choices
2. localise where possible, centralise where necessary (i.e. routine healthcare should be as close to people's homes as possible)
3. truly integrated care and partnership working, maximising the contribution of the entire workforce
4. prevention is better than cure
5. a focus on health inequalities and diversity

(Darzi 2007a: 6–8 and 41–3)

Eight reasons were identified for the proposed 'co-ordinated programme of change across London'. First, there was a need to improve health of Londoners and in particular focusing on London's specific health challenges, HIV, drug abuse, mental health, smoking and childhood obesity (Darzi 2007a: 3; 2007b: 16–17). Second, the Service was not meeting expectations with 27 per cent of Londoners dissatisfied with the running of the NHS compared to 18 per cent nationally, and Londoners giving their GP services a lower net satisfaction than people nationally (Darzi 2007a: 3; 2007b: 17–18). Third, that there were big inequalities within London in terms of both health outcomes, for example, life expectancy, infant mortality, and service provision, for example, funding per person and GPs per head of weighted population (Darzi 2007a: 4; 2007b: 18–20). Fourth, that while medical advances meant that more care could be provided locally than ever before, community services were not providing a satisfactory alternative to hospital (Darzi 2007a: 5). Fifth, more specialised care was needed, but also the rationalisation and centralisation of these services in fewer hospitals. Specialist services should cater for larger populations in order to ensure sufficient volumes of work and variety of cases to maintain specialist staff expertise, the range of diagnostic equipment and the sufficiency of experienced staff to allow comprehensive consultant care (Darzi 2007a: 6; 2007b: 22–4). Sixth, for London to be at the cutting edge of medicine there would need to be closer co-operation between hospitals and universities and the establishment of Academic Health Sciences Centres to ensure that research breakthroughs would lead to direct clinical benefits for patients (Darzi 2007a: 8; 2007b: 24–5). Seventh, there was a need to use the workforce more effectively since both hospital doctors and nurses were seeing relatively fewer patients than their counterparts in the rest of the country. In addition, there was an ageing health care estate which was being used ineffectively (Darzi 2007a: 9; 2007b: 26–7). Lastly, there was the need to make the best use of taxpayer's money, for example, if all London hospitals had achieved the English average length of stay this would save over £200 million and free up over 2,000 beds (Darzi 2007a: 10; 2007b: 27).

As part of the review, six clinical working groups were commissioned to look at six patient pathways and make recommendations for change. The patient pathways were as follows (with page references to Darzi 2007b):

- maternity and newborn care (key proposals on p. 43 and further details on pp. 43–9);
- staying healthy (key proposals on p. 49 and further details on pp. 49–55);
- acute care (urgent and emergency care) (key proposals on p. 60 and further details on pp. 60–6, including the development of urgent care centres on pp. 62–3);
- planned care (key proposals on p. 67 and further details on pp. 67–72);
- long-term conditions (key proposals on p. 72 and further details on pp. 72–8);
- end-of-life care.

In addition, the chief executives of London's mental health trusts helped develop proposals in their particular area (Darzi 2007b: 55, for key proposals, and 55–9, for further details). It was concluded that London did not have the infrastructure and facilities to provide the ideal care outlined by the clinical working groups with two particular needs identified as, first, a new kind of community-based care at a level that falls between the current GP practice and the traditional district general hospital; and, second, the development of hospitals that were more specialised, delivering excellent outcomes in complex cases with fewer, more advanced and more specialised hospitals to provide the most complex care (Darzi 2007b: 10).

This led to a proposal for seven models of provision for medical care. These models were informed by medical advances that indicate that more care than ever can be provided locally, for example, day surgery in local hospitals (Darzi 2007b: 21). The main thrust of the proposals was to remove from hospitals those medical care services that could more appropriately, clinically, economically and ethically, be provided in six primary care settings. The suggested settings were home, polyclinics, local hospitals, elective centres, major acute hospitals and specialist hospitals.

More health care should be provided at home, for example, including rehabilitation after a hospital stay and to prevent hospital admission, while new facilities, polyclinics, should be developed as the major vehicle for the provision of relocated services. The polyclinic would become 'the place where most routine health care needs are met, and ... from which further navigation through the healthcare system is provided' (Darzi 2007b: 91). GP practices will be based at polyclinics, but the range of services 'will far exceed that of most existing GP practices' (Darzi 2007b: 91) including pharmacies, other professionals, for example, opticians and dentists, and community services, for example, mental health. They could include outpatient services, minor procedures, diagnostics and the management of long-term conditions, allowing a shift of services out of hospital settings, but being more accessible and less medicalised than hospitals. The majority of 24-hour urgent care centres would be located there, acting as the 'front-door' for accident and emergency. For a population of 50,000, there could be one building or a federation of GPs based on already existing practice-based commissioning clusters or 'hub and spoke' arrangements. The intention was that the polyclinic would provide the main stop for health and well-being support, for example, access to ante-natal and postnatal care. The ideal outcome is the provision of truly integrated care, bridging the current divide between primary and secondary care, between those working within different disciplines, and between health care and social care (Darzi 2007b: 10, 12 and 92).

Hospitals would concentrate on secondary care with a hierarchy of hospital models, local, elective, acute, specialist, and a concentration of skills into critical masses predicated on raising the quality of services. Darzi gives a dramatic example of survival from stroke. If thrombolysis and a scan can be got to the stroke patient within three hours, survival rates are much higher than if they wait 24 hours for the same in a local hospital. Local hospitals should provide the majority of inpatient care including all non-complex inpatient and day case surgery in all but the most severe emergency cases. Elective Centres would be there for non-urgent booked operations, for example, cataract, this work being separated from emergency cases to achieve better results and lower infection risk. Some hospitals should be designated as major acute hospitals, handling the most complex treatments. These would treat sufficient patients to maintain the most specialised clinical skills of their teams. Specialist hospitals would remain for areas like paediatrics, ophthalmology and heart disease, as well as trauma, cardiac and end of life treatment. Academic health science centres would be created in large cities to bring together research findings from major teaching hospitals under one umbrella. Three such centres were created in London based on University College Hospital, King's College Hospital and Imperial College to be centres of clinical and research excellence (Darzi 2007b: para. 18) and to provide links between research and clinical practice.

One implication of the polyclinic would be the 'sizing up' of many primary care arrangements, particular relevant given that GP practices in London were still smaller than the England average, with 54 per cent having only one or two GPs compared with 40 per cent nationally and therefore often without the support and equipment to undertake treatments close to people's homes (Darzi 2007b: 22). At the same time, other models for secondary care allow for the 'sizing down' of hospitals, the down-sizing of well-established local hospitals. This is particularly the case if urgent care centres dealing with primary care conditions are placed at the 'front end of A&E'.

Darzi stated that NHS London, the strategic health authority for London, would need to co-ordinate the task of turning the vision into the reality of improving healthcare for London. He identified short-term activities that would be necessary to show that the NHS in London was serious about this Framework and these were the development of five to ten polyclinics by April 2009, the urgent London-wide reconfiguration of both stroke and trauma services and rapid work to further improve the skills and capacity of the already remarkable London Ambulance Service.

He noted the value of up-front investment to help put new services in place quickly and win public support for change. The Report also identified the longer-term drivers for change and improvement as follows (Darzi 2007a: 11–13):

- *commissioners* at all levels, from GPs as practice-based commissioners through to commissioners of highly specialised services, should lead change;
- *partnerships* to improve health, working with London boroughs, the Greater London Authority and the Mayor's Office, the voluntary and private sectors and the higher education sector;
- *public support*, the clinical case for change needed to be clearly publicised;
- *clinical leadership*, NHS London would need to identify clinical 'champions' to make the case for change;
- *training* and the workforce;
- *patient choice* and information;
- *funding flows* would need to be used to incentivise the best practice contained in this report, at its simplest this means commissioners defining the best, safest

practice for a patient pathway and then ensuring that this and only this is the practice they pay for; and

- *better use of the estates*: surplus or underused buildings and land could be used to finance new developments.

A full inequalities impact assessment was to be undertaken post-publication as part of the discussion period. Darzi's expectation was that in future systematic use would be made of health inequalities assessments to ensure improvements to help those who were currently least well-served by the NHS in London. The preliminary review indicated that the way in which the Framework was implemented would be the most important factor in reducing inequalities (Darzi 2007a: 7). A change in service provision would be required if health care was going to be available, accessible, acceptable and affordable. For example, *availability* would mean extended hours, *accessibility*, reduced waiting times, locations, choice of hospital, primary care or home, *acceptability*, quality of service and *affordability*, the efficient use of scare clinical resources.

Darzi acknowledged that implementing the proposals would be a major challenge and that in particular there could be opposition to the polyclinics (Darzi 2007b: 2). Indeed, it is the proposed 'polyclinic' which drew the most hostile criticism including views such as the 'end of general practice as we know it'. In particular, the one building serving 50,000 patients as the model for GPs was the most criticised, threatening, in the views of the critics, the end of 'continuity of care' as a general practice principle. Yet whilst described as a 'new idea', aspects of the polyclinic are reminiscent of earlier proposals in the 1920 Dawson Report (Chapter 2; Carrier and Kendall 2008b) of health centres in the early years of the NHS (Chapter 5) and of the Royal Commission (Chapter 10)

Darzi's Report emphasised the need to listen to the concerns of Londoners, to build a clinical consensus, to work with the Mayor and the London boroughs, and to provide evidence for any recommendations for change. He hoped for support from 'politicians of all parties' given the key aim of improving 'the quality and safety of the care patients receive'. He also saw NHS London as a key 'pan-London body to drive forward strategic changes in healthcare' and 'to take forward this review's recommendations'.

Following from Darzi's recommendations, NHS London had managed to introduce service change for stroke care and major trauma before the Secretary of State in the new coalition Government halted all reconfigurations in London immediately on assuming office. Darzi's 'flagship' 'polyclinics' (in purpose built health centres serving populations of 50,000 or more, or as a federation of GPs) were abandoned in the face of hostile professional opposition. With a new White Paper and the resulting implementation of the Health and Social Care Act 2012, London's health services were reconfigured again. Before the Bill became law, London Primary Care Trusts (PCTs) were clustered into six groups, each group covering five PCTs. This was to prepare the way for the introduction of Clinical Commissioning Groups (CCGs) charged with the commissioning of health care

services from a variety of providers. This clustering was an attempt to save management costs and streamline the NHS bureaucracy in London. This interim
change, before the advent of CCGs, resulted in the loss of skilled staff, redundancy
costs and even the re-employment of the same staff. The long-awaited strategic
planning body of London, NHS London, was abandoned. At the same time, the
long-running disputes about the reconfiguration of London hospitals continued,
for example, changes to Barnet and Chase Farm Hospitals. The development of
networks and collaboration between London hospitals were disrupted. The separation of commissioners and providers of medical services continued in preparation for the formal legal authorisation based on the new Act:

> During much of the twentieth century, the capital's hospital services, medi-
> cal education and clinical research have been fixed in a gridlock imposed by
> history, buildings, institutions and the fierce loyalties each has engendered.
>
> (King's Fund 1992a: 66)

> In relative terms, London is over-endowed with acute hospitals, poorly pro-
> vided with community health services and lacks the organizational capacity
> to deal with the complex issues it faces at a strategic level high enough to
> make the impact which is required.
>
> (Benzeval et al 1991: 25)

This review of health care in London shows how attempts to change existing patterns and distributions of care engender conflict. It has been extremely difficult
to achieve a planned and integrated service that meets the needs of a diverse and
often disadvantaged population. Health care needs in London are quite distinctive because alongside its significant resident population there are an additional
1 million daily commuters as well as an annual 13 million tourists (Darzi 2007b: 14
and 17) London also has a unique, for the UK, density of population, and range
and diversity of individuals. Extremes of poverty and wealth exist, as well as a high
proportion of people from other cultures for whom English is not a first language.

Until the establishment of the NHS, the lack of any coherent organisational
framework for health care in Britain was such that it was perhaps inevitable that
very little was done (Chapters 1 and 2). Unfortunately, the political compromises
associated with the establishment of the NHS and its organisational structure
(Chapters 4 and 8) and the politics of planning and cost containment (Chapters
5 and 6) severely limited the ability and willingness of successive Governments to
address the issues:

> The 'fragmentation of responsibility between a multiplicity of regional, dis-
> trict, family health services and special health authorities means that the
> development of a coherent plan for health services in the capital has proved
> extremely difficult.'
>
> (Benzeval et al 1991: 31)

There was a consistency of findings through the analysis of problems identified in the series of reports generated between 1892 and 1992, the House of Lords Committee and the King's Fund. There seemed to be an intractable quality about these problems despite their serious consequences for the quality of health care provided in London. The latter suggested that what was happening to London's hospitals at the time was 'the worst of all possible worlds' (King's Fund 1992a: 58), noting also continuing concerns about competition between and the duplication and fragmentation of specialist services. Continuing problems included the disparity of resources in London, in particular the over-provision of acute hospital services in Inner London and the under-provision of primary and community health services. Within the primary sector there were co-ordination problems between the agencies and professional workers who provide different elements of primary care. There would be different planning and budgetary cycles, different and incompatible forms of accountability, as well as differences in ideologies and values.

Addressing these problems was hampered by the multiplicity of authorities. It was the Turnberg Report (1998: 1) that included a recommendation for the establishment of a single London Regional Office, although it was not until July 2006 that NHS London was established. It was the sort of organisation that many advocates of the NHS might have hoped to see in place from the inception of the Service or to emerge from the lengthy series of publications and debates that had preceded the 1974 reorganisation (Chapter 8). Within an organisational framework that had been changed by incremental stages associated with incoming administrations, the arrival of a New Labour approach to public services with its emphasis on organisational rationality and critical mass (Chapters 11) may explain this long advocated and long awaited arrival of a single health authority for London. However, its existence was to prove relatively short-lived and it was to disappear as part of the significant organisational reforms to be introduced by the new coalition Government elected in May 2010.

# Part IV

# Conclusions

The principles identified by the King's Fund in 1992 as the basis for change in London would not have been problematic for those who argued for a national health service half a century ago in the following way:

> London's health services must be *planned* and managed to serve the population rather than to perpetuate institutions ... and ... Londoners should be much more actively involved in their own health and health care.
>
> (King's Fund 1992a: 75, emphasis added)

Indeed one of the King's Fund Commission's conclusions (1992a) restates some of the key arguments in favour of a national health service:

> We are also convinced that changes of ... (this) ... scale and depth ... will require *strategic guidance* and *co-ordinated development* at national, regional and local level. Success will depend on coherent, system-wide implementation.
>
> (King's Fund 1992a: 75, emphasis added)

There has been considerable potential for conflict over the development of health services in London, given the historic domination of the teaching hospitals in Inner London. New technologies and techniques afford opportunities for more effective use of expensive hospital resources, for example, day surgery, and there have been long-running and ongoing plans to reduce acute beds in Inner London. But there is also, and inevitably, professional self-interest, concern for threats to autonomy and job security, and conflicting views about consumers' interests which are also uncovered when change is mooted. The attempts to deliver high quality health care for London were frustrated by the difficulty of maintaining high clinical ideals underpinned by values of equity, of unimpeded access and high quality outcomes in the context of scarce resources and established institutions.

# Part V

# The NHS, 2010–2015

# Part V

# Introduction

Chapters 13, 14 and 15 take up the up the story of the significant and controversial organisational reforms introduced by the coalition Government which was elected in May 2010. This reform process is traced from the Election manifestos of 2010 through the publication of the White Paper, *Liberating the NHS* in 2010 (DoH 2010c), the publication of the Health and Social Care Bill (2011), the passage of the Health and Social Care Act 2012 and subsequent events up until the publication of *The NHS Five Year Forward View* in October 2014 (NHS England 2014a).

# The Coalition Government, May 2010 to September 2011

The result of the 2010 General Election was that none of the parties achieved an overall majority, with the Conservative Party having the largest number of seats in a hung Parliament. Coalition talks began immediately between the Conservative and the Liberal Democrats in which the National Health Service (NHS) 'barely featured' (Timmins 2012: 53). At the end of five days, Mr Cameron became Prime Minister on 11 May 2010, and the leader of the Liberal Democrat Party, Mr Clegg, became Deputy Prime Minister in a new Conservative/Liberal Democrat coalition Government. The Secretary of State for Health would be Mr Lansley, who had been acting as Shadow Secretary of State for the previous six and a half years.

The coalition Government was responsible for a major new piece of legislation relating to the NHS, the Health and Social Care Act 2012, which came into force on 1 May 2013. The passage of this legislation was fraught with political conflict, almost equivalent to that engendered by the debates which surrounded the seminal period in the history of the NHS from the publication of the Beveridge Report (1942) to the passage of the National Health Service Act 1946 and its vesting day on 5 June 1948 (Chapters 3 and 4). The debates began soon after the General Election in May 2010, with the establishment of the coalition Government and the speedy publication of a White Paper.

These debates, from the publication of the Bill through to the final legislative and binding framework of the Health and Social Care Act 2012, were reported upon almost daily in most newspapers. Reports from journalists, leading articles and correspondence columns followed the publication of the Bill through to the Third Reading and the passage of the Act. The context of this discussion has been taken from official Government documents (White Paper, Bill) and Hansard, as well as from the speeches of politicians and the published concerns of voluntary organisations. This rich mix of running commentaries gives insight into this major reorganisation of the NHS. It reminds us yet again that while all sides in the debate have subscribed to a consensus supporting the necessity of the NHS, sharp conflicts and divisions have appeared concerning how to deliver health care, its cost, its quality and its place in public service priorities.

## General Election (May 2010)

One of the most controversial aspects of the reform was that its scale was unanticipated. Whilst all the major parties had something to say about the NHS in their manifestos, these seemed to indicate that the NHS would not be a source of major political debate after the General Election. One commentator observed that there appeared to be a 'high level of consensus between the three main parties' with all of them aspiring to a 'more locally accountable, responsive NHS' (Thorlby and Maybin 2010). There were, in addition, shared commitments to a tax-funded NHS, free at the point of use, to choice and more information for patients, to better access to general practitioners (GPs), especially out of hours, and to improving public health. All could see a continuing role for the independent sector in the NHS, although the Conservative Party appeared most enthusiastic about seeking, and being willing to support, a much greater involvement of independent and voluntary providers as a key element in their commitment to the continuous improvement of the quality of services to patients. The future of the NHS played little part in the televised debates between the leaders of the three main parties.

There were, however, some commitments that were not shared between the three parties. The Conservatives and Liberal Democrats proposed cutting many current government targets, to remove 'unnecessary bureaucracy', but were not clear about which of these would go. The Liberal Democrats proposed cutting the size of the Department of Health (DoH) in half, whilst the Conservatives proposed reducing the costs of NHS 'management' by a third, transferring the resources to front-line services, and cutting significantly the number of health quangos. The Conservatives also proposed reforming the National Institute for Clinical Excellence (NICE). Conservatives and Liberal Democrats both proposed giving every patient the right to register with the GP of choice. The Conservative and Labour Parties also proposed giving patients the right to choose any health care provider that would meet NHS standards of quality at NHS costs when booking a hospital appointment. Specific Conservative proposals included the establishment of an independent board to run the NHS, including the allocation of resources and the provision of commissioning guidelines, strengthening the power of GPs by enabling them to commission care on behalf of their patients, establishing a new national body to represent patients, and moving to a system of value-based pricing, so that all patients could have access to the drugs and treatments their doctors think they need. They also proposed to stop the forced closures of accident and emergency departments and maternity units, and to guarantee that health spending would increase in real terms in each year of the new Parliament. Specific Liberal Democrats proposals included the establishment of elected Local Health Boards which in time could raise local taxes to fund the NHS, prioritising dementia research, and improving access to counselling for people with mental health issues (Party political manifestos for 2010 General Election).

There was an agreed commitment to increasing funding for the NHS in real terms in each year of the Parliament, but according to a senior Liberal Democrat:

We didn't have any other discussions about the NHS of any kind during those few days. We didn't discuss reform ... I think if I am honest the assumption was that the NHS was going to be an area where a degree of stability would be expected [and that the Conservatives] didn't mention anything about the NHS during the talks other than the budget situation. And therefore I think there was probably an assumption on both sides, or certainly on our side, that what we would be seeing in the NHS is incremental change within the tramlines set by existing policy.

(Timmins 2012: 53)

## A programme for government

The next challenge was to construct a programme for the new Government and this was produced within ten days (Cabinet Office 2010). The resulting text described the NHS as 'an important expression of our national values' and the new Government restated the commitment of previous governments to a Service that is free at the point of use and available to everyone based on need. The commitments included more democratic participation, with transparent account-ability for patients and the driving up of standards. Primary Care Trusts (PCTs) would act as a 'champion of patients' and would include directly elected indi-viduals making them 'a stronger voice for patients locally'. Detailed data about 'the performance of healthcare providers' would be made available online and hospitals would be required to be 'open about mistakes and always tell patients if something has gone wrong'. Patients would have the power to choose any health-care provider that meets NHS standards and the right to choose to register with the GP they want, with no restrictions linked to location.

The aim was the 'continuous improvement of the quality of services to patients'. The greater involvement of independent, voluntary and community sector providers was seen as part of the improvement of the quality of ser-vices. Government success would be measured on 'the health results that really matter', for example, improving cancer survival rates, extending best practice on improving discharge from hospital and reducing delays to operations. There should be better access to local services, 'enabling community access to care and treatments', including improved access to primary care and preventative healthcare for those in disadvantaged areas. A 24/7 urgent care service would be developed, including GPs' out-of-hours service and the provision of a single telephone number for every kind of urgent care (Cabinet Office 2010). Another important aim was better value for money by maximising the number of day-case operations, greater access to talking therapies to bring down long-term costs for the NHS, which would minimise duplication. The latter was seen as one element in reducing the resources spent on 'administration', used inter-changeably with the term 'management', thereby cutting costs by one-third and reallocating those resources to 'front-line care', 'supporting doctors and nurses on the front line'. These front-line staff would have 'more control of their working environment' ... they need to be able to 'use their professional judgement about what is right for patients' including patients having access to the drugs and treatment their doctors think will help them. GPs would be enabled to commission care on behalf of their patients with PCTs commissioning 'those residual services that are best undertaken at a wider level, rather than directly by GPs'. Action to promote public health would include ensuring that the responsibilities of PCTs involved 'improving public health for people in their area' and a renegotiation of GP contracts to provide greater incentives to tackle public health problems. An ambitious strategy to prevent ill-health would include encouraging behaviour change to help people live healthier lives and take responsibility for their own health. With regard to health and social care, the need to break down the barriers between health and social care was noted, as it had been by many previous Governments. There were also commitments to establish a Commission on long-term care, to help elderly people to live at home for longer, and to prioritise dementia research. Lastly, there was a guarantee that health spending would increase in real terms in each year of the new Parliament (Cabinet Office 2010).

The new Government also sought to distance itself from what it considered to be characteristics of the preceding Labour Governments. These included freeing NHS staff from 'political micromanagement' and to this end the new Government would stop 'top-down reorganisations' and the 'centrally dictated closure of A&E and maternity wards'. They would give control to local authorities and local 'health watch' and a centralised Commissioning Board. This new, independent NHS Board would allocate resources and provide commissioning guidelines (Conservative manifesto), it would also advise the Secretary of State on the composition of PCT boards. It would also cut the number of health quangos. At this stage, there appeared to be no intention to abolish PCTs or to diminish their significance. Indeed, they were intended to include directly elected individuals, to act as champions of patients, and to have responsibilities in commissioning and public health. There was no mention of abolishing Strategic Health Authorities (SHAs) (Liberal Democrat manifesto). This would seem to be in accordance with the restatement of the commitment to stop top-down reorganisations. At this point, therefore, there was no indication of the scale of the changes to the structure of the Service to come and this, taken with statements in the Queen's Speech, led to accusations of broken promises.

## The Queen's Speech

The Queen's Speech (27 May 2010) included a reference to a Bill, the purpose of which was to implement the Government's proposals for a sustainable national framework for the NHS, to support a patient-led NHS focused on outcomes and to deliver the commitment to reduce bureaucracy. The main benefits of the proposed Bill were identified as creating an NHS led by clinical decision makers that would be more responsive to patients and foster continuous quality improvements. There would be more focus on patients, ensuring that they would genuinely share in making decisions about their care and have more choice and control. The intention was to shape a health care system which would drive up standards of care, eliminate waste and achieve outcomes that are amongst the best in the world. The main elements of the Bill included the establishment of an independent NHS Board to allocate resources and provide commissioning guidance, allowing GPs to commission services on behalf of their patients. The overriding assumption was that efficiency and outcomes would be improved by strengthening the role of the Care Quality Commission (CQC) and developing Monitor into an economic regulator to oversee aspects of access and competition in the NHS. Lastly, the intention was to take forward proposals to significantly cut the number of health quangos thereby helping to cut the cost of NHS administration by one-third.

## Before the White Paper

On 2 June 2010, the Shadow Health Secretary, Andy Burnham summarised what he saw as the achievements of the previous Labour Government. The NHS had been 'substantially rebuilt and renewed'. Waiting times were at an 'all-time low', infection rates were 'right down', and patient satisfaction with the NHS was at an all-time high. He noted that the Government had made a commitment to 'increase health spending in every year of this Parliament' but that this was at the expense of 'other crucial budgets on which the NHS depends'. It was, he suggested, a 'judgement that had more to do with political positioning than with sound and good policy-making, and they will come to regret it'. He concluded that the previous Government had left the NHS in its 'strongest ever position' and that 'we do not want to see the progress made in the NHS lost in the coming months and years' (House of Commons 2010a: col. 539).

On 8 June 2010, the new Secretary of State, Andrew Lansley, made a speech in which he argued for 'not just change, but a clear, consistent, coherent strategy for our health and social care services', with 'patients at the heart of everything, as patients, there should be no decision about us, without us'. The intention was to 'empower professionals to deliver' since 'engaged and empowered professionals will deliver results'. He did not appear to have noticed that it has always been the powerful professionals that have stood in the way of any rationalisation of health and redistribution of resources, and that doctors and health professionals have not been trained to be managers and bureaucrats. He continued by saying that the aim was a consistent and sustainable strategy for reform to provide long-term stability. This would include disempowering 'the bureaucracy, the Primary Care Trusts and the Strategic Health Authorities' (DoH 2010a). These references to PCTs and SHAs sounded quite radical, although at this stage it was still not clear to those outside the DoH what this would mean for the future of these institutions given that the coalition Government's *Our Programme for Government* (Cabinet Office 2010), published less than three weeks previously, had identified a continuing role for PCTs and had made no mention of changing the position of SHAs. Furthermore, the new NHS Board announced in the Queen's Speech was going to produce guidelines to allow, not require, GPs to commission care. Indeed, a subsequent publication of the DoH (21 June 2011) included references to PCTs and SHAs, which seemed to indicate a continuing role for both sets of institutions, giving no indication of the far more radical proposals that were to emerge with the publication of the White Paper (DoH 2010c: 9–10). This new document identified significant changes in-year and signalled substantial changes for the future with the intention of driving up standards, supporting professional accountability, and delivering better value for money. The document also stated that the NHS 'must also maintain a relentless focus' on achieving 'efficiency savings' of £15 billion to £20 billion over the next four years (DoH 2010b: 5, per Sir David Nicholson). The task of achieving these savings was to remain a feature of discussions about the NHS over the next three years. This was perhaps inevitable given the scale of the desired efficiency savings, but the challenge seemed especially daunting when set alongside the proposals that were set out in the new White Paper. For many observers this appeared to constitute just the sort of 'disruptive, top-down reorganisation' which they had been led to believe would not feature in the coalition Government's programme for the NHS. It was from 10 June 2010 onwards that reports began to appear from various sources (*Health Service Journal*, *Financial Times*, NHS Confederation) indicating that the reforms to be set out in the forthcoming White Paper would be far more radical than had been anticipated.

## The White Paper

The White Paper (DoH 2010c) was produced with remarkable speed, appearing 62 days after the formation of the coalition Government, just as public satisfaction with the NHS and its services was being recorded as its highest ever by both the British Social Attitudes Survey and the DoH's own surveys. The reforms contained therein were described as 'challenging and far-reaching' and it was estimated there would be managerial job losses of 20,000 and a transitional cost of £1.7 billion.

First, the Labour Government's policy of getting all hospitals to achieve Foundation Trust status and separating out the provider arms of PCTs was to continue. Second, proposals in the Conservative Party manifesto to establish a new patient organisation called Healthwatch would be implemented, and the role of NICE would be limited in its power to recommend which treatments the NHS should and should not adopt. Third, the coalition Government's Programme would be implemented through a planned reduction of management costs, but this figure had now jumped from the one-third to 45 per cent, and the establishment of Health and Well-Being Boards (HWBs) at the local authority level would 'join up' the commissioning of health care, social care and public health improvement, limiting the powers of ministers with regard to day-to-day NHS decisions. An 'autonomous' National Commissioning Board would be established.

The White Paper also included proposals which would not have been anticipated by those who had read the relevant party manifestos, followed the General Election campaign and read the coalition Government's *Our Programme for Government* (Cabinet Office 2010). A new economic regulator to oversee choice and competition would be set up, with patients to be given the choice of any willing provider, with no reference to NHS standards of quality, and public health would be given back to local government, the arrangement before 1974. Perhaps most dramatically, all GPs were to be involved in commissioning consortia, with SHAs to be abolished in 2012 and PCTs to go in 2013. *Our Programme for Government* (Cabinet Office 2010) had referred to enabling, not requiring, GPs to commission care on behalf of their patients and had identified continuing roles for PCTs.

Lastly, the White Paper had little to say about whether the transitional costs of these reforms could be successfully contained at the quoted figure of £1.7 billion, given the unprecedented £20 billion efficiency savings also required of the NHS over the next four years, and whether the implementation of both the reforms and the efficiency savings could be carried through with what was now to be a 45 per cent reduction in management costs. In these 'challenging and far-reaching reforms' (White Paper), the entire superstructure of the NHS was to be abolished. This was proposed in a relatively brief White Paper that had been produced very quickly.

On 19 July 2010, and over a period of eight days, the Government published a suite of consultation papers. Where consultations were seen as appropriate, the period set was 12 weeks (closing date: 11 October 2010). The papers were all titled *Liberating the NHS* with the following sub-titles: *Transparency in Outcomes, a Framework for the NHS*; *Commissioning for patients*; *Local democratic legitimacy in health*; *Regulating health care providers*; and *Report of the Arm's Length Bodies Review* (DoH 2010d).

The implications of the reforms set out in the White Paper generated the beginning of significant coverage in the press. Whilst the White Paper received a warm welcome in some circles, for example, the National Association of Primary Care, there were more who expressed reservations. These included professional groups, such as the British Medical Association (BMA), the chief executives of large hospitals (*Financial Times*, 15 August 2010), at least one very well-known figure in the Liberal Democrat Party (Shirley Williams, *The Guardian*, 14 August 2010) and think tanks, not only the King's Fund and the Nuffield Trust, but also the pro-market think-tank Reform (Seddon, *Daily Telegraph* 12 July 2010). In *The Independent* (13 August 2010: 4 and 6), there was a reference to the 'huge NHS reform gamble' and to 'nervous GPs' being 'given charge of 80 per cent of the NHS budget'. The *British Medical Journal* published an article by Chris Ham (King's Fund) on 17 July 2010 which suggested that while the Government's proposals 'take forward reforms set out by the Labour Government ... in 2002' (Ham 2010a) and developed further by Darzi in 2008, they were 'much more ambitious and risky' (Ham 2010a: 111). He concluded that despite 'the promise in the Coalition Agreement published in May not to embark on top-down structural changes, this is precisely what is happening, and the effects of major organisational upheaval will be felt for three years' (Ham 2010a: 212). Later in July, Sir David Nicholson (Chief Executive, NHS) wrote to all the senior leaders of the NHS in England to outline what they needed to do to implement the huge changes proposed in the White Paper. He acknowledged that 'there is a significant risk, during this transition period, of loss of focus on quality, financial and performance disciplines as organisations and individuals go through change'.

On 7 September 2010 in the House of Commons (2010b: col. 162), Andy Burnham was again to make the point that these 'plans were not in the Conservative or Liberal Democrat manifestos'. A few days later, Sir David Nicholson sent his second letter to NHS chief executives on the subject of managing the transition. This paved the way for PCTs to be merged as a means to make significant savings while implementing the proposals. There was further commentary on the proposals in the *British Medical Journal* on 18 September 2010, in which Chris Ham concluded that the proposed reforms involved 'the most radical transformation of the NHS since its inception' whilst noting also that the 'history of NHS reform is littered with examples of radical plans that have delivered much less than they have promised'. Might the White Paper 'suffer a similar fate without meticulous attention to transitional arrangements' especially when the imperative to cut management costs 'will remove many of the managers who in the past have been at the forefront of carrying policies into practice?' (Ham 2010b).

On 12 October 2010, it was reported that the majority of responses to the White Paper from health sector organisations had warned about the scale and the pace of the proposed reforms (Steve Ford, *Health Service Journal*). A fortnight later (26 October 2010), the Office of the National Managing Director of Commissioning Development published the Government's response to the White Paper as *Local democratic legitimacy – a consultation paper that accompanied the White Paper 'Liberating the NHS'* (DoH 2010h). It identified the core purpose of the new HWBs to be joining up commissioning across the NHS, social care, public health and other services. The HWBs would be established on a statutory basis in every upper tier local authority with effect from April 2013 and there would be a duty placed on relevant GP consortia to participate in the work of the Board as statutory members. There would also be a statutory duty on local authorities and GP consortia to undertake Joint Strategic Needs Assessment (JSNA) through HWBs and there would be a new legal obligation on NHS and local authority commissioners to have regard to the JSNA in exercising their relevant commissioning functions. However, there would be no statutory guidance on the nature of these strategies, nor would the HWB be required to submit them to the DoH, the NHS Commissioning Board or any other central organisation, although they would be made public. HWBs would be able to consider whether the commissioning arrangements for social care, public health and the NHS, developed by the local authority and GP consortia respectively, were consistent with the JSNAs but would have no authority to sign-off GP commissioning plans. Health scrutiny functions would remain within the local authority. At the time, the DoH intended to write to local authorities in the near future, inviting interest in becoming an early (HWB) implementer, taking the form of non-statutory partnership arrangements until April 2013.

After the end of the period of consultation, the Conservative Chair of the new Health Select Committee, Stephen Dorrell, was expressing his concern about the implications of combining massive efficiency savings with very significant organisational reforms (*Health Service Journal*, 17 November 2010). At a Health Committee hearing on 23 November 2010, Sir David Nicholson conceded that PCTs were 'in meltdown' as staff took voluntary redundancy and as PCTs were being merged into clusters (House of Commons 2010c: Oral and Written Evidence, 23 November 2010). Subsequently, Robert Creighton, a PCT chief executive who had been Principal Private Secretary to Virginia Bottomley when she had been Health Secretary, was reported as saying that he was doing nothing but interview people for jobs in the reshaped clusters and that staff were doing 'nothing about patient care, money, or anything else' (*Financial Times*, 8 October 2010).

The day before Sir David Nicholson was appointed chief executive designate of the new Commissioning Board, he was quoted as saying that he had been consulting management gurus around the world and no one 'could come up with a scale of change like the one we are embarking on at the moment', with one commentator saying that it is the 'only change management system you can actually see from space' (*Financial Times*, 9 September 2010). In the same newspaper eight days previously, one Number 10 insider was quoted as saying that the Secretary of State has all the answers 'when he is asked the questions about how the implementation of all this will work. We are just not sure they are the right ones' (*Financial Times*, 1 December 2010).

The delayed formal response to the consultation was eventually published on 10 December 2010 (DoH 2010e). This paper contained very little change, despite the 6,000 responses received during the consultation paper, many of which were critical of various aspects of the proposed reforms. Dr Hamish Meldrum, Chair of the Council of the BMA, said that 'most of the major concerns that doctors and many others have raised about the White Paper seem, for the most part, to have been disregarded' and the 'Government also seems to have ignored the warnings of the BMA and many others about the pace and scale of these reforms' (*The Times*, 16 December 2010: 14).

On 14 December 2010, a report of the House of Commons Health Select Committee (House of Commons 2010c) concluded that the Government's spending plans will test NHS and social services in England to the limit and add to the growing concerns about whether the NHS can meet the financial challenge it faces at the same time as implementing the structural changes set out in the Government's Health White Paper. Stephen Dorrell issued a press release noting that:

> Those figures represent a requirement for the NHS to deliver a 4 per cent efficiency gain, four years running. There is no precedent for efficiency

gains on this scale in the history of the NHS nor has any precedent been found for any healthcare system anywhere in the world achieving anything similar.

(House of Commons Press Release, December 2014)

On the same day, the NHS Confederation noted that 'NHS trusts are grappling with unprecedented efficiency savings, major management cuts and radical structural reforms. It's a mixture that is causing real anxiety among NHS leaders' and for Unite (the largest union in the country) the Select Committee's report was 'another stake in the heart' of the coalition Government's claim that the NHS was safe in its hands. There were continuing commentaries in the press. A leading article in *The Times* (16 December 2010: 2) observed that the increased power for GPs promised in the Conservative manifesto will be accompanied by the abolition of PCTs and called this a 'surprising decision and rather a worrying one. It involves moving very quickly, and at considerable costs, to a new system whose merits are unproven'. In the same edition, there was an article by Dr Wendy Savage, a well-known gynaecologist and campaigner for women's rights in childbirth. Dr Savage noted that whilst a Bill has not yet been laid before Parliament 'Mr. Lansley is acting as if it is law, with staff made redundant and pathfinder GP consortiums set up'. Three days later, *The Observer* reported that in a letter from the Independent Challenge Group, the body set up by the Government to scrutinise its spending review process, the Chief Secretary to the Treasury, Danny Alexander, was told that the vast bulk of the planned annual savings in the health budget of £16 billion 'may not be achievable'.

The year ended with a warning from Nigel Edwards, acting chief executive of the NHS Confederation (which represents hospitals and trusts) that 2011 could be the 'toughest' the NHS has faced in its 62-year history, unless ministers can successfully manage their ambitious £15 billion to £20 billion efficiency drive alongside reorganisation of NHS structures (*The Independent*, 29 December 2010), and two days later Dr Wollaston, a GP, Conservative MP and member of the Health Select Committee, warned that the proposed changes opened up the NHS to the stringencies of EU competition law. In the two days immediately prior to the publication of the Bill, there were two items in the *Financial Times*. On 16 January 2011, Nigel Edwards emphasised the degree to which the state 'will be withdrawing from the day to day management of health care' so that the NHS will become more like a regulated industry, such as the water and energy industries, and on the following day Philip Stevens suggested that the NHS reforms could become 'Cameron's poll tax'.

The Health and Social Care Bill was published on 18 January 2011 and given its First Reading in the House of Commons the following day. The Bill was presented by the Secretary of State (Lansley) and its importance was emphasised by the presence of the Prime Minister, the Deputy Prime Minister, the Chancellor of the Exchequer, and other Ministers, Vince Cable, Michael Gove, Eric Pickles, Danny Alexander, Simon Burns and Paul Burstow. In marked contrast to the slimline White Paper that had instituted the reform process, the Bill was vast. It was the longest piece of health legislation since the establishment of the NHS, being three times the size of the National Health Service Act 1946. On Radio 4, Shirley Williams said she had 'never ploughed through so much', having read the Bill, the impact statements, and the quality statements. She went on to say that she had 'been in politics a very long time and I don't think I'd ever seen a bill that was so incomprehensible, so detailed, so long, so impossible to understand, and I've seen some pretty complicated bills' (Radio 4, 'David Cameron's Big Idea'). The Bill was seen as fundamentally altering 'the landscape of health care in England', abolishing several NHS bodies and layers of management, changing the way NHS services are commissioned and establishing local government powers to scrutinise services and promote public health (House of Commons 2011a).

On the day of its publication, the national press included a range of comments expressing reservations about the Bill. The reforms were categorised as 'rushed' (Martin Beckford, *The Daily Telegraph*; Rachel Sylvester, *The Times*), risky and 'costly' (Sarah Boseley, *The Guardian*). They could 'blow our NHS apart' (Polly Toynbee, *The Guardian*), 'destroy the NHS' (*The Independent*: 6) and 'seriously damage health' (Rachel Sylvester, *The Times*). There was an unsurprising reference to the one thing upon which health professionals agreed, that the NHS did not need another reform. There were also further references to the breaking of previous promises not to impose further organisational change on the NHS, that the proposed reforms were not mentioned in the relevant General Election manifestos and therefore lacked a mandate from voters, and that the reforms were not included in the coalition Government's *Our Programme for Government* (Cabinet Office 2010) (*The Times*). For Lord Robert Winston, the reforms represented a 'broken promise' which constituted a 'threat to the care of patients' (*Daily Mirror*). According to the BMA, the Bill represented a 'massive gamble' and Dr Laurence Buckman, chair of the BMA's GPs' committee, commented that 'we too are very concerned about the scale and pace of these reforms. The speed of the reforms means primary care trusts are imploding as staff leave in droves and those managers who are left are focused on delivering the reforms rather than efficiency savings and the maintenance of patient care. Meanwhile alongside all these reservations about the reforms the latest redundancy and transition costs were estimated at between £2 and £3 billion by the King's Fund' (*Daily Mirror*, 18 January 2011).

On same day, the House of Commons Health Select Committee (Third Report, Session 2010–11, Commissioning) also noted the discrepancy between what was said in the coalition Agreement and what was included in the White Paper a few months later. The Committee also expressed concern about the scale and speed of the reforms taking place alongside the challenging demands of up to £20 billion in efficiency savings and at a time when expertise was being lost as two tiers of management were scrapped. They also commented that the proposals to hand more power to family doctors was increasing costs and leading to poor decisions on care. The outcome foreseen by the Committee was one of 'significant institutional upheaval' and 'widespread uncertainty'. Chris Ham of the King's Fund commented that the Committee were 'right to highlight the risk these reforms pose to delivering the key priority facing the NHS in the period ahead, finding up to £20 billion in productivity improvements to maintain services and improve the quality of care'.

The Bill received its Second Reading in the House of Commons on 31 January 2011, with opinion 'divided as to whether the Bill marks a radical and risky departure or a logical and sensible extension of earlier policies' (House of Commons 2011a). It was clear from the contributions of MPs to the Debate on the Second Reading that the main theme of Government supporters was that the Bill was merely a logical and sensible extension of earlier policies. For the Opposition, the Bill was characterised as 'radical and risky', the untrammelled consequences of which would be to destroy the values, principles and known delivery systems of the NHS and replace it with commercial or 'economic' values and an uncertain future in the face of efficiency savings. John Healey, now Labour's health spokesman, declared that the 'more people learn about … (the proposed reforms) … the less they like them' (House of Commons 2011c: col. 619).

From 8 February 2011 to 31 March 2011, the Bill was considered by a Public Bill Committee. Meanwhile, there was continuing commentary in the Press, much of it expressing reservations about the proposals in the Bill. In *The Times* (28 February 2011), Shirley Williams expressed concerns about the role of the new GP consortia and price competition. She followed other commentators in noting how well the NHS scored in international comparisons of health systems, for example that published recently by the Commonwealth Fund (Davis et al 2010). She said that it amazed her why 'we dismember this remarkably successful public service for an untried and disruptive reorganization'.

On 2 and 3 March 2011, the Letters page of *The Times* included various concerns expressed by members of the medical profession. Professor Sir Dillwyn Williams of Cambridge wrote that 'those who wish to use market forces in the health service must realise that the regulation needed to ensure co-operation in a multi-unit health service run for profit will be both very difficult and very expensive' and described the reforms as 'based on unproven theory that was not in either manifesto, and would introduce expensive and irreversible changes to the detriment of patient care'. On 4 March 2011, four letters, all from doctors, expressed various concerns including whether 'postcode variation will become the norm' after the reforms, whether those GPs who are good at their job will want to practise medicine, not become administrators, and that the community/hospital divide was not being addressed at all in the proposals.

On 16 March 2011, a leading article in *The Guardian* stated that when the BMA calls its first emergency meeting in 19 years and votes to denounce Government plans as 'dangerous', as it did yesterday, there is bound to be a stir. GPs are 'fuming as they discover that every English GP is going to get involved in commissioning, thanks to a decision made in Whitehall'. On the same day, Andrew Milburn reported that he had refused Andrew Lansley's invitation for him to chair the new commissioning board (*The Independent*). A fortnight later, a leader in *The Times* was concluding that 'the right NHS reforms are essential, but GP commissioning looks like the wrong one'. It continued by describing Mr Lansley's reforms as 'a dangerous leap in the dark, opposed by those whose support they most urgently require. Even in a best-case scenario, it could be that, after maximum cost and maximum upheaval, the NHS ends up broadly where it started' and a consistent theme of commentaries on the reforms is that the 'Government's plans for the NHS were not in the Conservative manifesto at the last election, and nor did they feature in the coalition agreement' (*The Times*, 30 March 2011).

The Committee stage of the Bill was completed on 31 March 2011. On 4 April 2011, a Report of the Health and Social Care Committee (House of Commons 2011d) warned of three key issues which had to be resolved. These were the guarantee of making GPs more accountable given their control of 80 per cent of the NHS budget, increasing the number of those to be involved in budgetary decision making and curtailing the powers of the regulator, Monitor, to encourage competition. All these were major issues in the parliamentary debates. On the same day, the Secretary of State made a statement to the House of Commons about NHS modernisation (House of Commons 2011e). The statement consisted of an update on the number of GP-led consortia, a total of 200 groups representing 87 per cent of the country and covering 4.5 million patients. Some 90 per cent of local authorities were willing to lead on the creation of HWBs.

However, the dramatic news on 4 April 2011 was the announcement of 'a natural break in the passage of the Bill to pause, listen and engage with all those who want the NHS to succeed, and subsequently to bring forward amendments to improve the plans further in the normal way' (House of Commons 2011e: col. 767). The Secretary of State, with the backing of the Prime Minister and the Deputy Prime Minister, announced the formal procedure for a listening exercise which would involve the setting up of what would be known as the NHS Future Forum. Whilst the Secretary of State claimed that listening has already occurred, and plans improved by strengthening the Oversight and Scrutiny process, with amendments in Committee 'to make it absolutely clear that competition will be on the basis of quality not price. Patients will choose and GPs will refer on the basis of comparisons of quality, not price'. He also stated that 'we recognise that the speed of progress has brought with it some substantive concerns, expressed in various quarters' (House of Commons 2011e: col. 767). Some are 'misplaced … based on misrepresentations … but we must recognise that some of them are genuine. We want to continue to listen to, engage with and learn from experts, patients and front-line staff within the NHS and beyond and to respond accordingly' (House of Commons 2011e: col. 767). He identified areas for improvement in the Bill, based upon the criticisms and uncertainties exposed by Parliamentarians, NHS professionals and the public and in particular those relating to choice, competition and 'the involvement of the private sector'. These were defined by the Secretary of State as a 'means to improve service for patients, not ends in themselves' (House of Commons 2011e: col. 767). He referred specifically to accident and emergency and major trauma services that should never be based on competition, and that private companies cannot be allowed to 'cherry pick' NHS activity thereby 'undermining existing NHS providers, and that competition must be fair'.

The Secretary of State was adamant in responding to the constant criticism from all sides about the potential difficulties faced by GPs in commissioning groups whereby there could arise a conflict of interest between their clinical judgement and the financial interests of the commissioners. Such GP commissioning groups 'cannot have a conflict of interest, are (to be) transparent in their decisions, are (to be) accountable not only nationally, but locally, through the democratic input of Health and Well-being Boards'. 'People want to know that the patient's voice is genuinely influential, through Health Watch and in commissioning. Doctors and nurses in the Service have been clear, they want the changes to support truly integrated services, breaking down the institutional barriers that have held back modernisation in the past' (House of Commons 2011e: col. 768).

The Secretary of State continued as follows:

> As I told the House on 16 March, we are committed to listening, and we will take every opportunity to improve the Bill. The principles of the Bill are that patients should always share in decisions about their care, that front-line staff should lead the design of local services, that patients should have access to whichever services offer the best quality, that all NHS trusts should gain the freedoms of foundation trust status, that we should take out day to day political interference, through the establishment of a national NHS commissioning board and through strong independent regulation for safety, quality and effectiveness, and that local government should be in the lead in public health strategy. Those are the principles of a world-class NHS which command widespread professional and public backing. All those principles will be pursued through the Bill and our commitment as a coalition Government to them is undiminished.
>
> We support and are encouraged by all those across England who are leading the changes nationally and locally We want them to know that they can be confident in taking this work forward. Our objective is to listen to them and support them, as we take the Bill through. No change is not an option. With an ageing and increasing population, new technologies and rising costs, we have to adapt and improve. Innovation and clinical leadership will be the key. We want to reverse a decade of declining productivity. We have to make productive care and preventive services the norm, and we must continue to cut the costs of administration, quangos and bureaucracy. The House knows my commitment to the National Health Service and my passion for it to succeed. To protect the NHS for the future must mean change, not in the values of the NHS, but through bringing forward and empowering leadership in the NHS to secure the quality of services on which we all depend.

Change is never easy, but the NHS is well placed to respond. I can tell the House today that the NHS is in a healthy financial position. Waiting times remain at historically low levels as promised under the NHS Constitution. Patients with symptoms of cancer now see a specialist more quickly than ever before.

(House of Commons 2011e: col. 768)

Responding for the Labour Opposition, John Healey reiterated the issue of what was in the manifestos:

Will the Health Secretary tell us why the Tories did not tell the people before the election about the biggest reorganization in NHS history? Why did he not tell the Liberal Democrats about the reorganisation before the Coalition Agreement was signed?

(House of Commons 2011e: col. 769)

He went on to describe the proposed changes as 'a reckless and ideological upheaval in the health service … whatever the Government may say or do now, there is no mandate for this change'. His view of the proposed 'Pause' was that doing 'the wrong thing more slowly is not the answer' given growing criticism of the proposals from doctors, nurses, patient groups, NHS experts, the Health Select Committee, the Liberal Democrats and peers of all parties in the House of Lords. He went on to say that there were 'fundamental flaws' in what the Government is doing, not just in what it is saying, expressing his concern that the 'Pause' might just be 'a public relations exercise rather than an exercise that will lead to real changes in the current plan' (House of Commons 2011e: col. 770).

Labour MPs expressed concerns during the debate about lengthening waiting times and deteriorating quality of services (House of Commons 2011e: col. 771, per B. Bradshaw), large scale redundancies (House of Commons 2011e: col.772, per K. Barron), the position of health promotion (House of Commons 2011e: col.773, per Meg Mann), the accountability of health service managers who will be re-employed during the 'Pause' (House of Commons 2011e: col. 774, per Lucian Berger), and the rationale for having this 'so-called natural break' now, after the Bill has passed Committee stage (House of Commons 2011e: col. 775, per M. Wicks). A Conservative MP, Andrew Perry, while supportive of GP commissioning, pointed out to the Secretary of State that there was undoubtedly concern about the exact role of the private sector in the NHS and urged the Secretary of State 'to use these next few weeks or months to ensure that in the country and if necessary in the Bill, we make it perfectly clear that the private sector will not be allowed to undercut or undermine our local hospitals'. Lansley responded to this point by saying that choice is to be based upon quality not price and that 'there cannot be a race to the bottom on price … we make it very clear in the legislation, it is important to set this out, that the commissioners of local services will also, through designating services, be able to ensure that where patients need services to be maintained and need continuity of services they can set that out themselves' (House of Commons 2011e: col. 777).

This 'natural break' became known as the 'Pause'. Whether this was truly a 'natural' break in the process of seeing a contentious Bill through to completion may be doubted. Some might interpret this 'Pause' as a reaction to the gathering storm of opposition to the principles underlying the Bill, as well as the dramatic impact of an out-of-hours GP event which resulted in the death of an elderly patient through a wrong dose by an overseas doctor carrying out a locum visit in February 2008. The Fields and Colin-Thome Report of the Inquiry into the incident was published in 2010 (DoH 2010f), but the concern about it raised the prospect of a further problem that might be associated with market forces operating in GP care which might mean it could be undertaken by 'any *willing* provider'. This approach was later amended under pressure, in the passage of the Bill, to 'any *qualified* provider'.

Thus on 6 April 2011, the Secretary of State, with the backing of the Prime Minister and the Deputy Prime Minister, announced the formal procedure for the 'Pause'. The Listening Exercise would involve the setting up of what would be known as the NHS Future Forum. This announcement was preceded (the previous day) by the Health Select Committee (*The Times*, 6 April 2011); House of Commons 2011d, 2011e; Prime Minister's Office 2011). It was the Committee's view that the Government's plans to reform NHS commissioning needed to be changed significantly. The Committee proposed that representatives of nurses, hospital doctors, public health experts, social care professionals, and an elected member nominated by the local authority should all be involved as decision makers alongside GPs in NHS commissioning. They believed that these changes were vital to enable the NHS to meet the unprecedented challenges it faces in finding 4 per cent annual efficiency savings over the following four years, the so-called Nicholson challenge. They welcomed the extension of the health scrutiny powers of local authorities. It was their view that NHS commissioners should be given a legal obligation to consult Health Watch, and that Health Watch should have a legal obligation to consult with patients and patient representative bodies. All NHS commissioners should have a Chief Executive and a Finance Director, both of whom should be members of the Board.

All NHS commissioners should have an independent chair appointed by the NHS National Commissioning Board. Boards of NHS Commissioners should be required to meet in public, publish their papers and comply with the rules of the Committee on Standards in Public Life with regard to conflicts of interest amongst board members, the 'Nolan principles'. NHS Commissioners should be held to account by the new National Commissioning Board through a clear system of authorisation and assurance. All these Boards should be referred to as NHS Commissioning Authorities. Given these proposals, they considered there was no need to continue with the establishment of HWBs or to separate the commissioning of primary and secondary care. NHS Commissioning Authorities should be responsible for commissioning primary, secondary and community health care, as well as creating robust links with social care. Stephen Dorrell, the Chair of the Committee, commented as follows:

> Ever since 1948 the NHS has suffered from an artificial distinction between primary and secondary care. Instead of entrenching this distinction further, this is an opportunity to abolish it for good, and create a single, integrated health service which is able to provide properly coordinated health & social care to all patients. It is an opportunity to deliver greater efficiency and high quality at the same time. It is a 'win-win,' what is the argument against?
>
> (House of Commons 2011e)

Also on 5 April 2011, the Prime Minister's Office published *Working together for a stronger NHS* (Prime Minister's Office 2011). Given that there was supposedly a 'natural break' before the Bill entered its final stages in Parliament, the intention was to take this time to pause, listen and reflect on how to improve the Government's plans. However it also reiterated that 'no change is not an option' (Prime Minister's Office 2011: 2) and restated what the Government saw as some of its key themes, 'taking power away from the bureaucrats and giving it to the professionals' (Prime Minister's Office 2011: 9) in a health service that is 'truly local' (Prime Minister's Office 2011: 14) so that local communities have a 'clear say in changes to essential services (like A&E and maternity units)' (Prime Minister's Office 2011: 14), that choice was 'absolutely crucial to driving improvements in the NHS' (Prime Minister's Office 2011: 10), that real patient power was 'long overdue' (Prime Minister's Office 2011: 10) and perhaps most controversially in terms the debate thus far, that 'we are committed to going further in opening up the NHS to qualified providers' (Prime Minister's Office 2011: 13). The following day, the Government announced the establishment of an NHS Future Forum as an independent advisory panel (to be chaired by Professor Steve Field) to report back on what they had heard and to offer advice to the Prime Minister, the Deputy Prime Minister and the Secretary of State. From this point on commentators would refer to this period as the 'Pause', the Listening Exercise and the Futures Forum.

## The NHS Future Forum

The period in which the NHS Future Forum would accept evidence ended on 31 May 2011, an eight-week period of consultation. The group reported its findings and recommendations to the Government on 13 June 2011 (NHS Future Forum 2011a). Four core themes of the NHS Listening Exercise were identified as being choice and competition, clinical advice and leadership, patient involvement and public accountability, and education and training (NHS Future Forum 2011a: 14). The Forum identified fears of privatisation in the evidence they had reviewed concerning choice and competition and concluded that the Bill 'contained insufficient safeguards against cherry-picking and was not sufficiently clear that competition would only exist when it served the interests of patients not profit' (NHS Future Forum 2011a: 9). The Government 'should not seek to increase the role of the private sector as an end in itself' (NHS Future Forum 2011a: 11). Similarly, competition 'should never be pursued as an end in itself' and the role of Monitor in relation to 'promoting competition should be significantly diluted' (NHS Future Forum 2011a: 6). The 'primary duty' of Monitor to 'promote competition' should be removed from the Bill and the Bill should be amended to support 'choice, collaboration and integration' (NHS Future Forum 2011a: 11).

With regard to clinical advice and leadership the Forum was clear that the 'Secretary of State must remain ultimately accountable for the NHS' with the Bill 'amended to make this clear' (NHS Future Forum 2011a: 10). Experienced managers 'must be retained in order to ensure a smooth transition and support clinical leaders in tackling the financial challenges facing the NHS' (NHS Future Forum 2011a: 11). The Forum was clear that services 'must change in order to meet the needs of local populations' (NHS Future Forum 2011a: 6). It was 'right that GPs should take responsibility for the health of their local populations and the financial and quality consequences of their clinical decisions through a comprehensive system of commissioning consortia' but they 'cannot and should not do this on their own' (NHS Future Forum 2011a: 6). 'The Bill should require commissioning consortia to obtain all relevant multi-professional advice to inform commissioning decisions and the authorisation and annual assessment process should be used to assure this' (NHS Future Forum 2011a: 11). In addition 'multi-speciality clinical senates should be established to provide strategic advice to local commissioning consortia, Health and Well-being Boards and the NHS Commissioning Board' (NHS Future Forum 2011a: 11). The Forum also noted the importance of 'independent, expert public health advice at every level of the system' and advised against establishing Public Health England fully within the Department of Health' (NHS Futures Forum 2011a: 12). In addition, there had been 'too much focus on different parts of the system, GPs, hospitals, public health, and insufficient attention to how they all join up to provide the integrated care that patients need' (NHS Future Forum 2011a: 9). Concerns 'around integration came up time and time again' (NHS Future Forum 2011a: 20) and the Forum 'would expect to see the NHS Commissioning Board actively supporting the commissioning of integrated packages of care' (NHS Future Forum 2011a: 20), concluding that 'collaboration is essential for the delivery of high quality health and care in the future NHS' (NHS Future Forum 2011a: 21). There was a 'growing consensus' around the potential of HWBs (NHS Future Forum 2011a: 20–1) and it was recommended that the legislation should strengthen the role of these Boards, especially with regard to health and social care integration, meeting the needs of local population and of vulnerable people (NHS Future Forum 2011a: 12). The boundaries of local commissioning consortia 'should not normally cross those of local authorities' (NHS Future Forum 2011a: 12).

On the subjects of patient involvement and public accountability, the Forum noted that the 'importance and relevance of the NHS Constitution became increasingly apparent' (NHS Future Forum 2011a: 19) and that they were 'united in its support for the enduring values of the NHS and the rights of patients and citizens as set out in the Constitution' (NHS Future Forum 2011a: 19). They recommended that the Bill 'should be amended to place a new duty on the NHS Commissioning Board and Commissioning consortia to actively promote the NHS Constitution' (NHS Future Forum 2011a: 10). The Board, the consortia, Monitor and the CQC 'should all set out how they are meeting their duty to have regard to the NHS Constitution in exercising their functions in their annual reports' (NHS Future Forum 2011a: 19). Building on the NHS Constitution, the Commissioning Board and the Secretary of State 'should, following full public consultation, give a 'choice mandate' to the NHS Commissioning Board setting out the parameters for choice and competition in all parts of the service. A Citizens Panel, as part of Healthwatch England, should report to Parliament on how well the mandate has been implemented and further work should be done to give citizens a new 'Right to challenge' poor quality services and lack of choice' (NHS Future Forum 2011a: 11). There must be 'transparency about how public money is spent and how and why decisions are made and the outcomes being achieved at every level of the system' (NHS Future Forum 2011a: 9). The Bill should 'require commissioning consortia to have a governing body that meets in public with effective independent representation to protect against conflicts of interest. Members of the governing body should abide by the Nolan principles of public life' (NHS Future Forum 2011a: 10). 'The assessment of the skills, capacity and capability of commissioning consortia must be placed at the heart of the authorisation and annual assessment process' (NHS Future Forum 2011a: 11). 'The declaration of 'no decision about me, without me' must become a reality, supported by stronger and clearer duties of involvement written into the Bill' (NHS Future Forum 2011a: 10).

With regard to the education and training of the workforce 'more time is needed to get this right' (NHS Future Forum 2011a: 9 and 14), and overall the Chair of the Forum identified one of the main messages to the Government that the 'aim of making improvement in quality and health care outcomes the primary purpose of all NHS funded care' was 'universally supported' (NHS Future Forum 2011a: 6). Lastly, everyone involved in the listening exercise had 'agreed that the values of the NHS must endure and the NHS must continue to be a national institution of which patients, the public and staff alike are proud' (NHS Future Forum 2011a: 19; 2011b, 2011c, 2011d, 2011e).

Parliamentary procedures for considering the final stages of the Bill commenced following the presentation of the report of the NHS Future Forum and the Health and Social Care Bill was reintroduced to the House of Commons following the 'acceptance' of the findings of the Forum's report (DoH 2011a; House of Commons 2011f). The Futures Forum allowed all sides in the debate to draw breath and prepare their arguments for the final stages of the Parliamentary process. The House of Commons considered the remaining stages of the Bill from 28 June 2011 to 14 July 2011. From 6 to 7 September 2011, the Report Stage took place in the House of Commons before the Bill moved for discussion to the House of Lords. The reception of the Bill by the House of Lords demonstrated yet again the conflict between the major parties over the contents of the Bill and its consequences for the NHS if it became law in its current form.

## Conclusion

> At the British Pharmaceutical conference in 2009, in front of several hundred pharmacy and scientific colleagues, Mr. Lansley informed me, in response to a direct question, that no major NHS reorganization was planned. His reply was … surprisingly clear and unequivocal. So was the palpable sigh of relief among my 700 or so colleagues.
>
> (Brian Curwain, Letter, *The Observer*, 29 June 2014: 38)

Following a significant period of reform under the previous Labour Governments (1997–2010), it seemed that only some minor reforms would be expected from all parties. As a result, the NHS did not feature significantly in the 2010 General Election campaign. In addition, the Service continued to fare very well in inter-national comparisons of health care systems, whilst in the UK it was achieving its highest ever levels of public satisfaction as recorded by both the DoH and the British Social Attitudes Survey. This situation was not changed with the publication of the coalition Government's *Our Programme for Government* (Cabinet Office 2010). The new Government would stop top-down reorganisations and the role of PCTs, a particularly controversial feature of the reforms unveiled in the subsequent White Paper, seemed assured. With the addition of 'directly elected individuals', PCTs were identified as acting as 'champions of patients' with responsibilities for improving public health for people in their areas.

The publication of a relatively brief White Paper in July 2010 outlined a set of reforms described as 'challenging and far-reaching'. GPs may have anticipated being enabled to play a more significant role in commissioning care, but instead found that they would be required to commission care. As a result, rather than pursuing their role as patients' champions the PCTs were to be abolished along with RHAs. Allied to these changes, there would be a very substantial reduction in management costs. In addition, the reforms set out in the White Paper were to be introduced alongside substantial, and possibly unrealistic, efficiency savings, the latter being described by the House of Commons Health Select Committee as being without precedent not only in the history of the NHS but also in any other health care system anywhere in the world.

These unanticipated reforms were immediately the subject of considerable and continuing press commentaries, much of it critical. Reservations were also being expressed by the health care professions, patient groups, NHS experts, MPs and peers across the political spectrum and the House of Commons Health

Select Committee. Concerns included both the scale and the pace of the proposed reforms, especially when combined with unprecedented 'efficiency savings' and an equally unprecedented diminution of management costs and presumed loss of management expertise. Whilst the reforms unveiled in the White Paper were obviously a surprise to many both inside and outside the NHS, there was another surprise to come. Almost ten months after the publication of the White Paper, there was the very distinctive decision to propose a 'natural break in the passage of the Bill. This 'natural break' came to be known as the 'Pause'. The events leading up to the passage of the Health and Social Care Act 2012 are the subject of the next chapter.

# Chapter 14

# The Health and Social Care Bill, September 2011 to March 2012

In September 2011, the Constitution Committee reported on the Health and Social Care Bill (House of Lords 2011a). Their conclusion was that it was not clear whether the existing political and legal structures which were necessary to ensure accountability for the National Health Service (NHS) would continue to operate as before, if the Bill was enacted in its current form. The Bill was thus unlikely to have an easy passage through the House of Lords. The First Reading in the Lords was on 8 September 2011.

During the Second Reading on 11/12 October 2011 (House of Lords 2011b), Baroness O'Loan, a cross-bench peer, thought that 'The level of concern about this Bill must be virtually unprecedented'. Baroness Masham of Ilton, another cross-bench peer told the House 'we have before us a monster of a Bill. It is complex and confusing'. Lord Clinton-Davis asked, 'Why was none of this mentioned in the Conservative manifesto at the election' (House of Lords 2011b: col. 1472).

Earl Howe, the Parliamentary Under Secretary of State at the Department of Health (DoH), described the Bill as one of 'profound importance for the quality and delivery of health and care in England, for patients and for all those who care for them' and that it is 'quite rightly the subject of intense scrutiny'. In his opening statement, he reiterated support for the 'founding principles of the NHS', that it be a comprehensive service, free at point of use, regardless of ability to pay, and funded from general taxation, and that the Service should aspire to highest standards of service for all our citizens. He then restated the familiar set of challenges that had faced the NHS since its inception. They were rising demand from a growing and ageing population, the demographic reason, with its consequent increase in long-term conditions, rising expectations of patients relating to the availability of new drugs and treatments and the promises of high-tech medicine and the financial pressures associated with 'inexorably rising costs of providing services against an increasingly constrained budget' (House of Lords 2011b: col. 1469).

Earl Howe identified a familiar response to these challenges, the need to ensure maximum efficiency in the use of scarce resources. He also acknowledged 'the need to make the service patient-centred' (House of Lords 2011b: col. 1469) which had certainly been at the forefront of government statements about the Service for at least two decades. He claimed that the distance between the patient and the professional and 'the layers of administration which consume so much of the NHS budget' (House of Lords 2011b: col. 1470) were obstacles to achieving maximum efficiency with a patient-centred service. Again, this was certainly not the first time that politicians had homed in on some combination of the seemingly interchangeable categories of NHS administration, NHS bureaucracy and NHS management as being burdensome and counter-productive to the aims of the Service.

The Government's plans for the NHS were said to be 'focused on three main themes: accountability, efficiency and quality, keeping at the centre the most important theme of all, the interests of the patient' (House of Lords 2011b: col. 1470). The aim was to 'shift the balance of power from politicians to patients, through increased choice and information, and to doctors and health professionals, giving them real budgets and empowering them to use these resources in a cost-effective way to drive up quality ... the potential is truly enormous: allowing doctors, nurses, hospital specialists, social services and other professionals the freedom to design care pathways that are integrated, and to commission them on behalf of their patients will, we firmly believe, transform the quality of care and treatment that the service delivers' (House of Lords 2011b: col. 1471). He emphasised that 'outcomes' not 'processes' were the most meaningful way of measuring success.

In his opening statement, Earl Howe also attempted to counter the frequently voiced criticism that the Government lacked a democratic mandate for their proposals. He claimed that this mandate was 'absolutely clear' (House of Lords 2011b: col. 1471), having been laid out in various Conservative and Liberal Democratic publications from 2006 onwards, including a White Paper, 'in our own manifestos at the last election, the Coalition agreement and, finally, a Government White Paper from which the Bill directly stems' (House of Lords 2011b: col. 1471). He proceeded to outline the most important points of the proposed reforms. 'To define the functions and duties of every element in the chain of accountability within a reformed health care system' (House of Lords 2011b: col. 1471), so that the NHS would no longer be subject to change by a directive from the Secretary of State but change could only come about by parliamentary approval. Regulations and directions would now be covered by Statute. The savings required by the Nicholson challenge, £20 billion over the next four years, could be achieved through 'system wide change and the measures in the Bill' (House of Lords 2011b: col. 1472). Furthermore, there appeared to be an assumption that the reforms would yield additional savings, beyond those required to meet the Nicholson challenge, and that these could be 'ploughed back into patient care'.

This 'system wide change' involved 'liberating the NHS to work better and be more accountable to patients', streamlining the architecture of the NHS 'to make it more efficient and transparent' and 'creating a public health service ... configured to tackle the major challenges to the nation's health and well-being over the years ahead' (House of Lords 2011b: col. 1472). In particular, the commissioning powers for 'the bulk of the NHS commissioning budget', 80 per cent, would lie with local Clinical Commissioning Groups (CCGs), comprised of general practitioners (GPs). These CCGs had been operating in shadow form since October 2011 (clause 7 of the Bill). The creation of Healthwatch, nationally and locally, was seen as a way of empowering patients with regard to how local services were to be commissioned, provided and scrutinised (House of Lords 2011b: col. 1472) (clauses 178–186 of the Bill). Locally, Healthwatch was to be based on existing Local Involvement Networks but 'with added clout', while the organisation, Healthwatch England, would become a committee of the Care Quality Commission (CQC) so that the voice of patients is heard at 'the very heart of health and social care regulation'. In addition, the creation of local Health and Well-Being Boards (HWBs) was designed to meet the idea of a local democratic mandate for health care provision having as their main purpose the assessment of health and social care needs of a local area with a typical HWB to be comprised 'as a minimum' (House of Lords 2011b: col. 1471) of representatives from CCGs, social care, public health and patient groups, including local Healthwatch, plus elected representatives. Local CCGs would be 'required to have regard to them when preparing their commissioning plans'.

The local authorities were to become 'the hubs for commissioning and delivering public health led by Directors of Public Health and supported by a ring-fenced budget' and there would be a new executive agency, Public Health England, to bring together 'health protection functions alongside local authority – joined up public health strategies' (House of Lords 2011b: cols 1474–5). All DoH arm's length bodies would be streamlined and those no longer required would be abolished. The National Institute for Clinical Excellence and the NHS Information Centre would be made more secure through primary legislation.

For Foundation Trust hospitals, the proposal was to remove the private patient income cap, 'without jeopardising the NHS focus' and so generate income 'which can be deployed for the benefit of NHS patients' (House of Lords 2011b: cols 1473–4). This proposal was contained in clauses 148–177 of the Bill. With regard to the Independent Sector Treatment Centres, Earl Howe suggested that they did not operate on a level playing field, with guarantees and price subsidies, not available to the public sector. This would change with Monitor to be given a new role as a 'sector specific regulator' for the health service with duties and powers 'to bear down on unfair competition, conflicts of interest and unsatisfactory pricing' (House of Lords 2011b: col. 1474).

Earl Howe completed his opening speech on the Bill by referring to the Listening Exercise (the 'Pause') as suggesting 'widespread agreement for the key principles of our policies' and 'a shared view among professionals about the way those principles should be put into practice'. He also referred to the 'significant scrutiny' of the Bill 'in the other place' (the House of Commons). In total, the Bill's First Committee Stage lasted longer than any Bill in the past nine years (a total of 28 sittings). After the Report of the NHS Future Forum (2011a), a further 12 sittings in Committee took place. This scrutiny during 40 sittings was more than any other Public Bill between 1997 and 2010. Earl Howe summarised his commendation of the Bill thus:

> The case for change is clear and compelling, and I am personally in no doubt that the changes set out in this Bill are right for our NHS and, more importantly, right for patients. I hope very much that your Lordships, in reserving your powers to scrutinise the detail of the Bill with your usual care, will wish to endorse the ideas and the vision that it presents. This is a Bill with but a single purpose: to deliver for the long term, a sustainable NHS, true to its founding principles. It is on that basis that I am proud to commend this Bill to the House, and I beg to move.
>
> (House of Lords 2011b)

One hundred other peers spoke in the debate, which lasted for over 16 hours. Fifty-three of these brought their knowledge, skills and values from at least five backgrounds, some discrete, but often overlapping.

The first group, 17 peers, had professional experience in various aspects of health care. Some had been practising physicians and surgeons, and indeed some were still in practice. Some had held high office in their profession, as leaders of Royal Colleges or professional associations. Their contributions were critical in pointing out the issues that would arise during the implementation of the proposed reforms. The second group, eight, had been health ministers and civil servants responsible for health policy, administering the service, or being accountable for so doing. The third group, nine, was made up of members with 'pressure group' or quango and charity experience. Their main concerns focused upon the impact of the Bill upon these sectors and their work. The fourth group, eight, consisted of 'other politicians with special interests in health'. The fifth group, 11, did not have the background of the first four groups, but either supported a generalised view that the NHS needed reforming, or took the view that, although all was not always well in this public service, the principles upon which the NHS was based, universal coverage, comprehensive services wherever possible, paid for from general taxation and the absence of any link between ability to pay and receiving health and social care according to professionally defined need, were so obviously sound, practical and representative of highly ethical values in action, that any 'reform' would run the risk of well-meant means confounding value-based ends.

Of those who supported the Bill, the main arguments rested upon the opportunity in the Bill for the integration of health and social care, thus creating an atmosphere, a set of principles and a system that would be patient-centred, and would use the 'pathways' so created for the patient journey between seamless health and social care organisations, primary and secondary, or acute hospital care. Another key argument deployed was the relocation of public health expertise through Directors of Public Health and their staff returning to the local authority they had left in the 1974 reorganisation. This move, it was thought, would allow public health staff to deploy epidemiological intelligence to inform the Joint Strategic Needs Assessments used by local authorities in conjunction with Primary Care Trusts (PCTs), and later, CCGs, of the major health issues within their jurisdictions. The placing of public health within the local authority was therefore seen as a key plank in providing the HWBs with health status data, targeting health inequalities and justifying the decisions of CCGs. Most of the opposition to the Bill was based upon the following arguments.

The Nicholson Challenge was that the NHS should save £20 billion over the lifetime of this Parliament. In a period of austerity, with the need to make savings, this was not the right time to reorganise, especially given the proposed loss via redundancies of management skills. This meant the loss of the sort of 'institutional memory' skills required to enable the NHS cope with the unprecedented 'efficiency savings'. Indeed, by the time of the Debate, many of these redundancies had already occurred in preparation for the 'new world' after April 2013 when it was intended that the Bill would become law. Given their intended demise, groups of PCTs had now come together in 'clusters', with 'shadow' CCGs, to prepare the way for the Appointed Day and to keep the Service running in the meantime. This led to related concerns about the 'shadow' CCGs drawing on managerial and financial skills from either re-employing recently redundant NHS managers or from private sector organisations. Thus some of the presumed savings from the massive cuts in NHS bureaucracy would be nullified to some extent, especially in the short-run, via redundancy and re-employment costs. Lord Rodgers of Quarry Bank (Lib Dem) expressed a 'deep concern about whether the NHS can deliver greater efficiency and quality while overhauling the NHS structures in the Bill' especially given the scale of the proposed reforms, described by Lord Low as 'the most radical reorganisation of the National Health Service since it was founded over 60 years ago'.

There was the continuing issue, already raised in Parliament and widely featured in previous press comments, that the proposed reforms, and therefore the defining characteristics of the whole Bill, had not been published in the Conservative or the Liberal Democrat manifestos in May 2010 or in the printed coalition Agreement. This accusation raised the important question of whether the Addison-Salisbury convention could be invoked. This convention states that the Opposition should not put down 'wrecking amendments' if Bills reflected the manifesto commitments of the Government of the day. The reforms represented something that the electorate had been told would not happen, that there would not be another 'top-down' reorganisation of the NHS. Thus Lord Rea, a doctor, moved that 'this House declines to give the Bill a Second Reading, in the light of the statement in the Coalition Agreement that we will stop the top-down reorganisations of the NHS that have got in the way of patient care' (House of Lords 2011b: cols 1476–77).

Baroness Thornton, the Opposition spokesperson on health and social care in the House of Lords argued that 'the Government have no mandate for such a drastic change in the way the Bill is suggesting', because of the absence of a manifesto reference (House of Lords 2011b: cols 1479–83).

Lord Rea was also critical of the White Paper, *Equity and Excellence: Liberating the NHS* (DoH 2010c) 'for not preparing us for the Bill' (House of Lords 2011b: col. 1477) and for opening 'the door for the market and independent sector to play a bigger role in the National Health Service' (House of Lords 2011b: col. 1477). He also questioned whether the implementation of changes in the Service should have begun before the Bill's passage through Parliament, referring to Shirley Williams' article on this point in the *British Medical Journal* (Coombes 2011). In Lord Owen's view 'A Select Committee is the only procedure that can look at the complexity of this new relationship that we are trying to establish' (House of Lords 2011b: col. 1498). Lord Owen's final point was to predict that some Trust hospitals will fail, as will some commissioning groups, and the public would not accept that such a failure would be dealt with by a quango, the Chairman of the National Commissioning Board. Therefore:

> this is not a blocking measure … it would be an all-party, unanimous Select Committee …
>
> Cherish the fact that the NHS is one of the most popular public institutions in our country. Look hard at how we can retain that. Do not believe that, in adversarial debates across the floor of this House, you can get the balance right, the new balance that is needed for the Secretary of State for Health
>
> (House of Lords 2011b: col. 1498)

Baroness Kingsmill (Lab), the former deputy chairman of the Competition Commission, expressed 'grave anxieties that we are all going too far, too fast'.

Lord Low was concerned about 'the proliferation of bureaucracy required to administer the Byzantine commissioning and contracting process'. Baroness O'Loan (cross-bench) referred to the 'creation of the internal market so many years ago (when), we saw change of a much lesser kind, and it resulted in the creation of hundreds of new bodies which accelerated the cost of NHS administration over the year'. Lord Low also worried about the 'fragmentation of services and the difficulties of integrated planning and delivery across health, social care and health-related services, especially given 300–450 clinical commissioning groups in future, compared with the current 152 PCTs'. Baroness Masham of Ilton also feared 'that the service might become fragmented'. Baroness Kennedy of The Shaws (Lab) suggested that 'there will be a lack of transparency'.

Baroness Kingsmill (Lab), the former deputy chairman of the Competition Commission, said she was:

> not impressed by the regulatory mechanisms in the Bill and I am not impressed by Monitor. It seems at the moment to be a somewhat underpowered

regulator ... We do not do a good job of regulating our public services in this country. We have only to look at the railways to see that ... It would be entirely appropriate for us to have a Select Committee where people could come forward and give proper evidence, have it heard in public and televised if necessary so that a full and clear debate about these issues could be had, not simply rush through with the inadequate scrutiny we have had both in the other place and here.

(House of Lords 2011b)

Lord Patel of Bradford believed that the CQC:

has a third less funding that those bodies it replaced. It is currently being asked to cover 18,000 care homes and 400 NHS trusts and will now be asked to take on responsibility for GP practices and the yet-to-be-determined number of 'any qualified providers' who may be pressing for registration, all of which will once again distract the CQC from its vital inspection role.

(House of Lords 2011b)

Lord Rea challenged Earl Howe on Britain's health record by referring to John Appleby's King's Fund paper in the *British Medical Journal*, suggesting that Britain's health record 'is improving faster than any other country in the EU' (Appleby 2011).

Baroness Thornton, the Opposition spokesperson on health and social care in the House of Lords claimed that 'it will change the NHS from a health system into a competitive market, turning patients into consumers and patient choice into shopping ... Most critically it will turn our healthcare into a traded commodity' (House of Lords 2011b: cols 1479–83). Baroness O'Loan maintained that 'this is effectively unplanned, unstructured privatisation, with the attendant enormous difficulties of regulation'. Baroness Kennedy of The Shaws (Lab) claimed that:

Market competition in healthcare does not improve outcomes. The US has the highest spending in the world and the outcomes are mediocre. The US over diagnoses, over treats and over tests. Why? Because that increases revenue. You change the nature of the relationship between doctors and their patients. You get more lawsuits and doctors therefore practise defensive medicine. You ruin your system.

(House of Lords 2011b)

Baroness O'Loan argued that:

What is profoundly important is that reform is carried out following proper consultation with a clear mandate with properly costed and analysed resourcing decisions and with the support of service-users ... and of professional bodies that will have to implement the change. I have not seen any evidence to suggest that is the case in the Bill.

(House of Lords 2011b)

Lord Patel of Bradford also had 'serious reservations about the impact of the Bill in a number of areas: on commissioning, public health, integration with social care, service-user engagement and quality and safety'. A fair summary of the entire opposition case against the Bill is contained in Baroness Thornton's speech as follows:

> Nothing suggested wholesale dismantling of the structure of the NHS; nothing about the biggest quango in the world being created, the NHS Commissioning Board; nothing about the intention to allow £60 billion of taxpayers' money to be spent by GPs, originally on their own and now through clinical commissioning; nothing about the creation of a huge bureaucratic economic regulator, the new Monitor; and nothing about many other parts of the Bill, some of which is good and some less so. There is no mandate for this Bill. That is a serious constitutional issue for this House, which is signalled by us by, for example, the Constitution Committee report ... so, no mandate, no evidence, no support ... [for this] most significant [piece] of legislation that we are going to see in the whole of this Parliament.
>
> (House of Lords 2011b: col. 1480)

Earl Howe was unable to accept either the Rea or Owen/Hennessey amendments. He agreed with Lord Hennessy that the NHS 'is the nearest thing that this country has to institutionalised altruism' and that its delivery of high quality care is a 'product of the investment made by the previous Government (which) has contributed significantly to that quality'. But he said that, without reform, variations in quality and outcomes cannot be eliminated, and that the sustainability of the NHS over the next five, ten or 20 years has to be assured. He also said that with scarce resources, empowering commissioners will cut the cost of NHS administration by one-third. He reassured the House that the Minister's ultimate responsibility for the NHS, Ministerial accountability, would in no way be diluted. He concurred with the views of Lord Warner, a Minister of Health in the previous Labour Government, Lady Bottomley, a previous Secretary of State for Health, and Lady Murphy, formerly a Chief Executive of a Trust, and a psychiatrist, that for many years 'the Secretary of State [has] not directly provide[d] services himself'. Earl Howe re-emphasised the statutory duty of the Secretary of State to promote a comprehensive service and a duty to use his powers to secure the provision of such a service. Earl Howe suggested that the Secretary of State would carry out these duties by mandating the NHS Commissioning Board, the standing rules and the use of his powers to intervene in the event of 'failing' Trusts.

Lord Owen's concern about the response to a pandemic if the Bill were to become law was answered by referring to clause 44 of the Bill, giving the Secretary of State all the powers needed to take control in an emergency.

In reply to the concerns of Lady Williams and Lord Marks of Henley on Thames on the loss of the duty of autonomy of the Secretary of State, Earl Howe, quoting from the Report Stage on the Bill in the Commons, and the reply of the Minister for Care Services, repeated the commitment that:

> We (the House of Commons) are willing to listen to and consider the concerns that have been raised and make any necessary amendment to put it beyond doubt that the Secretary of State remains responsible and accountable for a comprehensive health services, which we all want to see.
>
> (House of Commons 2011b: col. 754)

Earl Howe's response to Baronesses Kennedy's and Bellingham's concerns, about the likely effects of competition, was to assert that the Bill 'does not introduce a free market place' or 'change or widen the scope of competition law'. The Bill 'introduces a framework to effectively manage competition, does not lead to privatisation, but creates a level playing field between efficient providers. The safeguards in this context are integration, service continuity and the prevention of cherry picking'. On the removal of the private income cap on Trusts, leading to a possible rise in waiting lists for admission to Trust hospital services, Earl Howe quoted the Minister of Health's contribution in the House of Commons debate one month earlier:

> We are proposing to explore whether and how to amend the Bill to ensure that Foundation Trusts explain how their non-NHS income is benefiting NHS patients. We will also ensure that governors of FTs can hold boards to account for how they meet their purpose and use that income. I hope that provides some reassurance.
>
> (House of Commons 2011b: col. 289)

Reassurance was also given to those concerned about the impact of the Bill upon education, training, research and innovation. A promise was given that a new duty for the Secretary of State with regard to education and training would be tabled in time for the Committee and that the Report of the Academy of Medical Royal Colleges would be taken forward.

Lords Rea and Owen had the final words in the debate. Lord Rea drew attention to the unease in the House and the 'tumultuous call from the country not simply to amend the Bill but to reject it entirely' saying that 'whole swathes of the population want the Bill sent back to the drawing boards' and that he thought that 'the NHS is the best public service in the world. It is horrific that its future is threatened'. He asked the noble Lords to accept his amendment which asked the House to decline to give the Bill a Second Reading. The House divided and his

amendment was rejected by 354 to 220 votes. Lord Owen, moving an amendment pointed out that he did not vote against the Second Reading, for Lord Rea's
amendment, because it was a 'blocking tactic'.

Instead, his case for a Select Committee was based upon the attendance of
constitutional experts and parliamentary draftsmen to guide members through a
complex Bill with many legal issues. As there was no agreement on the timetable,
and the Government would not risk delay to the Bill, the Owen amendment was
put before the House, and was lost in the Division by 330 to 262 votes. The Bill
was therefore read a second time and from late October to late December proceeded to the Committee Stage, where attempts to amend the Bill were made by
those opposed to the most contentious provisions.

In summary, supporters of the Bill suggested that it was not radical enough to
meet the patient-centred, high quality, efficient use of resources requirements of
the first half of a twenty-first century health service. The opponents of the Bill, on
the other hand, claimed that it was disruptive and destabilising, and demonstrated
a deficiency in its drafting. They thought the impact of the main clauses of the
Bill would be detrimental to the everyday efficiency, effectiveness and equity of
the NHS, in terms of resources, quality and raising the health status of the most
deprived to the accepted norms of a modern society. The debates surrounding
major scandals in the NHS provided the context for the long-running concern
with raising quality in health care. The Shipman Inquiry chaired by Dame Janet
Smith, which has already been mentioned (Smith 2002–05), primary care and the
role of the General Medical Council, the Francis enquiry into Mid-Staffordshire
Hospital Foundation Trust (Francis Report 2013) and the Maidstone and
Tonbridge C difficile mortality inquiry (Healthcare Commission 2007) all fuelled
these debates. The tragedy of Baby P, whose mother was convicted of neglect and
murder, drew attention to failings in social services. Added to this was the constant
stream of critical assessments by the CQC concerning the care of the elderly in
hospital, the treatment of dementia patients and the GP out-of-hours service. All
these incidents and reports fuelled the media's desire for stories about the 'ailing
NHS' which gave credence to the Government's contention that the NHS must
be 'liberated'.

From October 2011 until the Bill received the Royal Assent (27 March 2012),
commentaries of various sorts continued to appear in the press. The most persistent criticism was that the proposed reforms were not mentioned in the relevant
manifestos and reiterated by Lord Rea that 'we have a Bill that was expressly ruled
out by David Cameron and subsequently in the Coalition Agreement' (Letters to
the Editor, *The Independent*, 11 October 2011: 16). In *The Observer* (12 January
2012: 39), Andrew Rawnsley commented that a Prime Minister who 'took his
own promises more seriously might also have asked himself how he was going
to square such a dramatic shake-up of the NHS with his pre-election promise of
no more reorganisations'. There were references to 'this behemoth of a Bill' (*The
Independent*, 14 March 2012, Opinion: 14) as being 'almost unintelligible in its
original formulation' (Roland Watson and Chris Smyth, *The Times*, 8 February

2012: 9) and 'one of the most badly-drafted, over-complex and confused works of legislation ever put before Parliament' (Letters to the Editor, *The Independent*, 14 March 2012: 22).

There remained questions about the necessity of the reforms. If the PCTs were, as one journalist claimed, inefficient, some hospitals poorly managed and GPs take us for a ride, then the centrally elected government should reform the PCTs, transfer the best managers to the poor performers, and negotiate with less naivety when dealing with the pay demands of GPs, all the while pledging that every penny of taxpayers' money will be forensically audited. It should not be 'beyond the wit of a Health Secretary and his army of civil servants to sort this out under existing structures' (Steve Richards, *The Independent*, 9 February 2012: 17).

It was asserted that the reforms will 'cost billions to implement' (*The Independent*, 14 March 2012, Opinion: 14). Embarking on 'another major reorganisation, while simultaneously requiring £20 billion worth of savings, was ambitious to the point of irresponsibility' (*The Independent*, 8 February 2012, Opinion: 54). Radical reforms 'do not sit well alongside the £20 billion squeeze on NHS budgets' (*The Independent*, 14 March 2012, Opinion: 14).

There remained continuing widespread and serious misgivings about the proposed reforms amongst health and social care professionals and managers. A letter signed by 38 consultants and professors of medicine was published in *The Independent* on 11 October 2011 (p. 16) stating that despite 'the Prime Minister's claims to the contrary, it is a public fact that every single Royal College representing nurses, GPs and midwives maintains serious concerns about the Bill'. They called for 'the suspension of or significant amendment of the Bill so it can be supported by most of the medical profession and the British people who pay for, support and service our great NHS'. On the following day, and also in *The Independent* (p. 18), there was a letter signed by over 1,000 doctors writing to express their view that 'that the Health and Social Care Bill will irreparably undermine the most important and admirable principles of the National Health Service'. In the same paper on the same day (p. 5), it was reported that a survey of 1,890 psychiatrists found that only one in ten believe the plans will improve patient care. On 8 February 2012, *The Times* reported that 90 per cent of respondents to a poll in the *British Medical Journal* opposed the changes (p. 2). On the following day, Sue Hudgetts, Chief Executive of the Institute of Health Service Managers was quoted as saying that 'we can confidently say health and social care managers do not support this Bill' (*The Independent*, 9 February 2012: 12). On 12 February 2012, Andrew Rawnsley noted in *The Observer* that 'every Royal College of this or that is, at best, highly sceptical and, at worst, deeply hostile' (p. 39). Dennis Campbell and Toby Helm (*The Observer*, 26 February 2012: 14) reported that a new poll revealed that nine out of ten hospital doctors wanted the reforms scrapped. It was concluded that the Government had 'bungled the opportunity for change' especially with the 'spectacular failure to win the support of the professions that have to implement the changes' (*The Independent*, 14 March 2012: 14).

A policy aimed at reducing the amount of bureaucracy looked as though it would increase the number of 'mediating agencies' (Steve Richard, *The Independent*, 12 October 2011: 15) so that instead of 'less bureaucracy, we will end up with more' (Andrew Rawnsley, *The Observer*, 12 February 2012: 39). 'The former three-tier management structure is now replaced with a seven-tier system' (Letters, *The Independent*, 22 March 2012: 22) so the Bill results in 'increased layers of management', and at the centre of the Service will be 'the biggest unaccountable quango in the UK' (Leader in *The Independent*, 14 March 2012: 14). The planned reforms were depicted as a 'chaotic shambles' (*The Independent*, 2 December 2011: 24), and that 'chaos that is being imposed' (Steve Richards, *The Independent*, 24 January 2012: 19). The outcome being described variously as an 'unholy mess' (a joint editorial in the three leading health journals reported by Rachel Sylvester in *The Times*, 7 February 2012: 23) and 'an incoherent mess' (Andrew Rawnsley, *The Observer*, 12 February 2012: 39). It has, it was suggested, become 'increasingly clear that the Bill will lead to a disorganised NHS' (Oliver Wright and Jeremy Laurance, *The Independent*, 9 February 2012: 12).

In Lord Darzi's opinion, we now had 'health and well being boards, clinical commissioning groups, clinical senates, local health watches, the NHS Commissioning Board, a quality regulator and an economic regulator' but who would be 'responsible for making sure that the NHS saves more lives this year than last?' Who would be 'accountable for how its budget is spent?' and who would 'inspire NHS staff to lead the difficult changes?' (*The Independent*, 9 February 2012: 14–15). Concerns were also expressed that the new reforms would deliver less choice for patients (Andrew Rawnsley, *The Observer*, 12 February 2012: 39), would lead to increased health inequalities (Oliver Wright and Jeremy Laurance, *The Independent*, 9 February 2012: 12) and that the contracts for the new GP consortia would be 'nightmarishly complex and lawyers will charge a fortune to navigate on behalf of the consortia' (Steve Richards, *The Independent* 24 January 2012:19). Thus much of the commentary in the Press more than justified the comment that a 'year on from the Bill's introduction, it is more controversial than ever' (Opinion, *The Independent*, 8 February 2012: 54).

In a speech at Guy's Hospital London on 7 December 2011, Andrew Lansley made announcements on initiatives intended to improve patient results and give patients more control over their health care. The NHS 'has one ambition and one ambition alone, improving results for patients'. This is the change that the 'NHS Outcomes Framework ... will bring about'. The Secretary of State went on to identify 'five broad areas' where the Government 'was setting out what the objectives are for the NHS in delivering quality of care'. The intention would be to judge performance 'in terms of outcomes and the results delivered for patients' with regard to ... stopping people from dying prematurely ... improving the quality of life for people with long term, conditions ... and ... helping people to recover after they've been ill or been in an accident'.

Patients should also 'have as positive an experience of their care as possible' and 'be treated in a safe environment, free from harm'. The amount of information available would be significantly expanded by publishing (on NHS Choices) maps of GP surgeries 'to help you choose the GP that's right for you'. The associated media release says that there will be 'a new map of local health services which patients will be able to access through the "Any Qualified Provider" policy scheduled to start in April 2012'. Lansley did not actually say this in his speech, but he did say that 'Properly integrating care across the NHS and social care is essential' and 'I am an advocate of patient power'.

On 14 December 2011, the Constitution Committee reported that discussions between their officials and those of the DoH were based on these agreed criteria, as follows:

> The Bill is not intended to reduce the Secretary of State's overall accountability in respect of the NHS in England, even though it will change the way that such accountability works. There is a need for the Bill to be clear, so that the House and the public alike can understand exactly the accountabilities and responsibilities of the Secretary of State.
>
> The Bill should support the policy intention that ministers should not be involved in day-to-day operational management. The Bill should reflect the reality of what ministers actually do in practice. The Bill is not intended to weaken the legal protection afforded to individuals in respect of health services.
>
> (House of Lords 2011b)

Judged against these criteria the Constitutional Committee went on to recommend amendments to the Bill, which would address the concerns they had raised in their earlier report, and they commended them to the House.

On 27 December 2011, *The Times* reported (p. 1) that the latest amendment to the Health and Social Care Bill 'quietly introduced by ministers last week' states that 'hospitals can remain NHS foundation trusts as long as a majority of their income comes from public sources'. On the same day, the same paper (p. 6) reported that rows over health reforms look set to 'flare up again as Liberal Democrats warn that their battle with the Conservatives over the NHS is far from over'. The chairman of the Liberal Democrats' health committee, John Pugh, was reported as saying 'the time had come for an up-front debate about the true motivation behind the Tory plans for a massive reorganization of the NHS'.

The King's Fund and the Nuffield Trust called on the DoH and the NHS Commissioning Board to 'develop a consistent and compelling narrative that puts well co-ordinated care for people with complex needs at the heart of what is required of local NHS and social care organizations' (Goodwin et al 2012). On 24 January 2011, the Chair of the Health Committee, Stephen Dorrell commented:

> Our December 2010 Report on health expenditure expressed concerns then about the ability of the health service and local authorities to make the

demanding efficiency gains required of them by the 2010 Spending Review, while maintaining the quality of care. Both the NHS and local authorities are struggling to meet current targets in a sustainable, long-term manner that will maintain high quality, efficient care in the future.

The evidence submitted to the Committee is therefore unambiguous. The Nicholson Challenge can only be achieved by making fundamental changes to the way care is delivered ... we are convinced that the required level of efficiency gain will not be achieved without significant change in the care model ... The Committee believes that the distinction between healthcare and social care, which has its roots in institutional decisions made in the 1940s, is now a major cause of inefficiency and service breakdown.

(House of Commons 2012a)

He also claimed that:

The persistent failure of successive governments to address the requirement for more integrated, patient focussed care is creating powerful perverse incentives in the care system, which are driving up costs at the same time as undermining the ability of the system to meet the needs of its patients. It is also apparent that the contribution that social housing could make to a proper integrated service is also impeded by institutional structures.

(House of Commons 2012a: 7)

He continued:

While the separate governance and funding systems make full-scale integration a challenging prospect, health and social care must be seen as two aspects of the same service and planned together in every area for there to be any chance of a high quality and efficient service being provided which meets the needs of the local population within the funding available. We would like to see best practice in this rolled out across the Health Service and underperforming commissioners held to account for failure to engage in this necessary process of change.

(House of Commons 2012a: 8)

He referred to the 2010 Spending Review Increase in NHS cash funding of £12.5 billion by 2014/15:

What real terms growth there may be in the settlement is negligible at best ...

The reorganisation process continues to complicate the push for efficiency gains. Although it may have facilitated savings in some cases, we heard that it more often creates disruption and distraction that hinders the ability of organisations to consider truly effective ways of reforming service delivery.

(House of Commons 2012a: 20 and 25)

In spite of Government assurances, local authorities are having to raise eligibility criteria in order to maintain social care services to those in greatest need. ...

The Permanent Secretary at the Department of Health told us that the settlement was intended to 'hold the position steady' until a new funding system for social care was developed. The tightening of eligibility criteria demonstrates that the settlement is not sufficient to do this.

(House of Commons 2012a: 27)

Although the Committee welcomes the continuing interest and support for the priority by the NHS Future Forum to greater service integration, it found precious little evidence of the urgency which it believes this issue demands, on both quality and efficiency grounds.

(House of Commons 2012a: 31)

The reorganization process continues to complicate the push for efficiency gains. Although it may have facilitated savings in some cases, [in others,] we heard that it more often creates disruption and distraction that hinders the ability of organizations to consider truly effective ways of reforming service delivery and releasing savings.

(House of Commons 2012a: )

The above quotations are included to show that structural changes to the NHS contained in the Bill would be fraught with difficulty. The concern was that they might well act against the laudable purposes of integrated care which could only be achieved by partnership with other public agencies, already under pressure from reductions in public expenditure.

At the start of the Committee Stage in the House of Lords on 8 February 2012, *The Times* had the headline, 'Cameron defies critics and backs NHS reforms', and reported that 'as the Bill returns to the House of Lords today with more than 1000 amendments, the scale of opposition to the reforms is clearer'. Following this Stage, the Government tabled 137 amendments for Report, regarding the accountability of the Secretary of State, patient involvement, education and training, health inequalities and service integration (House of Lords 2012). Baroness Thornton (House of Lords 2012: col. 262) claimed that 'this Bill did not need to be in front of us at all because many of the changes that are taking place do not need primary legislation'. Lord Patel (House of Lords 2012: col. 264) believed that 'The amendment would place an explicit duty on the Secretary of State to promote parity of esteem between mental and physical health services.'

Baroness Finlay of Llandaff (House of Lords 2012: col. 278) tabled two amendments, specifying 'that all providers, whether NHS or private, must train clinical staff adequately. They seek to ensure that private providers of services for NHS patients cannot undercut NHS providers by failing to provide adequate training for their staff. All providers should ensure that clinical and other skills are kept up to current standards and that future generations of clinicians are also trained'. Lord Turnberg (House of Lords 2012: col. 2890) added that they were 'concerned specifically that private providers should not be able to shirk their responsibility for training. There is no doubt that training requires more time and money. If private sector providers are able to avoid training, they will have an unfair advantage over NHS providers'. Lord Hunt of Kings Heath supported this view:

> If, regrettably, the Government persists with this lunatic idea of a competitive approach within the health service, it is essential that when it comes to commissioning decisions all qualified providers contribute to education and training. It would be an absolute disgrace if clinical commissioning groups and the national Commissioning Board started to commission services from organizations that did not play their full part in education and indeed research.
>
> (House of Lords 2012: col. 285)

Baroness Thornton (House of Lords 2012: col. 290) expressed a general view that this was still a very bad Bill. She said it had 'no support from anywhere except in the Department of Health and possibly not even from everybody there. It still has no mandate'. She also claimed that the Prime Minister had come to the Bill's rescue because a Downing Street source yesterday was reported to threaten the very life of the Secretary of State for his failure to communicate the Bill and the Bill's policy (House of Lords 2012: col. 2910). She referred to 'the managerial jargon of … Mr. Lansley, which is as dense as the Bill itself' and claimed that 'the public's view of this Bill has shifted and hardened since we completed the Committee stage before Christmas'.

On 27 February 2012, Nick Clegg and Baroness Williams sent a letter on the NHS to all Liberal Democrat MPs and peers about the Health and Social Care Bill, which said:

> We secured a 'pause' in the legislation, which led to a number of substantial changes to the Bill, for instance that competition could only be on quality and not on price …
>
> An all-party consensus has now ensured that the Secretary of State will remain responsible and accountable for a comprehensive health service financed by taxpayers, accessible to all and free at the point of need …
>
> This is not the Bill that we debated as a party last March …
>
> We want to rule out beyond doubt any threat of a US-style market in the NHS. That is why we want to see changes that have been put forward by our Liberal Democrat team in the House of Lords to make sure that the NHS can never be treated like the gas, electricity, or water industry. First, we propose removing the reviews by the Competition Commission from the Bill to make sure that the NHS is never treated like a private industry. Second, we want to keep the independent regulator of Foundation Trusts, Monitor, to make sure hospitals always serve NHS patients first and foremost. Third, we will

introduce measures to protect the NHS from any threat of takeover from US-style health care providers by insulating the NHS from the full force of competition law. We will also insist that anyone involved with a commissioning group is required to declare their own financial interests, so that the integrity of clinical commissioning groups is maintained. Finally, we will put in place additional safeguards to the private income cap to make sure that Foundation Trusts cannot focus on private profits before patients ...

These changes will ensure that competition and diversity in the NHS will always be done in the interests of patients and not profits ...

(Clegg and Williams 2012)

Responding to questions from the Shadow Health Secretary, on 28 February 2012, Andrew Lansley confirmed that the Government supported the changes outlined in the letter and that 'we have been working together on [the amendments] in order to make sure there is further reassurance'. The Lords also agreed the introduction of a new clause providing a duty on the Secretary of State to have regard to the NHS Constitution when exercising his functions. Another clause was amended so that Healthwatch England would be added to the list of bodies the Secretary of State must keep under review.

The Report Stage in the Lords lasted from 8 February 2012 until 13 March 2012. The Third Reading of the Bill in the House of Lords took place on 19 March 2012, and the next day, 20 March 2012, the House of Commons considered the Lords' amendments. The Government agreed to a number of the amendments, the majority moved by the Liberal Democrat peers, relating to conflicts of interest, competition and the regulation of NHS Foundation Trust hospitals.

Although Ministers expressed some reluctance in agreeing to certain non-Government amendments, there had been only two defeats for the Government on division, once during Committee and once during the Report Stage. The first concerned the payment of VAT by charities providing NHS services, and the second emphasised the importance of mental health services.

There was considerable press coverage of the final passage of the Bill into law. Oliver Wright reported in *The Independent* that:

Liberal Democrat and Conservative Cabinet Ministers banged the table in jubilation yesterday after they were told the Government's Health Bill is almost certain to receive Royal Assent by next Tuesday ... But privately they concede the Government has a struggle to successfully implement the reforms in the face of stiff opposition from the medical profession and at a time when the NHS has to find savings of £20bn over the next four years ... One senior Conservative privately predicted that Andrew Lansley, the Health Secretary, was unlikely to survive in his job beyond the next reshuffle, expected in the Autumn, as David Cameron moves to repair relations with doctors' leaders and health groups who opposed the Bill.

(*The Independent*, 21 March 2012: 15)

In a brief item in its 'News Bulletin' (p. 2), *The Daily Telegraph* reported that the 'controversial health reforms were on course to be passed into law … after a last-ditch attempt to halt the Bill failed', and commented (p. 23) that 'This has been an object lesson in how not to reform a venerated public service.' Another journalist, Patrick Butler, wrote, 'The Government won, but no one is quite sure what kind of victory it has achieved, or at what price' (*The Guardian*, 21 March 2012: 7). Chris Ham, Chief Executive of the King's Fund was reported as saying that the danger was that 'doctors and managers would become preoccupied with the changes rather than concentrate on the efficiency and innovation the NHS needs'. *The Guardian's* main headline was 'After the fury, the cold reality: NHS bill passes its final hurdle.' Mike Farrar, chief executive of the NHS Confederation was quoted as saying, 'Let there be no doubt that this will be amongst the toughest projects the NHS has ever taken on. We will have to find our way through the considerable confusion and complexity that has been handed to us as we build and stress-test the new NHS system.'

*The Times* had the headline 'NHS Reforms overcome final challenge' (Michael Savage, 'News', 21 March 2012: 14), and reported that 'Andy Burnham, the Shadow health Secretary, said that a *Labour Government would repeal the reorganisation at the first opportunity*' (emphasis added). He also said that 'MPs and peers have been forced to take a 'gamble' on sweeping changes to the health service without knowing the risks', and 'the truth is, members will go through the lobbies tonight without knowing the full implications of what it means for the NHS in their constituencies'. 'NHS 1948–2012 KILLED BY THE COALITION' was the *Daily Mirror's* main headline. 'David Cameron celebrated the death of the NHS by banging the table in jubilation after his reforms cleared the final hurdle. The shameful Cabinet scenes came as the hated Health Bill was approved' (Jason Beattie, *Daily Mirror*: 1 and 4). 'Shadow health minister, Liz Kendall said that there had been 1000 Government amendments to the "disastrous" bill in the Commons and 374 in the Lords.' Brian Reade (p. 4) under the headline 'Shameful' wrote 'a cruel, ideological threat to the very existence of a fabled institution, many of us view as the true diamond in our nation's crown'. The reforms were described as a chaotic shambles and an unholy mess, disruptive and destabilising, leading to a disorganised NHS.

On 27 March 2012, the Bill received the Royal Assent.

# Chapter 15

# The Health and Social Care Act, April 2012 to January 2015

The Health and Social Care Act 2012 was probably 'by far the most controversial piece of legislation in more than two decades' (Timmins 2012: 2). It was fiercely debated in both the House of Commons and the House of Lords and in the committees of both Houses. The parliamentary process took from January 2011 to March 2012, 14 months in all. This included the so-called 'Pause' for the NHS Future Forum, from April until June 2011. There were 47 days of debate on the Bill and almost 2,000 amendments were agreed. The Government introduced major changes to its legislation in response to the recommendations of the NHS Future Forum in the summer of 2011 and at the Commons Report Stage. Before the Lords' Report Stage, the Government tabled 137 amendments regarding ministerial accountability, patient involvement, education and training, health inequalities and service integration. This followed intensive discussions with peers about their concerns and recommendations from the House of Lords Constitution Committee. Throughout the period between January 2011 and March 2012, there were criticisms in Parliament and the press, about this 'monster' of a Bill, which was variously described as incomprehensible, confusing, obscure, ambiguous and completely unintelligible. It was also noted by critics that the Bill was the largest piece of health legislation since the establishment of the National Health Service (NHS). The Bill completed its parliamentary process with Royal Assent on 27 March 2012, becoming law on 1 April 2013.

It is not uncommon for Bills dealing with social policy and welfare state issues to be hotly contested during their passage and this Bill was no exception, provoking a very large number of amendments, even including some tabled by the Government. Predictably, there were differences between the original Bill and the final Act and some of the most contentious clauses in the Bill were changed. However, the Primary Care Trusts (PCTs) did not survive this process, and their place was taken by Clinical Commissioning Groups (CCGs) which would be general practitioner (GP) led. This change was intended to meet two of the Government's objectives. These were reducing management and bureaucracy, and the involvement of GPs in the commissioning of health care for their patients. The membership of CCGs was to include other health professionals, and not solely GPs, thereby emphasising the multi-professional nature of commissioning. The income hospital trusts could derive from private patients would still be capped, although this was later changed for Foundation Trust (FT) hospitals. Monitor had to be satisfied that any such arrangements would not damage NHS provision. Monitor's remit was changed from promoting competition to preventing anti-competitive behaviour and it would continue to oversee FTs for the foreseeable future. Constitutional issues, especially with regard to the role of the Secretary of State, were also identified and clarified to ensure that key responsibilities would clearly remain with the holder of that office. Issues relating to research, education and training were addressed after parliamentary pressure, rather than left to be resolved at a later date.

The service providers were to be NHS Trusts, GP providers, dentists, opticians, pharmacists, walk-in centres, community services and independent sector treatment centres. It was intended that all hospitals would become FTs. Public health powers and duties were transferred back to local authorities, where they had been until the NHS reorganisation introduced by the 1970–1974 Conservative Government. One hundred and fifty-one PCTs were replaced by 211 CCGs, the latter intended to provide an increased role for GPs in commissioning services. At the time of writing, the wide-ranging commissioning powers and duties of CCGs include primary care, provided by GPs, and regional and national specialised services. These are all part of the remit of NHS England, previously known as the NHS Commissioning Board. In addition to GPs, the membership of CCGs includes nurses, allied health professionals and pharmacists. Between the PCTs and the Department of Health (DoH) there were ten Strategic Health Authorities (SHAs). NHS England has taken their place, with four regional commissioning offices, 19 commissioning support units and 27 NHS England Local Area Teams (LATs). These arrangements were put in place to produce significant cuts in administrative costs and bureaucracy in the NHS, but whether this will happen has yet to be seen.

At the national level, there remains the DoH but with the addition of NHS England and Public Health England. NHS England is to provide leadership for commissioning and will be accountable for the outcomes achieved by the NHS. Public Health England provides a national voice for public health, provides impartial advice to the Government, and advice and support to local authorities and CCGs (Davies 2013: 16–18, 29–30 and 37–41).

Major funding flows will be from the DoH to NHS England and to Public Health England. Funding will pass from the NHS England to CCGs and GPs. From Public Health England funding will pass to the public health departments based in the local authorities. CCGs will be responsible for approximately 60 per cent of the NHS budget. At the national level, NHS England will have responsibility for regulating and monitoring the quality of services. The National Institute for Clinical Excellence (NICE, now the National Institute for Health and Care Excellence) will be accountable to the DoH, with a remit extended to producing quality standards for social care. There is a strengthened Care Quality Commission (CQC) and a new 'consumer champion', Health Watch England, a statutory committee of the CQC. Monitor remains directly accountable to

Parliament and will continue to regulate FTs to 2016, but will also be developed further into an economic regulator to oversee aspects of access and competition in the NHS and to make sure that there is a level playing field for private companies and charities to compete with NHS organisations to provide care. At the same time, Monitor must provide assurances that competition does not have a detrimental impact on the service patients receive. It has a duty to protect and promote the interests of patients and to support the delivery of integrated services. The 211 CCGs will be accountable to 152 local Health and Well-being Boards (HWBs) and GPs will be accountable to NHS England's 27 LATs.

Performance management of the 211 CCGs will be the responsibility of NHS England and the LATs, both of which will also provide advice to the CCGs. Advice will also be provided by Health Watch England, NICE, the 152 HWBs, the local authority public health departments, 12 clinical senates, and the 152 local Health Watch organisations (Davies 2013: 19–22, 34–36 and 94–95). The Secretary of State will be responsible for the funding of Health Education England which then passes funding to the new Local Education and Training Boards (LETBs) replacing Deaneries, and to the new Academic Health Science Networks. The Parliamentary and Health Services Ombudsman (NHS complaints) and Local Government Ombudsman will remain. The latter will deal with complaints about adult social care, including private providers. Patient Advice and Liaison also remains (see Tables 15.1, 15.2 and 15.3).

For many of those who followed the passage of the Health and Social Care Act 2012, perhaps the most important parts of this Act, and those most easily understood, are the first eight sections in Part 1. The sections placed duties upon the Secretary of State to promote a comprehensive service (section 1), to improve the quality of services (section 2), to 'have regard' to the NHS Constitution (section 3), to reduce inequalities (section 4), to promote autonomy (section 5), to promote research (section 6), to secure an effective system for the planning and delivery of education and training (section 7), and to report on and review the treatment given by providers (section 8).

The first duty, 'to promote a comprehensive health service' is divided into four subsections, the first two of which are a restatement of section 1(1) of Part 1 (Central Administration) of the National Health Service Act 1946. Because

*Table 15.1* The NHS in England before the reforms

Department of Health
↓

Ten Strategic Health Authorities (SHAs)
↓↓↓↓↓↓↓↓↓↓

One hundred and fifty-one Primary Care Trusts (PCTs)
↓↓↓↓↓↓↓↓↓↓↓↓↓↓↓↓↓↓↓↓↓↓↓↓↓↓↓↓↓↓↓↓↓↓↓↓↓↓

Health services: primary care services and NHS Trusts/hospitals

*Table 15.2* The NHS in transition: January 2012–March 2013

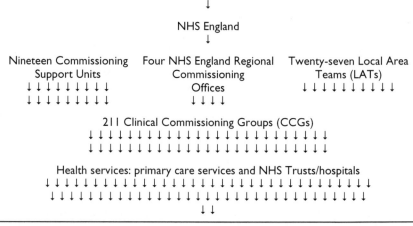

Department of Health
↓

Four merged Strategic Health Authorities (SHAs)
↓   ↓   ↓   ↓

Fifty Primary Care Trusts (PCTs) clusters
↓↓↓↓↓↓↓↓↓↓↓↓↓↓↓↓↓↓↓↓↓↓↓↓↓↓↓↓↓↓↓↓

Two hundred+ shadow Clinical Commissioning Groups (CCGs)
↓↓↓↓↓↓↓↓↓↓↓↓↓↓↓↓↓↓↓↓↓↓↓↓↓↓↓↓↓↓↓↓
↓↓↓↓↓↓↓↓↓↓↓↓↓↓↓↓↓↓↓↓↓↓↓↓↓↓↓↓↓↓↓↓

Health services: primary care services and NHS Trusts/hospitals
↓↓↓↓↓↓↓↓↓↓↓↓↓↓↓↓↓↓↓↓↓↓↓↓↓↓↓↓↓↓↓↓↓
↓↓↓↓↓↓↓↓↓↓↓↓↓↓↓↓↓↓↓↓↓↓↓↓↓↓↓↓↓↓↓↓↓
↓ ↓

*Table 15.3* The NHS: April 2013 onwards

Department of Health
↓

NHS England
↓

Nineteen Commissioning     Four NHS England Regional     Twenty-seven Local Area
Support Units              Commissioning                 Teams (LATs)
↓↓↓↓↓↓↓↓↓                  Offices                       ↓↓↓↓↓↓↓↓↓
↓↓↓↓↓↓↓↓↓                  ↓↓↓↓                          

211 Clinical Commissioning Groups (CCGs)
↓↓↓↓↓↓↓↓↓↓↓↓↓↓↓↓↓↓↓↓↓↓↓↓↓↓↓↓↓↓
↓↓↓↓↓↓↓↓↓↓↓↓↓↓↓↓↓↓↓↓↓↓↓↓↓↓↓↓↓↓

Health services: primary care services and NHS Trusts/hospitals
↓↓↓↓↓↓↓↓↓↓↓↓↓↓↓↓↓↓↓↓↓↓↓↓↓↓↓↓↓↓↓↓↓
↓↓↓↓↓↓↓↓↓↓↓↓↓↓↓↓↓↓↓↓↓↓↓↓↓↓↓↓↓↓↓↓↓
↓ ↓

Sources: Nuffield Trust (2012) *Evidence for Better Health Care*, London: Nuffield Trust; Nuffield Trust (2013) *The new NHS in England: structure and accountabilities*, London: Nuffield Trust; BBC News Health, *The changing NHS*, 1 March 2013; Peter Davies (2013) *The concise NHS handbook 2013/14: The essential guide to the new NHS in England*, London: NHS Confederation.

sections 9 and 10 of the Health and Social Care Act 2012 legislate for the creation of the NHS Commissioning Board and CCGs, it was important that the Secretary of State remained accountable, through ministerial responsibility, to Parliament. Hence, subsection (3) of the section 1 duty to promote a comprehensive health service states, 'the Secretary of State retains ministerial responsibility to Parliament for the provision of the health service in England'.

The second duty, 'as to improvement in quality of service', also contains four subsections. Each subsection builds upon the clinical governance principles stated as best practice in *A-first class service* (DoH 1998c) and in sections 18–25 of the Health Act 1999, 'a duty of quality'. The entire section also reinforces the remit of the CQC. The Secretary of State must exercise his functions in relation to the NHS with a view to securing continuous improvement in the quality of services provided to individuals for or in connection with the prevention, diagnosis or treatment of illness, or the protection or improvement of public health. The Secretary of State must also act with a view to securing continuous improvement in the outcomes that are achieved from the provision of the services and in particular outcomes relating to the effectiveness of services, the safety of the services, and the quality of the experience undergone by patients. In addition, the Secretary of State must have regard to the quality standards prepared by NICE.

The Secretary of State 'must have regard' to the NHS Constitution. This may be interpreted as giving the Secretary of State a degree of latitude and discretion as to the meaning of 'must have regard'. A future challenge may question the seriousness and degree of 'regard' exercised by the Secretary of State in preparing future legislation, or in situations where health service users claim that patients' rights under the Constitution have been compromised. The meaning of the NHS Constitution in the Health and Social Care Act 2012 is the same as that given in Part 1, section 1 of the Health Act 2009. The importance of this section lies in the 'regard to the NHS Constitution' all NHS bodies should have had when performing their functions. These bodies were the SHAs, PCTs, Special Health Authorities, and the CQC. This duty is now placed upon the new institutions that have come into existence as a result of the new legislation. This means that the seven principles of the NHS Constitution, that guide the NHS, published on 8 March 2010, remain in force (DoH 2010g). These are that the NHS should be:

(1) A comprehensive service, available to all, irrespective of gender, race, disability, age, sexual orientation, religion or belief,
(2) Based on clinical need not the individual's ability to pay, and
(3) Aspiring to the highest of standards of excellence and professionalism.
(4) The NHS 'must reflect the needs and preferences of patients, their families and their carers'.
(5) It will work across organisational boundaries … (with) partnerships in the interest of patients, local communities and the whole population.
(6) It must seek the best value for taxpayers' money and the most effective, fair and sustainable use of finite resources.
(7) It must be accountable to the public, communities and patients.

(DoH 2010g)

These principles may well be tested in the revised structure of the NHS, with challenges around the conflict of interests for CCG members, the role of the market with reference to 'any qualified provider', and the denial of some services through local policies of CCGs refusing to commission 'procedures of limited clinical effectiveness'. In exercising functions in relation to the health service, the Secretary of State must have regard to the need to reduce inequalities between the people of England with respect to the benefits that they can obtain from the health service' (section 4 of the Health and Social Care Act 2012). Again the phrase 'must have regard' allows the Secretary of State some flexibility as to how the reduction in inequalities could be measured. There is a large body of literature on this issue, covering decades of clinical and sociological research and speculation, so it is likely that controversies will be generated around the selection of criteria, the success and failure of health and social care policies, and the importance of the social and economic determinants of health status across social class, age, region and gender. Access to health care, the importance of the patient/professional relationship and advice, and differential outcomes and consequences for patients may result in this duty being the hardest to deliver and the most disputatious to resolve.

The duty under section 5 of the Health and Social Care Act 2012 'promoting autonomy' is a recognition of the conflict surrounding the various Ministers of Health between 1942 and 1948 (Chapters 3 and 4) and at other times since. These conflicts were concerned with the professional freedom of clinicians from 'state interference' and were sharpest in the period spanning the publication of the Beveridge Report (1942) and the National Health Service Act 1946 coming into force on 5 July 1948. Further conflict between the state and the medical profession in the mid-1970s resulted in the setting up of the Royal Commission on the NHS (1979). In the late 1980s, the National Health Service and Community Care Act 1990 generated controversy relating to 'fundholding GPs' (Chapter 10). The parliamentary and extra-parliamentary fierceness of the debate surrounding the main provisions of the Health and Social Care Act 2012 is the latest example of this conflict. It is therefore intriguing to wonder what the phrase 'that unnecessary burdens are not imposed on any such person' exercising health service functions, means (or will mean in practice). The Secretary of State's duties under section 1 of the Act (duty to promote a comprehensive service) are to be given priority over those in section 1(1) (section 5(1)(b)).

The duty as to research (section 6 of the Health and Social Care Act 2012) requires the Secretary of State to promote research on matters relevant to the health service, and the use in the health service of evidence obtained from research. It is hard to argue with this duty. However, what will constitute research on 'matters relevant to the health service' might stimulate debates as to the importance of non-clinical research which might improve the patient experience. There may also be controversy about 'the use in the health service of evidence obtained from research'. This academic terrain has always been beset by ethical, scientific and policy debates about the purpose of research, the ethical protection of research subjects, scientific methodology, funding and the translation of research findings into clinical practice, sometimes known as 'bench to bedside'. The legislative duty may not prevent these traditional controversies recurring.

With regard to education and training (section 7 of the Health and Social Care Act 2012) the Secretary of State's duty would be to exercise his functions under any relevant enactment so as to secure that there is an effective system for the planning and delivery of education and training to persons who are employed, or who are considering becoming employed, in an activity which involves or is connected with the provision of services as part of the health service in England. This duty has resulted in the creation of new education and training structures, especially Health Education England and LETBs. These organisations will control education and training resources and have some authority over curriculum matters and the number of trainers. Careful liaison with the General Medical Council concerning evaluation and standards will have to take place, as well as taking into account the interests of the Royal Colleges and professional associations.

Lastly, there is the Secretary of State's duty as to reporting on and reviewing the treatment of providers of services (section 8 of the Health and Social Care Act 2012). This requires the Secretary of State to report to Parliament on any matter which might affect the ability of health care providers to make available services which meet the requirements of the Act. The report should include recommendations as to how any differences in the treatment of NHS care providers could be addressed. This duty to report on and review the treatment of providers might be interpreted as the legislative authority given to the Secretary of State to ensure a 'level playing field' between traditional providers of medical care. After much debate an amendment was passed to change the Government's original intention from any 'willing provider' to 'any qualified provider', thereby placing quality standards above economic considerations in the health care market. This is the clearest indication that competition between providers will be scrutinised by Parliament and would involve making a remedy available to meet any violation of the rules overseen by the Competition and Co-operation Commission, now called the Competition and Markets Authority, whose task is to make markets work for the benefit of consumers, in this case patients, especially where hospital mergers are planned. This was arguably one of the most politically contentious sections of the Act, and the section most likely to emphasise the difference between the main political parties. The success of the Act may well be judged by the rigour with which the Secretary of State carries out the duties laid upon him in the first eight sections of the Act.

We have deliberately used national newspaper reports to illustrate changes as they occurred. Although these accounts and comments by journalists do not claim academic objectivity, they are too good a resource to be ignored as they both reflect and influence public opinion. So the comment, 'It is extraordinary that Andrew Lansley is still in position as Health Secretary having so monumentally mishandled the Government's NHS reforms' was a prediction of what was to come (Rachel Sylvester, *The Times*, 23 February 12: 7).

On 29 March 2012, Mr Lansley thanked NHS staff for their work over the last year and reassured them that the new legislation 'explicitly supports the core principles of the NHS'. He restated these as care provided free at the point of use, funded from general taxation, and based on need, not ability to pay. He also said that at the heart of the Health and Social Care Act 2012 were two simple principles, that patients should share in every decision about their care and that those responsible for patient care should have the 'freedom and powers to lead an NHS that delivers continually improving care'. In a letter to NHS staff, sent on the same date he wrote that:

> The Health and Social Care Act will, in reality, empower NHS clinicians to determine the type of health services needed in their local area, using their clinical expertise and their knowledge to ensure NHS services meet the needs of patients
>
> (DoH 2012a)

He also said:

> My ambition is for a clinically-led NHS that delivers the best possible care for patients. Politicians should not be able to tell clinicians how to do their jobs. I hope you and your colleagues in the NHS will take advantage of the new freedoms the Act has put in place
>
> (DoH 2012a)

A few days later (3 April 2012), Mr Lansley sent out four letters to CCGs clinical and managerial leads, to NHS trust chief executives, to NHS foundation trust executives, and to local authority chief executives, directors of adult services, and directors of children's services (DoH 2012b). He restated all the above points. In addition, he emphasised to CCGs their freedoms to 'use the NHS budget in the best interests' of their patients, 'to pursue innovative ways of delivering care that delivers better results' for their patients, 'to prioritise resources in ways that best suit the needs' of their populations, and to 'reinvest all efficiency savings' directly back into 'frontline patient care'. To both NHS trust chief executives and NHS FT chief executives he emphasised their 'genuine operational independence' and for FTs their 'far greater operational freedom to organise services in the ways you know will deliver better care for your patients'. FTs were also to be 'genuinely free from political interference'. For CCGs the hope was expressed that the CCG authorisation process would not 'replicate the burdensome and bureaucratic processes of the past' whilst FTs would be free from any 'burdensome legislative process'.

The letter to local authority chief executives and directors of services also concluded with a reference to them taking 'maximum advantage' of 'new powers and freedoms'. In other respects, it contained some distinctive points specifically for them. The Health and Social Care Act 2012 placed 'local government in its rightful place at the core of health and care services', stating that 'the ambitions we want to achieve in health and social care can only be realised with the enthusiastic contribution of local government'. Having emphasised the important new role for local authorities in commissioning public health services, the letter went on to say that for too long, local government has been 'left on the sidelines when it comes to health services' and that the new Act 'will help ensure you are no longer bystanders in the decisions that affect your local communities'. If taken seriously, with additional resources, this augers well for the future integration of the health and social care services for particular groups of the population.

In his first major interview following the passing of the Health and Social Care Act 2012 (Anushka Asthana, *The Times*, 14 April 2012: 32–3), Mr Lansley took the opportunity to rebut what he saw as unfair criticisms of the new legislation. There is nothing in the Act, he said, 'that permits or promotes privatisation' or 'that will lead to the fragmentation of the NHS'. However, the following month, he got an indication that his relationship with at least one key profession remained fraught. At the Royal College of Nursing (RCN) Conference he found himself being jeered by 'hundreds of disgruntled nurses' when 'he claimed that frontline staffing levels had increased under his watch'. The delegates also 'laughed when he told them to report to their superiors if there were not enough nurses to provide safe patient care', with some of the nurses shouting 'liar' when he claimed that 'staffing numbers had increased since the coalition took power' (N. Lakhani, *The Independent*, 15 May 2012: 2).

At the beginning of June 2012, polling data published by the King's Fund taken from the British Social Attitudes survey showed that public satisfaction with the NHS had fallen from 70 per cent in 2010 to 58 per cent in 2011. This was the biggest drop since the survey started 30 years earlier. The King's Fund chief economist, Professor John Appleby, noted that year on year increases in satisfaction had to end at some point but 'nevertheless it is something of a shock that it has fallen so significantly' (NHS Confederation press summaries, 12 June 2012 and relating to reports in *The Times*, *Daily Telegraph*, *Daily Mail*, *The Guardian*, *Financial Times*, *The Independent* and *The Sun*). Later the same month (26 June 2012), the CQC published a report on residential care provided for people with learning disabilities. Their conclusion was that people with learning disabilities were twice as likely to receive unsafe and poor quality care in privately run institutions compared with care provided by the NHS. Only one in three private hospitals and homes inspected by the regulator was providing acceptable standards of care and adequately protecting vulnerable residents from abuse (*The Independent*, 26 June 2012: 10).

In each of the four letters sent out by the Secretary of State on 3 April 2012, he stated that everyone was at 'only the beginning of a journey'. In his interview published in *The Times* later in April, Mr Lansley was reported as insisting that 'his job as Health Secretary is not over' and that 'actually we've got more to do'. He went on to say that 'the day may come when I can say OK, the things we have come into office to do have been done. But I'm not at that place yet' (*The Times*, 10 April 2012: 33). If NHS commissioners and providers were indeed at the 'beginning of a journey', Mr Lansley was not to continue with them in his role as Secretary of State for Health. Within five months, on 4 September 2012, he was replaced by

Jeremy Hunt. Mr Lansley, as Shadow Health Secretary for many years, knew a great deal about the NHS, but he was not adept at explaining the changes necessary to realise his vision for the NHS. Jeremy Hunt, on the other hand, can be seen as a more accomplished communicator.

At the October 2012 Conference of the Royal College of General Practitioners, Sir David Nicholson, chief executive of the NHS, told them he was concerned that 'big, high-profile, politically driven objectives and changes like this almost always end in misery and failure'. He told GPs that he believed competition could be healthy but also that it is 'very effective when used as a rifle shot to deal with specific issues rather than a carpet bombing' (Daniel Boffey, *The Observer*, 14 October 2012: 3). Before the end of the month, there was a report by the House of Commons Public Accounts Committee which noted that 'one in five NHS trusts is in serious financial trouble' and that 'there is a real concern that some will fail' (Jeremy Laurance, *The Independent*, 30 October 2012: 4).

On 13 November 2012, the NHS mandate was published by the NHS Commissioning Board (DoH 2012c). A mandate is the vehicle through which authority and responsibility is delegated from a higher strategic authority to an operational authority, the latter being charged with delivering a specified set of outcomes. Where legislation involves duties, a mandate raises expectations. In the case of the NHS mandate, the Secretary of State formally defined a number of objectives, based on five domains, which were mandated for the NHS Commissioning Board to deliver (DoH 2012c). This was the first mandate to the NHS Commissioning Board published by the Secretary of State, and set the Board the task of achieving those objectives, from April 2013 to the end of 2015. The domains were identified in the NHS Outcomes Framework and were 'informed by a wide range of organisations and stakeholders across the health and care system'.

Section 1 of the mandate referred to the prevention of ill health and providing better early diagnosis and treatment for conditions such as cancer and heart disease. Success in this area of health care should improve both the longevity and quality of the population's health.

Section 2 referred to the management of long-term conditions, both physical and mental health. This domain was concerned with preventing where possible, but also treating, the rising numbers of those prone to, or suffering from dementia, diabetes and depression. It was not surprising that the mandate saw the joining up of all professional and organisational participants in this, involving GPs, midwives, district nurses, hospitals and, of more recent concern, care homes, as a priority.

Section 3 of the mandate concentrated upon the means to be employed to aid recovery from episodes of minor or potentially catastrophic conditions such as stroke or the consequences of injury. A good model of service was the concentration of stroke services in specialist units in response to the Darzi recommendations for London (Darzi 2009) which has been successful in improving survival rates. Section 4 made an important distinction between 'treatment' and 'care'. High quality treatment was a reasonable expectation, with research findings being used in the clinical setting. But the deserved outcry concerning poor treatment and care at the Mid-Staffordshire Hospital Foundation Trust (Mid-Staffs) and the Winterbourne View private care home had drawn attention to the key components of care, besides clinical excellence, those of compassion, dignity and respect. Mid-Staffs has by now been merged with a larger hospital trust and its identity as a separate entity no longer exists. The provision of safe care ought to be a *sine qua non* of any experience of NHS patients. However, MRSA and C difficile infections have raised concerns about such expectations.

Domain 5 is therefore a reminder of the importance of infection prevention and control in hospitals, which goes back to the days of Florence Nightingale and Semmelweiss, ensuring the treatment of all in the cleanest and safest of NHS settings, so that while it is not possible to eliminate all risks, the lowest possible risks to patients from infections, blood clots or bed sores is seen as feasible and reasonable.

There were eight specific key objectives in the mandate which supported the five domains. The first was the improvement in care standards alongside treatment with special reference to the care of the elderly. The second, addressing the rise in the long-term condition of dementia, was the better diagnosis, treatment and care for this group of citizens. The third stressed the importance of personalised care for women during pregnancy through a named midwife. This had long been a benchmark of the ante- and post-natal care of mother, foetus and baby. This key objective will certainly have professional and public support. The fourth, and in many ways an original key objective, was the introduction from April 2013 of a friends and family test. This would enable patients to report on their experience in the hospitals, with respect to in-patient wards, accident and emergency departments and maternity units which provide the best care. The test was based on the question as to whether a patient would recommend the hospital service they have received to their family and friends. Results are already being published nationally on the findings of these tests and unofficial 'league tables' are being constructed upon this subjective understanding of quality by the lay public. It is likely that these findings will be referred to by the CQC. This objective was a pre-emptive recognition of the Mid-Staffs findings. The claim was that:

> Working in partnership with national agencies, including the Care Quality Commission and Health Watch England, Monitor, the professional regulators and Royal Colleges, the NHS Commissioning Board and Health Education England, the Government will bring about a response that is comprehensive, effective and lasting. It will be important to ensure there is a credible, robust and independent inspection regime across the entire health and care system.
> (DoH 2012c: 16, para. 4.4)

This objective also included a reference to 'the appalling abuse that was witnessed at Winterbourne View private hospital' and that the NHS Commissioning Board's objective 'is to ensure that CCGs work with local authorities to ensure that vulnerable people, particularly those with learning disabilities and autism, receive safe, appropriate, high-quality care (DoH 2012c: 16, para. 4.5).

The fifth key objective referred to the use of online technology for patients to book GP appointments, and their prescriptions, or to receive advice from their GPs by electronic means. The sixth was a statement about placing mental health on an equal footing with physical health, especially with regard to the timeliness and quality of treatment. The seventh objective, reducing the number of preventable deaths from the biggest killers, was clearly linked to Domains 1, 2 and 3. The eighth objective referred to 'finding out how well (everyone's) local NHS (is doing)' in providing the care they need through the results the local NHS achieves on objective four, the friends and family test. Whether this objective will lead to the further creation of league tables, with all their attendant benefits and disadvantages, only further research over a number of years will tell.

A debate took place in the House of Commons on the day the mandate was published (House of Commons 2012b: cols 177–91). The debate lasted for 51 minutes with 28 speakers. The Secretary of State, Jeremy Hunt, opened the debate by stating that the 'NHS is the country's most precious creation. We are all immensely proud of the NHS and the people who make it what it is'. He went on to identify the essence of the NHS as its values of 'universal and comprehensive health care that is free and based on need and not on the ability to pay' (House of Commons 2012b: col. 177). He continued:

> Today, I am proud to publish the first ever Mandate to the NHS Commissioning Board. From now on, Ministers will set the priorities for the NHS, but for the first time, local doctors and clinical staff will have the operational freedom to implement those priorities using their own judgment as to the best way to improve health outcomes for the people they look after. That independence comes with a responsibility to work with colleagues in local authorities and beyond, to engage with local communities to create a genuinely integrated system across health and social care that is built around the needs of individual people.
>
> (House of Commons 2012b: col. 177)

He went on to say that the priorities in the mandate 'closely reflect the four key priorities I have identified to Parliament as my own'. The first of these was 'to reduce avoidable mortality rates for the major killer diseases' (House of Commons 2012b: col. 177). The second priority was 'to build a health and care system where quality of a person's care is valued as highly as the quality of their treatment'. The third priority was to 'improve dramatically care for the third of people in England who live with a long-term condition such as asthma, diabetes or epilepsy' (House of Commons 2012b: col. 178). The final priority was identified as caring for 'older people, specifically those with dementia' (House of Commons 2012b: col. 179). He also identified other 'important areas of NHS performance' that were covered by the mandate. These included 'research, partnership working, the armed forces covenant and better health services for those in prison' (House of Commons 2012b: col. 179). An 'important objective for the board (NCB) is therefore to ensure good financial management, as well as unprecedented and sustainable improvements in value for money across the NHS'.

The Secretary of State concluded by stating that England is 'the first country in the world to set out our ambitions for our health services in a short concise document' and claiming that its 'clarity and brevity will bring accountability, transparency and stability to the NHS' (House of Commons 2012b: col. 179). The mandate 'signals the end of top down political micro-management of the NHS' and 'will make it easier for Ministers to hold the health and care system to account, and easier for Parliament to hold Ministers to account for their steward-ship of the system'. He concluded by claiming that the mandate is 'a historic step for the NHS' (House of Commons 2012b: col. 179).

For the Opposition, the Shadow Secretary of State for Health, Andy Burnham, described the mandate as 'an impressive wish list' but that Mr Hunt's statements were 'dangerously at odds with the reality on the ground' and risked 'raising unrealistic expectations' (House of Commons 2012b: col. 180). Mr Burnham's key theme centred on a concern voiced with the publication of the White Paper (DoH 2010c) and throughout the parliamentary process, the combination of a radical reorganisation with a set of 'efficiency gains' unprecedented in the history of the NHS or any other modern health care system. He described this as a 'toxic mix of reorganisation and real-term cuts' which risked 'plunging the NHS into a tailspin' (House of Commons 2012b: col. 180). In support of his theme he made the following points:

> Across England, services are under severe pressure with ambulances queue-ing outside A and E, patients left on trolleys in corridors for hours on end, and increasing numbers of A and E and ward closures. No wonder nurses' leaders today warn that the NHS is 'sleepwalking into a crisis.'
>
> (House of Commons 2012b: col. 180)

To listen to the Secretary of State, however, it was as if none of this is happening (House of Commons 2012b: col. 180). 'While the NHS front line takes a batter-ing, the Government keep throwing money at a back-office reorganization that nobody wanted' (House of Commons 2012b: col. 180). Mr Burnham's criticism of the Mandate was crystallised in what he calls 'the new language of the Coalition NHS, in which competition and contracts replace care and compassion' (House of Commons 2012b: col. 181) and expressed his concern that the Government 'have put the NHS on a fast track to fragmentation (House of Commons 2012b: col. 181).

In the debate that followed, questions asked and points made tended to follow on predictable party political lines. A GP, Sarah Wollaston (Totnes, Cons), concluded her contribution by asking the Secretary of State to 'reassure the House that, in these challenging times, efficiency savings made in the NHS will be genuinely reinvested in patient services' (House of Commons 2012b: cols 185/186). The Secretary of State responded by saying that 'the budget for the NHS is protected, but demand for services is going up, so we need to make these changes' (House of Commons 2012b: col. 186).

## The Francis Report

On 6 February 2013 the *Report of the Mid-Staffordshire NHS Foundation Trust Public Inquiry* was published (Francis Report 2013). It provided a detailed analysis of the failings in care at Mid-Staffs between January 2005 and March 2009. It addressed a range of issues of concern to NHS managers, clinical staff and patients. These included the recruitment, training and competence of staff, the regulation of care services, the science of quality measurement, the role of the public voice and oversight, and the degree to which those working in the NHS feel empowered and engaged. The Report's key recommendations were that the patient must be put at the centre of everything the NHS does, and the CQC should take over some of Monitor's functions so there is a single regulator for patient safety, quality, finance and governance. Regulators and professional bodies should share information and NICE should have an increased role in setting standards, working with professional bodies. With regard to management, there should be a 'fit and proper' test for directors.

The Report introduced a 'duty of candour' which should be both contractual and subject to criminal proceedings in certain circumstances, ensuring that when patients are harmed by a health care service, they are informed of the fact and an appropriate remedy is offered, whether or not a complaint or a question is asked about it by the patient or his or her representative. It was recommended that a statutory duty should be imposed on health care providers and registered medical and nursing practitioners to observe the 'duty of candour' (Francis Report 2013: Executive Summary, 75, paras 1.177 and 1.181). Legislation has been drafted on this particular recommendation, reinforcing the duty of care towards the patient by all who work in the NHS (see below).

A difficult to define but commonly agreed characteristic of nursing, compassion, should be embedded in training. In addition, there should be staffing level guidance based on a ratio of nurses to patients, as well as the regulation of health care assistants. Also recommended was an appraisal and revalidation system for staff, bolstering the role of ward sister. The RCN was asked to consider splitting the role of education and training, thereby emphasising the difference between the acquisition of nursing knowledge and the operational skills of the nurse applied to the patient. Education and training should only take place where a good care model can be observed. The education and training division will rely heavily on there being a greater integration between Deaneries, now LETBs and the regulators. Further recommendations refer to the embedding of quality and a stronger clinical input into the commissioning of services. To facilitate this, the creation of information hubs in hospitals adhering to common standards and the introduction of electronic patient records would be a necessary change. The CQC's response to the Report was reticent and guarded, probably feeling unable to take on increased responsibilities at this stage for overseeing the main Francis recommendations.

The initial Government response from the Prime Minister, on 7 February 2013 (Prime Minister's Office 2013), was a commitment to create a single 'failure regime' where suspension of the Hospital Trust Board could be triggered by failure in care, as well as failure in finance. Don Berwick, who had advised President Obama on this issue, was commissioned to make zero harm a reality in the NHS. Nurses should be hired and promoted on the basis of having compassion as a vocation as well as academic qualifications. The hospital inspections regime should be improved so that it does not only look at numerical targets but examines the quality of care and makes an open, public and explicit judgement. The CQC would create a new post, a Chief Inspector of Hospitals, to take personal responsibility for this task. Professor Sir Bruce Keogh was asked to conduct an immediate investigation into the quality of care in those hospitals with the highest mortality rates and to check that urgent remedial action is taken (Keogh Review 2013). Tricia Hart, MP for Cynon Valley, with the Chief Executive of South Tees Hospitals NHS Foundation Trust, would investigate how hospitals should handle complaints. The Prime Minister was directly critical of the RCN as being 'ineffective both as a professional representative organization and as a trade union'.

There was a more detailed response from the Secretary of State on behalf of the Government on 26 March 2013 (House of Commons 2013). The Government accepted the 'essence' of the Francis Report and promised a line-by-line response in due course. It was agreed that a priority should be to prevent problems occurring. A culture of zero harm and compassionate care was needed. Previously, the success of a hospital was not focused on patient experience. As promised, there would be a Chief Inspector of Hospitals reporting to the CQC, and a rating system would be introduced for every hospital Trust, which would capture the complexity of hospital services, so that patient experience is central at department and ward level. A Chief Inspector of Social Care would also be established and consideration would be given to the appointment of a Chief Inspector of Primary Care. In the light of the Berwick Review findings the Government would consider a statutory duty of candour on providers and professionals, and the CQC enforcement powers would be transferred to Monitor so there is no conflict of interest (Berwick Report 2013). On 26 March 2014, the DoH stated that:

> The duty is being introduced as part of the fundamental standard requirements for all providers. It will apply to all NHS trusts, foundation trusts and special health authorities from October and the government plans to implement the standards for all other providers by April 2015, subject to parliamentary approval
>
> (DoH 2014)

Swift action was promised. If fundamental standards were not being met, the hospital would not get a good rating. If action is not taken the hospital would go on to a failure regime. With regard to accountability legal sanctions were promised for organisations withholding information, as well as consultation on a barring system for managers. Professional regulators were asked to tighten processes for doctors and nurses that breach standards, training for student nurses would include a year on the ward, and health care assistants would have minimum standards, but not professional regulation. The DoH would be the first department where civil servants get experience on the front line.

Andy Burnham pressed the Government on the duty of candour. Would it cover professionals and all types of providers? The Government confirmed it would cover all providers. The appointment of a Chief Inspector of Hospitals was not a Francis recommendation. Francis recommended creating a uniform structure for Local Health Watch to provide patients with a meaningful voice. The Government did not commit to this, nor would it agree to regulate health care assistants in spite of the Francis recommendation. Burnham drew attention to hospital staffing levels, that one in ten hospitals did not have adequate staffing, that cutting front-line staff had gone too far and a minimum patient-to-staff ratio was needed. Lastly, he asked what was to be future of Stafford Hospital. The reply was that the Government will support Monitor's review of local services in Stafford.

Robert Francis QC issued a statement regarding the Government's response, saying that it indicated a determination to make positive changes to the culture of the NHS, in part by adopting some of his recommendations and in part through other initiatives. He looked forward to seeing the Government's fully developed response. The overall effectiveness of the response would have to be judged on the detail developed over the next few months, and the decisions taken about other recommendations. Many of his recommendations did not require Government intervention or legislation to proceed, and he expressed his hope that all those involved in health care throughout the NHS would give real consideration to what they can do to turn his recommendations into reality. He sensed a real commitment to make the necessary changes now, although six months later, Katherine Murphy (Chief Executive of the Patients Association) noted that 'there remains no clear time frame, or even commitment, by the Government to deliver the recommendations of the Francis inquiry' (*The Independent*, 12 September 2013: 22).

## The NHS Constitution (2013) and further mandates

A new version of the NHS Constitution was published in March 2013 subtitled *The NHS belongs to us all* (DoH 2013a). The first version in January 2009 was a result of Lord Darzi's Report *High Quality Care for All* (Secretary of State 2008), which had been published on the sixtieth anniversary of the founding of the NHS (Chapter 11). The new Constitution did not create any new rights or responsibilities, but rather brought them all together in one document. The purpose of the NHS, stated in red print in the first paragraph, said nothing new, but made explicit what had been almost always taken for granted in theory, but was often ignored or denied in practice. All the conflicts and debates that have been discussed in earlier chapters were based on the best way to deliver the Beveridge principles. Now the purpose, principles and values were stated clearly, with rights and responsibilities to match. They were enshrined in law, with a promise that they would be regularly reviewed, and can only be altered after a 'full and transparent debate with the public, patients and staff' (DoH 2013a: 2).

The document restated the guiding principles of the NHS. It is to be comprehensive, free at the point of need, with the highest standards, with 'patients at the heart of everything it does', 'in partnership with other organizations', providing best value for taxpayers' money and accountable to 'the public, communities and patients that it serves'. It refers to 'involvement', 'respect', 'commitment', 'quality', 'compassion', 'improving lives' and that 'everyone counts' (DoH 2013a: section 2).

The new Constitution was not so very different from many other documents issued by Governments over the years and statements by medical officers of health. Yet, like the 'Nolan principles' of public life (CSPL 1995), which made explicit for the first time things that many people had always taken for granted but not always observed, this was intended to make sure that no one could be in any doubt about what is to be expected of the NHS. Section 3a enlarged on patients' rights and the Service's commitment, while section 3b stated the responsibilities of patients. Section 4a set out the rights of NHS staff and section 4b their corresponding responsibilities. It met the criticisms about the 'nanny state' by emphasising individuals' responsibilities, as well as collective ones. In return for the rights and benefits, the patients and staff have specific obligations, even if each of those of patients is respectfully preceded by the word 'please'. All NHS bodies, and any providers supplying them with services, have a legal duty to refer to the Constitution in all that they do. The Health and Social Care Act 2012 placed a duty on the NHS Commissioning Board and the new CCGs to have regard to it.

At the same time, the DoH produced two further mandates. One was directed to the NHS Commissioning Board (DoH 2013b), renamed NHS England on 1 April 2013, and the other to Health Education England. In a Foreword to the first, the Secretary of State promises to offer 'health professionals more power and space' and 'to make sure the NHS responds decisively' to the things that matter most. The NHS Commissioning Board is entrusted with the NHS budget and shares a legal duty with the Secretary of State to promote a comprehensive health service (DoH 2013b: para. 4). The mandate wants to release 'the energy, ideas and enthusiasm of frontline staff and organizations' and the hope is expressed that 'by March 2015 improvement across the NHS will be clear' (DoH 2013b: para. 8). The Mandate focuses on seven objectives, matching the NHS Outcomes Framework. These are preventing people from dying prematurely, enhancing the quality of life for people with long-term conditions, helping people to recover from episodes of ill-health or following injury, ensuring that people have a positive experience of care, treating and caring for people in a safe environment and protecting them from avoidable harm, freeing the NHS to innovate, and the broader role of the NHS in society.

This may be read as a repetition of all the value statements made by various governments since the 1940s, and although important, there was little that was new, except a few pointers to the view that there could be privatisation by stealth, for example in the sixth objective, freeing the NHS to innovate. 'The Commissioning Board's objective by 2016 is to have ... supported the creation of a fair playing field, so that care can be given by the best providers, whether from the public, independent or voluntary sector.' The NHS's procurement is also to be 'more open and fair' allowing 'providers of all sizes and from all sectors to contribute, supporting innovation and the interests of patients'.

The second mandate is addressed to Health Education England (DoH 2013c), a new body with responsibility for education and training all medical and health care staff. This responsibility has been transferred from the strategic health authorities, which have been abolished, to local education and training boards (LETBs). The mandate uses the terms 'education' and 'training' interchangeably without any definition of either. There are plenty of objectives, and references to the Secretary of State's priorities, as well as emphasis on learning values and behaviours, along with technical and academic skills. One of the more contentious suggestions is that 'every student who seeks NHS funding for nursing degrees should first serve up to a year as a healthcare assistant' (DoH 2013c: para. 3.2). LETBs will be responsible for commissioning education and training but it seems that this will be mostly from existing providers and 'stakeholders'.

## The Cavendish Review

This Review, published on 10 July 2013, was an independent review into Health Care Assistants (HCAs) and social care support workers in the NHS and social care (Cavendish Review 2013). It was set up as a result of the findings at Mid-Staffs and at Winterbourne View. The Secretary of State asked Camilla Cavendish, a non-executive director of the CQC, to carry out the Review and in particular she was asked to look at what could be done to ensure that unregistered staff treat all patients and clients with care and compassion. The final report made a total of 18 recommendations, taking note of what the best employers are already doing with the objective of reducing complexity and overlap. The best organisations in health and social care recognise that HCAs are a strategic resource, critical to ensuring the safety of patients or clients. Recruiting people for their values and commitment to caring, investing in induction, training and development and supporting line managers to lead and engage with their teams is crucial. However, in all of the conversations about values, standards and the quality of care a view was formed that the support workforce has received the least attention.

The HCAs and support workers are largely invisible to the public and policy makers, but they may have more contact with the patient than the professional staff. The members of the Cavendish Review found HCAs and social care support workers to be largely 'dedicated, sometimes fierce, advocates for the people they look after'. Many in this group were also frustrated at what they feel is a lack of recognition from managers, employers and commissioners. The public image of this workforce is outdated. Working with vulnerable people with sometimes multiple and complex conditions and ensuring they are treated with dignity and compassion is, in the opinion of the Cavendish Review, about 'basic' care. This is because roles have evolved, with increased levels of responsibility but a lack of clarity on expected standards, and this needs to be resolved. This can both help the individuals and employer and enable them both to be held accountable. There is a huge, unnecessary divide between health and social care, and in some cases between HCAs and registered nurses. If these could be bridged it was felt that it would help create a more effective team approach to delivering care and reduce duplication of effort. Thus it was proposed that all HCAs and social care support workers should have the same training, based on best practice and should have a certificate of fundamental care before being allowed to work unsupervised.

## The Keogh Review

Following the inquiry into Mid-Staffs, the Prime Minister asked Sir Bruce Keogh, Medical Director of NHS England, to conduct a review of the quality of care and treatment provided by those NHS Trusts and NHS FTs that were persistent 'outliers' on mortality indicators (Keogh Review 2013). A total of 14 hospital Trusts were investigated as part of this Mortality Review. The Review was guided by the NHS values set out in the NHS Constitution (DoH 2013a) and underpinned by the key principles of patient and public participation, listening to the views of staff, openness and transparency and co-operation between organisations. The Review considered the performance of the hospitals across six key areas: mortality, patient experience, safety, workforce, clinical and operational effectiveness, and leadership and governance. The Review team found that none of the 14 hospitals were providing consistently high quality care to patients. For all the Trusts visited, the Review team uncovered previously undisclosed problem areas in care. They identified patterns across many of the hospitals including professional and geographical isolation, failure to act on data or information that showed cause for concern, the absence of a culture of openness, a lack of willingness to learn from mistakes, and ineffectual governance and assurance processes. In many cases, Trust Boards were unaware of the problems discovered by the Review team.

As a result of this the Secretary of State announced that 11 of the 14 Trusts reviewed would be placed in 'special measures for fundamental breaches of care'. In addition, all 14 trusts have been ordered to act on the recommendations made by Sir Bruce.

This Report set out eight 'ambitions' for the wider NHS in light of its findings:

(1) To reduce the numbers of avoidable deaths using early warning systems for deteriorating patients and to introduce more accurate statistical measurement of mortality rates.

(2) Expertise and data on how to deliver high quality care should be shared between NHS trusts more effectively.

(3) Patients, carers and the public should be more involved, and should be able to give real time feedback

(4) Patients should have more confidence in the regulator, the CQC, with wider participation of patients, nurses and junior doctors on review teams.

(5) Hospitals in remote areas should not be left isolated, with staff from better-performing hospitals used to train and inspect others.

(6) Nurse staffing levels and mix of skills should be appropriate to the patients being cared for on any given ward.

(7) Medical directors should tap into the latent energy of junior doctors and include them in review panels.

(8) NHS employers should make efforts to ensure staff are 'happy and engaged'.

## The Berwick Report

The Berwick Report (6 August 2013) used the findings of the Francis Report (2013) as a template upon which to suggest 'cultural' rather than 'rule-based' changes to improve the quality of treatment and care in the NHS. The Report emphasised the need to re-examine what the NHS does and determine how it can improve further. It said that the only conceivably worthy honour due to those who have been harmed would be to make changes that will save other people and other places from similar harm. 'Our job has been to study the various accounts of Mid-Staffordshire, as well as the recommendations of Robert Francis and others, to distil for Government and the NHS the lessons learned, and to specify the changes that are needed.'

Berwick concluded that patient safety problems exist throughout the NHS as with every other health care system in the world. He said that NHS staff were not solely to blame. In the vast majority of cases it was systems, procedures, conditions, environment and constraints that led to patient safety problems:

> Incorrect priorities do damage: other goals are important, but the central focus must always be on patients ... In some instances, including Mid Staffordshire, clear warning signals were present and were not heeded, especially the voices of patients and carers ... Where responsibility is diffused, it is clearly not owned: with too many in charge, but no one being responsible. Improvement in quality of care requires a continuing and supportive system of support for all staff. The NHS needs a considered, resourced and driven agenda of capability-building in order to deliver continuous

improvement ... Fear is toxic to both safety and improvement. To address these issues the system must recognise with clarity and courage the need for systematic change, abandon blame as a tool and trust the goodwill and good intentions of the staff, reassert the primacy of working with patients and carers to achieve health care goals.

(Berwick Report 2013: 4)

Berwick's strongest advice concerned using quantitative targets with caution. Such goals would have an important role en route to progress, but should never displace the primary goal of better care. 'Culture trumps rules, standards and control strategies every single time.'

His ten recommendations were as follows:

(1) The NHS should continually and forever reduce patient harm by embracing wholeheartedly an ethic of learning.
(2) All leaders concerned with NHS health care – political, regulatory, governance, executive, clinical and advocacy – should place quality of care in general, and patient safety in particular, at the top of their priorities for investment, inquiry, improvement, regular reporting, encouragement and support.
(3) Patients and their carers should be present, powerful and involved at all levels of health care organisations from wards to the boards of Trusts.
(4) Government, Health Education England and NHS England should assure that sufficient staff are available to meet the NHS's needs now and in the future. Health care organisations should ensure that staff are present in appropriate numbers to provide safe care at all times and are well-supported.
(5) Mastery of quality and patient safety sciences and practices should be part of initial preparation and lifelong education of all health care professionals, including managers and executives.
(6) The NHS should become a learning organisation. Its leaders should create and support the capability of learning.
(7) Transparency should be complete, timely and unequivocal. All data on quality and safety, whether assembled by Government, organisations, or professional societies, should be shared in a timely fashion with all parties who want it, including, in accessible form, with the public.
(8) All organisations should seek out the patient and carer voice as an essential asset in monitoring the safety and quality of care.
(9) Supervisory and regulatory systems should be simple and clear. They should avoid diffusion of responsibility. They should be respectful of the goodwill and sound attention of the vast majority of staff. All incentives should point in the same direction.
(10) Responsive regulation of organisations would be supported, with a hierarchy of responses. Recourse to criminal sanctions should be extremely rare, and should function as a deterrent to wilful or reckless neglect or mistreatment.

Place the quality of patient care, especially patient safety, above all other aims. Engage, empower, and hear patients and carers at all times. Foster whole-heartedly the growth and development of all staff, including their ability and support to improve the processes in which they work. Embrace transparency, unequivocally and everywhere, in the service of accountability, trust and the growth of knowledge.

## The controversies continue: the Nicholson challenge and the 'winter crisis'

Between July 2013 and the publication of *The NHS Five Year Forward View* in October 2014 (NHS England 2014a), a number of concerns were reported which echoed those made during the passage of the Health and Social Care Act 2012. There was continuing evidence of major financial pressures in the NHS as the Service sought to contend with the demands of the so-called 'Nicholson Challenge'. In July 2013, Sir David Nicholson, still NHS Chief Executive at this time, was reported as stating that hospitals are 'staring down the barrel' of having to cut the jobs of doctors and nurses (Oliver Wright, *The Independent*, 11 July 2013: 22). In November 2013, *The Times* reported that more 'than a million people have had to sit in A&E departments for longer than four hours', noting at the same time that, whilst there may have been 'perverse consequences' from some of the previously imposed targets, 'removing one form of pressure to perform, and replacing it with nothing, will ensure that performance declines' (*The Times*, Leading article 'Winter Crisis', 11 November 2013: 30). The following day it was reported that Freedom of Information requests submitted by the RCN to dozens of NHS hospitals had exposed 'a hidden workforce crisis' that had been missed by government statistics. The RCN was reported as stating that there were thousands more nursing vacancies than indicated by official figures because 'hospitals have not been replacing staff that have retired or moved on due to reduced budgets' (Charlie Cooper, *The Independent*, 12 November 2013: 4). In April 2014, Richard Murray, the director of policy at the King's Fund, was reported as saying that the scale of the slowdown in NHS funding under the coalition Government was unprecedented (*The Independent*, 18 April 2014: 1 and 11). In June 2014, Stephen Dorrell, a former Conservative health secretary, Sarah Wollaston, Tory MP and Paul Burstow, a former coalition health minister, stated that 'with the economy growing the NHS must receive a real terms increase in spending over the next five years if it is to function properly' (*The Observer*, 29 June 2014: front page). On 24 July 2014, the Audit Commission expressed concern about the number of Trusts being referred to the Secretary of State as in financial difficulty, and on 8 September 2014, *The Independent* reported that two-thirds of NHS hospitals were 'in the red', the source being reports of the health-sector watchdogs Monitor and the Trust Development Authority. In the FT sector a significant number of NHS organisations had gone into overall deficit for the first time ever (*The Independent*, 20 September 2014: 27).

Also in September 2014, a study was published by the Health Services Management Centre of the University of Birmingham (Exworthy 2014). Using interviews with clinicians, GPs, public health experts and patients, they found 'cancer services under mounting pressure after years of efficiency savings and the recent NHS reforms'. These services were described as being at a 'tipping point' with front-line staff warning that quality care is 'already deteriorating because of a funding squeeze'. Cancer Research UK, which had commissioned the study, called for urgent increased investment in NHS cancer services to help staff keep services viable for patients (Adam Sherwin, *The Independent*, 8 September 2014). *The Independent* published a copy of a letter sent to the Prime Minister, the Leader of the Opposition and the Deputy Prime Minister. It was from Dr Mark Porter, chair of council, British Medical Association; Dr Peter Carter, chief executive and general secretary, Royal College of Nursing; Professor Jane Dacre, president, Royal College of Physicians; Dr Maureen Baker, chair, Royal College of General Practitioners; Cathy Warwick, chief executive, Royal College of Midwives; Dr Hilary Cass, president, Royal College of Paediatrics and Child Health; Dr David Richmond, president, Royal College of Obstetricians and Gynaecologists; Professor Caroline MacEwen, president, Royal College of Ophthalmologists; Jeremy Hughes, chief executive, Alzheimer's Society; Henny Braund, chief executive, Anthony Nolan; Michelle Mitchell, chief executive, the MS Society; Lesley Anne Alexander, chief executive, Royal National Institute of Blind People; Siobhan Dunn, chief executive of Teenage Cancer Trust; Dr Peter Swinyard, GP Swindon and national chairman, The Family Doctor Association; Moira Auchterlonie, chief executive, Family Doctor Association; and Dr John Middleton, acting president, Faculty of Public Health. Their letter expressed their view that 'our NHS has just been through the longest, and most damaging budget squeeze in its history' and they reported that 'major accident and emergency departments in England have failed to meet their waiting times targets for an entire year' (*The Independent*, 6 September 2014).

The case for important reforms in the way the NHS delivered services was made in another Report from Sir Bruce Keogh, on urgent care and emergency medicine (Keogh 2013). This proposed that the majority of patients with minor conditions should be treated 'as close to home as possible', while treatment for the most serious emergencies should be concentrated at a small handful of high-performing 'major emergency centres'. GPs, local pharmacists and the NHS 111 telephone triage service should all do more to keep people out of hospital. Under the plans, between 40 and 70 accident and emergency units with the most specialist equipment and expertise will become the first port of call for around 5 per cent of patients with the most serious conditions that may not require specialist intervention, while another 70–100 will be known as emergency centres to treat serious conditions that may not require specialist intervention. The plan was based on successful reforms on the way the NHS handles heart-attack patients in a small number of specialist centres and the concentration of London's stroke services from 32 to eight hospitals – both of which had dramatically improved survival rates (see report in *The Independent*,

Charlie Cooper, 13 November 2013: 4). The following year, in his first day as the new Chief Executive of the NHS, it was reported that Simon Stevens would call for a fundamental overhaul of disjointed services that are not focused on patients. 'Our traditional partitioning of health services, GPs, hospital outpatients, A&E departments, community nurses, emergency mental health care, out of hours units, ambulance services and so on, no longer make much sense' (Oliver Wright, *The Independent*, 1 April 2014: 16.). These themes would be taken up in *The NHS Five Year Forward View* (NHS England 2014a: 21–2, para. 10).

There was the issue of whether the NHS, since the passing of the Health and Social Care Act 2012, was now organised to enable the service to address the need for these reforms. In July 2013, the previous NHS Chief Executive, Sir David Nicholson, was reported as predicting that unless politicians and the public accepted the need to shut and centralise services such as accident and emergency, cardiac surgery and maternity units, the NHS would no longer be able to cope with demand. Sir David was backed up in his remarks by Sir Bruce Keogh, and Jane Cummings, the Chief Nursing Officer (Oliver Wright, *The Independent*, 11 July 2013: 22). Sir David Nicholson was reported as saying that hospitals were being held back from making changes that made 'perfect sense from the point of view of patients' because they did not meet new strictures governing competition between health care providers (Charlie Cooper, *The Independent*, 26 September 2013: 2). He would elaborate on this theme in November 2013, explaining to the House of Commons Health Select Committee that competition, a key tool, allegedly, for improving quality, increasing productivity, driving down costs and widening choice for patients, was proving an expensive impediment to change as lawyers battle over the details of competition law and procurement on a 'scale and nature' never anticipated (*The Observer*, 10 November 2013). Subsequently, the former Conservative health secretary, Stephen Dorrell, who chaired the All-Party Select Committee on Health, was reported as suggesting that patients' lives were at stake, and called on NHS England to drive through improvements and to make sure patient care took precedence. Sir David Nicholson had told Dorrell's select committee that 'it is causing great frustration for people in the service about making change happen. That may be because of the way in which we are interpreting the law … but it maybe because that is the law, in which case to make integration happen we will need to change it' (Toby Helm, *The Observer*, 17 November 2013: 1 and 4). The following year, the study published by the University of Birmingham (Exworthy 2014; noted above) would also warn of the 'fragmentation of commissioning across the patient pathway', with Mike Hobday, Director of Policy and Research at Macmillan Cancer Support saying that 'these findings are consistent' with their own research and that 'cancer commissioning is in a state of utter confusion and uncertainty' (Adam Sherwin, *The Independent*, 8 September 2014). This would be identified in *The NHS Five Year Forward View* (NHS England 2014a), referring to situations in which the manner in which 'improvement and clinical engagement happens can be fragmented and unfocused' (NHS England 2014a: 25).

The relationship between health care and social care was still an issue. In April 2014, *The Times* reported that according to research conducted by the Royal Voluntary Service charity, 15 per cent of patients over the age of 75 are readmitted to hospital within 28 days of being discharged. There are 150,000 people over 75 who are discharged from hospital with no care plan in place. It was also noted that the Nuffield Trust and the Health Foundation have reported that readmissions for patients who have had hip fractures has risen by 60 per cent over a decade. 'The trouble is that cuts to local authority services have been randomised. The central NHS budget has been protected for political reasons and this has meant that local councils have taken the brunt of austerity. The care they provided for post-discharge patients has been one of the services to suffer' (Leading article 'Duty of Care', *The Times*, 1 April 2014: 26). Just over six months later, Kate Barker, who had chaired the Commission on the Future of Health and Social Care in England, which was established by the King's Fund, was reported as saying that the 'present health and social care system is not fit for purpose. It lacks transparency, is inefficient and creates distress and confusion for users and their carers'. The Commission had concluded that to 'make health and social care work better together they should be funded from a single ring fenced budget, and commissioned by a single body' and that 'without such a change it is hard to see how a seamless service could be delivered' (*The Independent*, 7 October 2014: 7). The important goal of breaking down barriers between health and social care was emphasised by *The NHS Five Year Forward View* (NHS England 2014a: 3, para. 6).

In June 2014, the Commonwealth Fund published its periodic comparative study (Davis et al 2014). In this update, the UK ranked first out of the 11 nations evaluated (the other ten countries being Australia, Canada, France, Germany, the Netherlands, New Zealand, Norway, Sweden and the USA). The criteria utilised related to quality care, access, efficiency, equity and healthy lives. The UK's lowest ranking, tenth out of 11, related to the healthy lives category, but as we have already noted issues relating to the health of the population are a function of much more than the organisation of health care delivery. In the previous year, another major study of health care systems in Europe was published (Pavolini and Guillen 2013a). In their Conclusions, the editors noted that National Health Services, like the UK, tended to 'perform better in terms of medical, social and economic efficiency objectives than the Social Health Insurance ones' (Pavolini and Guillen 2013b).

## *The NHS Five Year Forward View* and the Dalton Review

*The NHS Five Year Forward View* was intended to represent 'the shared view of the NHS national leadership' and to reflect an emerging consensus amongst patient groups, clinicians, local communities and frontline NHS leaders (NHS England 2014a: 2). Significantly, it is described as a 'view' and not a 'plan', and leaves room for local discretion to be used to meet local needs while still being bound by NHS quality standards. It sets out how the health service needs to change 'arguing for a more engaged relationship with patients, carers and citizens so that we can pro-mote wellbeing and prevent ill-health' (NHS England 2014a: 2). It makes it clear that 'some critical decisions, for example on investment, on various public health measures and on local service changes, will need explicit support from the next government' (NHS England 2014a: 3).

The authors' analysis suggests that 'a radical upgrade in prevention and public health' is needed, with patients having 'far greater control of their own care, including the option of shared budgets combining health and social care' (NHS England 2014a: 3). The 'decisive steps' needed to provide integrated care would mean breaking down the barriers 'in how care is provided between family doctors and hospitals, between physical and mental health, between health and social care' (NHS England 2014a: 4, para. 6). For organisational purposes this would not mean a 'one-size fits all care model', but neither would the answer be 'to let a thousand flowers bloom' (NHS England 2014a: 4, para. 7). The intention would for different local health communities to be 'supported by the national NHS lead-ership' in choosing from amongst a 'small number of radical new care delivery options' (NHS England 2014a: 4).

One of these 'new care delivery options' would be multi-speciality community providers, a new concept where groups of GPs will be permitted to combine with 'nurses, other community health services, hospital specialists and perhaps mental health and social care to create integrated out-of-hospital care' (NHS England 2014a: 4). It was noted that early versions of this model are already emerging in different parts of the country, but that 'they generally do not yet employ hospital consultants, have admitting rights to hospital beds, run com-munity hospitals or take delegated control of the NHS budget' (NHS England 2014a: 4 and 19–20). Amongst other options referred to were primary and acute care systems which involve 'combining general practice and hospital services, similar to the Accountable Care Organisations now developing in other countries' (NHS England 2014a: 4 and 20–1). There would also be new options for smaller hospitals to remain viable including partnerships with other hospitals and at the same time the redesign of urgent and emergency care and the development of high quality specialised hospital care and there are examples of the possible 'new care models' (NHS England 2014a: 4 and 22–5).

With regard to organisational arrangements, the focus of so much change and discussion since 2010, the authors of *The NHS Five Year Forward View* say that they 'will back diverse solutions and local leadership, in place of the distraction of further national structural reorganization' (NHS England 2014a: 4). It was their view that 'across the NHS we detect no appetite for a wholesale structural reorganisation' (NHS England 2014a: 28). They continued:

> In particular, the tendency over many decades for government to repeatedly to tinker with the number and functions of the health authority/primary care trust/clinical commissioning group tier of the NHS needs to stop. There is no 'right' answer as to how these functions are arranged, but there is a wrong

answer, and that is to keep changing your mind. Instead, the default assumption should be that changes in local organisational configurations should arise only from local work to develop new care models [noted above], or in response to clear local failure and the resulting implementation of special measures.

(NHS England 2014a: 28)

Whilst this statement is clearly critical of the incessant top-down reorganisations imposed by successive governments, it does not rule out the need for changes in organisational arrangements for local work on the new care delivery options or because of local failures. The organisational arrangements introduced in the recent legislation were working well in some parts of the country so that they 'will be able to continue commissioning and providing high quality and affordable health services using their current care models' (NHS England 2014a: 25). However, 'many areas will need to consider new options' requiring 'a new perspective where leaders look beyond their individual organisations' interests and towards the future development of whole health care economies, and are rewarded for doing so' (NHS England 2014a: 25). In these circumstances 'we will therefore now work with local communities and leaders to identify what changes are needed in how national and local organisations best work together' (NHS England 2014a: 25). *The NHS Five Year Forward View* was followed by the Dalton Review, published in December 2014 (NHS England 2014b). Without suggesting major organisational change, the Review identifies five themes to raise the quality of service through integrated care models, but deliberately eschewing wholesale (organisational) change. The five themes were that one size does not fit all; quicker transformational change is required; ambitious organisations with a proven track record should be encouraged to expand their reach and have greater impact; overall sustainability for the provider sector is a priority; and a dedicated implementation programme is needed to make change happen. The urgent nature of these changes is best expressed by Dalton as follows 'the extent of variation of standards of care across the country and the challenges all providers of NHS services face, must be addressed as soon as possible'. *The NHS Five Year Forward View* signposts organisations to consider new and innovative solutions to address quality and financial challenges; the recommendations of this review complement *The NHS Five Year Forward View* and support providers to deliver the changes required (NHS England, 2014a: Conclusions).

The expectation is that innovative models of care will encourage collaborative, contractual and consolidated relationships to be formed between service providers demonstrating clinical and financial viability, and at the same time encouraging the development of integrated patient care through integrated services across all providers in the NHS. This approach deliberately avoids large-scale and top-down reorganisation and is meant to enhance local autonomy within a national framework of quality and financial sustainability.

This autonomous freedom for local providers should be read within the context of the regulatory framework for health and social care in England. In November

2014, two regulations came into force by law: Regulations 5 and 20. The first concerned all trust directors being 'fit and proper persons' 'to be in senior decision-making positions in the NHS. The second, 'the duty of candour', is a consequence of recommendation made in the Francis Report (2013). This duty requires all who work within the NHS to report inappropriate staff behaviour which may endanger patient safety or quality of services (Francis Report 2013: Recommendations, 181 and 182).

In an interview with *The Independent* (11 January 2014: 13), the Shadow Secretary of Health had repeated his pledge to revoke the Health and Social Care Act 2012 which introduced the Government's health reforms. Although he went on to say he would keep the new institutional arrangements so as to avoid further disruption, but the law that forces commissioners to put all NHS services out to tender would be repealed, and the income NHS hospitals could make through charging patients would be reduced.

Mr Burnham's qualification was important since it did not seem incompatible with the key issues being raised by critics even after the passage of the Health and Social Care Act 2012. These included the fragmented and confused state of some commissioning arrangements and the continuing failure to address the health and social care divide. This would be the focus for the integration of health and social care services. The outgoing Chief Executive of the NHS had also claimed that the faith of the coalition Government in competition was a faith that was not 'anchored in evidence', and expressed serious misgivings about the impact of competition, describing it as an impediment to the changes needed in the Service. If the already significant costs of competition were not simply due to the interpretation of the law but to the law itself, then it was his view that the latter needed to be changed. This view was expressed at the end of his tenure as Chief Executive, a real dilemma for a civil servant, when a government policy was in conflict with his professional opinion.

The authors of the *Five Year Forward Review* also observed that there was evidence that the way in which service improvement and clinical engagement was happening could be fragmented and unfocused. They proposed that changes in local organisational arrangements may be needed in some areas to introduce some of the new care models which they were advocating.

In terms of sustaining a comprehensive, high quality NHS, they are clear that 'action will be needed on all three fronts, demand, efficiency and funding' and that less 'impact on any one of them will require compensating action on the other two' (NHS England 2014a: 5). However, they conclude that there is nothing in their analysis to suggest that 'continuing with a comprehensive tax-funded NHS is intrinsically un-doable' and that 'there are viable options for sustaining and improving the NHS over the next five years' (NHS England 2014a: 5). *The NHS Five Year Forward View* is written in a more analytical style, making suggestions for change to improve services to patients but at the same time recognising the importance of 'local solutions', flexibility and discretion, whilst adhering to *the* fundamental *national* health service principles.

## Conclusions

The Health and Social Care Act 2012 became law in April 2012. Key areas of change introduced by the new Act included the transfer of public health powers and duties back to local authorities. It strengthened the CQC and set up a new 'consumer champion' Health Watch England, and gave a new role to GPs to commission services. One of the intentions was to make significant reductions in administrative costs and bureaucracy in the NHS.

Given its controversial passage through both Houses of Parliament, it was not surprising that the final Act differed from the original Bill in various ways. For example, while the PCTs were dissolved, the new organisations replacing them, the CCGs, would be GP-led, with the involvement of other health professionals, rather than solely GP-run. Other changes included the remit of Monitor which was changed from promoting competition to preventing anti-competitive behaviour, as well as continuing to oversee FTs for the foreseeable future. There were also constitutional issues to be resolved with regard to the role of the Secretary of State. These were identified and clarified so that key responsibilities would clearly remain with the holder of that office. Some other features of the NHS would remain essentially unchanged. So the seven principles of the NHS Constitution published on 21 January 2009 by the DoH remained in force until a more recent version of the Constitution was published in March 2013. This new Constitution did not create any new rights or responsibilities, but brought them all together in one document.

Andrew Lansley, the Secretary of State, who had instigated the Health and Social Care Act 2012, was replaced by Jeremy Hunt in September 2012. In Mr Hunt's first year of office, a major series of documents were published, from an updated *Never events policy framework* on 26 October 2012 (DoH 2012d) to the Berwick Report (*A Promise to Learn*) on 6 August 2013. The other documents were the Francis Report (6 February 2013) the Cavendish Review and the Keogh Review (both published in July 2013). These inquiries and their findings had in common issues concerning the quality of treatment and care in the NHS which had first been raised in 1997 and in the Health Act 1999, which laid upon all in the NHS a 'Duty of Quality'. The criteria of quality has come to dominate debates about what patients can expect if the reissued NHS Constitution is to become a reality. The views of Francis, Cavendish and others make sober reading because of the challenges they pose to the quality of treatment and care, which has always been taken for granted as the bedrock of the NHS. The recommendations contained in the reports of these independent and expert external assessors may take years to embed and work through. They will cost money, make assumptions about the commitment and motivation of all staff in the NHS and expect patients to understand and accept, but also to challenge their treatment where necessary. To embody a set of high level values in law will necessitate taking seriously Professor Berwick's view about culture always trumping rules. It may be that culture, rules, standards and control strategies are of equal importance, but perhaps only time will tell.

*The Five Year Forward View* (NHS England 2014a) includes an optimistic conclusion about the potential to maintain an improving NHS based on its essential principles. However optimistic their view, the salutary reminder of the action needed to contain demand, improve efficiency, and guarantee stable and sustainable funding arrangements, while at the same time maintaining and improving the quality of services, will require recognition of the balance to be struck between public, professional and political expectations. Each group will have their own interpretation of what is needed. For the public, responsive, high quality health and social care is the top priority. For the professional groups, the flexibility to practise their skills and apply their knowledge without the 'interference' of the state, while at the same time accepting the limits of autonomy within a national system is a long standing defence of professional freedom and unlikely to diminish. For the politicians, facing the dilemma between what the economy can 'afford' in the light of the drive for raising the quality of health and social care services, is a long-standing issue, which has faced all governments since the inception of the Service in 1948. The public, the professionals and the politicians must face these dilemmas in the context of the major changes that have taken place in British society since the end of the Second World War. These are a radical shift in the demographic structure of the country in the last few decades, the constant comparisons between the expectations and demands created by a consumer society with the clinical and social needs defined by health and social care professionals, especially the challenges of modern technology as applied to medicine, and the willingness of government to fund the consequences of these changes.

It is clear that the passing of the Health and Social Care Act 2012 did not mean there would be an end to some of the controversial issues raised during its passage. Sir David Nicholson was just one of the individuals as well as organisations registering concern about the impact of the radical efficiency gains that had been expected of the NHS and the extent to which these were turning into real cuts in services and deterioration in the quality of care. In January 2014, in its *Quarterly Monitoring Report*, the King's Fund reported that 'as we approach 2014/15, just under two thirds of trust finance directors rated the risk of failure to meet the (Nicholson) challenge as high or very high' (King's Fund 2014).

In February 2015, a further report from the King's Fund (Ham et al 2015) described the coalition Government's health reforms as the 'biggest and most far-reaching legislation in the history of the NHS' (Ham et al 2015: 4) but that the Health and Social Care Act 2012 created 'confused accountabilities' (Ham et al 2015: 20–2) and that both governance and accountability had become 'more complex' as a result of the reforms. The massive restructuring of the NHS was described as 'damaging and distracting' and in particular one significant conclusion was that 'it seems likely that the massive organisational changes that resulted from the reforms contributed to widespread financial distress and failure to hit key targets for patient care'.

# Chapter 16

# Conclusions

There seems to be a common predilection to construct peaceful and serene 'golden ages' to set against contemporary 'crises' and so we have placed considerable emphasis on the conflict-laden history of health and medical care within the UK. This continuing and lengthy history of conflict is of more than academic interest. Long running conflicts that successive generations have failed to resolve may involve irreconcilable aims and interests. This may seem a rather obvious point, but has been often ignored in the not infrequent pursuit of 'single best solutions' to the organisation and delivery of health care.

The provision of health care was a source of conflict long before there was any substantial state intervention in the provision of such care. There were conflicts about costs, and in relations between lay and professional personnel, between professionals and bureaucrats and between the various professional disciplines. Whilst these conflicts may have assumed particular and distinctive forms as state intervention in health care was extended, their origins seem to lie more in the emergence of something we would recognise as modern health care and modern professional groups. There has never been a golden age of conflict-free health care to which we might return if we abandoned our commitment to a national health service (Chapter 1).

Some degree of state involvement in health care has a very long history which can be traced back even before the Poor Law Amendment Act 1834. More extensive state intervention was the subject of Rumsey's *Essays on State Medicine* in 1856. Indeed, social and economic circumstances appear to have drawn the state into significant intervention in aspects of health care, for example, public health, Poor Law medical services, and the asylums (Chapter 1) long before the more overt reformism of New Liberalism and the Labour Party formulated 'national health' legislation in 1911 (Chapter 2) and 1946 (Chapters 3 and 4).

As soon as the state was drawn into something more than a minimal state model of 'less eligibility' and institution-based health care, successive Governments became embroiled in some of the fundamental conflicts of modern health care (how much is it costing and can we afford it?) and of modern state welfare (who should benefit and who should pay?) Over virtually 100 years, from nineteenth-century Poor Law and public health reforms to the Medical Planning Commission of the 1930s, conflict was endemic between the participants and Government (Chapters 1 and 2).

The National Health Service (NHS) came into existence in an atmosphere of conflict generated by the strong ideological commitment of the post-Second World War Labour Government, and the opposition of the Conservative Party as well as some sections of the medical profession. The Service was perceived as the most symbolic of socialist aspirations, a universally available, comprehensive, centrally planned and free at the time of need, medical care service. The state's acceptance of financial responsibility for health care could be sustained by a range of arguments based on efficiency, equity, the welfare of the community, the support of the community and the limitations of the alternative institutions, such as private charity and endowments (Chapters 3 and 4). These arguments did not allay the concerns of politicians regarding the costs of a national health service, especially when it seemed as though the costs of the new service had been seriously underestimated (Chapter 5). The outcomes were predictable. Only 21 months went by before the first cash limits were introduced in the NHS (AbelSmith 1990: 12), and the first major committee of enquiry into the new service was concerned with its cost (Guillebaud Report 1956). The latter was the most obvious indication that the initial Conservative opposition to the passage of the Bill would not disappear. But the main conclusions of the Guillebaud Report were that far from the NHS being over-resourced and wasteful, it was on the contrary under-resourced and efficient given its objectives and the unsympathetic economic environment in which it was established. However, its publication became the launching pad for another area of potential conflict, between the old fashioned public administration of the NHS and the new concern with managing such a Service. Between the twin concerns of money and management, other more 'technical' changes were affecting the Service, all of which raised sharply the economic and management questions for professionals, politicians, planners and eventually the public.

Throughout its history, the Service has been beset by problems concerning funding, administration and management. The conditions of service, including payment of general practitioners, were a general concern. There were also issues about the equality of resources between social groups and regions of the country, and the balance between acute, chronic and preventive medicine. The competing needs of priority groups, such as elderly people and people with mental health problems, and those acutely sick people who required technological intervention such as dialysis and transplants, were to become a dilemma in priority setting, which continues to the present day. This was part of the long-running saga of a powerful medical profession that wished for an arm's length relationship with Government and the state over its clinical autonomy, yet at the same demanded automatic access to the corridors of power to make its case for more resources. At the same time, the values of a consumer-conscious society were subtly being applied to the judgement of professional services, resulting in an overt and official commitment to consumer (patient) choice.

If conflict in the Service seemed to increase after 1974 with the introduction of indicative planning, managerialism and the use of specifically economic criteria to measure health service performance and outcomes, this could be attributed in part to a clearer commitment to 'real NHS principles', such as equity in resource allocation, in less than propitious economic circumstances. Subsequent structural change produced new administrative cadres, such as general managers, efficiency criteria being used to measure the performance of the Service, with much criticism of the validity of the measures used, and public expectations rising inexorably along with the mass production and distribution of medical knowledge about what was feasible, such as DNA testing, genetic engineering and technological applications in medicine.

At the same time, the elderly population could be seen as a 'burden' upon the resources of the Service, as mortality was delayed and 'medicated survival' became a costly process. So even though the political battle was won to establish the Service, conflicts and arguments have dominated the Service since its inception to the present day. Basic questions about individual and collective responsibility and the role of the state were posed by the public health debate in the nineteenth century (Chapter 1). If we can identify, in the first 40 years of the twentieth century, elements of health care which would be incorporated in the NHS, such as compulsory health insurance and municipal health services, we can also, in that same period, identify the origins of later conflicts about costs, remuneration, clinical freedom and (again) the role of the state (Chapter 2).

There are also the conflicting roles of different specialties of the medical profession. The profession has been a major source of innovatory ideas about health care reforms and could be described as 'progressive' rather than 'conservative'. Where Governments have been reluctant to provide medical care on a continuing and open basis, the role of the medical profession has been critical, as for example, the contribution of Poor Law medical officers in the nineteenth century (Chapter 1), and Lord Dawson's Report in 1920. The role of the British Medical Association (BMA) and the Socialist Medical Association (now the Socialist Health Association) in the 1930s (Chapter 2) and the influences of the Royal Colleges in the late 1980s and early 1990s (Chapter 10) are further examples of professional persuasion, influence and pressure on British Governments. At the same time, the profession has also been a major source of opposition to health care reforms, regardless of the political party forming the Government, but especially in battles to influence and delay the establishment of National Health Insurance before 1913 (Chapter 2) and the NHS before 1948 (Chapter 4). In 1990, the BMA took a strong stand against the introduction of the so-called 'internal market' thus providing an example of a so-called 'conservative' profession in direct opposition to a Conservative Government (Chapter 10). Few of the conflicts identified in contemporary debates are entirely new.

Also, there is the dichotomy between centralised control, to maintain standards, and local autonomy, to meet local needs. One radical but simple organisational solution to this problem would have been to unify the NHS under the control of local government. Not only would this have bridged the divisions between hospital and community health care, but it would also have afforded the opportunity for a consistent and co-ordinated approach to health and related social care services. But the medical profession was opposed to local government control of the NHS. The resulting limitations of the 1948 tripartite structure exacerbated the inevitable difficulties of recasting the balance between institution-based and community-based health and social care. The later culmination of a lengthy period of discussion about organisational reform (1962–1974) replayed some of these issues. Central government did not want to transfer the NHS to local government for fear of losing control of public expenditure on health (the cost-containment issue), whilst the medical profession did not want local government to control the NHS for rather similar reasons to those expressed before 1948 (the professional autonomy issue). In addition, the social workers did not want social care services to become part of the NHS for fear of being controlled by another profession (another professional autonomy issue). The result of the NHS and personal social service restructurings following legislation in 1970 and 1974 were that policies for community care were still hampered by what was to become known as the health social care divide. Health care services such as home nursing and day hospitals remained the responsibility of the NHS. Social care services, such as home helps and day centres, were the responsibility of local authority social services departments.

Sir Roy Griffiths, in the early 1980s, was critical of an administered NHS. He detected an absence of managerial authority and with this therefore a lack of visible accountability for the deficiencies in resource management and the quality of services. His solution was to insist on the NHS becoming a managed Service with a core group of specialised health service managers. The NHS changed from an administered service based on professional goodwill to a managed service with unprecedented bureaucratic regulation. NHS critics have tended to blame all deficiencies in the delivery of health care on the bureaucracy, administration and management of the NHS, and this distrust is shared by professionals, politicians, patients and the general public. Although the terms are often used interchangeably, bureaucrats, administrators and managers have different tasks. Bureaucracy is concerned with oversight of due process, fairness, complaints and redress, while administration is responsible for the application of centrally directed rules. Management's skill is to use discretion, for example in the use of scarce resources to deliver a service in line with clinical priorities.

With hindsight, it may have been inevitable that the 1948 compromise between a state administered service and professional freedom, struck by Bevan and the leaders of the medical profession, could not be sustained in the era of rising costs. As Klein argues:

> As in the United States, clinicians feel oppressed by what they see as managerial encroachment on their autonomy and as excessive demands for

accountability that have flowed from the Government's emphasis on quality control. They see themselves as over appraised and over inspected

(Klein 1995a: 941)

Regardless of how we divide up and compartmentalise the history of health care in the UK, most periods seem to contain within themselves major differences of opinion about the rationale, the methods and the outcomes of providing and judging medical care in a national health service. All were contentious in their time and all have in common the uneasy relationship between professional definitions of adequate health care, government funding and organisation of such care, and the actual and potential expectations of patients. Perhaps one of the challenges and achievements of the NHS has been the management of conflicts and changes within the broad parameters of a near consensus about the concept of a national health service which Beveridge captured in his Report (1942). Given the scarcity of 'conflict-free golden ages' we should perhaps be more accepting of the conflicts engendered by the attempt to contain within the institutional arrangements of the NHS a number of dissident and potentially conflicting elements.

We have now had over 100 years of statutorily recognised health care in the UK. With the establishment of the NHS, Britain became the first country in the world to offer free medical care to the whole population. The principle of universality, of providing the same rights to services to all residents, has since been emulated by many other countries. Given agreement on the revolutionary nature of the NHS (universal provision and access, comprehensive coverage, absence of a cash nexus, retention by professionals of independence within a state system) and a context of scarcity with the necessity to reconstruct a war-battered society, it seems remarkable that within a decade the NHS had become an accepted and well regarded social institution, resting upon public and collective rather than private and individual values (Eckstein 1958). Even with the introduction of managed, quasi-market, arrangements the NHS retained the key principles of a national system, financed by taxation, with comprehensive coverage and no explicit limits on health care. Indeed, the concentration on continuing episodes of conflict, whether between Government and the profession, or between Government and organised pressure groups, runs the danger of ignoring or forgetting what to a non-British visitor has been a remarkable consensus surrounding the delivery of health care through the NHS. Overseas visitors still comment on the simplicity of funding arrangements and the guarantee of medical care based upon need not purchasing power. The NHS is well-established within British social and political arrangements, having been in existence for 67 years. This may be, in part, because some of its characteristics, for example, health care that is largely free at the point of consumption, were present in the arrangements for health care before the Service was established (Chapters 1 and 2). It is taken for granted that there will be a medical care response to a whole range of health threatening episodes, from the most minor visit to an accident and emergency department to major transplant surgery or long-term care. There is a long-standing near-consensus with regard to the citizenship right to adequate health care which we might represent as 'minimising the gap between new biomedical knowledge and its application and availability to the community as a whole' (Carrier and Kendall 1990c: 10). For the moment, the rights of NHS users and the responsibilities of the state remain broadly unchanged, the key issue remains the volume of resources the state is willing to commit to the NHS in recognition of these rights and responsibilities.

This is a history of health *care* rather than health, but concerns regarding the latter have been, as one might expect, a feature of the former. We should note in particular the Liberal reforms, the case for health care reform in the 1930s, and the Beveridge Report (1942). One widely shared assumption from the Beveridge Report was that the introduction of the NHS would improve the health status of the population, would moderate inequalities in health status between sections of the population and would be a powerful force for the elimination of disease and sickness through prevention, as well as health promotion and advice. However, it has become apparent that the relationship between health care and health status is a more complex one. Health care and health status are related, but the relationship is mediated through the impact of social divisions, lay/professional relationships and attitudes towards health and sickness. From a simple equation attributing improvements and variations in morbidity to improvements and variations in health care, a more diverse picture has emerged since the establishment of the NHS. A more efficient and equitable health care system does not translate simply into improved health status for the population as a whole, or of fewer inequalities in health status between locations and social groups. The citizenship right to adequate health care is not identical with a citizenship right to adequate health, and the former cannot be taken as a guarantee of the latter.

This complex relationship between health status and health care does provide vindication for another view expressed in the Beveridge Report. That policies to improve the health status of the population, as a whole or of sections thereof, require an inter-sector approach based upon a recognition of the significance of a range of external (environmental), personal (genetic) and public (state and voluntary activities) policies in addition to policies for health care. As Beveridge indicated in identifying his 'Five Giants', the contribution from public policies would involve more than health care but would also include education, housing and social security. Social, economic, environmental and lifestyle factors are at the root of much ill-health and disability. These include many factors over which the NHS has little or no control, although other state activity may have the potential to impact on some of these factors, for example, other service provision or regulatory regimes.

In the period leading up to the establishment of the NHS, the hope was expressed that an efficient and effective national health service could be developed that would bring to the entire population a clinically effective, economically efficient and equitably just service. Sufficient resources for such a service might be afforded in part by diminishing the incidence of disease and disability (Beveridge Report 1942: 105, para. 270(3); 158, para. 426; 162, para. 437). This outcome did not materialise. However, it has been the more market-orientated health care systems that have experienced greatest difficulties with cost-containment, the over-prescription of drugs and over-use of surgical intervention. The example of Canada, where a switch to a universal and largely government-funded system led to a levelling off of health care costs by comparison with the increasingly competitive and commercial US system, is a one example of this point (Timmins 1988: 77). It is unrealistic to expect the NHS to deliver stable or declining health care costs, but there is also equally abundant evidence that 'socialised medicine' (the NHS model) provides a most cost-effective means of delivering such health care.

There is no doubt that clinical autonomy remains an important dimension of the NHS. Indeed, given the enduring popularity of a Service that has placed considerable emphasis on that autonomy, it may be that it still represents an appropriate basis for decisions if suitably informed by research, guided by ethical considerations and moderated more by concerns about economic costs to the community than the economic benefits to the individual professional or health care provider. It may be that economic theory is best left in the text books where it works, and used rather sparingly in the real world of health care, given the propensity of health care markets to depart significantly from the text book.

For the moment at least, the NHS remains a very popular public institution and one for which most people seem prepared to pay. The British Social Attitudes Survey has found that despite all the political exhortations in recent years, which stress the desirability of cutting State spending, the public still wants Government expenditure on the NHS to be increased, '... there remains persistent, and indeed increasing, support for the idea of a universal service (Bosanquet 1989: 102; Klein 1995a: 157).

The NHS has been considered to be the most publicly valued and politically discussed of all British welfare state arrangements. This book has shown that from the difficult days beginning with Beveridge's promise (Beveridge Report 1942: paras 426–7) through to Brown's White Paper (Ministry of Health 1944) and Bevan's triumphant speech during the Third Reading (April 1946) (House of Commons 1946: cols 43–63), that whatever Government has been in power and whatever the concerns, and sometimes sheer over-statement of the threat to professional independence in a state-run service, nevertheless the Service has survived to provide one of the most comprehensive, high quality, free at point of need, medical care systems in the world (Davis et al 2014):

> The basic principle of the NHS is simply that comprehensive, high quality medical care should be available to all citizens on the basis of professionally judged medical need without financial barriers to access. The same aspiration is to be found in nearly all economically developed societies outside the United States.
>
> (Weale 1998)

Are these aspirations compatible with increasing health care costs or do they represent an 'inconsistent triad?' Can we have only two of Weale's triad of a comprehensive, high quality and universally available service? The US solution, high quality comprehensive care not available to all, is described as a 'poor solution' by Weale in 1998, with up to 20 per cent of citizens at that time either underinsured or uninsured, and non-existent primary care service for the poor. The successful passage of the 'Obama Care' Bill after the ruling by the Supreme Court in the case of *National Federation of Independent Business v Sebelius* was decided on 28 June 2012. There was a 5 to 4 ruling to uphold the Affordable Care Act. This has not resolved the strong ideological conflict around the statutory obligation of the American public to insure themselves against ill-health and thereby gain access to medical care. Those who are insured face 'spiralling costs and defensive medicine', as well as efforts on the part of insurance companies to evade or diminish their insurance obligations. Isaiah Berlin warned in 1959 that 'value conflicts are the essence of public policy … To suppose that we can escape this conflict of values by retreating to an ideologically and organisationally simpler world casts a veil of deceit over the choices that must be made' (Berlin 1959: 167–72).

In his discussion of health care politics in the USA, Alford put forward a theory of health care being influenced by the structural interests of the 'professional monopolists' (the medical profession), 'corporate rationalisers' (insurance companies and health care managers), and 'equal health care advocates' (the 'repressed' community). The structure of the system is dependent upon the relationship between and dominance of one of those interests over the other. While the idea of structural interests may not be immediately transferable to the NHS, nevertheless a similar interest can be detected before the advent of and during the growth of the NHS, with the rise in the community of expectations resting upon the primary care system in the UK to challenge the dominance of hospital-based, acute care systems, and the post-Griffiths evolution of management.

The system reforms set in motion by the Health and Social Care Act 2012 supported Steven's idea that the NHS was in for a period of 'constructive discomfort' (Stevens 2004).

Although Weale's article was published in 1998, nevertheless its main theme, 'Can we have all three?' still dominates current discussions of the state's health care offer to its citizens in England and Wales. Of course in conditions of scarcity, some rationing devices are necessary. For state health care, the question is how do you ration with equity and retain the support of the disappointed, preventing the disappointed becoming the disenchanted and ultimately the disaffected? The argument then becomes that the presence of state provision of health care allows the disappointed the opportunity to challenge with possible scope for redress. By contrast, the presence of competing markets reinforces the dispossession of the disappointed. This viewpoint is quite well summed up in Titmuss's vision of a society, which lets market relations dominate in the areas we have come to view as subject to state welfare activities, 'There is nothing permanent about the expression of reciprocity. If the bonds of community giving are broken the result is not a state of value neutralism. The vacuum is likely to be filled by hostility and social conflict … the myth of maximising economic growth can supplant the growth of social relations' (Titmuss 1970: 198–9).

So what would the situation be like without the NHS? This might be said to constitute the *key* but *unanswerable* question about any form of welfare, state or non-state. But although it cannot be answered in any definitive sense, it is susceptible to some comment and the production of some plausible answers. One set of answers might be derived from comparative analysis. What has been the effect of different models of state welfare in other societies? Have they, for example, been markedly more or less 'successful' in solving 'health care problems'? Another set of answers may be derived from the analysis of empirical evidence. Welfare spending in general 'is notably more egalitarian than income distributed through the market' (O'Higgins 1983: 181) and evidence for health care, especially the comparison with the USA, suggests health care spending through the NHS is more egalitarian than health care distributed through the market.

Sir George Godber's assessment 40 years after the appointed day is still relevant. Although he was a great supporter of the NHS, he recognised the imperfections of the NHS in that it did not have an in-built review of quality at that time, and was often less effective than he hoped it would be. He felt it was under-funded and too much focused on reducing costs. Yet he could still say that the NHS it had, in its first 40 years:

> achieved more for the resources invested in it, than any other service that I know. It has one great advantage in its firm basis of multi-disciplinary primary care. It has been restricted by lack of funds, savagely in the 1980s, but no country can have all the resources that could be used to advantage, and at least in the NHS we share in accordance with need, and, so far, not in accordance with ability to pay.
>
> (Godber 1988)

Judged against the 'real world' of 'real social institutions' in Britain and elsewhere, there is much to be said in support of one judgement that the NHS is 'a striking success story' (Klein 1995a: 226) and to concur with another judgement that the 'NHS was and remains one of the finest institutions ever built by anybody anywhere' (Hennessey 1992: 144). Bevan's comment may be idealistic but it is shared by many. Society becomes more wholesome, more serene, and spiritually healthier, if it knows that:

> its citizens have at the back of their consciousness the knowledge that not only themselves, but all their fellows have access, when ill, to the best that medical skill can provide. But private charity and endowment, although inescapably essential at one time, cannot meet the cost of this. If the job is to be done, the state must accept financial responsibility.
>
> (Bevan 1978: 100)

He also maintained that 'a free Health Service is a triumphant example of the superiority of collective action and public initiative applied to a segment of society where commercial principles are seen at their worst' (Bevan 1978: 109). His view was that 'the field in which the claims of individual commercialism come into most immediate conflict with reputable notions of social values is that of health' (Bevan 1978: 98). 'The National Health Service is the nearest Britain has ever come to institutionalising altruism' (Hennessey 1992: 132).

What perhaps we need is an intellectual equivalent of the emotional experience involved in the final scenes of Frank Capra's film *It's A Wonderful Life* in which George Bailey discovers what life would have been like if he had not lived (Capra 1946). George Bailey's life had, in some respects, never quite worked out as he hoped. For example, he never got away from his home town of Bedford Falls, but Bedford Falls would have turned into a significantly different and worse place without his 'wonderful life' that is to say, Pottersville, a town dominated by that evil go-getter, Potter.

Perhaps in the end, the judgement on the NHS would not be as positive as that on George Bailey. But drawing on international and historical comparisons, and making what we can of the non-state alternatives and the residual model of state welfare, we might at least conclude that the NHS remains 'the least worst alternative' that any society might choose. Indeed, in many respects, it may offer us our best hope of getting equity, effectiveness and efficiency in the allocation and utilisation of health care. It may compensate for discrepancies in welfare even if it does not always enhance status and psychological well-being, which may only come through total individual self-sufficiency. It may not have the profound impact on inequalities hoped for by its founders, but it may significantly moderate the impact which economic inequalities would have on inequalities in health and health care, especially the latter where there would be a denial of applied knowledge in the health field to those unable to purchase it, even though this knowledge was collectively known. It may not convey the full sense of citizenship its founders hoped for, but it may at the very least limit the sense of non-citizenship that would otherwise be more pervasive for more vulnerable groups in our sort of society. In this way, and in its impact on inequalities, the NHS may contribute to a more socially just society than we would have in its absence. Lastly, and in contrast to the concerns of those who feared for the sense of community and professional commitment when a virtual state monopoly took over health care and displaced voluntary institutions, the NHS may have fostered both levels of individual altruism and standards of professional ethics that have eluded other health care systems both past and present.

## Postscript

We were completing this book in the months leading up to the General Election of 7 May 2015.

In the usual political turmoil preceding a General Election, the current state and future of the NHS was, as expected, high on the political agenda. The manifestos of all political parties included claims and counter-claims about how safe the NHS would be in the hands of the competing parties. Whatever the outcome of the Election, the Service is likely to remain one of the dominant concerns of the public.

These concerns can be grouped under the following questions, which fall under the general categories of the sustainability of the NHS and the quality of the health care to be expected.

Will enough money be spent to meet the health care needs of the population?
Does the NHS need to be 'reorganised' again in order to deliver the most efficient and equitable care?
Lastly, will the values that underpinned the creation of the NHS remain inviolate no matter which government is in power and whatever the state of the economy?

In facing these questions, future Secretaries of State would be well advised to note the relative success of the NHS exemplified by the recent judgment of the American Commonwealth Fund in its comparative studies of eleven health care systems in the developed world (Davis et al, 2014, Exhibit 2.11, p.12). The Fund ranked the UK first for the quality of care (measured by effective care, safe care, co-ordinated care and patient-centred care), first for access (measured by cost-related access problems and timeliness of care), first for efficiency, second for equity, but tellingly tenth out of the eleven countries for healthy lives (raising serious questions concerning the long-standing issue of investment in public health services, especially those social determinants of health identified in the Beveridge Report).

# Bibliography

Abel-Smith, B. (1959) 'Trends in social policy: social security'. In Ginsberg, M. (ed.) *Law and Opinion in the Twentieth Century*, London: Stevens.

Abel-Smith, B. (1964) *The Hospitals 1800–1948: a study in social administration in England and Wales*, London: Heinemann.

Abel-Smith, B. (1971) 'The Politics of Health', *New Society*, 29 July 1971.

Abel-Smith, B. (1972) 'The History of Medical Care'. In Martin, E. W. (ed.) *Comparative Developments in Social Welfare*, London: Allen & Unwin.

Abel-Smith, B. (1976) *Value for money in health services*, London: Heinemann.

Abel-Smith, B. (1978) *National Health Service: the first thirty years*, London: HMSO.

Abel-Smith, B. (1990) 'The first forty years'. In Carrier, J. and Kendall, I. (eds) *Socialism and the NHS: Fabian Essays in Health Care*, Aldershot: Gower.

Abel-Smith, B. (1994) *An introduction to health: policy, planning and financing*, Harlow: Longman.

Abel-Smith, B. and Glennerster, H. (1995) 'Labour and the Tory health reforms', *Fabian Review*, Vol. 107, No. 3.

Abel-Smith, B. and Titmuss, R. M. (1956) *The Cost of the National Health Service* (National Institute of Economic and Social Research Occasional Papers 18), London: Cambridge University Press.

Abrams, P. (1977) 'Community Care: Some Research Problems and Priorities', *Policy and Politics*, No. 6, pp. 125–51.

Acheson Report (1988) *Public Health in England*, Cm. 289, London: HMSO.

Alford, R. (1975) *Healthy Care Politics: Ideological and Interest Group Barriers to Reform*, London: University of Chicago Press.

Allsop, J. (1984) *Health Policy and the National Health Service*, London: Longman.

Allsop, J. (1995) *Health Policy and the NHS: Towards 2000* (2nd edn), London: Longman.

Appleby, J. (2011) 'Which is the best health system in the world?' *British Medical Journal*, 4 October 2011, 343:d6267.

Audit Commission (1986) *Making a Reality of Community Care*, London: HMSO.

Audit Commission (1992) *Lying in Wait: The use of medical beds in acute hospitals*, London: HMSO.

Audit Commission (1994) *Trusting in the Future: Towards an Audit Agenda for the NHS Providers*, London: HMSO.

Audit Commission (1995) *A Price on their Heads: measuring management costs in NHS Trusts*, London: HMSO.

Audit Commission (1997) *The Coming of Age*, London: HMSO.

Ayers, G. (1971) *England's First State Hospitals and the Metropolitan Asylums Board 1867– 1930*, London: Wellcome Institute of the History of Medicine.

Baggott, R. (1994) *Health and Health Care in Britain*, Basingstoke: Macmillan.

Ball, D. (1972) 'Health', *New Society*, 3 August 1972, p. 241.

Bartlett, W. and Harrison, L. (1993) 'Quasi-markets and the National Health Service Reforms'. In Le Grand, J. and Bartlett, W. (eds) *Quasi-markets and social policy*, Basingstoke: Macmillan.

Barnett, C. (1986) *The Audit of War; The Illusion and Reality of Britain as a Great Nation*, London: Macmillan.

Barr, A. and Logan, R. F. L. (1977) 'Policy alternatives for Resource Allocation', *The Lancet*, 7 May 1977, pp. 994–6.

Barton, R. (1976) *Institutional Neurosis* (3rd edn), Bristol: J. Wright.

Bayley, H. (1995) *The Nation's Health*, London: Fabian Society.

Bean, P. and MacPherson, S. (eds) (1983) *Approaches to Welfare*, London: Routledge & Kegan Paul.

Beardshaw, V. and Morgan, U. (1990) *Community Care Wars*, London: Mind Publications.

Beaver, M. W. (1973) 'Population, infant mortality and milk', *Population Studies*, Vol. XXVII, No. 2, pp. 243–54.

Benzeval, M., Judge, K. and New, B. (1991) 'Health and Health Care in London', *Public Money and Management*, Vol. II, No. 1, pp. 25–32.

Beresford, P. (1978) 'More Camberwells?', *New Society*, 21/28 December 1978, pp. 700–2.

Berlin, I. (1988) *Four Essays on Liberty*, Oxford: Oxford University Press.

Berwick Report (2013) *A promise to learn*, London: Department of Health.

Bevan, A. (1978) *In Place of Fear*, London: Quartet Books.

Beveridge Report (1942) *Social Insurance and Allied Services*, Cmd. 6404, London: HMSO.

Black Report (1980) *Inequalities in Healthy: Report of a Research Working Party*, London: Department of Health and Social Security.

Booth, C. (1903) *Life and Labour of the People in London*, London: Macmillan.

Booth, T. A. (1981) 'Collaboration between the Health and Social Services: Part II, A Case Study of Joint Finance', *Policy and Politics*, Vol. 9, No. 2, pp. 205–26.

Bosanquet, N. (1989) 'An ailing state of National Health'. In Jowell, R., Witherspoon, S. and Brook, L. (eds) *British Social Attitudes, The Fifth Report*, Aldershot: Gower.

Boswell, D. and Wingrove, J. M. (eds) (1973) *The Handicapped Person in the Community*, London: Open University Press.

Brand, J. (1965) *Doctors and the State*, Baltimore: John Hopkins Press.

Brenton, M. and Ungerson, C. (1986) *Yearbook of Social Policy 1985–86*, London: Routledge & Kegan Paul.

Briggs, A. (1978) 'The achievements, failures and aspirations of the NHS', *New Society*, 23 November 1978, pp. 448–51.

Bristowe, J. S. and Holmes, T. (1863) *The Hospitals of England and Wales*, Sixth Report of the Medical Officer of the Privy Council, London: P.S. King and Son.

British Hospitals Association (1937) *Report of the Voluntary Hospitals Commission* (Sankey Report), London: British Hospitals Association.

British Medical Association (BMA) (1930) *Proposals for a General Medical Service for the Nation*, London: BMA.

British Medical Association (BMA) (1938) *A General Medical Service for the Nation*, London: BMA.

British Medical Association (BMA) (1942) *Medical Planning Commission*, London: BMA.

Brown, M. (1977) *An Introduction to Social Administration*, London: Hutchinsons.

Brown, M. and Baldwin, S. (1978) *The Year Book of Social Policy in Britain 1977*, London: Routledge & Kegan Paul.

Brown, R. G. S. (1972) 'Reorganising the Health Service'. In Jones, K. (ed.) *The Yearbook of Social Policy in Britain 1971*, London: Routledge & Kegan Paul.

Brown, R. G. S. (1975) *The Management of Welfare: a study of British social service administration*, Glasgow: Collins.

Brown, R. G. S. (1979) *Reorganising the National Health Service*, Oxford: Basil Blackwell.

Bruce, M. (1961) *The Coming of the Welfare State*, London: Batsford.

Burdett, H. (ed.) (1893a) *Burdett's Hospital Annual and Year Book of Philanthropy*, London: The Scientific Press.

Burdett, H. C. (1893b) *Hospitals and Asylums of the World*, London: Churchill.

Burkitt, D. P. (1973) 'Diseases of modern economic development'. In Howe, G. M. and Loraine, J. A. (eds) (1973) *Environmental Medicine*, London: Heinemann.

Butler, J. R. and Vaile, M. (1984) *Health and Health Services: An Introduction to Health Care in Britain*, London: Routledge & Kegan Paul.

Buxton, M. (1976) *Health and Inequality*, Milton Keynes: Open University Press.

Buxton, M. and Klein, R. (1975) 'Distribution of Hospital Provision: Policy Themes and Resources Variations', *British Medical Journal*, Vol. 307, 8 February 1975, pp. 345–9.

Buxton, M. and Klein, R. (1978) *Allocating Health Resources: a commentary on the Resource Allocation Working Party*, Royal Commission on NHS Research Paper, No. 3, London: HMSO.

Cabinet Office (2010) *The Coalition: Our Programme for Government*, London: HMSO.

Calder, A. (1971) *The People's War*, London: Granada.

Campbell, J. (1987) *Nye Bevan and the Mirage of British Socialism*, London: Weidenfeld & Nicolson.

Capra, F. (dir.) (1946) *It's A Wonderful Life*, RKO/Liberty Films.

Carrier, J. (1978) 'Positive discrimination in the allocation of NHS resources'. In Brown, M. and Baldwin, S. (eds) (1978) *The Year Book of Social Policy in Britain 1977*, London: Routledge & Kegan Paul.

Carrier, J. (1980) 'London's health'. In Hall, P. (ed.) (1980) *A Radical Agenda for London*, London: Fabian Society.

Carrier, J. and Kendall, I. (1977) 'The Development of Welfare States: the production of plausible accounts', *Journal of Social Policy*, Vol. 6, No. 3, pp. 271–90.

Carrier, J. and Kendall, I. (1986) 'The Griffiths Report'. In Brenton, M. and Ungerson, C. (eds) (1986) *Yearbook of Social Policy 1985–86*, London: Routledge & Kegan Paul.

Carrier, J. and Kendall, I. (eds) (1990) *Socialism and the NHS: Fabian essays in health care*, Aldershot: Gower.

Carrier, J. and Kendall, I. (1990a) 'Working for patients?'. In Carrier, J. and Kendall, I. (eds) *Socialism and the NHS: Fabian essays in health care*, Aldershot: Gower.

Carrier, J. and Kendall, I. (1990b) *Medical negligence: complaints and compensations*, Aldershot: Gower.

Carrier, J. and Kendall, I. (1990c) 'At its best without equal'. In Carrier, J. and Kendall, I. (eds) *Socialism and the NHS: Fabian essays in health care*, Aldershot: Gower.

Carrier, J. and Kendall, I. (1995) 'Professionalism and inter-professionalism in health and community care: some theoretical issues'. In Carrier, J., Owens, P. and Horder, J. (eds) (1995) *Interprofessional issues in Community and Primary Health Care*, London: Macmillan.

Carrier, J. and Kendall, I. (2008a) 'Lord Darzi Interview: A Policy Perspective', *London Journal of Primary Care*, Vol. 1, pp. 45–7.

Carrier, J. and Kendall, I. (2008b) 'Twas ever thus: why Darzi is 90 years too late', *Health Service Journal*, 28 February 2008, pp. 16–17.

Cavendish Review (2013) *An independent review into Healthcare Assistants and Support workers in the NHS and social care settings* (Chair: Camilla Cavendish), 10 July 2013, London: Department of Health.

Checkland, S. G. and Checkland, E. O. A. (eds) (1974) *The Poor Law Report of 1834*, Harmondsworth: Pelican.

Clarke, M. (1976) 'Community as dustbin', *New Society*, 29 July 1976, p. 235.

Clegg, N. and Williams, Baroness (2012) 'Letter to all Social Democratic MPs and Peers', *The Independent*, 27 February 2012.

Cochrane, A. (1972) *Effectiveness and Efficiency: random reflections on health services*, London: Nuffield Provincial Hospitals Trust.

Cohen, S. (1979) 'Community Control – a new utopia', *New Society*, 15 March 1979, pp. 609–11.

Committee on Standards in Public Life (CSPL) (1995) *The 7 Principles of Public Life*, London: CSPL.

Coombes, R. (2011) 'Shirley Williams: still a rebel', *British Medical Journal*, 4 October 2011, 343:d6359.

Cranbrook Report (1959) *Report of the Maternity Services Committee*, London: HMSO.

Crosland, C. A. R. (1956) *The Future of Socialism*, London: Jonathan Cape.

Crossman, R. (1969) *Paying for the Social Services*, London: Fabian Society.

Curtis Report (1946) *Report on the Care of Children*, Cmnd. 6922, London: HMSO.

Darzi, Lord (2007a) *Health Care for London: Case for Change*, London: NHS London.

Darzi, Lord (2007b) *Healthcare for London: A Framework for Action*, London: NHS London.

Darzi, Lord (2009) *High Quality Care for All. NHS Next Stage Review. Final Report*, Cm. 7432, Norwich: The Stationery Office.

Davies, B. (1968) *Social Needs and resources in local services: a study in variations in standards of provision of personal social services*, London: Michael Joseph.

Davies, P. (2013) *The Concise NHS Handbook 2013/14, The essential guide to the new NHS in England*, London: NHS Confederation.

Davis, K., Stremikis, K., Squires, D. and Schoen, C. (2010) *Mirror, Mirror on the Wall: How the performance of the US health care system compares internationally*, New York: Commonwealth Fund.

Davis, K., Stremikis, K., Squires, D. and Schoen, C. (2014) *Mirror, Mirror on the Wall, 2014 update: How the US health care system compares internationally*, New York: Commonwealth Fund.

Dawson Report (1920) *Interim Report on the future of the Medical and Allied Services*, Cmd. 693, London: HMSO.

Day, P. and Klein, R. (1987) *Accountabilities: five public services*, London: Tavistock.

Department of Health (DoH) (1989a) *Working for Patients*, Cm. 555, London: HMSO.

Department of Health (DoH) (1989b) *Caring for People: Community Care in the Next Decade and Beyond*, Cm. 849, London: HMSO.

Department of Health (DoH) (1990) *Community Care in the Next Decade and Beyond: Policy Guidance*, London: HMSO.

Department of Health (DoH) (1992) *The Health of the Nation*, Cm. 1523, London: HMSO.

Department of Health (DoH) (1993) *Making London Better*, Cm. 2812, London: HMSO.

Department of Health (DoH) (1995) *A policy framework for commissioning services: a report by the Expert Advisory group on Cancer to the Chief Medical officer of England and Wales* (Calman-Hine Report), London: HMSO.

Department of Health (DoH) (1997) *The New NHS*, Cm. 3807, London: Stationery Office.

Department of Health (DoH) (1998a) *The Future of London's Health Services*, London: DoH.

Department of Health (DoH) (1998b) *Our Healthier Nation*, London: HMSO.

Department of Health (DoH) (1998c) *First-class service: quality in the NHS*, London: HMSO.

Department of Health (DoH) (2000) *NHS Plan: a plan for investment, a plan for reform*, Cm. 4818, London: HMSO.

Department of Health (DoH) (2002) *Reforming NHS financial flows, payment by results*, London: HMSO.

Department of Health (DoH) (2004) *Choosing Health: making healthy choices easier*, Cm 6374 (White Paper), London HMSO.

Department of Health (DoH) (2005) *Health reform in England: update and next steps*, London: HMSO.

Department of Health (DoH) (2006a) *Our Health, Our Care, Our Say: a new direction for community services*, London: HMSO.

Department of Health (DoH) (2006b) *Commissioning a Patient-led NHS*, London: HMSO.

Department of Health (DoH) (2010a) Speech by the Rt. Hon Andrew Lansley CBE MP, Secretary of State for Health, 8 June 2010: 'My ambition for patient-centred care', 18 June 2010, London: DoH.

Department of Health (DoH) (2010b) *Revision to the Operating Framework for the NHS in England 2010/11*, 21 June 2010 (sent to all Chief Executives cc to all Chairs), London: DoH.

Department of Health (DoH) (2010c) *Equity and Excellence: Liberating the NHS*, July 2010, Cm. 7881 (White Paper), London: HMSO.

Department of Health (DoH) (2010d) *Liberating the NHS consultation papers*, July 2010 (*Transparency in Outcomes, a framework for the NHS*; *Commissioning for Patients*; *Local democratic legitimacy in health*; *Regulating health care providers*; *Report of the Arm's Length Bodies Review*), London: DoH.

Department of Health (DoH) (2010e) *Liberating the NHS: legislative framework and next steps*, Cm. 7993, London: HMSO.

Department of Health (DoH) (2010f) *General Practice Out of Hours Service, Project to consider and assess current arrangements. A review by Dr. Colin-Thome and Professor Field*, February 2010, London: HMSO.

Department of Health (DoH) (2010g) *The NHS Constitution for England*, London: HMSO.

Department of Health (DoH) (2010h) *The Government's response to the 2010 Consultation on NHS reform*, London: HMSO.

Department of Health (DoH) (2011a) *Government response to the NHS Future Forum report*, Cm. 8113, London: HMSO

Department of Health (DoH) (2011b) 'Andrew Lansley, A patient centred NHS', Transcript of speech at Guys and St. Thomas Hospital, 7 December 2011, London: DoH.

Department of Health (DoH) (2012a) 'Letter from Andrew Lansley', 29 March 2012, London: DoH, www.dh.gov.uk/health/2012/03/lansley-letter (accessed 4 May 2015).

Department of Health (DoH) (2012b) 'Letters from Andrew Lansley: Dear colleague letters' (Ambition for clinically-led NHS), 3 April 2012, London: DoH.

Department of Health (DoH) (2012c) *The Mandate: A mandate from the Government to the NHS Commissioning Board: April 2013 to March 2015*, London: DoH.

Department of Health (DoH) (2012d) *Never events policy framework: an update to the never events*, 29 October 2012, London: DoH.

Department of Health (DoH) (2013a) *The NHS Constitution: The NHS belongs to us all*, London, DoH.

Department of Health (DoH) (2013b) *A mandate from the government to the NHS Commissioning Board April 2013 to March 2014*, London: DoH.

Department of Health (DoH) (2013c) *A mandate from the government to Health Education England*, London: DoH.

Department of Health (DoH) (2014) *Statutory duty of candour for health and adult social care providers*, 26 March 2014, London; DoH.

Department of Health/Office of Population Censuses and Surveys (DoH/OPCS) (1994) *Departmental Report: The Government's Expenditure Plans 1994–95 to 1996–97*, Cm. 2812, London: HMSO.

Department of Health/Office of Population Censuses and Surveys (DoH/OPCS) (1995) *Departmental Report: The Government's Expenditure Plans 1995–96 to 1997–98*, Cm. 2812, London: HMSO.

Department of Health and Social Security (DHSS) (1970) *The Future Structure of the National Health Service* (Second Green Paper), London: HMSO.

Department of Health and Social Security (DHSS) (1971a) *National Health Service Reorganisation: Consultative Document*, London: HMSO.

Department of Health and Social Security (DHSS) (1971b) *Better Services for the Mentally Handicapped*, Cmnd. 4683, London: HMSO.

Department of Health and Social Security (DHSS) (1972a) *Hospital Advisory Service: Annual Report*, London: HMSO.

Department of Health and Social Security (DHSS) (1972b) *National Health Service Reorganisation: England*, Cmnd. 5055, London: HMSO.

Department of Health and Social Security (DHSS) (1972c) *Management arrangements for the Reorganised National Health Service (Grey Book) Report of the Management Study Steering Committee* (Chairman: Sir Philip Rogers), London: HMSO.

Department of Health and Social Security (DHSS) (1972d) *Statistical and Report Series No. 3: Census of Mentally Handicapped patients in Hospitals in England and Wales 1970*, London: HMSO.

Department of Health and Social Security (DHSS) (1974) *Democracy in the NHS*, London: HMSO.

Department of Health and Social Security (DHSS) (1975a) *The First Interim Report of the Resource Allocation Working Party (RAWP)*, London: HMSO.

Department of Health and Social Security (DHSS) (1975b) *Better Services for the Mentally Ill*, Cmnd. 6233, London: HMSO.

Department of Health and Social Security (DHSS) (1976a) *Priorities for Health and Personal Social Services in England: A Consultative Document*, London: HMSO.

Department of Health and Social Security (DHSS) (1976b) *The Final Report of the Resource Allocation Working Party (RAWP)*, London: HMSO.

Department of Health and Social Security (DHSS) (1976c) *The NHS Planning System*, London: HMSO.

Department of Health and Social Security (DHSS) (1976d) *Prevention and Health*, Cmnd. 7047, London: HMSO.

Department of Health and Social Security (DHSS) (1977) *The Way Forward: Further Discussion of the Government's National Strategy*, London: HMSO.

Department of Health and Social Security (DHSS) (1978) *Prevention and Health: Everybody's Business*, Cmnd. 247, London: HMSO.

Department of Health and Social Security (DHSS) (1979) *Patients First*, London: HMSO.

Department of Health and Social Security (DHSS) (1981a) *Growing Older*, Cmnd, 8173, London, HMSO.

Department of Health and Social Security (DHSS) (1981b) *Consultative Document: Care in Action*, London: HMSO.

Department of Health and Social Security (DHSS) (1981c) *Consultative Document: Care in the Community*, London: HMSO.

Department of Health and Social Security (DHSS) (1983) *NHS Management Inquiry Report*, London: HMSO.

Department of Health and Social Security (DHSS) (1985) *Government Response to the Second Report of the Social Services Committee (Session 1984–85) Community Care with special reference to adult mentally ill and mentally handicapped people*, Cmnd. 9674, London: HMSO.

Department of Health and Social Security (DHSS) (1987) *Promoting Better Health – the government's programme for improving primary health care*, Cm. 249, London: HMSO.

Department of Health and Social Security (DHSS) (1988) *Report of the Committee of Inquiry into the Care and Aftercare of Miss Sharon Campbell*, London: HMSO.

Dillner, L. (1993) 'London's specialist centres cut by half', *British Medical Journal*, Vol. 306, 24 June 1993, pp. 1709–10.

Dixon, J. and Mays, N. (1997) 'New Labour, New NHS?', *British Medical Journal*, Vol. 315, 20–27 December 1997, p. 1639–40.

Doll, R. and Kinlen, L. J. (1972) *Epidemiology as an aid to determining the causes of cancer*, 49th Annual Report of the Cancer Research Campaign, London: Cancer Research Campaign.

Donaldson, L. (1993) 'Maintaining excellence: the preservation and development of specialist services'. In Smith, J. (ed.) (1993) *London after Tomlinson: Reorganising Big City Medicine*, London: BMJ Publishing.

Dorrell, S. (1990) Keynote Address to North East Thames Regional Health Authority (NETRHA).

Doyal, L. (1979) *The Political Economy of Health*, London: Pluto Press.

Draper, P., Grenhom, G. and Best, G. (1976) 'The Organisation of Health Care: A Critical View of the 1974 Reorganisation of the National Health Service'. In Tuckett, D. (ed.) *An Introduction to Medical Sociology*, London: Tavistock.

Durkin, E. (1972) *Hostels for the Mentally Disordered*, London: Fabian Society.

Eckstein, H. (1955) 'The Politics of the British Medical Association', *Political Quarterly*, Vol. XXVI, No. 4, pp. 345–59.

Eckstein, H. (1958) *The English Health Service: its origins, structure and achievements*, Cambridge, MA: Harvard University Press.

Enthoven, A. C. (1985) *Reflections on the Management of the National Health Service*, London: Nuffield Provincial Hospitals Trust.

Evans, N. (dir.) (1981) *Silent Minority*, ATV, London.

Evans, N. (1994) 'A Poisoned Chalice? Personal Social Services Policy'. In Savage, S., Atkinson, R. and Robins, L. (eds) (1994) *Public Policy in Britain*, Basingstoke: Macmillan.

Exworthy, M. (2014) 'The paradox of health policy: revealing the true colours of this "chameleon concept"', *International Journal of Health Policy and Management*, Vol. 3, No. 1, pp. 41–3.

Flowers Report (1980) *London Medical Education, A New Framework*, London: University of London.

Foot, M. (1975) *Aneurin Bevan 1945–1960*, St Albans: Paladin.

Foster, A. (2006) *The regulation of the non-medical healthcare professions, A review by the Department of Health*, London: DoH.

Francis Report (2013) *Report of the Mid-Staffordshire NHS Foundation Trust Public Inquiry*, 6 February 2013 (Chair: Robert Francis QC), HC 947, London: HMSO.

Frankel, S. and West, R. (eds) (1993) *Rationing and Rationality in the National Health Service: The Persistence of Waiting Lists*, Basingstoke: Macmillan.

Fraser, D. (1973) *Evolution of the British Welfare State*, London: Macmillan.

Fries, J. F. et al (1993) 'Reducing health care costs by reducing the need and demand for medical services', *The New England Journal of Medicine*, Vol. 329, No. 5, pp. 321–4.

Gilbert, B. B. (1966) *Evolution of National Insurance in Great Britain*, London: Michael Joseph.

Gilbert, B. B. (1970) *British Social Policy 1914–1939*, London: Batsford.

Gilderdale, S. (1971) 'The feeble-minded in hospital', *New Society*, 8 April 1971, p. 584.

Ginsberg, M. (ed.) (1959) *Law and Opinion in the Twentieth Century*, London: Stevens.

Glennerster, H. (ed.) (1982) *The Future of the Welfare State: Remaking Social Policy*, London: Heinemann.

Glennerster, H. (1995) *British Social Policy since 1945*, Oxford: Blackwell.

Glennerster, H. and Le Grand, J. (1997) 'The NHS is not dead yet', *The Guardian*, 10 October 1997.

Glennerster, H., Cohen, A. and Bovell, V. (1996) *Alternatives to fundholding, Welfare State Programme No. 123*, London: STICERD.

Glennerster, H., Matsaganis, M. and Owens, P. (1994) *Implementing GP fundholding: wild card or winning hand?* Buckingham: Open University Press.

Godber, G. (1988) 'Forty years of the NHS, Origins and early development', *British Medical Journal*, Vol. 297, 2 July 1988, pp. 37–43.

Goffman, E. (1961) *Asylums: essays on the social situation of mental patients and other inmates*, London: Penguin.

Goodwin, N., Perry, C., Dixon, A. and Ham, C. (2012) *Integrated Care for patients and populations; Improving outcomes by working together*, London: King's Fund.

Goodwin. S. (1989) 'Community Care for the Mentally Ill in England and Wales: Myths, Assumptions and Reality', *Journal of Social Policy*, January, pp. 27–52.

Gostin, L. (1975) *A Human Condition: The Mental Health Act from 1959–1975*, Vol. 1, London: Mind.

Green, M. (1993) 'Clinical research'. In Smith, J. (ed.) (1993) *London after Tomlinson: Reorganising Big City Medicine*, London: BMJ Publishing.

Griffiths, R. (1988) *Agenda for Action, A Report to the Secretary of State for Social Services*, London: HMSO.

Guillebaud Report (1956) *Committee of Enquiry into the Cost of the National Health Service*, Cmnd 553, London: HMSO. Hall, P. (1975) 'The development of health centres'. In Hall, P., Land, H., Parker, R. and Webb, A. (1975) *Change, Choice and Conflict in Social Policy*, London: Heinemann.

Hall, P. (ed.) (1980) *A Radical Agenda for London*, London: Fabian Society.

Hall, P., Land, H., Parker, R. and Webb, A. (1975) *Change, Choice and Conflict in Social Policy*, London: Heinemann.

Ham, C. (1992) *Health Policy in Britain: the politics and organisation of the National Health Service* (3rd edn) Basingstoke: Macmillan.

Ham, C. (1997) 'New British Labour Government: A turning point for NHS funding?', *LSE Health*, Vol. 3, No. 2, pp. 27–28 (London: LSE Health and European Health Policy Research Network).

Ham, C. (1998a) 'Forward through fusion', *The Guardian*, 7 January 1998, p. 2.

Ham, C. (1998b) 'Financing the NHS', *British Medical Journal*, Vol. 316, 17 January 1998, pp. 212–13.

Ham, C. (2004) *Health Policy in Britain* (5th edn), Palgrave, Basingstoke.

Ham, C. (2010a) 'Coalition's plans for the NHS in England', *British Medical Journal*, Vol. 341, No. 7764, 17 July 2010, p. 111.

Ham, C. (2010b) 'Why the plans to reform the NHS may never be implemented', *British Medical Journal*, Vol. 341, No. 7773, 18 September 2010, p. 586.

Ham, C., Baird, B., Gregory, S., Jabbal, J. and Alderwick, H. (2015) *The NHS under the Coalition Government, Part One: NHS Reform*, London: King's Fund

Harris, J. (1977) *William Beveridge: A Biography*, Oxford: Oxford University Press.

Harris, J. (1979) 'Caring for the sick: a look back at the voluntary tradition', *New Society*, 9 September 1979, pp. 287–90.

Harris, J. (1990) *Enterprise and Welfare States: A Comparative Perspective*, London: Transactions of the Royal Historical Society.

Harrison, P. (1973) 'Careless Community', *New Society*, 28 June 1973.

Harrison, S. and Wistow, G. (1992) 'The Purchaser/Provider Split in England Health care: towards explicit rationing', *Policy and Politics*, Vol. 20, No. 2, pp. 123–30.

Health and Safety Executive (HSE) (1996) *Good Health in Good Business*, London: HSE.

Healthcare Commission (2007) *Investigation into outbreaks of Clostridium Difficile at Maidstone and Tunbridge Wells NHS Trust*, London: HMSO.

Healthcare Commission (2008) *Report: State of Health Care*, London: Stationery Office.

Health Education Council (1987) *The Health Divide*, London: Health Education Council.

Heginbotham, C. (1990) 'The future of community care'. In Carrier, J. and Kendall, I. (eds) *Socialism and the NHS: Fabian essays in health care*, Aldershot: Gower.

Hennessey, P. (1992) *Never Again: Britain 1945–51*, London: Jonathan Cape.

Heywood, J. (1965) *Children in Care: the development of the service for the deprived child* (2nd edn), London: Routledge & Kegan Paul.

Hills, J. (1993) *The Future of Welfare: A Guide to the Debate*, York: Joseph Rowntree Foundation.

Hills, J. (1997) *The Future of Welfare: A Guide to the Debate*, London: Joseph Rowntree Foundation

HM Treasury (1976) *Public Expenditure to 1979–80*, Cmnd. 6393, London: HMSO.

HM Treasury (1977) *The Government's Expenditure Plans*, Cmnd. 6721, London: HMSO.

Hodgkinson, R. (1967) *The Origins of the National Health Service: The Medical Services of the New Poor Law 1834–1871*, London: The Wellcome Historical Medical Library.

Honigsbaum, F. (1979) *The Division in British Medicine: A History of the Separation of General Practice from Hospital Care 1911–1968*, London: Kogan Page.

Honigsbaum, F. (1989) *Health, Happiness and Security – the creation of the National Health Service*, London: Routledge.

House of Commons (1942) *Official Report: Fifth Series: Parliamentary Debates 1941/1942*, Vol. 383, London: HMSO.

House of Commons (1943) *Official Report: Fifth Series: Parliamentary Debates 1942/1943*, Vol. 386, London: HMSO.

House of Commons (1946) *Official Report: Fifth Series: Parliamentary Debates 1945/46*, Vol. 422, London: HMSO.

House of Commons (1985) *Second Report from the Social Services Committee (Session 1984– 85) Community Care with special reference to adult mentally ill and mentally handicapped people*, Vol. 1, London: HMSO.

House of Commons (1995a) *Parliamentary Debates (Hansard)*, Vol. 257, No. 86, 5 April 1995, London: HMSO.

House of Commons (1995b) *Parliamentary Debates (Hansard)*, Vol. 259, No. 102, 10 May 1995, London: HMSO.

House of Commons (1997) *Official Report, Parliamentary Debates (Hansard)*, Vol. 584, No. 76, 9 December 1997, London: HMSO.

House of Commons (2010) *Report of Health Select Committee Session 2009–10, 4th Report, Commissioning*, HC 268-I, London: HMSO.

House of Commons (2010a) *Parliamentary Debates (Hansard)*, Vol. 510, No. 8, 2 June 2010, cols 540–3, London: HMSO.

House of Commons (2010b) *Parliamentary Debates (Hansard)*, 6/7 September 2010, London: HMSO.

House of Commons (2010c) *Report of Health Select Committee, Session 2010–11, 2nd Report, Public Expenditure*, London: HMSO.

House of Commons (2011a) *House of Commons Research Paper 11/11, House of Commons Library, Health & Social Care Bill: Bill 132 of 2010–11, 27 January 2011* (Thomas Powell, Manjit Gheera), London: HMSO.

House of Commons (2011b) *Third Report, Session 2010–11*, HC 513, 18 January 2011, London: HMSO.

House of Commons (2011c) *Parliamentary Debates (Hansard)*, Vol. 522, No. 100, 31 January 2011, cols 605–707, London: HMSO.

House of Commons (2011d) *House of Commons Health Committee, Fifth Report, Commissioning: further issues*, HC 796-I and HC 796-II, London: HMSO.

House of Commons, (2011e) *Parliamentary Debates (Hansard)*, Vol. 526, No. 145, 4 April, 2011, cols 767–86 (NHS Reform) London: HMSO.

House of Commons (2011f) *Parliamentary Debates (Hansard)*, Vol. 529, No. 169, 14 June 2011, cols 645–70, London: HMSO.

House of Commons (2012a) *Report of House Commons Health Committee, Session 2010–12, 13th Report, Public Expenditure*, HC 1499, London, HMSO.

House of Commons (2012b) *Parliamentary Debates (Hansard)*, Vol. 533, No. 69, 13 November 2012, London, HMSO.

House of Commons (2013) *Parliamentary Debates (Hansard)*, Vol. 560, No. 137, 26 March 2013, cols 1472–87, London, HMSO.

House of Lords (2011a) *Constitution Committee, 18th Report, 2010–12, Health and Social care Bill*, HL Paper 197, London: HMSO.

House of Lords (2011b) *Health and Social Care Bill, Second Reading*, Vol. 730, No. 202, 11 October 2011, cols. 1470–518, London, HMSO.

House of Lords (2011c) *Health and Social Care Bill, Second Reading*, Vol. 730, No. 203, 12 October 2011, cols. 1671–711, London, HMSO.

House of Lords (2011d) *Constitution Committee, 22nd Report, Health and Social Care: follow up*, 14 December 2011, London: HMSO.

House of Lords (2012), 8 February 2012, cols 260–74, London: HMSO.

Howe, G. M. and Loraine, J. A. (eds) (1973) *Environmental Medicine*, London: Heinemann.

Illich, I. (1976) *Limits to Medicine: Medical Nemesis: The Expropriation of Health*, London: Marion Boyars.

Illich, I. (1978) *The Right to Useful Unemployment: Professional Enemies*, London: Marion Boyars.

Illsley, R. (1986) 'Occupational class, selection and the production of inequalities in health', *Quarterly Journal of Social Affairs*, Vol. 2, No. 2, pp. 151–65.

Inner London Health Authority Chief Executive (ILHACE) (1995) *Hospital Services for Londoners*, London: ILHACE.

Israel, S. and Telling-Smith, G. (1967) 'The submerged iceberg of sickness in society', *Social and Economic Administration*, Vol. 1, No. 1, pp. 43–56.

Jacobson, B. (1993) 'Public health in Inner London'. In Smith, J. (ed.) *London after Tomlinson: Reorganising Big City Medicine*, London: BMJ Publishing.

Jaehnig, W. (1979) *A family service for the mentally handicapped, Fabian Tract 460*, London: Fabian Society.

James, P. (1998) 'Food is a public health issue', *British Medical Journal*, Vol. 316, 7 February 1998, p. 416.

Jarman, B. (1981) *A Survey of Primary Care in London*, London: Royal College of General Practitioners.

Jarman, B. (1993) 'Is London Overbedded?', *British Medical Journal*, Vol. 306, 10 April 1993, pp. 979–82.

Jarman, B. (1994) 'The Crisis in London Medicine: How many hospital beds does the capital need?', Special University Lecture, London: University of London.

Jenkins, P. (1963) 'Bevan's Fight with the BMA'. In Sissons, M. and French, P. (eds) *Age of Austerity*, London: Hodder and Stoughton.

Jones, K. (1955) *Lunacy, Law and Conscience*, London: Routledge & Kegan Paul.

Jones, K. (1960) *Mental Health and Social Policy*, London: Routledge & Kegan Paul.

Jones, K. (1972a) *A History of the Mental Health Services*, London: Routledge & Kegan Paul.

Jones, K. (ed.) (1972b) *The Yearbook of Social Policy in Britain, 1971*, London: Routledge & Kegan Paul.

Jones, K. (ed.) (1974) *The Yearbook of Social Policy in Britain, 1972*, London: Routledge & Kegan Paul.

Jones, K. (ed.) (1975) *The Yearbook of Social Policy in Britain, 1974*, London: Routledge & Kegan Paul.

Jones, K. (1983) 'Services for the mentally ill: the death of a concept'. In Bean, P. and MacPherson, S. (eds) *Approaches to Welfare*, London: Routledge & Kegan Paul.

Jowell, T. (1993) 'Community care in London: The prospects'. In Smith, J. (ed.) *London after Tomlinson: Reorganising Big City Medicine*, London: BMJ Publishing.

Judge, K. (1995) 'Income distribution and life expectancy: a critical appraisal', *British Medical Journal*, Vol. 311, 11 November 1995, pp. 1282–5.

Kennedy Report (2001) *The report of the public inquiry into children's heart surgery at the Bristol Royal Infirmary 1984–85: learning from Bristol* (Chairman: Professor Ian Kennedy), Cm. 5207, London: HMSO.

Keogh, Sir B. (2013) *Transforming Urgent and Emergency Care Services in England, 1st Report*, London: Department of Health.

Keogh Review (2013) *Review into the quality of care and treatment provided by 14 hospital trusts in England and Wales* (Chair: Sir Bruce Keogh KBE), 16 July 2013, London: Department of Health.

King's Fund (1987) *Planned Health Services for Inner London, Back to back planning*, London: King's Edward Hospital Fund for London.

King's Fund (1992a) *London Health Care 2010, Changing the Future of Services in the Capital, King's Fund Commission on the Future of London's Acute Health Services*, London: King's Fund Initiative.

King's Fund (1992b) *London Health Care 2010 – Review*, London: King's Fund.

King's Fund (1994) *London Monitor No. 1*, London: King's Fund.

King's Fund (1995a) *London Monitor No. 2*, London: King's Fund.

King's Fund (1995b) *Tackling Health Inequalities: An Agenda for Action*, London: King's Fund

King's Fund (2005) *Independent Audit of the NHS under Labour (1997–2005)*, London: King's Fund.

King's Fund (2014) *King's Fund Quarterly Monitoring Report, January 2014, Health and social care surveys, The £20 billion productivity challenge*, London: King's Fund

Klein, R. (1973) *Complaints against doctors*, London: Charles Knight.

Klein, R. (1976) 'The Politics of Redistribution', *British Medical Journal*, Vol. 2, No. 6040, 9 October 1976, p. 893.

Klein, R. (1983) *The Politics of the National Health Service*, Harlow: Longman.

Klein, R. (1993) 'Dimensions of rationing: who should do what?', *British Medical Journal*, Vol. 307, 31 July 1993, pp. 309–11.

Klein, R. (1994) 'Can we restrict the health care menu?', *Health Policy*, Vol. 27, pp. 103–12.

Klein, R. (1995a) *The New Politics of the NHS* (3rd Edn) Harlow: Longman.

Klein, R. (1995b) 'Big Ban Healthcare Reform, Does It Work?: The Case of Britain's 1991 National Heath Service reform', *Milbank Quarterly*, Vol. 73, No. 3, pp. 299–337.

Klein, R. (1998) *Labour's Third Way: 'Solution or Delusion?*, Parliamentary Brief, March 1998, p. 32.

Klein, R. (2004) 'Britain's National Health Service Revisited', *New England Journal of Medicine*, Vol. 350, No. 9, pp. 937–42.

Last, J. M. (1963) 'The iceberg: "Completing the Picture" in General Practice', *The Lancet*, Vol. 282, No. 7927, 6 July 1963, pp. 28–31.

Lawson, N. (1993) *The View From No. 11: Memoirs of a Tory Radical*, London: Corgi.

Lindsey, A. (1962) Socialised Medicine in England and Wales, London: University of North Carolina Press.

London Advisory Group (1981) *Reports* (Chair: Sir John Habakkuk), London: Department of Health and Social Security.

London Health Planning Consortium (LHPC) (1980) *Acute Health Services in London*, London: HMSO.

London Health Planning Consortium (LHPC) (1981) *Primary Health Care for Inner London* (Chairman: Sir D. Acheson), May 1981, London: HMSO.

London Implementation Group (LIG) (1993) *Specialty reviews, Reports of Independent Reviews of Specialist Services in London: Cancer; Cardiac; Children; Neurosciences; Plastics and Burns; Renal,* June 1993, London: HMSO.

Martin, F. M. (1984a) *Between the Acts: Community Mental Health Services 1959–1983*, London: Nuffield Provincial Hospitals Trust.

Martin, J. P. (1984b) *Hospitals in Trouble*, London: Basil Blackwell.

Matthew, H. C. G. (1984) 'The Liberal Age (1851–1914)'. In Morgan, K. O. (ed.) *The Oxford Illustrated History of Britain*, Oxford: Oxford University Press.

Maxwell, R. (1990) 'London's Health Services', *Christian Action Journal*, Special Edition, Autumn.

Maxwell, R. (1994) *What next for London's health care?* London: King's Fund.

Maynard, A. and Tingle, R. (1975) 'The objectives and performance of the mental health services in England and Wales in the 1960s', *Journal of Social Policy*, Vol. 4, No. 2, pp. 151–68.

Mays, J., Forder, A. and Keidan, O. (eds) (1975) *Penelope Hall's Social Services of Modern England*, London: Routledge & Kegan Paul.

McDougall, K. (1959) 'The Mental Health Bill', *Political Quarterly*, Vol. 30, No. 2, pp. 120–30.

McKeown, T. (1967) 'Medical and Social Needs of Patients in Hospitals for the Mentally Subnormal', *British Journal of Preventative and Social Medicine*, Vol. 21, pp. 115–21.

McKeown, T. (1976) *The Role of Medicine: Dream, Mirage or Nemesis?* London: Nuffield Provincial Hospitals Trust.

McKeown, T., Garratt, F. N. and Lowe, C. R. (1958) 'Institutional care of the Mentally Ill', *The Lancet*, Vol. 271, No. 7022, 29 March 1958, pp. 682–4.

Mental Health Task Force London Project (MHTFL) (1994) *Priorities for Action: a report by the Mental Health Task Force London Project*, London: MHTFL.

Milburn, A. (1997) 'For a healthier Britain', *Fabian Review*, Autumn/Winter, p. 22.

Ministry of Health (1921) *Voluntary Hospitals Committee (Cave Committee) Final Report*, Cmd. 1335, London: HMSO.

Ministry of Health (1944) *A National Health Service*, Cmd. 6502, London: HMSO.

Ministry of Health (1946) *National Health Service Bill*, Cmd. 6502, London: HMSO.

Ministry of Health (1962) *Hospital Plan for England and Wales*, Cmnd. 1604, London: HMSO.

Ministry of Health (1963) *Plans for Health and Welfare Services of the Local Authorities in England and Wales*, Cmnd. 1973, London: HMSO.

Ministry of Health (1968) *The Administrative Structure of the medical and related services in England and Wales* (First Green Paper), London: HMSO.

Mittler, P. (1965) *Mental Health Services*, London: Fabian Society.

Mooney, G. (1992) *Economics, Medicine and Healthcare* (2nd Edn) London: Harvester Wheatsheaf.

Morgan, K. O. (1984a) Editor's Foreword. In Morgan, K. O. (ed.) *The Oxford Illustrated History of Britain*, Oxford: Oxford University Press.

Morgan, K. O. (1984b) *Labour in Power 1945–1951*, Oxford: Clarendon Press.

Morris, J. N. et al (1953) 'Coronary Heart Disease and Physical Activity of Work', *The Lancet*, Vol. 2, 21 November 1953, pp. 1053–7.

Mumford, L. (1940) *The Culture of Cities*, London: Secker & Warburg.

National Audit Office (1987) *Use of Operating Theatres in the National Health Service*, HC 143, London: HMSO.

NHS England (2014a) *The NHS Five Year Forward View*, London: NHS England.

NHS England (2014b) *Examining new options and opportunities for providers of NHS care* (The Dalton Review), London: NHS England.

NHS Executive (1993) *Managing the New NHS: a background document*, Leeds: Department of Health.

NHS Executive (1994) *NHS Responsibilities for meeting long term health care needs*, HSG (94) London: Department of Health.

NHS Executive (1997a) 'Letter: NHS Priorities and Planning Guidance', EL (97) 39, Leeds: Department of Health.

NHS Executive (1997b) *The Commissioning Process for 1998/99*, Leeds: Department of Health.

NHS Executive (1997c) *Priorities and Planning Guidance for the NHS: 1998/99*, Leeds: Department of Health.

NHS Executive (1997d) 'Letter: Health Action Zones – Invitation to Bid', EL (97) 65, Leeds: Department of Health.

NHS Future Forum (2011a) *Summary Report on proposed changes to the NHS* (Chair: Professor Steve Field), London: Department of Health.

NHS Future Forum (2011b) *Choice and Competition: Delivering Real Choice, A report from the NHS Future Forum*, London: Department of Health.

NHS Future Forum (2011c) *Clinical Advice and Leadership, A report from the NHS Future Forum*, London: Department of Health.

NHS Future Forum (2011d) *Education and Training, A report from the NHS Future Forum*, London: Department of Health.

NHS Future Forum (2011e) Patient Involvement and Public Accountability, A report from the NHS Future Forum, London: Department of Health.

Nicholls, G. (1854) *History of the English Poor Law*, London: King.

North East Thames Regional Health Authority (NETRHA) (1990) *Better out than in?* Report from the 5th Annual Conference of the Team for the Assessment of Psychiatric Services, London, NETRHA.

North East Thames Regional Health Authority (NETRHA) (1994) *Institution to Community: Friern Lessons Pack*, London: NETRHA.

O'Higgins, M. (1983) 'Issues of Redistribution in State Welfare Spending'. In Loney, M., Boswell, D. and Clarke, J. (eds) *Social Policy and Social Welfare*, Milton Keynes: Open University Press.

Packman, J. (1975) *The Child's Generation: Child Care Policy from Curtis to Houghton*, Oxford: Basil Blackwell.

Parker, J. (1965) *Local Health and Welfare Services*, London: Allen & Unwin.

Parker, J. (1975a) *Social Policy and Citizenship*, London: Macmillan.

Parker, R. (1975b) 'Social administration and scarcity'. In Butterworth, E. and Holman, R. (eds) *Social Welfare in Modern Britain*, London: Fontana.

Parry-Jones, W. L. (1987) 'Asylum for the mentally ill in historical perspective', *Bulletin of the Royal College of Psychiatrists*, pp. 407–10.

Parston, G. and McMahon L. (1998) 'A third way? England – yes Scotland – maybe', *British Medical Journal*, Vol. 316, 17 January 1998, p. 213.

Paulus, I. (1974) *The Search for Pure Food: a sociology of legislation in Britain*, London: Martin Robertson.

Pavolini, E. and Guillen, A. (eds) (2013a) *Health Care Systems in Europe under Austerity: Institutional Reforms and Performance*, Basingstoke: Macmillan.

Pavolini, E. and Guillen, A. (2013b) 'Conclusions'. In Pavolini, E. and Guillen, A. (eds) *Health Care Systems in Europe under Austerity: Institutional Reforms and Performance*, Basingstoke: Macmillan.

Phillimore, P., Beattie, A. and Townsend, P. (1994) 'Widening inequality of health in northern England 1981–1991', *British Medical Journal*, Vol. 308, 30 April 1994, pp. 1125–8.

Phillips Report (1954) *Report of the Committee on the Economic and Financial problems of the Provision for Old Age*, Cmd. 9333, London: HMSO.

Phillipson, C. (1990) 'A Policy for Health Care for Older People'. In Carrier, J. and Kendall, I. (eds) *Socialism and the NHS: Fabian Essays in Health Care*, Aldershot: Gower.

Pinker, R. (1966) *English Hospital Statistics 1861–1938*, London: Heinemann.

Pinker, R. (1971) *Social Theory and Social Policy*, London: Heinemann.

Pollock, A. (2004) *NHS plc: The Privatisation of our Health Care*, London: Verso Books.

Porritt Report (1962) A *Review of the Medical Services in Great Britain*, London: Social Assay.

Powell, E. (1961) 'Speech by the Minister of Health, the Rt. Hon. Enoch Powell', in *Report of the Annual Conference of the National Association for Mental Health*, London.

Powell, M. (1992a) 'The geography of English hospital provision in the 1930s: the historical geography of heterodoxy', *Journal of Historical Geography*, Vol. 18, No. 3, pp. 307–16.

Powell, M. (1992b) *Hospital Provision before the National Health Service: A Geographical Study of the 1945 Hospital Surveys*, London: The Society for the Social History of Medicine.

Power, C. (1994) 'Health and Social Inequality in Europe', *British Medical Journal*, Vol. 308, 30 April 1994, pp. 1153–6.

Powles, J. (1973) 'Science, Medicine and Man', *Social Science and Medicine*, Vol. 1, pp. 1–30.

Prime Minister's Office (2010) *Queen's Speech, 25 May 2010: bills and topics mentioned*, London: HMSO.

Prime Minister's Office (2011) *Working together for a stronger NHS*, 5 April 2011, London: HMSO.

Prime Minister's Office (2013) *Francis report: Prime Minister's Statement on the Mid-Staffs Public Inquiry*, 6 February 2013, London: HMSO.

Redfern Report (2001) *Report of the Royal Liverpool Children's Inquiry* (Alder Hay Inquiry) (Chair: Michael Redfern QC), London: HMSO.

Ritchie Inquiry (2000) *Inquiry into Quality and Practice within the NHS arising from the actions of Rodney Ledward 1999–2000* (Chair: Jean Ritchie, QC), London: Secretary of State for Health (HMSO).

Robb, B. (ed.) (1967) *Sans Everything*, London: Nelson.

Roberts, N. (1967) *Mental Health and Mental Illness*, London: Routledge & Kegan Paul.

Robinson, D. (1973) *Patients, Practitioners and Medical Care: aspects of medical sociology*, London: Heinemann.

Robinson, R. and Le Grand, J. (eds) (1994) *Evaluating the NHS Reforms*, London: King's Fund Institute.

Rowntree, S. (1901) *Poverty: A Study of Town Life*, London: Macmillan & Co.

Royal Commission on Local Government in England (1969) *Report* (Chair: The Rt. Hon. Lord Redcliffe Maud), Cmnd. 4040, London: HMSO.

Royal Commission on Local Government in Greater London (1960) *Report* (Chair: Sir Edwin Herbert), Cmnd. 1164, London: HMSO.

Royal Commission on Medical Education (1968) *Report* (Chair: Lord Todd), Cmnd. 3568, London: HMSO.

Royal Commission on National Health Insurance (1926) *Report*, Cmd. 2596, London: HMSO.

Royal Commission on NHS Research Paper 1 (1978) *The Working of the National Health Service*, London: HMSO.

Royal Commission on the Law Relating to Mental Illness and Mental Deficiency (1957) *Report* (Chair: Lord Percy of Newcastle), Cmnd. 169, London: HMSO.

Royal Commission on the NHS (1979) *Report* (Chair: Sir Alec Merrison), Cmnd. 7615, London: HMSO.

Rumsey, H. (1856) *Essays on State Medicine*, London: John Churchill.

Ryan, J. and Thomas, F. (1980) *The Politics of Mental Handicap*, Harmondsworth: Penguin.

Sand, R. (1935) *Health and Human Progress: an essay in sociological medicine*, London: Kegan Paul, Trench, Trubner & Co.

Savage, S. and Robins, L. (1990) *Public Policy under Thatcher*, Basingstoke: Macmillan.

Scammells, B. (1971) *Studies in Social Administration: Administration of Health and Welfare Services*, Manchester: Manchester University Press.

Scull, A. (1979) *Museums of Madness: the social organisation of insanity in the nineteenth century*, London: Allen Lane.

Secretary of State (2008) *High Quality Care for All*, London, HMSO.

Secretary of State for Scotland (1997) *Designed to Care*, Edinburgh: Stationery Office.

Sedgwick, P. (1982) *Psycho-politics: Laing, Foucault, Goffman, Szasz and the future of mass psychiatry*, London: Harper Row.

Seebohm Report (1968) *Report of the Committee on Local Authority and Allied Personal Social Services*, Cmnd. 3703, London: HMSO.

Seedhouse, D. (1987) 'Does the National Health Service have a purpose'. In Bryne, P. (ed.) *Medicine in Contemporary Society*, London: King's Fund.

Simey, T. S. and Simey, M. B. (1960) *Charles Booth: Social Scientist*, London: Oxford University Press.

Sissmons, M. and French, P. (eds) *Age of Austerity*, London: Hodder and Stoughton.

Smith, Dame Janet (2002–05) *Independent Public Inquiry into the issues arising from the case of Harold Frederick Shipman* (Chair: Dame Janet Smith, OBE); six reports were published between July 2002 and January 2005 (including Cm. 5853, Cm. 5854, Cm. 4249 and Cm. 6394) London: HMSO

Smith, J. (1993a) 'Introduction'. In Smith, J. (ed.) *London after Tomlinson: Reorganising Big City Medicine*, London: BMJ Publishing.

Smith, J. (ed.) (1993b) *London after Tomlinson: Reorganising Big City Medicine*, London: BMJ Publishing.

Smith, R. (1989) 'Words from the source: interview with Alan Enthoven', *British Medical Journal*, Vol. 298, 29 April 1989, pp. 1166–8.

Social Services Committee (1985) *Second Report from the Social Services Committee (Session 1984–85) Community Care with special reference to adult mentally ill and mentally handicapped people*, Vol. 1, London: HMSO.

Social Services Committee (1988) *Resourcing the NHS: Short Term Issues, Volume One*, London: HMSO.

Social Services Committee (1989) *Fifth Report: Resourcing the NHS: the Government's White Paper: Working for Patients*, London: HMSO.

Stark Murray, D. (1971) *Why a National Health Service?* London: Pemberton Books.

Stern, J. (1983) 'Social mobility and the interpretation of social class mortality differentials', *Journal of Social Policy*, Vol. 13, No. 1, pp. 27–44.

Stevens, R. (1966) *Medical practice in Modern England – the impact of specialisation and state medicine*, New Haven: Yale University Press.

Stevens, S. (2004) 'Reform Strategies for the English NHS', *Health Affairs*, Vol. 23, No. 3, pp. 37–44.

Szreter, S. (1988) 'The importance of social intervention in British mortality decline c. 1850–1914: a reinterpretation of the role of public health', *Social History of Medicine*, Vol. 1, No. 1, pp. 1–37.

Taylor, D. and Taylor, J. (1989) *Mental Health in the 1990s: From Custody to Care?* London: Office of Health Economics.

Thane, P. (1982) *The foundations of the welfare state*, Harlow: Longman.

Thatcher, M. (1993) *The Downing Street Years*, London: Harper Collins.

Thomas, N. and Stoten, B. (1974) 'The NHS and local government'. In Jones, K. (ed.) *The Yearbook of Social Policy in Britain, 1973*, London: Routledge & Kegan Paul.

Thorlby, R. and Maybin, J. (eds) (2010) *A high performing NHS? A review of the evidence 1997–2010*, London: King's Fund.

Timmins, N. (1988) *Cash, Crisis and Cure: Guide to the NHS Debate*, London: Newspaper Publishing.

Timmins, N. (1995) *The Five Giants: A Biography of the Welfare State*, London: Harper Collins.

Timmins, N. (2012) *Never Again? The Story of the Health and Social Care Act 2012*, London: King's Fund.

Titmuss, R. M. (1950) *The Problems of Social Policy*, London: HMSO.

Titmuss, R. M. (1961) 'Community care: Fact or Fiction'. In Titmuss, R. M. (ed.) *Commitment to Welfare*, London: George Allen & Unwin.

Titmuss, R. M. (1963) *Essays on the Welfare State*, London: George Allen & Unwin.

Titmuss, R. M. (1968) *Commitment to Welfare*, London: George Allen & Unwin.

Titmuss, R. M. (1970) *The Gift Relationship*, London: George Allen & Unwin

Titmuss, R. M. (1974) *Social Policy: An Introduction*, London: George Allen & Unwin

Titmuss, R. M. (1987) *The Philosophy of Welfare*, London: George Allen & Unwin

Tomlinson, D. (1991) *Utopia, Community Care and the Retreat from the Asylums*, Milton Keynes: Open University Press

Tomlinson Report (1992) *Report of the Inquiry into London's Health Service, Medical Education and Research*, London: HMSO.

Tooke, Sir John (2007) *Aspiring to Excellence, findings and recommendations of the independent inquiry into modernising medical careers*, London: Aldridge Press.

Tooth, G. C. and Brook, E. M. (1961) 'Trends in the mental hospital population and the effect on future planning', *The Lancet*, Vol. 277, No. 7179, April 1961, pp. 710–13.

Townsend, P. (1962) *The Last Refuge: a survey of residential institutions and homes for the aged in England and Wales*, London: Routledge & Kegan Paul.

Townsend, P. (1973) *The Social Minority*, London: Allen Lane.

Trombley, S. (1989) *Sir Frederick Treves: The Extra Ordinary Edwardian*, London: Routledge.

Tudor-Hart, J. (1971) 'The Inverse Care Law', *The Lancet*, Vol. 297, No. 7696, 27 February, pp. 405–12.

Turnberg, L. (1998) *Health Services in London – A Strategic Review*, London: Department of Health.

Tutt, N. (1974) *Care or Custody: community homes and treatment of delinquency*, London: Darton, Longman & Todd.

Walker, A. (1982a) 'A Caring Community'. In Glennerster, H. (ed.) (1982) *The Future of the Welfare State: Remaking Social Policy*, London: Heinemann.

Walker, A. (1982b) 'Dependency and Old Age', *Social Policy & Administration*, Vol. 16, No. 2, pp. 115–35.

Walker, A. (1983) *Community Care*, London: Macmillan.

Wanless, D. (2002) *Securing our Future Health: Taking a Long-Term View* (The Wanless Review), London: HM Treasury.

Wanless, D. (2004) *Securing Good Health for the Whole Population*, London: HMSO.

Wanless, D. and Forder, J. (2006) *Securing Good Health for Older People*, London: King's Fund.

Wanless, D., Appleby, J., Harrison, A. and Patel, D. (2007) *Our Future Health Secured? A review of NHS funding and performance*, London: King's Fund.

Watkin, B. (1978) *The National Health Service: The First Phase 1948–1974 and After*, London: George Allen & Unwin.

Weale, A. (1998) 'Rationing health care – a logical solution to an inconsistent triad', *British Medical Journal*, Vol. 316, 7 February 1998, p. 410.

Webb, B. and Webb, S. (1910) *English Poor Law Policy*, London: Longman.

Webster, C. (1988) *The Health Services since The War, Volume 1, Problems of Health Care, The NHS before 1957*, London: HMSO.

Webster, C. (1990) 'Conflict and Consensus: Explaining the British Health Service', *Twentieth Century British History*, Vol. 1, pp. 115–51.

Webster, C. (ed.) (1991) *Aneurin Bevan on the National Health Service*, Oxford: Wellcome Unit for the History of Medicine.

Webster, C. (1995) 'Local government and health care: the historical perspective', *British Medical Journal*, Vol. 310, 17 June 1995, pp. 1584–7.

White, A. (1901) *Efficiency and Empire*, London: Methuen & Co.

Wilensky, H. (1975) *The Welfare State and Equality: structural and ideological roots of public expenditures*, London: University of California Press.

Wilensky, H. (1981) 'Democratic Corporation, Consensus and Social Policy'. In *The Welfare State in Crisis: An account of the conference on Social Policies in the 1980s*, 20–23 October 1980, Paris: OECD, pp. 191–2.

Wilkinson, R. G. (1992) 'Income Distribution and Life Expectancy', *British Medical Journal*, Vol. 304, 18 January 1992, pp. 165–8.

Wilkinson, R. G. (1995) 'Commentary: A reply to Ken Judge: mistaken criticisms ignore overwhelming evidence', *British Medical Journal*, Vol. 311, 11 November 1995, pp. 1285–7.

Willcocks, A. (1967) *The Creation of the National Health Service*, London: Routledge & Kegan Paul.

Williams Report (1967) *Caring for People*, London: HMSO.

Wilson, N. (1938) *Public Health Services*, London: William Hodge.

Wilson Report (1994) *Being Heard: The report of a review committee on NHS complaints procedure*, London: HMSO.

Woodward, J. (1974) *To do the sick no harm: a study of the British voluntary hospital system to 1875*, London: Routledge & Kegan Paul.

World Health Organization (WHO) (1948) *WHO Constitution, Official Records, No. 2,* June 1948, Geneva: WHO.

World Health Organization (WHO) (1973) *Better Food for a Healthier World,* Geneva: WHO.

Yates, J. (1987) *Why Are We Waiting?* Oxford: Oxford University Press.

Young, F. G. (1968) 'The origin and development of the University of London with particular reference to medical education'. In *Royal Commission on Medical Education,* Cmnd. 3569, London: HMSO, Appendix 14.

# Index